Marion County Tennessee

DEED BOOK B

1827–1830

WPA RECORDS

Heritage Books
2024

HERITAGE BOOKS

AN IMPRINT OF HERITAGE BOOKS, INC.

Books, CDs, and more—Worldwide

For our listing of thousands of titles see our website
at
www.HeritageBooks.com

A Facsimile Reprint
Published 2024 by
HERITAGE BOOKS, INC.
Publishing Division
5810 Ruatan Street
Berwyn Heights, MD 20740

Originally published 1938

International Standard Book Number
Paperbound: 978-0-7884-8925-9

WPA RECORDS

The WPA Records are, for the most part, carbon copies of the original
that was typed on onion skin paper during the Depression. Since these
records were typed on poor machines by people who did not type well
either and read by persons not always sure of the older handwritten
material, the results are often less that perfect.

We have made every attempt to make as good a copy as can be made from
these older papers. Sometimes there are water stains and burned edges
around the paper.. This is the results of a fire at the home of one of
the workers, Mrs. Penelope Allen, who was over most of the project.

The WPA Records are now very scattered between the State Archives, various
Public and Private Libraries and other collections. Some day, there is
a hope that all of these can be collected and stored in one place. In
spite of their many mistakes and problems, these are still the most complete collection of Tennessee records found anywhere.

TENNESSEE

RECORDS OF MARION COUNTY

DEED BOOK VOLUME B OF A & B
1819 - 1830

HISTORICAL RECORDS PROJECT
OFFICIAL PROJECT NO. 465-44-3-115

COPIED UNDER WORKS PROGRESS ADMINISTRATION

MRS. JOHN TROTWOOD MOORE
STATE LIBRARIAN & ARCHIVIST, SPONSOR

ELIZABETH D. COPPEDGE
STATE DIRECTOR OF WOMEN'S & PROFESSIONAL PROJECTS

PENELOPE JOHNSON ALLEN
STATE SUPERVISOR

CAROLINE SMALL KELSO
SUPERVISOR

NELL LAWSON
COPYIST

MAY MANNING
TYPIST

APRIL 18, 1938

A   Page

Abraham	332
Abram	375
Akein, James P.	391
Aken, J. H.	350
Alabama, State of	249,250,251,263
	296,303,368,395
Alexander, Fancher	239
Alexander, George	238
Alexander, Thos.	239
Alley, Eramus	358,359,369,412
Amos	324
Anderson, James	329
Anderson, Samuel	243
Anderson, William	309
Armstrong, Dury P.	291,292
Armstrong, Robert	345
Arnett, William	283,327,360
	361,367,368
	395,398,417
Arnett, Wm	248,309
Ashburn, Joshua	307,340
Ashburn, Joshua T.	372,373
Austin, Hezekiah	373,374

B

Baer, John T.	65
Bailey, Thomas	373
Baker, Daniel O.	394
Baker, John	313,314
Baker, Mary	330,397
Ball, John	375
Baltimore	264
Barbary	331
Barbee, Mathew	293,296
Barker, Howell	330
Barker, James	337
Barnes, John	325
Barnes, William	325,342
Basham, Alex	309
Basham, Nancy	309
Bass, Andrew	402,403,404
Bathel, Larkin	308

       Page

Battle Creek	133,234,251,275
	276,278,279,281
	282,293,294,300
	301,303,308,311
	316,317,325,334
	343,344,347,350
	390,396,402,403
	405,407
Battle of Water	353
Baxin, John	266
Bean	266
Bean, Obediah	252,277,279
	280,335,350
Bean, Robert Jr.	277
Bean, Robert	335,350
Bear, Robert	351
Becky,	323
Beene, Benjamin	280
Beene, Jesse	281
Beene, John	280,281
Beene, Lemuel	280,281
Beene, Obediah	249,276,281,294
	295,342,351
Beene, Robert	280,351
Beene, Robert Jr.	280,348
Beene, Robert Sr.	295
Beene, Samuel	342
Beene, William	281
Belch, John	401
Belcher, David	351
Belcher, Wiley	336
Belfast	396
Belsher, Allen	417,418
Belsher, Allen Jr.	395
Belsher, Ferrell	349,394,395
	403,417,418
Belsher, Salley	417
Belsher, Wiley	317,355,403
	417,418
Belsher, Wiley	316
Berry	394
Berry, James	379
Bethel, Bedford	339

B	Page
Bethel, Blyford	340,402,403
Bethel, Larkin	317,318,396
Betsy,	338,403,417
Bible, John	273
Bible, Phillip	405
Big Cynthia	403,417
Blackburn	323
Blackburn, Jesse	329
Bledsoe	238,373
Bledsoe, A.	250
Bledsoe, County of	242,250,257
	271,287,360
	408,409,411,413
Blevins Cove	373
Blevins, Elizabeth	374
Blevins, James	407
Blevins, Jonathan	295,296
Blevins, Luke	257
Blevins, Nancy	374
Blevins, Richard	256,257
Blevins, Stephen A.	240,274,293
	296,338,373
Blevins, S. A.	356
Blevins, Tailton	395
Blevins, Wm	367
Boon Creek	396,397
Box, Henry	296
Box, John	296
Bradford, Alexander B.	312
Branches:-	
Allisons Spring	319,320
Dry	390
Dry Rocky	306
Halls	240,319,338,407
Spring	260,320,356
Brannon, Ephriam	356,357,393
Branson,	319,388
Branson, Andrew	338,339,349
	387,388
Branson, Col	315
Branson, Jarard	386
Branson, Jarrett	274
Branson, John	228,266,267
	274,275,387
Branson, Thomas	240,262,407
Branson, Valentine	315
Brantly, Thomas	325,333,386,388
Brewer, B.	400
Brewer, Benjamin	399,413,414
Brewer, Sallie L.	399
Brewer, Sallie S.	400,413,414

	Page
Bridge, Caldwell	417
Bridge, Kellys	338
Bridgeman, J.	409,411
Bridgeman, John	241,242,291
	375,376,377,416
Briggs, George	238,239
Brock, George	335
Brock, George A.	237,315,351,352
Brock, George E.	294
Brooks, Joseph	250
Brown, Benjamin	339
Brown, G. W.	285
Brown, Samuel	262,263
Brown, William	285
Bruce, Eliza	377,378
Brumby, J. B.	292
Brumley, William	354,356,358,385
Burnetts, John	364
Bryant, Jno	364,365,371
Bullin, Thos.	407
Burgess, John	258,314,399
Burk, County of	253
Butler, T. H.	364,397

C	
Caggard, Jesse	270
Caldwell	396
Calhoun, John	363
Callaham, Hugh	296
Campbell, James	264,265,369
Campbell, Lewis	289
Campbell, Thomas I.	379
Campbell, Thomas J.	344
Campbell, William	360,361
Carroll, George	340
Carroll, Jacob	340
Carroll, William	281,290,293,344
Carroll, William Jr.	340
Carter, A. M.	391,396,400,414
Carter, County of	381,399,413,414
Carter, George W.	399,400,413,414
Carter, London	334
Carter, William B.	399,413
Carter, Wm. D.	400
Chambers, Elijah	415
Chambers, George	392
Chandion, Isaac	350
Chandion, James	254,289,290,334
	349,359,360,385
Cheek, A.	373

	Page
Cheek, Anderson	274,338,362.365
Cherokee Nation	362,365,366,418
Childs, John	366
Chilton, John	305
Chilton, Felatich	377,398
Chimney, Stone	236
Cinthia, Little	417
Cities:-	
Murfreesboro	281,282,290,291
	292,294,344
Nashville	373
Norfolk	375,403,415
Pikeville	377,411
Washington	344,363,368
Winchester	264
Clayton, Ewin	272,273
Clemons, Adair	343
Clipper, James	300,311,339,349
Clipper, James Jr.	299
Clipper, John	297,311,339,340
Cobb, Pharoah	246
Cochran, John	297,311,339,340
Coffelt, Abraham	354,356,357
Cohorne, John	273,309
Conaster, Daniel	338
Conaster, Henry H.	337
Condra, James	330
Conn, Robert B.	338
Cooper, Burton	389
Cooper, Cannon	329,330,366
Cooper, Isaac	263,319,407
Cooper, Isabella	355,388,390
Cooper, William	290,408,410
Corlexan, Polly	397
Corner, Trussell	304
Cornett, John	368
Coulter, A.	340
Coulter, Abraham	359
Coulter, Alexander	240,254,255,293
	299,308,356
	358,359,363
Counties:-	
Burk	253
Carter	381,399,413,414
Franklin	193,251,255,286,
	294,310,315,317
	330,335,343,351
	363,398,399
Grey	299
Green	363,365,381,400
	401,414,415
Grundy	414
Irwin	417

	Page
Jackson	249,260,262,368
Morgain	395
Rhea	378
Richmond	398
Warren	271
Washington	387,396
White	308
Coves:-	
Blevins	273
Mullins	286
Sweetens	251,276,277,278
	279,294,295,303
	335,347,350
Coward, John	259
Cox, Amos	229
Cox, Polly	269,274,275,387
Cox, Thomas	267,328
Cozzart, Jesse	271
Crabtree, William	238
Cravens, E. H.	418
Creeks:-	
Battle	122,224,251,275,276
	278,279,281,282,293
	294,300,301,303,308
	311,316,317,325,334
	342,343,344,347,350
	390,396,402
	403,405,407
Boone	396,399
Crow	238,250
Dry	279,287,334
Farmer	283,357
Fiery Gizzard	243,273,309
	310,343,435
McBee	252
Mud	368
Saquachee	378,400,408,410,415
Sweetens	294,335,351
Crockett, Jonathan	282
Crockett, Nathan	281
Croft, Philipp J.	235
Cross, Izikier	303
Cross, Joel	303
Crow Creek	238,250
Cumberland Mountain	262,272,343
	361,381,396,406
Cunningham, John	293,294
Cynthia	403

D

Daiforth	273
Dame, John	267

	Page
Darvin, William	363,364
Davenport, Thomas	353,354,379,380
David, Nathaniel	253,374,396
Davidson County	316
Davis, James	286,381
Davis, Nathaniel	253,375,382
Davis, William	416
Deakins, Absolom	281,284,285,286
	399,400,401
Deakins, Jas.	286
Deckard, Benjamin	309,310,311
Deckard, Jonathan	399
Deckard, John	399
Deckard, Mathew	310
Deckard, P. L.	310
Denry, Joseph	243
Dixon, Mathew L.	310,311,330,331
Doss, John	263,295,296
Doss, John Jr.	262
Douglass, William	245
Drain, James	343
Drain, Will	234
Dry Creek	279,287,334
Dudley, Leonard	245
Dunaway, Wm.	282
Dunlap, James	385
Durham, Nathan	311

E

Easterly, Moses	333,334
Eaves, Jonathan	279,303
Eaves, William Jr.	279
Eaves, William Sr.	279,280
Elder, I. W.	395
Elder, Lockhart	395
Ellidge, James	283
Everett, J. C.	253,271,412
Everett, John	395
Everett, L.	271
Eves, William	351
Eves, Jonathan	347,350,357
Exertt, John	404

F

Fancher, Alexander	268
Farmer, Bird	335
Farmers Creek	283,367
Favis, James	381
Ferguson, Alexander	268
Fiery Gizzard Creek	243,273,309
	310,345,455
Fishtrap, Ford	289

	Page
Forster, C. F.	286
Forster, George	286,310
Foster, J. A.	286
Frank, Jno.	307
Francis, J. L.	390
Francis, Joseph	389
Francis, Samuel C.	389,390
Franklin, County of	198,251,255
	286,294,310
	315,317,330
	335,343,351
	363,398,399
Frederick, Reo	373
Frogge, Arthur	383

G

Gauf, Edmond	351,354,356
	357,358
Garderner, James	285
Gardner, Jennie	324
Gaskew, Joseph	253
Gavock, F. M.	93
Geer, Simon	340
Georgia, State of	396,417
Gibson, Phebe	324
Gibson, Sallie	324
Gibson, Wm	325
Gillespie, Eliza M.	399,400,413
	414,415
Gillespie, George P.	401
Gillespie, George T.	283,284,285
	286,399,400
	413,414,415
Glazier, Westley	343
Bocher, Henry	303
Goodlet, John H.	352
Goodwin, John	331,364
Gordon, George	293,325
Gordon, Robert C.	293
Gotcher, Henry	251,252,286,347
Gott, Clairborn	366
Gott, Samuel	229,242,257,258
Graham, Daniel	281,282,291,292
	293,294,344,378
Granville District	352
Gray, County of	399
Gray, George	296
Gray, William	296
Grayson, Henry	340,341,373,381
Grayson, Jesse	405,406
Green, Christopher A.	296
Green, Robert	325
Green, County of	283,295,381,400

Page

Green, County of (Cont'd) 407, 414
415
Griffith, Amos 240, 261, 265, 263
260, 266, 267, 268.
271, 301, 312, 313
341, 361, 362, 367
368, 375, 381, 382
404, 405, 406, 417
Griffith, Arden 392, 393
Griffith, David 392, 393
Griffith, John 361, 417
Griffith, Polly 323
Griffith, Thos 299
Griffith, William 362
Griffith, Wm C. 361
Grundy, County of 414
Gunter, James C. 303

H

Hackworth, Austin 303, 304
Hafner, Daniel 343
Hall, John 271, 365, 372, 393
Hall, William 305
Hall, Adam 401, 403
Hall, Davis 401, 402
Hall, Elijah M. 395
Hall, Enoch P. 259, 260, 264, 265
288, 289, 313, 329
Hall, James 403, 404
Hall, John 340, 371
Hall, Roswell 256, 258, 260, 261
263, 264, 265, 266
299, 301, 302, 316
317, 327, 328, 336
417
Hamilton, Harvey 380
Hands, Nichols 359
Hargiss, Abner 390, 391
Harris, Benjamin F. 316, 317
Harris, Charles 317
Harris, George 297, 305, 306
Harris, Lasater 340
Harris, Samuel 241, 316, 317
Harris, William 403
Harris, Wm C. 316
Harrison, Hilet 372
Harrison, John 229
Haslering, Thomas J 248, 254
259, 363
Hasting, Thos. J. 313

Page

Hatfield, H. 337
Hatfield, John 297, 298, 409
Harrow, Henry H. 374
Hawkins, William 314, 315, 318
Heard, John 410
Heard, Mary 392
Hick, S. 254
Heirs, Carter 399
Henderson, Alford 399
Hendrix, David 324, 325
Hendrix, Fannie 323
Hendrix, Fetherie 324
Hendrix, Luke 254, 285, 269, 274
281, 282, 324
373, 374, 337
Hendrix, Mark 371, 372
Hendrix, Wash 397
Hendrix, William 302, 303
Hards, John 298
Hickey, James 361
Hickey, John 244, 245
Hickey, W. R. 358
Hicks, Elijah 301, 306, 307
Hicks, Isaac 276, 301, 306, 307, 330
Hicks, Stephen 247, 248, 262, 263
270, 275, 284, 286
288, 289, 308, 317
333, 337, 346, 347
360, 370, 391
Hickson, Prigmore 331
Hill, Daniel 343, 405
Hilliard, Joel 339, 358
Hixon, Ephriam 242, 257, 258
270, 271, 301, 307
Hixon, Houston 242, 257, 258
301, 327
Hoag, Jas. H. 266
Holt, Polly 383
Hopkins, John 274, 275
Hopkins, T. 291, 368
Hornbeck, Elijah 276, 342, 371, 412
Hornbeck, James 342, 343, 370, 371
House, William 301
Houston, Horace B. 332, 344
Houston, R. 345
Houston, Samuel 378
Hudgins, Berry K. 398
Hudgins, Dawson 398
Hudgins, Emily 398
Hudson Creek 363
Hugar, Daniel 353

Page

Halvey, Conrod	273, 309, 310
Humble, Jepe	265
Humble, Jesse	269, 370, 313, 334
	346, 347, 375
Hunt, Nathel	310, 311
Hitchins, Mark	261

I

Indian Nation	296
Irwin, County of	417
Island Ford	337
Ives, John	377

J

Jackson, Churchwell	393
Jackson, County of	249, 250, 262, 368
Jackson, James	381, 382, 393
Jackson, John	207
Jackson, Samuel	334, 335
Jackson, Sam. Jr.	273, 274
Jall, Roswell	264
James Lloyd	241
Jefferson, (Negro Boy)	313
Johnson, Andrew R.	325, 348
Johnson, James	343, 344, 402
Johnson, Lewis	358, 366, 392
Jones, Dury	236, 237
Jones, Hercules	332, 348, 349
Jones, James	240, 241, 256, 257
	263, 292, 293, 388
Jones, John	240, 371
Jones, Joseph	240, 319, 341, 342
Jones, Morgan	300, 311
Jones, Thomas	332, 333, 348, 349
Jones, Wm	263, 293, 398
Jones & Blevins	319

K

Kell, Rober	381
Kell, Thomas	332, 413, 414
Kell, Thomas Jr.	381
Kell, Thomas Sr.	380
Kelly, Alexander	239, 241, 242
	243, 247, 250
	252, 257, 269
	272, 278, 287, 289
	290, 298, 308, 319
	322, 330, 346, 359

Page

Kelly, Alexander	360, 365, 370, 372
(Cont'd)	388, 391, 406, 410
Kelly, Jno	224, 235, 237, 238, 239
	240, 241, 242, 243, 244
	245, 246, 247, 248, 249
	250, 252, 253, 254, 255
	256, 257, 258, 259, 261
	262, 263, 264, 265, 266
	268, 269, 270, 272, 274
	275, 277, 278, 279, 280
	281, 284, 285, 287, 288
	290, 294, 295, 296, 297
	298, 299, 300, 301, 302
	303, 305, 306, 307, 308
	309, 312, 313, 314, 315
	318, 319, 320, 321, 322
	323, 325, 326, 327, 328
	330, 331, 332, 333, 334
	335, 336, 337, 338, 339
	340, 341, 342, 343, 344
	345, 346, 347, 348, 350
	351, 352, 354, 355, 356
	357, 358, 359, 360, 361
	362, 363, 364, 365, 366
	367, 370, 371, 372, 373
	374, 375, 377, 382, 383
	384, 385, 386, 387, 389
	390, 391, 392, 393, 394
	395, 396, 397, 398, 399
	402, 404, 405, 406, 407
	408, 411, 412, 417, 418
Kellys Turnpike Road	411
Kelly, William	241, 330, 392
Kennedy, Daniel	414, 415
Kenton, David	375
Kentucky, State of	401
Kerklen, Allen	298, 409, 410, 411
Kerklin, Elisha	297, 408, 409
	410, 411
Keys, Elizabeth	368, 369
Keys, Isaac	368, 369
Kilgore, Charles	408
Killen, A. S.	411
King, John	272
King, Thomas	308
King, William	247, 254, 289
	322, 346, 359
	370, 372
Kraft, Philip	260, 264, 266
	289, 369, 412

L	Page
Lackey, Thomas	350
Lamb, Adam	292
Lamb, Alexander	408, 410
Landing, Blakely	400
Lane, David	407
Lane, George	313, 314, 341
	342, 383
Lane, John	274
Lasey, Elizabeth	252
Lavron, Gabriel	393
Lowrery, George	224
Lawrence, Henry	392, 393
Layne, George	315, 318
Leeper, M.	359, 392
Lemon, Samuel	406, 407
Lewis, Archbald	320
Lewis, George W.	408
Lewis, James	296
Lewis, John T.	352
Lincon, County of	339
Little Sequatchie	265, 267, 269
	340, 386
Lloyd, James	242, 243, 257
	258, 298, 332
Long, Arther	278
Long, Henry	286, 287, 305, 306
Looney, John	329, 330, 358
Looney, Peter	357
Looney, Robert	256
Lowery's, Ferry	295
Lowery, George	282, 344
Lowery, James	353
Lowery, Susan	343, 405
Lyda, Henry	405, 406

M	
Malaway, Robert	401
Maloney, Robert	414
Malory, Robert	400
Mannel, Fleet	343
Marabel, Stephen	333
Marcum, Carter	243, 244
Marcum, William	358
Marsel, William	250
Marshall, Wm	343
Martin, Brice	294
Martin, David	273, 309, 405
Martin, Joseph	394
Martin, Uria	294, 295
Mathews, Burgess	240, 247, 254, 288
	289, 290, 322, 346
	347, 349, 350, 356

	Page
Mathews, Burgess (Cont'd)	359, 370, 371, 372
	373, 374, 385, 386
	391
Mathews, James	250
Mathews, William	267, 328
Mathis, Arthur	250
Maxwell, John	315, 347, 348, 351, 383
Maxwell, Thomas	252, 291, 314, 315
	318, 347, 348, 351
	352, 354, 370, 371
	383, 389, 390
May, Leroy	318, 331
Maybee, Phillip	322
Mayfield, Elisha	253, 254, 337
Mayo, I.	292
Mayo, James	241, 284, 285, 306, 307
McAllister, Ezekiel	320
McBee Creek	252
McBee, Obediah	279, 280
McBee, Samuel	294, 335, 347, 350, 351
McBride, Pleasent	305, 306
McCain, Jas.	297, 343
McCallis, Andrew	329
McCord, David	371
McCoy, John	243
McDaniel, John	272, 273
McDaniel, Rachel	272
McDowell, Rober	335
McDowell, Robert	251, 252, 277
	279, 351
McGavack, D.	281, 282, 291
	294, 344, 378, 382
McGavack, E.	344
McGavack, F.	282
McGavack, H.	281, 344
McGavack, T.	282, 291, 293
McGavan, John	241, 243, 244
	295, 314, 317
McHarry, Wm	394
McIntuff, Jasper	300
McIver, John	284, 329, 376
	377, 409, 411, 413
McLaughlin, William H.	315, 316
McMinn, County of	320
McMurray, John	297
McNatt, F.	270
McNeil, Churchwell	407, 408
McReynolds, James	271
McReynolds, Joseph	308
McReynolds, Samuel	308
McRinch, James	142
Mead, Samuel B.	329, 368, 369, 391

	Page			Page
Merritt, John	331	Nelms, John B.		260,366
Merritt, Nancy	332	Nelms, John R.		418
Merritt, Samuel	331	Newman, John		272,273
Metcalf, William	253,254	Newman, Jonathan		234,236,237,343
Miller, David	247,254,273,274	Newman, Lewisa		237
	289,290,297,300	Newman, S. D.		33
	311,343,346,347	Nichols, David		240,248,249
	352,363,359,360			293,338,373
	370,372,391,	Nicholson, Samuel		162
Miller, Francis	252	Norfolk, City of		375,408,415
Millsapp, John	349	North America		378
Minor, Anthoney B.	348	North Carolina, State of		186,235
Minor, J. B.	332,333,361			253,255,284
Minor, Joseph D.	348			320,352,355
Missouri, State of	316			405
Mitchell, Amos	411			
Mitchell, Harold	418			
Mitchell, Howell	268	**O**		
Mitchell, J. C.	319,320,389			
Mitchell, Joel D.	308,309	Oats, David		247,253,254,271,280
Mitchell, John	320			289,322,323,330,331
Mitchell, Warren	269			346,347,359,360,364
Mitchell, William	237,241,308,309			365,370,372,374,375
Montgomery, Benjamin R.	404			382,388,391,406
Montgomery, H.	361	Oats, Davis		252
Moore, Anthony W.	332,333	Oglesby, Ruth		352
Moore, George	262	Orear, William		317,318
Morgain, County of	395	Overturf, Adam		402,403
Morris, John	352,379	Overturf, John		304,305,333
Morrow, William	286,287,306	Owens, Enoch		345,246
Mountains:		Oyler, Fredrick		285
Cumberland	262,272,343,361			
	381,395,405	**P**		
Rocky	395			
Rocky Ridge	385	Pack, Betsey		299
Mud Creek	368	Pack, Elizabeth		362,363
Murfeesboro	281,282,290,291	Pankey, John		182
	292,294,344	Pankey, Smith		359
		Patterson, Andrew		401,414,415
N		Patton, John		277,280,281
		Payne, Thomas		334
Nahaley	334	Payne, William		311
Nancy, Big	417	Peck, Elizabeth		344
Nancy, Little	417	Pendleton, District of		352
Nashville	378	Perry, Alexander		379,380
Nations:		Petty, James		318
Cherokee	362,363,368,418	Philips, Abner		354,355,389
Indian	296	Philips, Richard		354,355
Neal, Joseph	253	Picketts, John		326,327
Neal, P.	253	Pikeville		377,411
Neene, Lenanal	281	Pond, Spring		294
		Pope, Jonathan		255,337

Page

Price, Charles   275
Price, Hugh   248
Price, Isaac W.   274, 275, 276, 359
Price, J. N.   256
Pryor, Greene   232, 247, 253,
                       275, 316, 337
Pryor, G. N.   239
Pryor, Mathew   247
Pryor, Mathew, Jr   245
Pryor, Mathew Sr. 237, 238, 245, 246
Pryor, P. M. Sr.   246
Pryor, Phillip   245
Pryor, Samuel   380
Pryor, Samuel M.   367
Pryor, Samuel N.   238, 246, 265
                            366, 383
Pryor, Seth   238, 247
Pryor, Williams   321, 322

           R

Ragsdale, Will H.   290
Raines, C. B.   397
Raines, Rolla   266, 369
Raines, Rollie P.   364
Rankin, David   255, 256, 257, 258
                   263, 327, 336, 340
                   348, 350, 355, 356
                   366, 367, 372, 386
                            387, 388
Rankin, James   386, 388
Rankin, Wm   264, 365, 387, 388
Ramsay, Thos. A.   320
Rawlings, Asable   377, 378
Rawlings, Asheal   379
Rawlings, Daniel R.   248, 363
                            388, 412
Ray, Hannah   334, 335
Ray, Thomas   335
Read, Charlie   268, 366
Read, Isaac   396
Reece, George   328
Reed, Charley   256, 325, 393
Renfro, W. D. L.   295
Renfro, W. H. S.   265, 296
Rhea County   370
Rice, G. W.   287, 289, 290, 294, 295
                298, 299, 302, 309, 312
                313, 314, 315, 318, 319
                320, 321, 322, 324, 325
                326, 327, 328, 330, 331

Page

Rice, G. W.   340, 341, 342, 346, 347
                348, 350, 351, 352, 353
                354, 355, 356, 357, 358
                359, 360, 361, 362, 363
                364, 366, 367, 368, 369
                371, 372, 373, 374, 375
                380, 381, 382, 383, 384
                385, 386, 387, 388, 389
                390, 391, 392, 393, 394
                396, 397
Rice, John   367, 368, 387
Rice, Joseph   383
Rice, William   336, 356, 386, 388
Richardson, Marget   324
Richmond, County of   398
Riggle, David 247, 249, 308, 398, 399
Riggle, Jacob   418
Riggle, Sand D.   398
Riggle, Solomon   247, 248, 308
                            398, 399
Rivers:
   Sequachie   288, 376
   Big Sequachie   315, 354
   Little Sequachie   302, 323
   Tennessee   206, 268, 287, 305
                 316, 343, 344, 377
                      378, 395, 411
Roads:-
   Georgia   289, 344
   Kelly's Turnpike   411
   Valley   381
Roberson, Eleph   378, 379, 381
Roberson, Elijah   378
Roberson, Sam W.   340
Roberts, Isaac   355
Roberts, I. H.   297, 350, 405
Roberts, Jesse C.   296
Roberts, Susan   355
Rocky Mountain   395
Rodgers, Jesse   341
Rogers, Emmuel   408
Rogers, Fountain   275, 284, 285
Rogers, James   409, 10
Rogers, Jesse   381, 382
Rogers, Joseph   377
Rollins, Daniel R.   369
Ross, A.   373
Ross, Fredrick   353
Roy, George W.   394
Russell, E.   296
Rutledge, Henry M. 343, 353, 363, 365

S	Page		Page
Salmon, C. W.	304,305,379,391	Spangler, Bennett	333
Schoolfield, Aaron	382,415	Spangler, Elizabeth A.	333
Seay, Sam'l	359	Sprigg, Rigen	352
Selab, William	417	Spring Pond	234
Selman, Benjamin	281	Spyker, Jonathan	310,311,399
Selman, Jesse	280	Standifer, Alford	323,349,395
Sequachie	283,298,341,348	Standifer, C.	251
Sequachie Creek	378,400,408	Standifer, H.	334
	410,415	Standifer, Isaac	250,251,312,321
Sequachie River	219,228,237,239		323,324,346
	242,244,245,248		348,350,387
	252,253,257,261	Standifer, James	261,281,282,287
	262,263,266,267		288,290,302,332
	269,270,271,274,		338,339,346,382,385
	284,285,288,289	Standifer, James Jr.	316
	291,292,301,302	Standifer, James M.	250,251
	312,314,318,319	Standifer, Jane	321,324
	320,321,322,323	Standifer, Jemima	312,313,323
	327,328,329,330		349,375
	331,334,337,338	Standifer, Jesse H.	250,251
	340,341,346,349	Standifer, John	291
	352,355,358,359	Standifer, J. P.	370
	363,365,366,367,	Standifer, Luke	298,299,302,312
	370,371,372,373,		323,346,360,361
	374,376,380,381	Standifer, Samuel	261,262,299,312
	382,383,384,385,389		313,333,345
	390,393,400,405,407		346,359,375
Sevier, John	284,376,400,405	Standifer, Shelton	321
	406,408,410	Standifer, Skelton	250
Sevier, V.	414,415	Standifer, William	239,250,252,253
Sharp, Richard	293		312,321,323,324
Shelton, Richard	243		327,345,346,349
Shelton, William	353,354,366		374,375,382,393
	367,380	Standifer, William I.	251,261,262
Sherley, Thomas	239,244,265,268		266,309,313,338
Sherley, Thomas Jr.	235,236,237		375,379,385,386
	267,269		387,403,404
Sherley, Thomas Sr.	362		405,406,407
Sherley, Wm. D.	283		408,412,416
Shropshire, John	362		418
Simiming, S.	300	Stanfield, David	303,304
Simms, James	281,282	Stanfield, John	305
Skillen, A.	377	States:-	
Smith, Aaron	408	Alabama	249,250,251,283
Smith, James	275,392,393		296,308,368,395
Smith, John	315,316	Georgia	396,417
Smith, Thomas	244,245,246,304,305	Kentucky	401
	314,337,356,357	Missouri	316
Southgate, John	375,376,377,400	North Carolina	186,235,253,255
	408,409,410		284,320,352,355,405
	411,415,416	Tennessee	240,281,282,290,291
Spangler, Bena	333		292,293,294,343,344,378

Page

States:- (Cont'd)
   United States   281,291,293,294
   Virginia   309,376,398,408,415
Steele, Isaac   262,263,382
Stephens, Williams   247,289,290
   322,347,370
   372,391
Stevens, Michal L.   287
Stevens, William   346,354,359,360
Stewall, William   415
Stewart, David   381
Stewart, George   285,399,400,401
Stewart, James   319,320,380
Stewart, John   250
Stewart, Joshua   401,402
Stewart, Samuel   379
Still, Andrew   283,284,405
Stinnett, Hiram   302,303
Stinnett, Jesse   302
Stinnett, Reuben   269,270
Stinnett, Samuel   240
Stinson, Michal L   287,288,289
Stone, Burt   317
Stone, John   326,327
Stone, Ludwall   237
Stone, Noble L.   404
Stone, Richard W.   367,368
Stone, William   247,254,289,290
   322,333,334,346
   347,359,360,370
   372,391,404
Stone, Gen'l William   283
Stovars, Isaac   298
Street, Anthony   411,412
Street, John   403
Stubblefield, Absolomon   250
Sulphur, Gen Spring   271
Summer, I. I.   378
Sween, V.   401
Sweetens, Creek   335,351
Swiney, Hopkins L.   301

T

Tate, John K.   405
Taylor, James P.   399,400,413,414
Taylor, May C.   399,400,413,414
Tennessee River   206,262,287,305
   316,343,344,377
   378,395,411
Terry, Hopkins L.   395

Page

Terry, Scott   271,292,366,372,377
   399,409,411,416
Thomas, Benjamin Jr.   383
Thomas, Burnett   396
Towson, John   314,354,357
Trussell, W.   300
Trussell, Asher   407
Trussell, Benjamin   364
Trussell, Elizabeth   333
Trussell, Mathew   359
Trussell, William   340,406,407
Turney, Hopkins L.   313,336
   337,359,398
   398,399

U

United States   281,291,293,294

V

Vale, Samuel   298
Valley Road   381
Vaulx, Wm.   316
Virginia, State of   309,376
   398,408,415

W

Walker, George   381
Walker, John   394,395,417
Walker, William C.   352,353
Wamack, Abner C.   235,249,277,278
Wamack, Isham   249,277,278
Wamack, Levi   276,280,281,353
Ward, Heiziah   366
Ward, John   388
Warren, County of   271
Washington, County of   381,396
Washington, City of   344,363,368
Washington, John   402
Watkins, Geo   381
Watson, Aaron   394
Watson, Henry   330
Watson, Jacob   393,394
Watson, Thomas   394
Watson, William   394,405
Wayne, County of   417
Webb, John   389
West, Humphreys   386,387
White, Abraham   252
White, County of   308

	Page
Whiteside, James	391
William, Arnett	239
William, George	400, 414
Williams, Hardin	249
Williams, John	322
Williams, Mathew	341
Williams, Oscar	396
Williams, William	285, 321, 322
Wilson, Andrew	366
Wilson, Arden	393
Winchester, Tennessee	264
Woffenburger, Samuel	351
Wood, G. W.	270, 289, 313, 369
Wood, William	315
Woodley, John	271

	Page
Woody, Robert	398
Wooten, Jesse	339
Wooten, John	339, 402
Worthington, Robert	256
Wynn, John	294, 295, 347, 348
Wynn, Mathew	303, 355
Wynn, Susan	355
Wynn, Thomas	295

Y

	Page
Yarnell, Henry	258, 259, 383
	384, 385
Yarnell, Naomi	323
Young, Henry	351

P. 234

Lease of Land From
Dury Jones
To)   VS
Jonathan Newman
100 acers of land.

This indenture made the twenty
third day of December in the year
of our Lord One Thousand eight
hundred and eighteen between Dury

Jones of the one part and Jonathan Newman of the other part, both of the
State of Tennessee and County of Marion,

WITNESSETH, that the said Dury Jones for and in consideration
of the said covenants and agreement herein- after- after- mentioned, reserved and contained on the part and behalf of the said Dury Jones his executors administrators and assigns to be paid down and performed here and
each of them hath granted demised, leased set and to form letter and
by this presents do and each of them doth grant, demised lease set on to
form let unto the said Johnathan Newman his executors administrators and
assigns; One hundred acres of land lying and being in the said County
above mentioned including one half of the survey where the said Newman
now lives and running as follows to wit:

down the Spring branch to the divide between Richard Blevins
and said Newman thence running with their divide to said Jonathan line
thence coming down towards improvements running so as to include One hundred acres Including Newman improvements and houses and meanders the mountain and dry branch and all and singular appurtenances thereunto belonging.

To have and To Hold all and singular the said demise, premises
with them every of them appurtenances unto the said Jonathan Newman his
executors administrators and assigns from the twenty fifth day of Dec.
being the date of said demise of said deed on title and unto the full
use and tenor of nine and Forty years from thence and next ensuing the
date of said deed of title and fuly to be complete and under yeilding
Oh said Newman shall for him his heirs, executors and administrators build
a dwelling house two story high with a shingle roof and stone chimney and
a good barn and out houses and said Newman is to plant two hundred fruit
trees and leave the place under good repair further more said Newman
is to pay the said Jones two hundred dollars to be paid quarterly ensuing
the date of said Jones Deed or title from him the said Drury Jones and
his heirs executors and administrators to him the said Jonathan Newman
and his heirs executors administrators.

To Have and To Hold from him the said Drury Jones and his heirs
and the said Drury Jones and his heirs and the said Drury Jones shall
warrant and defend from himself his heirs executors and administrators
and assigns and from all manner of person or persons whatsoever the said
Newman wherein I the said Drury Jones do bind himself, his heirs and executors, administrators in the sum of One Thousand Dollars if in case I
should fail in my part of the within interest whereunto I have set my hand
and affixed my seal the 23rd day of Dec. 1818 signed and retained in the
presents of us Richard Blevins Luke Blevins his mark.

his

Dury Jones X   (Seal
mark

P-237. Know ye that I the said Jonathan Newman held and firmly bound unto Dury Jones in the sum of One Thousand Dollars to be void on condition that the said Newman shall comply with the within mentioned and deliver the same to the said Dury Jones or his heirs executors administrators the end of the Forty nineth year from the date of his Deed then to be void and of no effect otherwise to remain in full force and virtue according to law whereunto I have set my hand ans cal this 23 day of December 1818.

                                               Jonathan Newman (SEAL)

      his
Richard X Blevins
      mark
            his
Luke Blevins X
          mark.

STATE OF TENNESSEE
MARION COUNTY COURT FEBRUARY TERM 1827.

Then was the within deed of Lease from Dury Jones to Jonathan Newman for One Hundred acres of land duly acknowledged in open court by the said Dury Jones and ordered to be certified for registration.
Given under my hand and private(seal) at office in Jasper the 19th. of Feb. 1827.

                               Jno. Kelly Clk.

For value recieved I assign the within lease of land to Luvisa & Lucinda Newman.

      Witness my hand & seal on the Deed this day of
                         Registered 1st. Oct. 1837.

Mathew Pryor Sr.
    To Deed of Conveyance
Conatser Daniel.

      This indenture made on the 23rd. day of December 1825 between Mathew Pryor Sr. of the County of Marion & State of Tennessee of the one part and Daniel Conatser of the County and State aforesaid of the other part.
    Witnesseth:
      That the said Mathew Pryor Sr. for and in consideration of the one half of sixty acres of land which Green H. Pryor, entered & surveyed for him upon the halfves and the said Green H. Pryor having soll his half which is thirty acres to the said Conatser and the said Mathew Pryor Sr. doth by these presents convey & relinguish to the said Daniel Conatser all the right & title vested in him the by the State of Tenn. his heirs &c the aforesaid Thirty acres of land be the same more or less.
    Situated in Marion County on the South east si nde of Sequachee River bounded as follows (viz).
    Beginning at a maple on the bank of a Drean the beginning corner of a seventy acre survey of said Conaster;thence East sixty three and a half poles & bending in part on a Sixteen acre survey of said Mathew Pryor Sr. to a stake and pointers on a line of the same; Thence North running with a line of said M. Pryor line seventy four poles to a stake & pointers on a line of the said sixty acre survey; thence west bending in part on forty acre survey of William Mitchell sixty three and a half

poles to a poplar Said Conatser corner; thence South with his line
seventy four poles to the beginning. And the said Mathew Pryor Sr. doth
convey and relinquish unto the said Daniel Conatser and his heirs &c the
above described thirty acres of land be the same more or less.

To Have and To Hold all the said Mathew Pryor doth by these
presents forever warrant and defend from himself his heirs unto the s'd
Daniel Conatser but not against any other person or persons whatsoever.

IN WITNESS WHEREOF, the said Mathow Pryor Sr. hath hereunto set his
hand & seal the date & date first above written.
P-238.

Mathew Pryor Sr.

Signed in presence of us
        Saml. N. Pryor
        Seth Pryor.

STATE OF TENNESSEE
MARION COUNTY COURT NOVEMBER
TERM
1826.

Then was this execution of the within Deed of conveyance from
Mathew Pryor Sr. to Daniel Conatser for thirty acres of land duly acknowledged in presents by s'd. Pryor and ordered to be certified and
admitted for registration.

Attest Jno. Kelly Clk.

Registered 28th. Dec. 1827.

BRIGGS GEORGE
        To Deed of Conveyance
ALEXANDER GEROGE and LUDWELL STONE.

        This Indenture made this Seventeen day of September in the year
of our Lord One Thousand eight hundred and twenty two, between George
Briggs of the County of Wilson of the One Part and George Alexander of
and Ludwell Stone of the other part both of the County of Marion and
all of the State of Tennessee.
        WITNESSETH:
                That the said George Briggs for and inconsideration of the
sum of two hundred to him in hand paid by the said George Alexander and
Ludwell Stone at and before the sealing and delivery of those presents
whereof he doth hereby acknowledge himself fully satisfied and paid
hath granted bargained and sold and confirmed and by these presents doth
grant, bargain, sell and confirm unto the said George Alexander and
Ludwell Stone one certain trat or parcel of land lying and being in the
County of Marion and State aforesaid on Crow Creek containing One
Hundred acres the same more or less, and bounded as follows to wit:-
        Beginning at two beeches and a hickory in William Crabtree con-
ditional line near the Mountain running thence North sixty four deg. E.
thiarty poles to two beeches and a hickory on the West bank of Crow
Creek thence South Forty Deg. E. down said Creek twenty two poles to a
bunch of White Walnuts on the bank of said cree; thence south eighty deg.
E. down said creek to a Sycamore; thence S. ten deg. West, down said
Creek twenty eight poles to a large poplar; thence South down said creek
twenty eight poles to a large poplar; thence S. fifty E. down said Creek
thirty poles to apoplar; thence S. twenty five E. down said creek thirty

down said creek thirty two poles to a poplar; thence S. twenty five
East down said creek thirty two poles to a poplar thence south eighty
seven E. twenty two poles to a cluster of Beeches on the bank of s'd
creek; thence S. forty deg. E. twenty four poles to a large hackberry
at the mouth of a small branch; thence S. thirty deg. E. thirty nine
poles to a box elder on the bank of said creek; thence South sixty deg.
West Eighty poles to a stake on the side of the mouth; thence N. forty
three West one hundred and eighty poles to the beginning—

    With the hereditaments and appurtenances. To Have and To, Hold
the said tract or parcel of land with all the rights and priviliges
belonging thereunto together with all the woods, water, mines, and min-
erals that are belonging unto the said George Alexander and Ludwell
Stone with tract or parcel of land I do covenant and forever defend from
me my heirs and assigns. We and all person or persons whatsoever.
    IN WITNESS WHEREOF

P-239. I have hereunto set my hand and affixed my seal this day and date
above written.

    Signed sealed and delivered in the presence of

                             Geo. Briggs (SEAL)

Alexander Tho's.
    Harrison John.   Attest.

                        STATE OF TENNESSEE
             MARION COUNTY COURT AUGUST TERM
                  ————1823————

    Then was the within deed of conveyance duly proven in open court
by the oaths of Thomas Alexander and John Harrison subscribing witnesses
thereto. Ordered to be certified and admitted to record.
    Given under my hand and seal not having an official seal at office
this 23rd. March , 1825.

                      Jno. Kelly   Clk.
                      By A. Kelly   D.C.

Registered 29th. Dec. 1827.

Arnett William	This Indenture made this 25th. day of
and Shirley Thomas	August in the year of Our Lord 1824 by and
To Deed of Conveyance	between William Arnett & Thomas Shirley
Fancher Alexander	of the One part & Alexander Fancher of the
	other par, all of the County of Marion &

State of Tennessee.
    Witnesseth:-

        That for and in consideration of the sum of three hundred
dollars to us paid the reciept of which is hereby acknowledged the
said William Arnett & Thomas Shirley hath this day bargained and sold
conveyed and confirmed and by these presents doth bargain sell convey
& confirm unto the said Alexander Faucher a certain tract or parcel of
land containing fifty acres more or less situated lying and being in
the county of Marion & State aforesaid, on the North west side of
Sequachee river it being a part of a tract of land granted by the State
of Tennessee to William Stadifer for One hundred and sixty acres by
Grant No. 15386 it being the tract whereon the said Alexander Faucher
now lives as follows to wit:-

Beginning on a hickory the south east corner of the said survey of One Hundred and sixty acres: thence with the line of the same North five Hundred and thirty three and one fourth poles to pointers the north East corner of said Survey then west with another line of the same forty poles to pointers: then S. sixteen deg. west One hundred and forty poles to pointers the S. boundary of said survey and with the same E. to the beginning.

To Have and To Hold the aforesaid land with the appurtenances to the said Alexander Faucher his heirs executors administrators and assigns from the claim and demise of all and every person claiming by through from under the said William Arnett & Thomas Shirely.

IN WITNESS WHEREOF we have hereunto set our hands and seals the day and year first above written.

William Arnett (Seal)
Thomas Shirley (Seal)

Signed, sealed and
delivered in the presence
of:

    Jno. Kelly
    G.N. Pryor.

STATE OF TENNESSEE
MARION COUNTY COURT- FEBRUARY TERM
------------1826------------

Then was the within execution of the within Deed of Conveyance from William Arnett & Thomas Shirley to Alexander Faucher for forty acres of land duly acknowledged in open court by the said Arnett & Shirley and ordered to be certified for registration.

Given under my hand & private seal (not having an official seal) at office in Jasper the 20th. day of February 1826.

(SEAL)

    Registered December 29th. 1827.

Jno. Kelly Clk.

P-240.

Jones James Sheriff to To) Deed of Conveyance Blevins Stephen A.	This Indenture made this 18th. day of September in the year of Our Lord One Thousand eight Hundred and twenty three between James Jones Sheriff of Marion County and State of Tennessee

of the one part and Stephen H. Blevins of the County and State afore said of the other part.

    Witnesseth:-

        That whereas it appears from the records of Marion County Court that Burgess Mathews Esquire issued two writs of fier facies from two judgments, Simon Grear obtained against Samuel Stinnett on the 31st. day of December 1820 before the said Mathew on which fier facies Joseph Jones Deputy Sheriff made his return to the worshipful court of pleas and quarter session for Marion County at November Term 1821 that no goods and chattels of the defendants was to be found in his County & levied on two tracts of land of eight acres each on both fier facies whereupon two orders of sales issued from said Court commanding the Sheriff of said Marion County to expose to public sale according to law the afore said tract of land so much thereof as would satisfy the said Plantiff debt &c therefor I James Jones Sheriff of Marion County as aforesaid by my deputy Alexander Coulter having given legal notice as the law requires of the time and place of sale did on the 18th. day of February 1822 at the Court House in the town of Jasper proceed to sell the afore said tract of land whereupon James Standifer bid the sum of one hundred and thirty five dollars and twenty five cents that being the highest and best bid for the aforesaid tracts of land and at the time of levy and sale the number of acres and No. of entry was not correctly under stood byas the said Stinnett had but two Entry's in said County on examination found them to be Eighty acres by Entry No. 5932 founded on certificate No. 1501 and the other for Eighty four acres by Entry No. 5933 on certificate 5933 founded on certificate No. 1504 both issued by the Register of East Tennessee bounded as follows adjoining lands of David Nichols on a branch known by the name of Hall's branch beginning at a stake and pointers it being a corner to said Nichols and running with line S. 14 deg. E. 46' poles to a stake and pointers then S. 88deg. E. 59 poles to a black gum Then S. 8 deg. E. 88 poles to pointers then E. 120 poles to black oak having crossed said Hall's branch at 84 deg. poles, then N. 101 poles to white oak on fork of said Hall's branch then N. 57 or 72 poles to a dogwood & sweet gum; then N. 20 deg. W. 87 poles to a sweet gums on the East bank of another fork of said branch S. 66 deg. W. 56 poles to hickory having crossed said branch; then a direct line to beginning and whereas by order of said Standifer who became the purchaser of the land directed me to convey the same to the said Blevins & James Jones Sheriff as aforesaid do hereby convey one hundred and sixty acres of the aforesaid tract of land to the said Stephen A. Blevins his heirs &c free from the right title claim and demand of him the said Samuel Stennett his heirs and assigns of all other as far as I as Sheriff aforesaid by reason of the Judgment execution levy and order of sale afore said and the law of the land I am bound to convey and warrant and defend but no other manner whatever.

IN TESTIMONY WHEREOF, I, the said James Joens Sheriff as aforesaid have hereunto set my hand and seal the day and date first above written signed sealdd and delivered in presence of

    Thomas Branson
    John Doss.

                           James Jones Sheriff
                           Marion County.

P*241.

STATE OF TENNESSEE
MARION COUNTY COURT MAY TERM
————1824————

Then was the within Deed of Conveyance duly acknowledged in open Court by James Jones, Ordered to be certified and admitted to record.

Given under my hand and private seal not having an official seal at office this the 23rd. March, 1825.

    (SEAL)

                         Jno. Kelly Clk.
                         By- A. Kelly D. Clk.

Revocation of Letters of Attorney from
S. Harris
  To
John McGowan

                           STATE OF TENNESSEE
                           MARION COUNTY.

Whereas the 2nd. day of April in the year of Our Lord 1822 I,
Samuel Harris form under my hand and seal did constitute and appoint
John McGowan my true and lawful attorney in fact for me and in my
name to settle and recieve from the commissioners in trust for the
town of Jasper the amount due and owing to me by virtue of a contract
made by and between myself and said commissioners for the building of
a jail for the county of Marion and to do all things there is concerning
the same for me in such manner as by said power of Attorney he the said
John McGowan was authorized to do, and whereas for reasons sufficient
moving me hereto,

Know all men by these presents that I the said Samuel Harris of
the County and State aforesaid do by these presents revoke the said
power of attorney made and executors on the said 2nd. Day of April 1822
to the said John McGowan and every article and thereof,

IN TESTIMONY whereof I, have hereunto set my hand and seal this
22nd. day of November 1822.

Sam Harris   (SEAL)

STATE OF TENNESSEE
MARION COUNTY COURT NOVEMBER TERM
————————1822————————

Then was the within revocation of a power of Attorney from
Samuel Harris to John McGowan acknowledged in open court by the Harris
and ordered to be certified and ordered for registration.

Given under my hand and private seal (not having an official
seal at office) this the 22nd. day of November 1622.

Jno. Kelly.

Registered December 29, 1827.

P-241.   Lloyd James
            To Deed of Conveyance   This indenture made the 11th.
            John Bridgman.   day of August One Thousand Eight
                                               Hundred and twenty three be-
tween James Lloyd of the one part and John Bridgeman of the other part.
Both of the County of Bledsoe and State of Tennessee.
            WITNESSETH:—
                      That the said James Lloyd hath this day bargained and delivred
unto John Bridgeman a certain tract or parcel of land in Marion County
and State aforesaid for the sum of two hundred and ten dollars the
reciapt of which is hereby acknowledged lying and bounded as follows:—
            Beginning at a post oak the north west corner of said tract
joining Wm. Kelly & James Mayhs 500 acre survey then along their line
84 deg. E. 46 poles to a black oak, thence S. 5 deg. E. 111 poles to a
poplar; Thence S. 35 deg. W. 150 poles to an ash Then west 88 poles to
pointers on William Mitchell line and with the same N. 25 deg. E. 266
poles to pointers on William Mitchell line and with the same N. 25 deg.
E. to the point of beginning,
            To Have and To Hold the same forever including one hundred
and thirty acres be the same more or less with and singular the wood
water water courses profits, commodities hereditaments and appurtenances
whatsoever
P-242.

P-242. to the said tract of land belonging the said James Lloyd doth
forever warrant and defend unto the said John Bridgman and his heirs
forever for himself and all persons claiming under him whatsoever
and his heirs and none other signed sealed and delivered in presence
of the

WITNESSETH the day and date above written.

James Lloyd   (SEAL)

STATE OF TENNESSEE
MARION COUNTY COURT AUGUST TERM
————1823————

Then was the within deed of conveyance from James Lloyd to John
Bridgman duly acknowledged in open court by the said Lloyd. Ordered to
be certified and admitted to record. Given under my hand and private
seal (not having an official seal) this 25th. March 1825.

Jno. Kelly   Clk.
By- A. Kelly D. Clk.

Registered Dec. 29th. 1837.

P- 242.   Lloyd James   ◊   This Indenture made the 18th.
To- Deed of Conveyance   ◊   day of August in the year of Our
Huston Hixon   ◊   Lord Eighteen Hundred and twenty
three between James Lloyd of the
County of Bledsoe and State of Tennessee of the one part and Huston Hixon
of the County of Marion and State aforesaid of the other part.
WITNESSETH:-

That for and in consideration of the benefits of nine and
and one fourth acres of land warrant the reciept of which is hereby
acknowledged hath and by these presents doth grant bargain alien and
confirm unto the said Huston Hixon a certain tract or parcel of land
containing nine and a fourth acres situated lying and being in the said
County of Marion on the South east side of Sequachee River and adjoining
Ephraim Hixon and Sam H. Gott, it being part of a tract of land granted
by the State of Tennessee to the said Lloyd for 160 acres by grant No.
16170 bearing date the 8th. day of November 1821.

Beginning at a large white oak on the South boundary of said tract
then along said Gotts line North seventy degree west one hundred poles
to stake and pointers on said E. Hixon line and with same south ten
degrees E. thirty four poles to stake and sweet gum then E. to the
beginning including 9 1/4 acres be the same more or less, with and singular
the wood water water courses, profits commodities hereditaments to the
said tract or parcel of land belonging or in any wise appertaining and
the remainder and remainders rents of and issues and all the estate
right title interest property claim and demand of in and to the same
and every part and every parcel thereof either in law or equity.

To Have and To Hold unto the P. Huston Hixon his heirs and assigns
forever the aforesaid tract or parcel of land with its appertances from
me my heirs &c will warrant and forever defend from all manner of persons
claimed from by or under me or my heirs forever but it is further under
stood by the parties that if the said tract of land should be hereafter
by any older or better title than the one by these presents conveyed that
this one is that case the said Lloyd is not bound for any consideration
cost or damages then he has red'd in consideration only the benefit of

of the warrant above stated which is by virtue of these presents.

IN WITNESS whereof I hereunto set my hand and seal the day and date above written.

James Lloyd   (Seal)

Sam H. Gott.   )
Epian Hixon   ) Witnesses.

STATE OF TENNESSEE
MARION COUNTY COURT NOVEMBER TERM
-----1824-----

Then was the within Deed of Conveyance duly acknowledged in open court by James Lloyd. Ordered to be certified and admitted to record.

Given under my hand and private seal not having an official seal at office this 22nd. March 1825.

(SEAL)   Jno. Kelly   Clk.
                                By- A. Kelly D. C.

John Cochran   )
To Deed of Conveyance)   This Indenture made this tenth day of May
Samuel Anderson   )   in the year of Our Lord One thousand Eight
                               Hundred and twenty six between John Cochran
and Samuel Anderson both of the County of Marion and State of Tennessee.

WITNESSETH:-

That the said John Cochran for and in consideration for the sum of thirty dollars to him in hand paid the reciept of which is here by acknowledged hath given granted bargained and sold unto the said Samuel Anderson and his heirs and by these presents doth grant, bargain and sell unto him the said Anderson & his heirs a certain tract or parcel of land lying and being in the County of Marion aforesaid on the waters of Fiery Gizzard Creek containing Thirty acres be the same more or less and bounded as follows to wit:-

Beginning at a stake below a field of said Andersson then west fifty poles to a sweet gum at the foot of the mountain thence with the same as it meanders N. 57 deg. west One Hundred and fifteen poles thence N. 66 west. 44 poles thence N. 25 poles to a bunch of lynns at the foot of said Mountain thence crossing the cave to an elm at the foot of the mountain thence with the same as it meanders to a stake thence S. 60 poles to the beginning.

To Have and to Hold and enjoy the above mentioned premises and the said John Cochran and his heirs will warrant and forever defend the title of the above mentioned tract from him and his heirs and no other person unto the said Samuel Anderson and his heirs forever .

IN TESTIMONY whereof the said John Cochran hath hereunto set his hand and affixed his seal the day and year first above written.

SIGNED? SEALED, and DELIVERED in the presence of us:
John McCoy
Joseph Denny   John Cochran (SEAL)

STATE OF TENNESSEE
MARION COUNTY COURT AUGUST TERM
-----1826-----

Then was the execution of the within Deed of conveyance from John Cochran to Samuel Anderson for thirty acres of land duly acknowledged in open court by the said Cochran and ordered to be certified for registration.

Given under my hand and private seal (not having an official seal at office) this the 21st. day of August 1826.

(SEAL)   John Kelly Clk.
    Registered January 1st. 1828.

P-243. Revocation of Letters of Attorney from
    Carter Marcum
        To
    John McGowan

STATE OF TENNESSEE
MARION COUNTY.

WHEREAS, I,Carter Marcum from under my hand and seal did constitute and appoint John McGowan my true and lawful attorney in fact for me and in my name to settle and relieve for the commissioners. in trust for the town of Jasper the amount due and owing to me by virtue of a contract made by and between my self and said commissioners for the building a jail for the said
P-244. County of Marion said to do all things concerning the same for me in such manner as by said power of attorney he the said John McGowan was authorized to do and whereas for reasons sufficient to me here moving

Know all men by these presents that I the said Carter Marcum of the County and State aforesaid do by these presents make the said power of Attorney made and executed as aforesaid to the said John McGowan and every article and clause thereof.

IN TESTIMONY whereof I have hereunto set my hand and seal this 22nd. day of November 1822.

                        his
           Carter X Marcum
                mark.

Test: Thos. J. Campbell.

STATE OF TENNESSEE
MARION COUNTY COURT NOVEMBER TERM
**********1822**********

Then was the within revocation of a power of attorney from Carter Marcum to John McGowan acknowlddged in open court by the said Marcum and ordered for registration.

Given under my hand and private seal (not having a seal of office) this 22nd. Nov. 1822.

(LS)   Jno. Kelly   Clk.
    Registerd Jan. 1st. 1828.

Hickory John
To Deed of Conveyance
Smith Thomas

This Indenture made this twenty ninth day of September One Thousand eight hundred and twenty six, between John Hickory of the County of Marion and State of Tennessee of the one part and Thomas Smith of the County and State aforesaid of the other part.
    WITNESSETH:
    That the said John Hickory for and in consideration of the sum of fifteen hundred dollars to him in hand paid the reciept whereof

is hereby acknowledged hath and by these presents doth bargain and sell
alien enforce and convey unto the said Thomas Shirely his heirs and
assigns forever a certain tract or parcel of land containing two hundred
and sixty three acres be the same more or less lying and being in the
County of Marion on the South E. side of Sequachee River.

Beginning at two black gums then S. thirty eight and a half poles
to pointers then E. 44 poles to pointers then N. 29 E. 22 poles to a
post oak then N. 5 deg. E. 64 poles to pointers then 60 then E. 29
poles to a hickory and poplar then N. 71 poles to a black oak then W.
59 poles to a stake then N. 90 poles to a white oak then W. seventeen
poles to a stake field then N. 58 poles to a white oak then W. 58 poles
to a white oak then S. 67 poles to pointers, then W. 58 poles to a
black oak on the bank of a branch then S. 5 W. 18 poles to a post oak
on the bank of a dry branch then up said branch as it meanders S. One
and a half W. 22 poles to a post oak then S. 16 and a half w. 30 poles
to a stake then S. 26 W. 15 poles to a black oak on the bank of said
branch then S. 130 poles to pointers then a direct lien to the beginning together with all and singular the hereditaments and appurtenances
to the said tract or parcel of land belonging.

To Have and to Hold to the said Thomas Smith his heirs and assigns
forever the said 263 acres of land with the hereditaments and appurtenances
against the said John Hickory and his heirs and against all and ever
person and persons whatsoever will warrant and forever defend.

IN WITNESS whereof the said John Hickory hath
P-245. hereunto set his hand and seal the date and date above written.
Signed, sealed, & delivered

John Hickory   (SEAL)

John Street
            his
John Baker   X
            mark.

STATE OF TENNESSEE

MARION COUNTY COURT NOVEMBER
SESSION
—— 1826 ——

Then was thw within deed of conveyance from John Hickory to
Thomas Smith for two hundred and sixty acres of land duly acknowledged
in open court, by the said Hickory and ordered to be certified for
registration.

Given under my hand & private seal (not having an official
seal) at office in Jasper the 21st. day of November 1826.

Jno. Kelly   Clk.

(SEAL)

Registered for registration, Jan. 9th. 1821.

P-245. Enoch Owens ⟩
    To Deed of Con. ⟩   This Indenture made the 25th. day of February
    Thomas Smith ⟩   1826 between Enoch Owens of the County of
                       Marion and State of Tennessee of the one part

and Thomas Smith of the County and State aforesaid of the other part.
WITNESSETH;

That the said Enoch Owens for and in consideration of the
sum of five hundred dollars to him in hand paid by the said said Thomas
Smith before the scaling and delivery of these presents the reciept of
which is hereby acknowledged hath granted bargained and sold and by
these presents doth grant bargain and sell unto the said Thomas Smith
his heirs and assigns a certain tract or parcel of land situated in the
County and State aforesaid on the south E. side of Sequachee River containing One hundred and forty seven acres 47 po adjoining lands of Mathew
Pryor Sr. Richard Shelton Leonard Dudley William Duglass Phillip Pryor
the Schooll land and the land that said Smith bought of Mathew Pryor
Jur.

Beginning at a hickory and pointers on the bank of the branch
heretofore called the dry branch a condition made between Mathew Pryor Sr.
and Enoch Owens thence with said condition S. 71 deg. E. 21 poles to
pointers; then S. 22 poles to a black oak on said Shelton line then
with the same line of his line E. 20 poles to pointers; then N. 20 degs.
E. 60 poles to a sweetgum then E. 87 poles to a black oak a corner of sd d
Dudleys land then with his lien N. 16 deg. E. 160 poles to a stake on
said Dudley line; then with his line W. 30 poles to a small plum bush;
then N. 4 poles to a stake said P. Pryor corner then with his line W.
117 poles to a stake & pointers on the E. boundary of the School land
then with the same S. 87 poles to a stake on said branch having passed
the S. E. corner of said School land nine poles then down said branch
with its different meanders as a condition heretofore made between
said John H. Pryor in the occupant entry to the beginning including
the place and premises which said Thomas Smith now lives together with
all and singular the tenements appurtenances and hereditaments thereto
appurtaining or belonging to have and to hold the said above described
tract or parcel of land hereby granted bargained and sold every part and
parcel thereof with all the tenements and appurtenances thereunto belonging the proper use and benefit of the said Thomas Smith
P-246. his heirs and assigns forever and the said Enoch Owens for himself
and his heirs all and singular the premises hereby granted bargained and
sold with the tenements and appurtenances &c unto the said Thomas Smith
his heirs and assigns against him the said Enoch Owens his heirs and
every and all other person or persons whatever shall and will forever
warrant and defend the same.

IN WITNESS whereof I, the said Enoch Owens have hereunto set
my hand and seal the day and date above written.
Signed, sealed and delivered in presence of
Sam'l N. Pryor   his
Mathew Pryor Ser.   Enoch X Owens   (SEAL)
                                          mark.

STATE OF TENNESSEE
MARION COUNTY COURT MAY SESSION
———— 1826 ————

Then was the execution of the foregoing Deed of conveyance from
Enoch Owens to Thomas Smith for One hundred and forty seven acres and forty
seven poles of land duly proven in open court by the oath of Samuel N.
Pryor Sr. the subscribing withess thereto. Ordered to be certified for
registration.

Given under my hand and private seal (not having an official seal)
at office in Jasper the 18th. day of May 1826.

(SEAL) Registered January 10th. 1828.

Jno. Kelly. Clk.

P-246. John H. Pryor
    To) Deed of Conveyance
    Mathew Pryor Sen.

This Indenture made this Seventeenth
day of February in the year of Our
Lord One Thousand eight hundred and
twenty eight, between John H. Pryor of the County of Marion and State
of Tennessee of the one part and Mathew Pryor Ser. of the County and
State aforesaid of the other part.
    WITNESSETH:
        That the said John H. Pryor for and in consideration of
twenty dollars to him in hand paid the reciept of which is hereby acknowledged, hath granted bargained and sold and by these presents doth
give grant bargin and sell unto the said Mathew Pryor Sen. his heirs and
assigns one tract of land lying and being in Marion County, Tennessee
aforesaid on the S. E. side of Sequachee River containing 42 acres be
the same more or less and bounded as follows to wit:-
        Beginning at a hickory & white oak on the E. boundary of said
Mathew Pryors 100 acre survey S.E. of his house where Pharoah Cobbs
lives of 49 1/2 acre survey joins the same; then E. wth Cobbs line
22 poles and an arrow pointer corner to a 21 acre survey of Richard
Shirley; then with the same N. 48 poles to pointers on a conditional
line said Mathew Pryor and Enoch Owens; then with the same N. one
deg. w. 22 poles to a stake in the branch then up the general course
of said branch N. 25 deg. E. 39 poles to a stake in s'd branch near
an ash on a conditional between athow Pryor and P. Jno. H. Pryor
then N. 71 deg. W. 22 and a half poles to a stake near a dogwood;
then W. 53 poles to a stake near a red oak then N. 68 poles to a stake
and pointers on the School land line the with the same W. 74 poles to
pointers; then S. 70 poles to pointers, then E. binding in on the lines
of S&d 100 acre survey of P.M. Pryor ser. One hundred and twenty seven
pole to a dogwood corner to said 100 acre survey, with the same S.
93 poles to the beginning.
        To Have and To Hold
P-247. the above mentioned granted and bargained premises P. Mathew
Pryor Sr. his heirs and assigns forever and the said John H. Pryor his
heirs &c do and will forever warrant and forever defend the title to
the said land to the said Mathew Pryor Sr. his heirs and assigns forever
against the claim of mine and his heirs and no other person.
        IN TESTIMONY whereof he hath hereun o set his hand and affixed
his seal the day and year first above written.
        Signed sealed and delivered in presence of us:
Green H. Pryor
Seth Pryor & John   John H. Pryor   (SEAL)

                    STATE OF TENNESSEE
                MARION COUNTY COURT AUGUST
                        SESSION
                ------   1826   ------

    Then was the within deed of conveyance from John H. Pryor to
Mathew Pryor Sr. for 42 acres of land duly acknowledged in open court,
by the oaths of said Pryor. Ordered to be certified and admitted to

record.

Given under my hand and private seal not having an official seal of office in Jasper the 22nd. Aug. 1826.

(SEAL)

Jno. Kelly Clk.

Registered January 12,1828.

By- A. Kelly D. C.

P-247. Commissioners &c.

      To Deed of Conveyance   This Indenture made the 2nd.

      Riggle D. & S.   day of May one thousand eight hundred and twenty six between William Stone &

David Oats

Burgess Mathews

Alexander Kelly

William King

William Stephen

David Miller   Commissioners in trust of the one Part;

      and   AND:-

S. & D Riggle of the county of Marion and State of Tennessee of the other part.

    WITNESSETH:

That for and in consideration of the sum of One hundred and Eighty dollars to us in hand paid the reciept whereof is hereby acknowledged hath and by these presents doth grant, bargain aline enforoff and confirm unto the said S. & D. Riggle their heirs and administrators two certain lots of land in the town of Jasper known and designated in the original plan of said town by Lots No. 49 & 50 containing one quarter of an acre each sold at public auction as the law directs.

To Have and To Hold the aforesaid lots of land with all and singular the rights title and profits emoulments and appurtenances belonging or in any wise appertaining to the same to the only use and behoof of them the said S. & D. Riggle their heirs &c and the said commissioners in trust as aforesaid and will as far as they are authorized as commissioners forever warrant and defend to the said S. & D Riggle their heirs etc. the above recited lots against the right title interest and demand of all and every person or persons whatever.

IN TESTIMONY whereof we hereunto set our hand and seald this the day and date first above written.

S. Hicks   Attest.   Wm. Stone   (Seal)

Jno. Kelly   David Oats   (Seal)

                                Burgess Mathew(Seal)

                                Alex. Kelly   (Seal)

                                Wm. Stephen (Seal)

                                David Miller (Seal)

STATE OF TENNESSEE

MARION COUNTY COURT MAY TERM

———— 1826 ————

Then was the execution of the within deed of Commissioners in trust for the town of Jasper

P-248.

P-243. to Solomon & David Riggle for lots No. 49 & 50 in said town was proven in open court by the oaths of Stephen Hicks & John Kelly the subscribing witnesses thereto & ordered to be certified for registration. Given under my hand and private seal (not having an official seal) at office in Jasper, 15th. day of May 1826.
(SEAL)

Jno. Kelly Clk.

Price Hugh
To
Rawlings & Haslering

This Indenture made this 21st. day of March In the year of Our Lord One Thousand Eight Hundred and twenty six by and between Hugh Price of the County of Marion and State of Tennessee of the one part and Daniel R. Rowlings and Thomas I Haslering, Merchant trading under the firm name and partnership style of Rawlings and Haslering of the same county and State of the other part.

WITNESSETH:
That for and in consideration of the sum of three hundred dollars to me in hand paid by the said Rawlings & Haslering I the said Hugh Price have and doth by these presents grant bargains sell and confirm unto the said Rawlings & Halsering a certain spot or place of land situated lying and being in the town of Jasper in said County of Marion containing One quater of an acre the same being known and designated in the general plan of said town as lot No. 4.

To Have and To Hold the aforesaid lot or parcel of land with the appurtenances to the said Rawlings & Haslering and their heirs forever from the claim and demand of all and every person or persons claiming by through from or under me the said Hugh Price from the claim and demand of all and every person or person whatever.

IN TESTIMONY whereof I the said Hugh Price have hereunto set my hand and seal the day and year herein written.

Hugh Price (SEAL)

Signed, sealed and delivered in
presence of:
      G. Hicks
      Wm. Arnett.

STATE OF TENNESSEE
COUNTY OF MARION COURT MAY
SESSION
———— 1826 ————

Then was the within deed of execution from Hugh Price to Rawlings & Haslering for lot No. 44 in the town of Jasper duly acknowledged in open court, by the said Price and ordered to be certified and admitted for registration.

Given under my hand and private seal (not having an official seal) at office in Jasper the 16th. day of May 1826.

Jno. Kelly Clk.

Registered January 15th. 1828.

P-248. David Nichols

To Deed of Conveyance

Rawlings & Haslering

This Indenture made this 21st.
day of August 1826 by and between
David Nichols of the County of
Marion and State of Tennessee of the
one part and Rawlings & Haslering of the County and State aforesaid of
the other part.

WITNESSETH:-

That for and in consideration of the sum of thirty dollars
hand paid the Rect of which is hereby acknowledged that David Nichols
hath this day bargained sold and conveyed unto the said Rawlings &
Haslering a certain spot or piece of land with its appurtenances situated
lying and being in the town of Jasper in said County of Marion Known
and designated in the orginal plan of said town by Lot No. 42 containing One quater of an acre.

TO Have and To Hold the aforesaid sport or piece of land with its
appurtenances to the said Rawling & Haslering and their heirs and assigns forever from the claim and demand of all and every person or persons
whatsoever I the said David Nichols do bind myself my heirs and
assigns firmly by these presents.

In Testimony whereof I have hereunto set my hand and seal the
day and date above written.

Signed, Sealed & delivered in our presents:-
David Riggle
Michal Nichols.

David Nichols (SEAL)

STATE OF TENNESSEE
MARION COUNTY COURT AUGUST TERM
———— 1826 ————

Then was the within deed of conveyance from David Nichols to
Rawling & Haslering for lot No. 42 in the above town of Jasper duly
acknowledged in open court by the said Nichols and ordered to be certified for registration.

Given under my hand and private seal Not having an official seal
at office in Jasper this the 21st. day of August 1826.

(LS)   Reg. Jan. 15,1828.

Jno. Kelly   Clk.

P-249. Isham Wamack

To Deed of Conveyance

Hardin Williams

This Indenture made the Eleventh
day of April One Thousand eight hundred and twenty five between Isham
Wamack of the State of Tennessee and County of Marion of the one part
and Hardin Williams of Jackson County and State of Alabama of the other
part.

WITNESSETH:

That the said Isham Marmack for and inconsideration of the
sum of Four Hundred Dollars to him in hand paid by the said Hardin
Williams the reciept whereof is hereby acknowledged hath given granted
bargained and forever a certain tract or parcel of land situated lying
and being in the County of Marion afroresaid on the waters of Battle
Creek in Sweetens Cove it being on a equal formity of one hundred and
and eighty acre tract granted to the said Isham Warmack by the State of

Tennessee it being the west half of said tract.

To Have and To Hold the aforesaid land with all and singlular
the hereditaments and appurtenances of in and to the same belonging
or in any wise appertaining to the only proper use and benefits and
behoofs of him the said Warmack for himself his heirs and assigns for
ever and the said Isham Warmack for himself his heirs and executors
and administrators and assigns doth covenant and agree to and with
the said Hardin Williams his heirs or assigns that the before recited
land he will warrant and forever defend against the right title interest
or claim of all and every person or persons whatsoever.

In Testimony whereof the said Isham Warmack have here unto set
his hand and affixed his seal the day and year first above written.
Signed Sealed, and delivered in presence of Obediah Beans.

Abne C. Warmack

Isham Warmack   (SEAL)

STATE OF TENNESSEE
MARION COUNTY COURT AUGUST SESSION
————1825————

Then was the execution of the foregoing deed of conveyance from
Ish m Warmach to Hardin Williams for fifty four (54) acres of land duly
acknowledged in open court by the P.Warmack and ordered to be certified
for Registration.

Given under my hand & private seal (not having an official seal)
at office the 15th. day of August 1825.

Jno. Kelly   Clk.

Reg. Jan. 16th. 1828.

P-250. Absolem Stubbfield   This Indenture made the 9th. day of
       To Deed of Conveyance   August in the year of Our Lord
       James Mathews   One Thousand Eight Hundred and twenty
                                 three between Absolem Stubbfield
assignee of Joseph Brooks of the County of Marion and State of Tennessee
of the one part and James Mathews of the other part and county and
State of Alabama.
      WITNESSETH:
      That for and in consideration of Five Hundred dollars in
hand paid the reciept of which is fully acknowledged have bargained
and sold and by these presents doth bargain sell and deliver unto the
P. James Mathews one hundred acres of land situated lying and being in
the said county of Marion and State of Tennessee on said west fork
of Crow Creek.
      Beginning at a beech at the foot of the Mountain on a conditional
line between the said Stubblefield and A. Bledsoe; thence with said
line S. 45deg. E. crossing said Creek at 60 poles in all 46 poles to large
poplar at the foot of the opposite mountain thence S. 81 E. 50 poles
to a stake at the foot of the mountain, thence S. 68 E. 50 poles to two
white oaks and three beeches at the foot of the mountain thence S. 8 deg.
E. 136 poles the mountain to a stake, Thence S. 14 deg. W. 48 poles to

to the creek thence S. 20 deg. E. 62 poles to a sugar tree and two
beeches in the conditional line of John Stewart thence S. 87 deg. W.
with the same crossing at twenty poles in all sixty six poles to a
large poplar and beach thence N. 19 deg. W. 310 poles to the beginning
with the meanders of the mountain &c,

To Have and To Hold the above mentioned land and premises with
all and every part thereof I the said Absolem Stubblefield do for
myself my heirs and assigns forever warrant and defend to the singly
right and behoof of the said James Mathews his heirs and assigns by
these to be fully enjoyed forever.

In Witness whereof I have hereunto set my hand and seal the day
and date above written.

In presence of:
William Marsee
William Mathews   Attest.   Absolem Stubblefield
Arthur Mathis

STATE OF TENNESSEE
MARION COUNTY COURT AUGUST TERM
———— 1823 ————

Then was the within deed of Conveyance from Absolem Stubblefield
and order to be certified, to James Mathew duly acknowledged in open
court by the said Stubblefield and admitted to record.

Given under my hand and private seal not having an official
at office this the 24th. March 1825.

Jno. Kelly Clerk.
By- A. Kelly D. Clk.

Registered Jan. 17th. 1828.

P-250. Standifer William   )
       To Deed of Gift   ) This Indenture made the 5th. day
       Willaim Standifer & others.   ) of October in the year of Our Lord
                                                one thousand eight hundred and
twenty, between Willaim Standifer Senior of the County of Marion and
State of Tennessee of the one part and I,
       William Standifer
       Luke C. Standifer
       Jesse H. Standifer
       S. K.   Standifer
       James M. Standifer
grandsons of the said William Standifer Sr. of the County of Bledsoe and
State aforesaid of the other part,
       Witnesseth:-
       That the said William Standifer Ser. as well for and in con-
sideration of the natural love and affection which he hath and beareth
unto the said William I. Standifer, Luke C. Standifer, Jesse H. Standifer
Skelton C. Standifer and Jesse M. Standifer as the better maintainance
and preferment of the said William I. Standifer, Luke C. Standifer,
Jesse H. Standifer, Skelton C. Standifer and James M. Standifer, hath
given and granted and by these presents doth give and grant unto the said
William I. Standifer his heirs and assigns forever a certain Negro girl
named Syle about twenty six years old.
       To Have and To Hold the above named Negro Girl to the only pro-
per use and behoof of him the said William I. Standifer, his heirs and

assigns forever . Also the P. Willi'm Standifer Ser. hath given granted
and by these presents doth give grant unto the said Luke C. Standifer
Jesse M. Standifer, Skelton C. Standifer and James M. Standifer, their
heirs and assigns forever a certain Negro girl named Lucinda about five
years old.

In Testimony whereof I the said William Standifer doth hereunto
set his hand and seal the date and day first above written.

William Standifer   (SEAL)

Amos Griffith
Isaac Standifer   Attest.

STATE OF TENNESSEE
MARION COUNTY COURT NOVEMBER TERM
———————— 1825 ————————

Then was the above Deed of gift from William Standifer Sr. to
William Standifer, Luke Standifer, Jesse H. Standifer Skelton C. Standifer
and James M. Standifer, for two negro girls named Syle and Lucinda was
proven in open court by the oaths of Amos Griffith & Isaac Standifer
subscribing witnesses thereto and ordered to be certified for registration.

Given under my hand andprivate seal not having an official seal
at office in Jasper the 21st. day of November 1825.

Jno. Kelly Clk.

(LS)   Registered January 19,1928.

P-251.   Thomas Maxwell   )
To Deed of Conveyance   )   This Indenture made the Fourth day
Henry Gotcher   )   of August in the year of Our Lord One
                                        Thousand Eight Hundred and twenty
three between Thomas Maxwell of the State of Tennessee and County of
Marion of the one part and Henry Gotcher of the State   of Alabama and
Franklin County of the other part;
WE NESSETH:—
        That the said Thomas Maxwell for and in consideration of the
sum of three hundred dollars to him in hand paid by the said Henry Gotcher
at or before the sealing & delivery of these presents the recippt whereof
is hereby acknowledged have given granted, bargained, sold and released
and by these presents doth give grant bargain sell & release a certain
quanity of land contain fifty two acres more or less it being a part of
two surveys Originally granted to Robert McDowell and Samuel McBee and
by them deeded to George A. Brach and from s'd Bruch to the above named
Thomas Maxwell situated lying and being in the said State of Tennessee and
Marion County aforesaid on Sweetens Creek waters of Battle Creek in
Sweeten Cove butting and bounding as follows:—
        Beginning at pointers at the foot of the mountain thence South
eight poles to a holly it being Robert Bear Sr. N. W. corner thence
on said Bean line South sixty poles to pointers; thence West eighty two
poles to Robert McDowells west boundary line to pointers; thence North
fifty five poles to a sugar tree it being Samuel McBee; South east corner;
thence
P-252.   thence west to the mounting of McBee creek; thence up said creek
with all its meanders to a horn bean coener it being a conditional corner

between the said Thomas Maxwell his son John Maxwell; thence Northwardly on the conditional line betwixt the said Thos. and John Maxwell to the Mountain where their spring branch comes down the mountain to McDowell N. boundary line thence with said Mountain south sixty nine East to said North boundary line to the beginning.

To Have and To Hold the aforesaid tract of land with all & singular the rights profits & apportenances there and unto the same beglonging or in any wise appertaining to the only proper use and behoof of him the said Henry Gotcher his heirs & assigns that before recited and forever) and bargained premises he the said Thos. Maxwell witll warrant and forever defend the right and title of said land from himself his heirs executors administrators & assigns and from all other persons whatsoever.

In Witness whereof I the said Thomas Maxwell have hereunto set my hand and affixed my seal this day and date year first above written.
IN prexence of:
Obidah Bean
Robert McDowell   Attest.   Thomas Maxwell (SEAL)

STATE OF TENNESSEE
MARION COUNTY COURT AUGUST TERM
——————1823——————

Then was the within deed of conveyance from Thomas Maxwell to Henry Gotcher duly acknowledged in open court by the said Maxwell. Ordered to be certified and admitted to record.

Given under my hand and private seal not having an official seal this 24th. day of March 1825.
(LS)   Reg. Jan. 19,1828.   Jno. Kelly Clk.
                                              By- A. Kelly   D. Clk.

P-252.   Wm. H. Standifer,   )
         To Deed of Conveyance   )   This Indenture made the 19th. day of
         Oats & Davis   )   September in the year of Our lord One
                                               Thousand eight hundred and twenty five
between William H. Standifer of the County of Marion and State of Tenn. of the one part and David Oats & Nathaniel Davis of the claim and county and State aforesaid of the other part.
WITNESSETH:-
That the said Wm. H. Standifer for and in consideration of the sum of Nine Hundred and eighty dollars to me in hand paid the reciept whereof is hereby acknowledged hath and by these presents, doth grant, bargain sell and confirm unto the said David Oats and Nathaniel Davis their heirs and assigns forever a certain tract or parcel of land containing two hundred and two acres be the same more or less, Lying and being in the county of Marion of the South Ease side of Sequachee River adjoining the school land Lot No. 2nd. and land of Abraham White Fredrick A. Ross, Elizabeth Rasey & Francis Miller-

Beginning on a beech and hickory at the N. E. corner of the School land lot No. 2 West with the same one hundred and fifty six poles to a white oak on the bank of the river; thence up the same as it meanders N. 53 deg. E. 26 poles; thence N. 28 deg. E. 50 poles; thence N. 35 deg. E. 42 poles; thence N. 19 Deg. 6 poles to a sweet gum; thence E. 80 poles to a dogwood; thence 36 deg. E. 38 poles to a post oak white's corner; thence 130 poles to a black gum; thence S. 52 poles to pointers and dogwood on Elizabeth Masys line; thence W. 22 poles to pointes at a branch; thence down the branch with the meanders of the same S. 45 deg.

West ten poles; Thence S. 8 deg. West 25 poles
P-253. thence S. 16 deg. W. 45 poles thence S. with East on East line
from the beginning will intersect it with all and singular the wood
water water courses profits, commodities herediatments, and appurtenances
whatsoever to the said tract belonging or appertaining and revision and
revisions and remainder and remainders rents and issues thereof and
all the estate right title interest and prifits claim and demand of him the
said William H. Standifer his heirs and assigns forever in and to same and
every part or parcel thereof either in law or equity.

To Have and to hold the said two hundred and two acres of land
with appurtenances unto the David Oats and Nathaniel David their heirs
and assigns forever against any lawful title claim or demand of all and
every person or persons whatsoever will warrant and forever defend by
these presents.

In Witness whereof the said William H. Standifer hath hereunto
set his hand and seal the date and year above written.

Signed, sealed and delivered in the presence of:

```
    I. C. Everett   )                    Wm. H. Standifer   (SEAL)
    Joseph Haskew   )   Attest.
```

STATE OF TENNESSEE
MARION COUNTY COURT NOVEMBER TERM
———————— 1827 ————

Then was the within deed of conveyance from William H. Standifer
to David Oats and Nathaniel Davis for two hundred and two acres of land
duly acknowledged in open court by the said Standifer and ordered to be
certified for registration.

Given under my hand and private seal not having an official seal
at office in Jasper 18th. day of January 1828.

(LS) Reg. Jan.19,1828.   Jno. Kelly Clk.

P-253.   Elisha Mayfield   0
         To Deed of Conveyance   0   STATE OF TENNESSEE
         Joseph Neal   0   MARION COUNTY.

This Indenture made the 18th. day of November 1825, betwixt
Elisha Mayfield of the State and County aforesaid of the one part and
Joseph Neal of the State of North Carolina Burk County of the other part.
WITNESSETH;-

That for the sum of Three Hundred dollars s'd Mayfield hath
sold & bargained & by these presents doth convey & deliver to P. Neal
one tract or parcel of land in the State of Tennessee Marion County on the
waters of Sequachee River beginning on a stake and pointers on the line
a tract of school land on the east side of the river then East with s'd
school line 138 poles to 2 sourwood then N. 171 poles to a white oak, a
corner of Green Pryor's farm then W. with the same line 138 poles to
white oak on the bank of the river then down the river as it meanders to a
stake and pointers then S. 46 poles to the beginning corssing the river
twice thirty acres of the above tract being accepted as already conveyed by E. Mayfield to William Matcalf square of the south & lower end
and s'd Mayfield doth by these presents bind himself his heirs and assigns

forever against all claim of any person claiming or to claim the above land or any one part of it.

In Testimony whereof of which s'd Mayfield hath hereunto set his hand and seal the date above.

Signed, sealed, & delivered in presence of:

Wm. D. Shirley.

William Metcalf   Attest.   Elisha Mayfield X

P-254.   STATE OF TENNESSEE
                   MARION COUNTY COURT FEBRUARY
                              TERM
                    ————— 1327 —————

Then was the within deed of conveyance from William Mayfield to Joseph Neal for thirty acres of land proven in open court by the oaths of William Metcalf one of the subscribing witnesses thereto and ordered to be certified and admitted for registration.

Given under my hand and private seal not having an official seal at office in Jasper this the 18th. day of Jan. 1828.

(LS) Reg. Jan. 19,1828.   Jno. Kelly   Clk.

P-254. Commissioners &c.   0
        To Deed of conveyance   0   This Indenture made the 21st. day
        James Chaudions   0 of February in the year of Our Lord
                                         0 One Thousand eight hundred and twenty

seven between William Stone a   0
        David Oats   0
        Burgess Mathews   0
        Alexander Kelly   0
        William King   0
        William Stevens   0
        David Miller   0   Commissioners in trust for the County
of Marion and Town of Jasper, Tennessee, and their successors in office
of the one part:-
                AND:-
     James Chaudions of the County of Marion and State of Tennessee
of the other part,
     WITNESSETH:-

That for and in consideration of the sum of forth three dollars to us in hand paid the reciept whereof is hereby acknowledged hath and by these presents doth grant bargains sell alino enforce and confirm unto the said James C. Chaudions his heris executors and administrators a certain lot of land in the town of Jasper, known and designated in the original plan of said town of said town by Lot No. 79 containing one quater of an acre sold at public auction as the law directs.

To Have and To Hold the aforesaid lot of land with all and singular the rights and prifits emoluments and appurtenances thereto belonging or in any wise appertaining to the same to the only use and behoof of him the said James Chaudions his heirs &c the said commissioners in trust as aforesaid and will as far as they are authorized as commissioners for ever warrant and defend to the said James Chaudions his heirs &c the above recited lot against the right title interest and demand of all and every person or persons whatsoever.

In Testimony whereof we hereunto set our hand and seal the day and

and date above written.
      Hock S.
      Kelly Jno.   Attest.

William Stone	(SEAL)
Burgess Mathews	(SEAL)
Alex. Kelly	(SEAL)
William Stephen	(SEAL)
David Oats	(SEAL)
David Miller	(SEAL)

STATE OF TENNESSEE
MARION COUNTY COURT FEBRUARY
TERM
———— 1827 ————

Then was the within deed of conveyance from the commissioners in trust for the County of Marion and town of Jasper to James Chaudions for lot No. 79 in Jasper this day duly proven in open court by the oaths of Jno. Kelly and S. Heck subscribing witnesses thereto and ordered to be certified for registration.

Given under my hand and private seal the 18th. day of January 1828.
(SEAL)   Registered January 21st. 1828.

                                        Jno. Kelly   Clk.

P- 254. Alexander Coulter   ◊ This Indenture made the 2nd. day of
        To   Deed of Convey-   ◊ January in the year of Our Lord One
        Luke Hendrix   ◊ Thousand eight hundred and twenty six
                                      between Alexander Coulter of the County
of Marion and State of Tennessee of the one part and Luke Hendric of
the County and State aforesaid of the other part.
      WITNESSETH:
            That for and in consideration of the sum of twelve hundred
dollars to him the said Coulter
P-255. hand paid the reciept whereof is hereby acknowledged hath and by
these presents doth grant bargain sell alien encoff and confirm unto the
said said Luke Hendrix a certain tract or parcel of land containing one
hundred and seventy one acres situated lying and being on the west side
of Little Sequachee adjoining lands of the said Hendri x and others it
being part of a tract of land granted by the State of Tennessee to the
said Alexander Coulter for two hundred and fourteen acres by patent No.
22839 bearing date the 4th. day of December 1824.
            Beginning at a beech on the N. W. bank of said Little Sequachee the
beginning corner of the original survey and corner to said Hendrix and
running with his line N. 23 deg. W. 43 poles to pointers S. 77 deg. W.
5 poles to a beech N. 110 poles to pointers N. 53 W. 7 poles to a holly
N. 19 deg. W. 48 poles to an ironwood N. 33 deg. E. 70 poles to a stake
N. 30 deg. W. 7 1/2 poles to pointers N. 59 deg. E. 54 poles to pointers
and sycamore s'd Hendrix corner on bank of said Sequachee then down the
same along Popes and Jones line S. 20 poles N. 83 deg. E. 25 poles N. 52
deg. E.46 poles to a Spanish Oak. Then S. 4 deg. W. 40 poles S. 3 deg.
E. 40 poles S. 26 deg. W. 40 poles to an ash then down the same to begin-
ing the center of the creek being the line including one hundred and
seventy one acres be the same more or less; With all and singular the wood
water water courses profits and commodities hereditaments and appurtenances
thereunto belonging or in any wise in either law or equity.
            To Have and to Hold unto the said Luke Hendrix his heirs and assigns
forever against the lawful title claim and demand of him the said Alexander
Coulter and his heirs will warrant and forever defend the aforesaid One

Hundred and Seventy One acres of land as above described, be the same more or less. Against the lawful title claim and demand of any person or persons whatever claiming by or under me or my heirs and it is further and expressly understood and agreed upon by the parties that in case the aforesaid tract of land and premises should hereafter be taken by any older title from any grant issued from the State of North Carliona that then and in that case the said Alexander Coulter is not liable or reponsible to the said Hendrix or his heirs for any part of the condiseration by him recieved for said land as he was only bound to relinquish the state title .

In Testimony whereof I have herunto set my hand and affixed my seal this day and date above written.

Signed, sealed and delivered in presance of:

Amos Griffith

Jno. Kelly   Attest.   Alex. Coulter   (SEAL)

STATE OF TENNESSEE
MARION COUNTY COURT FEBRUARY TERM
——————— 1826 ———————

Then was the within deed of conveyance from Alexander Coulter to Luke Hendrix for One Hundred and seventy one acres of land in Marion County court, duly acknowledged in open court by the said Coulter and ordered to be certified for registration.

Given under my hand and seal (not having an official seal at office) in Jasper the 18th. day of January, 1828.

(LS) Reg. 21st. Jan. 1828.   Jno. Kelly   Clk.

P-255. Wallis Estelle Jr.
        To Deed of Conveyance   This Indenture and entered into
        David Rankins   19th. day of January in the year of
                                        Our Lord One Thousand eight hundred
and twenty seven by and between Wallis Estelle Jr. of the County of Franklin and State of Tennessee
P-256. of the One Part and David Rankin of the County of Marion and State aforesaid of the other part,

WITNESSETH:-

That for and inconsideration of the sum of One Hundred and fifty dollars to me in hand paid the reciept whereof is hereby acknowledged hath and by these presents doth grant bargain sell alien encoff and confirm unto the said Daid Rankin his heirs and assigns forever one certained undivided monority of lot of land known and designated in the origingal of the town Jasper by Lot No. 62 it being the one half of said lot it being conveyed by the said commissioners trust for the town of Jasper jointly to said Estill and Rowell Hall containing one fourth part of an acre.

To Have and To Hold the aforesaid one undivided monority or half of said Lot No. 62 with all and singular the rights and profits emoulments and appurtenances belonging or in any wise appertaining to the same to the only use and behoof of him the said David Rankin his heirs &c and I the said Wallis Estello Jr. for myself my heirs and will forever warrant & defend to the said David Rankin his heirs &c the before recited undivided half of said lot against the lawfuly title interest property claim and demand of a manner of person or persons whatever.

In Testimony whereof I hereunto set my hand and seal this day and year first above written.

J. N. Price: Witness.   Wallis Estele Jr. (SEAL)

STATE OF TENNESSEE
MARION COUNTY COURT FEBRUARY TERM
—————— 1827 ——————

Then was the within deed of conveyance from Wallis Estele Jr.
to David Rankin for one undivided monority of Lot No. 62 in the town of
Jasper duly acknowledged in open court by said E stile and ordered to
certify for registration.

Given under my hand and private seal at office in Jasper this the
18th. day of January 1828.
(LS) Reg. Jan. 22nd. 1828.   Jno. Kelly Clk.

P-256. James Jones Sheriff   ◊   This Indenture made the 15th. day of
=   To Deed of Conveyance   ◊   December in the year of Our Lord One
        David Rankins   ◊   Thousand Eight Hundred and Twenty four
                                        between James Jones Sheriff of Marion
County said State of Tennessee by his deputy William Jones of the one part
and David Rankin of the Same County and State of the other part.
        WITNESSETH:-

That by virtue of an order of sale the said James Jones directed
from the worshipful County Court of Marion County as aforesaid at the
instant of Robert Worthington against Robert Looney therefore I James
Jones by my deputy as aforesaid having giveing legal notice of the time
and place of sale did on the 15th. day of Dec. 1824 at the Court House
in the town of Jasper proceed to sell a certain tract of land containing
ten acres lived on by Charley Reed one of the acting Constable on said
County and made return to said Court as the property of said Robert Looney
the said W. M. Jones proceeded to sell aforesaid tract of land and David
Rankin being the last and highest bidder at two dollars in redy cash.

Now thereofr I Jones Sheriff as aforesaid in consideration of the
premises do hereby bargain sell enforce and convey unto the said Rankin
his horis and assigns forever the aforesaid tract of land containing ten
acres as aforesaid in said County bounded as follows to wit:-

Beginning at a stake & East near the foot of the mountain South
eastwardly from where Cannon
P-257. Cooper now lives Thence N. 28 1/4 poles to a hickory thence W. 56
poles to a stake & black bum thence S. 28 1/2 poles to a bak oak thence
E. to the beginning.

To Have and To Hold the same also the house and spring where said
Cooper now lives free from the right title interest claim and demand of
him the said Looney his heirs and assigns &c all others as far as I as
Sheriff as aforesaid order of the judgment levy and sale as aforesaid
and the law of the land I am bound to convey warrant and defend but in
no manner otherwise .

In witness whereof I the said James Jones Sheriff as aforesaid
has hereunto set his hand and seal the day and date first above written.
Written in the presence of A. Kelly J.P. and W. M. Rice

                                James Jones Sheriff of Marion Co.

STATE OF TENNESSEE
MARION COUNTY COURT FEBRUARY TERM
———— 1827 ————

  Then was the within deed of conveyance from James Ones to David
Rankin for 10 acres pf land duly acknowledged in open court by said
Jones and ordered to be certified for registration.
  Given under my hand and private seal not having an official seal
at office in Jasper this the 18th. day of January, 1828.
(LS) Reg. 22nd. 1828.

                Jno. Kelly Clk.

P-257. James Lloyd
    To Deed   This Indentured made the 18th. day of August
    Samuel Gott   in the year of Our Lord One Thousand eight hund-
            red and twenty three between James Lloyd of the
County of Bledsoe and State of Tennessee of the one part and Samuel H.
Gott of the County of Marion and State aforesaid of the other part.
    WITNESSETH:-
  That for and in consideration of the benefit of the said Gott
occupant claim which he was entitled to by a purchase from Jno. Dame the
reciept of which is hereby acknowledged hath and by these presents doth
grant bargain alien enforce and confirm unto the said Samuel H. Gott
a certain tract or parcel of land containing seventy four acres of land
containing seventy four acres of land situated lying and being in said
County of Marion on the Southeast side of Sequachee River adjoining
lands of Huston Hixon and Ephraim Hixon it being a part of a tract of
land granted by the State of Tennessee to the said Lloyd for one
hundred and sixty acres by Grant No. 16170 bearing date the 8th. of Nov.
1821 beginning at a hickory at the foot of the mountain it being the
Southeast corner of said tract then W. 99 poles to a large White Oak
a corner of Huston Hixon tract of 9 1/4 acres then along his North line
70 deg. W. 100 poles to a stake and pointers on the said Ephraim Hixon
line and with the same N. 10 deg. W. 56 poles to pointers then E. 71 poles
to stake and black gum then N. 65 deg. E. 65 poles to a stake at the
corner of said Gotts field then S. 59 deg. E. 34 poles to balck Oak to foot
of said mountain it being another corner to said tract then along said
mountain S. 15 W. to the beginning, including 74 acres be the same more
or less with all and singular the wood water water courses profits commodities hereditaments and appurtenances to the said tract of land belonging
or nay wise apportaining and the rivision and rovisions remainder
P-258. and remainedrents and issues and all the estate right title and
interest property claim and demand of in and to the same #th in law or
equity.
    TO HAVE AND TO HOLD unto the said Samuel H. Gott his heirs &c
will warrant and forever defend from all manner of person claiming from
by or under me or my heirs whatever but it is further plainly understood
by the parties that if the said tract of land should be hereafter taken
by an older or better title than his by these presents conveyed that then
and in that case the said Lloyd is not to be liable for any consideration
cost or damages above stated as he has recieved no benefit only the benefits of the porface as above stated.
    In Witness whereof I have hereunto set my hand and seal the day
and year first above written.
    Witness:-   James Lloyd (SEAL)

    Horton Hixon
    Ephraim Hixon

STATE OF TENNESSEE
MARION COUNTY COURT NOVEMBER TERM
———————1824———————

Then was the within deed of conveyance duly acknowledged in open court by James Lloyd and ordered to be certified and admitted to record.

Given under my hand and seal not having an official seal at office this the 15th. day of November 1824.

(LS)
Reg. Jan. 27, 1828.

Jno. Kelly Clk.
By- A. Kelly D. C.

P-258. John Burgess
    To Deed of Convy.
    David Rankin.

This Indenture made and entered into and by and between David Rankin if the County of Marion & State of Tennessee of the one part and John Burgess of the County and State aforesaid of the other part.

WITNESSETH:-

That for and in consideration of the sum of ten dollars to me in hand paid the reciept whereof is hereby acknowledgded I have this day bargained sold aliened and confirmed unto the said David Rankin a certain lot or parcel of land in the town of Jasper known designated in the original plan of said town by Lot No. 77.

To Have and To Hold the said Lot for himself heirs &c from em and my heris &c I do forever warrant and defend the said Lot from me my heirs &c forever.

In Testimony hereof I have hereunto set my hand and seal this 22nd. day of February 1827.

John Burgess (SEAL)

Jno. Kelly
W.M. Rice Witnesses.

STATE OF TENNESSEE
MARION COUNTY COURT FEBRUARY TERM
——————— 1827———————

Then w as the within deed of conveyance from John Burgess to David Rankin for Lot No. 77 in the town of Jasper duly acknowledged in open court by said Burgess and ordered to be certified for registration.

Given under my hand and private seal not having an official seal at office in Jasper this the 15th. day of January 1828.
(LS) Reg. Jany. 23rd. 1828.

Jno. Kelly Clk.

P-258. Henry J. Yarnell
    To Deed of Convey.
    Amos Griffith

This Indenture made this the 15th. day of August in the year of Our Lord Oen Thousand eight hundred and twenty six between Henry J. Yarnell of the County of
P-259. Marion and State of Tennessee of the oen part and Amos Griffith of the County and State aforesaid of the other part.

WITNESSETH:-

That for and in consideration of part of an entry money paid by the said Amos Griffith for entering the land from which the title is above to be conveyed was founded the reciept of which is hereby ack-

nowledged hath and by these   presents doth grant bargain sell alien
enforce and convey unto the said Amos Griffith his heirs and assigns for
ever a certain part of a tract of land granted the State of Tennessee to
the said Henry J. Yarnell for one hundred and twenty five acres by
Grant No. 89193 bearing date the fifth day of April 1824 situated lying
and being in the said County of Marion and bounded and described as
follows :-

Beginning at a pointers North East corner of said Amos Griffith
tract of our hundred sixty acr es at the foot of the mountain then along
a line of the same E. One Hundred and thirty eight poles to a beech;
then along another line of the same S. One hundred and six poles to a
stake and white oak pointer to said Amos Griffith survey of One hundred
and forty acres; then East along the same thirty three poles to a white
oak; then N. Ninety two poles to pointers; then N. 64 deg. W. ninety poles
to passing near the beech corner above mentioned to pointers corner to the
said Amos Griffith survey of ten acres then along a line of the same West
forty poles yo the foot of the mountain to the beginning including thirty
one acres be the same more of less together with all and singular the
wooods water water courses profits commodities hereditaments and appurtenances
to the aforesaid tract of land.

To Have and To Hold to the said Amos Griffith his heirs and assigns
forever from and case of the lawful title claim and demand of him the said
Henry J. Yarnell or any person claiming from or under his or his heirs
forever will warrant and defend the aforesaid tract to the same Amos
Griffith so far as the right of the same is vested in him the said Henry
Jm Yarnell by the Grant from the State of Tennessee as above specified .

In Witness whereof I the said Henry J. Yarnell hath hereunto set
my hand and seale the day and year first above written.

Signed sealed and acknowledged in the presence of:

Tailiton Hendrix
John Coward   Henry J. Yarnell (SEAL)

                    STATE OF TENNESSEE
             MARION COUNTY COURT FEBRUARY TERM
                 ----------1827----------

Then was the within deed of conveyance from Henry J. Yarnelll to
Amos Griffith for 31 acres of land duly proven in open court by the oaths
of John Coward and Tarliton Hendrix subscribing witnesses thereto and
ordered to be certified for registration.

Given under my hand and private seal not having an official seal
at office in Jasper the 13th. day of January 1828.

                                        Jno. Kelly Clk.

(LS) Reg. Jan. 24th. 1828.

P-259. Roswell Hall   o
            To Deed of Conveyance   o   This Indenture made the 12th. day
        Enoch P. Hale   o   of April in the year of Our Lord One
                                          Thous nd Eight Hundred and twenty six
between Roswell Hall of the one part and Enoch P. Hale of the other part,
both of the County of Marion & State of Tennessee.

Witnesseth:—

That for and Inconsideration for the sum of two hundred dollars to him in hand paid the reciept whereof is hereby
P-260. acknowledged hath and by these presents doth grant bargain alien enforce and confirm unto the Enoch Hale his heirs executors and administrator a certain lot of land in the town of Jasper known and designated in the original plan of said Town by Lot No. 12 containing one quarter of an acre.

To Have and To Hold the aforesaid lot of land with all and singular the rights and profits emoulments and appurtenances belonging or any wise appertaining to the same to the use and behoof of him the said Enoch P. Hale his heirs &c and the said Roswell Hall will forever warrant and defend to the said Enoch P. Hale his heirs &c the above recited lot against the right title claim and demand of all and every person whatever.

In Testimony whereof I have hereunto set my hand and seal the day and date first above written.

                                        Roswell Hall   (SEAL)

        James H. Gogg
        James B. Nelms   Witness.

STATE OF TENNESSEE
MARION COUNTY COURT FEBRUARY TERM
————————— 1827 —————————

Then was the within deed of conveyance from Roswell Hall to Enoch P. Hale for Lot No. 12 in the town of Jasper this day duly acknowledged in open court by said Hall and ordered to be certified for registration.

Given under my hand and private seal not having an official seal of office in Jasper this 18th. day of January.

                                        Jno. Kelly   Clk.

(LS) Reg. Jan. 25, 1828.

P-260. Roswell Hall
       To Deed of Conveyance   This Indenture made the 12th. day of
       Philip Kroft.   April in the year of Our Lord One
                                      Thousand Eight Hundred and twenty six
between Roswell Hall of the one part and Phillip Kroft of the other part both of the County of Marion and State of Tennessee.
       WITNESSETH:—

That for and in consideration of the sum of three hundred dollars to him in hand paid the reciept whereof is hereby acknowledged hath and by these presents doth grant, bargain alien, enforce and confirm unto the said Phillip Kroft his heirs executors and administrators a certain lot of land in the town of Jasper Known and designated in the original plan of said town by Lot No. 72 containing one quarter of an acre.

To Have and To Hold the aforesaid lot of land with all and singular the rights profits emoulments and appurtenances belongining or any wise appertaining to the said to the only use and behoof of him the said Phillip Kroft his heirs &c and the said Roswell Hall will forever warrant and defend to the said Phillip Kroft his heirs &c the above recited lot against the right title interest claim and demand of all and every person whatever.

In Testimony whereof I have hereunto set my hand and seal the day and date first above written.

James H. Hogg

John B. Nelma Witnesses.   Roswell Hall (SEAL)

STATE OF TENNESSEE
MARION COUNTY COURT FEBRUARY
TERM
———— 1827 ————

Then was the within deed of conveyance from Roaswell Hall to Enoch P. Hale for Lot No. 12 in the town of Jasper this day duly proven in open court by said Hall and ordered to be certified for registration.
Given under my hand and private seal, not having an official seal, at office in the town of Jasper this 18th. day of January.
Jno. Kelly .

P-261.   Roaswell Hall
         To Deed of Conveyance
         Mark Hutchins

> For and in consideration of the sum of five hundred dollars to me in hand paid the reciept whereof is hereby

acknowledged, I have bargained and sold unto Mark Hutchins one negro worman Surlina between the age of twenty & thirty years the said negro I do warrant and forever defend I also warrant her being a sound negro so far as I know as witness my hand & mark seal this 28th. day of Sept.1826.

                                Roswell Hall   (SEAL)

Jas. H. Hogg   Attest.

STATE OF TENNESSEE
MARION COUNTY COURT MAY SESSION
————————1827————————

Then was the within Bill of Sale from Roswell Hall to Mark Hutching for a negro woman Surlina duly proven in open court by the oaths of James Hogg a subscribing witness thereto, and ordered to be certified for registration.
                                Jno. Kell   Clk.

Reg. Jan. 15,1829.

P-261.   Samuel Standifer
         To Deed of Conveyance
         Amos Griffith

> This Indenture made the 2nd. day of May in the year of Our Lornd One Thousand eight hundred and twenty seven

between Samuel Standifer of the County of Marion and State of Tennessee of the one part and Amos Griffith of the County and State aforesaid of the other part.
WITNESSETH:-
That for and in consideration of the sum of Five Hundred dollars to him the said Samuel Standifer in hand paid the reciept whereof is hereby acknowledged, hath and by these presents doth grant bargain alien enforce and confirm unto the said Amos Griffith his heirs and assigns forever a certain tract or parcel of land containing one hundred

and Seventy five acres situated lying and being in the County of Marion aforesaid on the northwest side of Sequachee River adjoining lands of the said Griffith Luke Standifer, and Alford or the widow Standifer beginning at a black gum the north west corner of a tract of land the said Griffith purchased of James Standifer then along Luke Standifer's line of forty five acres N. 56 deg. W. 98 poles to pointers on the west boundary of the original survey thence along the same N. 26 poles to a dogwood then East 16 poles to an ash and and ironwood at the foot of the mountain then along the same as it meanders S. 77 deg. E. 64 Poles then N. 77 deg. 54 poles then N. 52 E. 68 S. 30 Deg. E. 40 poles then S. 58 deg. E. to a branch or wash that runs out of the mountain and with the same down as it meanders the main dry creek to the South boundary of said tract on said Griffith's line then with the same West to the beginning including the aforesaid one hundred and twenty five acres. Be the same more or less it being part of a tract of land granted by the State of Tennessee to William Standifer for 180 acres of by Grant No. 16093 with all and singular the woods water water courses profits commodities hereditaments & appurtenances whatsoever to the said tract of land belonging or in any wise appertaining and the reversion & reversions and remainder and remainders rents and issues thereof and all the estate right title interest property claim and demand of him the said Samuel Standifer his heirs & assigns forever either in law or equity.

To Have and To Hold One (1) hundred and twenty five acres of land with its appurtenances unto the said Amos Griffith his heirs and assigns forever will warrant and forever defend against the lawful claims and demand of all and every person whatever.

In Testimony whereof I hereunto set my hand and seal the day and date above written.

Signed and acknowledged in presence of:

William I. Standifer
John Kelly   Samuel Standifer (SEAL)

P-262.   State of Tennessee

                                                      February Term 1827

          Marion County Court

Then was the within deed of conveyance from Samuel Standifer to Amos Griffith for One Hundred and twenty five acres of land duly proven in open court by the oaths of William Standifer and John Kelly subscribing witnesses thereto, and ordered to be certified for registration.

Given under my hand and private seal not having an official seal at office in Jasper the 25th day of January 1828.

                                                      Jno. Kelly Clk.

(LS) Reg. Jan. 29th. 1828,

P-262.   John Doss Jr.
                   To   Deed of Con.   This Indenture made this 21st
                Isaac Steele   day of May 1827 by and between
                                            John Doss Jr. of the County of
Marion and State of Tennessee of the one Part and Isaac Steele of the

same County and State of the other part.

WITNESSETH:-

That for and in consideration of the sum of two hundred dollars to me in hand paid the receipt of which is hereby acknowledged I the said John Doss both me both by these presents grant bargain sell and convey & confirm unto the said Isaac Steele and his heirs and assigns forever a certain tract or parcel of land containing fifty acres more or less situated lying & being in the County of Marion on the Northwest side of Sequachee River adjoining lands of the said Doss and Thomas Branson un. bounded as follows to-wit:-

Beginning at a stake and pointers Doss; Southwest corner and on the North boundary of Branson 100 survey; thence with Branson lying West 10 poles to pointers on Bransons west boundary lion; thence W. 30 poles to a black Oak at the foot of Cumberland Mountain; thence along the same North 10 poles North 31 deg. East 94 poles to a stake in the West boundary Doss survey thence South with the same to the beginning.

To Have and To Hold the aforesaid tract of land to the said Isaac Steele his heirs administrators and assigns from the claim and demand of all and every person or persons whatsoever I the said John Doss will warrant and forever defend.

In Testimony whereof I the said John Doss have hereunto set my hand and seal the day and year first above written.

Signed, sealed and delivered in the presence of George Moore.

Attest, S. Hicks.   John Doss   (SEAL)

P-262.   State of Tennessee

                                                  May Term 1827

               Marion County Court

Then was the within deed of conveyance from John Doss Jr. to Isaac Steele for fifty acres of land acknowledged in open court by said Doss and ordered to be certified for registration.

Given under my hand and private seal not having an official seal at office in Jasper the 25th. day of Jan. 1828.

                                             Jno. Kelly Clk.

(LS) Reg. 29th. day of Jan. 1828.

P-262.   John Doss   This Indenture made this the
                  Deed of Con.   11th. day of August 1825 be-
                Isaac Steele   tween John Doss for the Coun-
                                                ty of Marion and State of Ten-
nessee of the one part and Isaac Steele of the County of Mackson and State of Alabama of the other part.

WITNESSETH:-

That for and in consideration of the sum of seven hundred and twenty five dollars to me in hand paid the receipt of which is hereby

P-262. acknowledged, I he said John Doss hath and doth by these Presents grant bargain sell and convey unto the said Isaac Steele a certain
tract or parcel of land containing one hun red and no one hundredths
acres, lying and being

P-263. in the County of Marion and State aforesaid on the Northwest side
of Sequachee River adjoining lines of Samuel Broam and James Jones and
bounded as follows to wit:-

Beginning at a poplar an ash on the west bank of a branch
at the foot of the mountain then along the same S. 43 deg. W. 20 poles to
a white oak then S. 22 deg. W. 25 poles to a black oak; thence S. 142
poles to pointers then 838 poles to black oak then N. 36 poles to a
poplar & Elm on the East side of a branch then up the same with Brown
and Jones line N. 38 deg. W. to the beginning.

To Have and To Hold the aforesaid Tract or parcel of land
with the appurtenances unto the said Isaac Steele his heirs and assigns forever from the claim and demand of all and every person or
persons claiming by or through or under me the said John Doss and from
the claim and demand of any and every person or persons whatsoever,
I the said John Doss will warrant and forever defend.

In Testimony whereof I the said John Doss have set my hand
and seal the day and date first above written.

Signed, sealed and delivered in the presence of:

W. M. Jones

Isaac Cooper   John Doss   (SEAL)

S. Hicks.

P-262.   State of Tennessee

                                                   May Term 1827
               Marion County Court

Then was the within deed of conveyance from John Doss Jr.
to Isaac Steele for one hundred and no one hundredths acres of land
acknowledged in open court by said Doss and ordered to be certified
for registration.

Given under my hand & private seal not having an official
seal this 25th day of January, 1828.

                                     (LS)

                              Jno. Kelly.

Reg. 29th. day of Jan. 1828.

P-263. Roswell Hall

      To Deed of Conveyance

David Rankins

This Indenture Made and entered into this the 7th day of July in the year of Our Lord One thousand eight hundred and twenty six by and between Roswell Hall of the County of Marion and State of Tennessee of the one Part and David Rankins of the County and State aforesaid of the Other Part

      Witnesseth That for and in consideration of the sum of one hundred and ten dollars to Me in hand Paid the receipt Whereof is hereby Acknowledged hath and by these Presents doth grant bargain sell and alien enforce and Confirm unto the Said David Rankin his heirs and assigns forever one Certain Undivided Mority of a lot of land known and designated in the Original Plan of the town of Jasper by Lot No. 62 It being the one half of said Lot it being conveyed by the Commissoners in TRust for the town of Jasper jointly to said Hall and Wallis Estill Containing one fourth of an Acre

      To have and to hold the aforesaid one undivided Mority or half of said lot No. 62 With all and singular the rights and Profits emoluments and appurtenances belonging or any wise appertaining to the same to the only use and behoof of him the said David Rankin his heirs &c and the said Roswell Hall for myself My heirs &c Will forever Warrant and forever defend to the Said David Rankin his heirs &c the above recited One Undivided half of said Lot Against the lawful title interest Property Claim and demdn of all Manner of Persons

(P-264) Whatever

      In testimony Whereof I have set my hand and seal the day and Year first herein Written.

Thos. J. Haslering

Wm. Rankin Witness

        Roswell Hall   (Seal)

State of Tennessee

Marion County Court

        November Term 1826.

      Then Was the Within deed of Conveyance from Roswell Hall to David Rankin for One undivided Morety of Lot of land in the town of Jasper Acknowledged in Open Court by said Hall and ordered to be Certified for registration.

      Given under my hand & Private seal not having an official seal of office in Jasper this the 5th day February 1828.

                Jno. Kelly Clk.

P-264. Roswell Jall

      / To Deed of Trust

James Campbell

This Indenture Made the 19th day of February in the Year of Our Lord eighteen hundred and twenty seven beteen Roswell Hall of Jasper in Tennessee of the one Part and Enoch P. Hall & Philip Kroft of the Second Part and James Cambell of Winchester in Tennessee of the third Part

Witnesseth that the said Roswell Hall for and in Consideration of the Sum of Two Thousand Seventy Eight Dollars to him in hand Paid hath bargained and sold and by these Presents doth bargain and sell to the said James Campbell his heirs & legal representative a Certain Lot or Parcel or piece of ground situated in the said Town of Jasper and known & designated in the Plan of said town as lot No. 64 being the Corner lot in said town on Which said Hall lives and the stre house Which is now occupied by Hail Hog & Kroft excepting and reserving the Part of said lot Which is covered by the Old log house built by W. M. M. Rankin And now occupied by said Kroft fronting on the street With all its Appurtenances

To have and to hold the said lot or Piece of ground With all its Appurtenances to the said James Campbell & his heirs to the sole use and benefit of him the said James Campbell and his heirs forever, The said Roswell Hall for himself and his heirs doth covenant With said James Campbell And his heirs that the sid Roswell Hall his heirs executor & Administrator of said lot or Piece of Ground With all its appurtenances with the said James Campbell & his heirs Against the Claims of all Persons Whatever shall Warrant and forever defend and that the title hereby conveyed to the said James Campbell of said lot is good & Valid in trust Nevertheless, that

Whereas on the 14th day of October 1825 at Baltimore Roswell Hall executed to John Baxins his Note of that date for two thousand & seventy eight dollars & eighty eight cents due twelve Months after date the Amount of Which Note With interest from the time it fell due to now justly owing from the said Hall and said Baxin

Now if the said Roswell Hall shall on or before the first day of April 1828 well and truly Pay one half of said debt and all the balance of said debt in one Year thereafter together With the expenses of Proving and registering this deed or if the said Haile and Kroft Will Pay said said note for him then this indenture & every Part thereof shall be null and void

in further trust that if the Said Hall & Kroft shall fail to Pay one half

(P-265) of said debt 1st of April 1828 & the other half on 1st April 1829 then Whenever Such failure shall happen it shall & May be lawful for the said Trustee to Procede to sell the Above described lot & Appurtenance for ready Money to the highest bidder before the Court house door in the town of Jasper after Giving ten days Notice of the time of sale by Putting up an advertisement for that Purpose for that space of time at the Court house door in Jasper & at Such other Places as the said trustee shall think best & out of the Proceeds of said sale to pay Whatever may remain unpaid of the debt aforesaid & all Necessary expenses & Charges incurred in executing this trust & the over Plus if any to be Paid to the said Hall or his legal representative & the said trustee is to convey the Property so sold to the Purchasers in fee Simple and the said Haile & Croft hereby Covenant with the said John T. Baer that they Will Pay the debt aforesaid & the interest in one & two years from the 1st of April next for the fulfiment of which they bind themselves their heirs Exec. & Adms. and the said James Campbell bind himself in the event said Haile & Croft Pay Said debt that the Will Convey the title of said lot herby Conveyed to him to them and the Hall in the event said Haile & Croft Pay Said debt binds himself to rerelease to them his right of redemption in said lot & to convey to them his interest therein

in Witness Whereof the said Roswell P. Hall Philip Croft & James Campbell have hereunto set their hands & Seal this day & Year first above Written.

Signed sealed and delivered in Presence of

Thos Sherley Wist	E. P. Hall	(seal)
Jupe Humble	Roswell Hall	(seal)
N. H. S. Renfro, Wist.	Philipp T. Croft	(seal)
	James Campbell	(seal)

P-265.   State of Tennessee   At the Court house of Pleas
                                   & Quarter Session held for
       Marion County Court   Marion County this 19th day of
                                     February 1827 this Deed of Trust
from Roswell Hall to James Campbell for lot No. 64 in Jasper & the Agreement therein contained Was duly Proven in Open Court by the Oaths of Thomas Shirley & William H. S. Renfroe Subscribing Witness thereto to be the act and deed of the said Roswell Hall E. P. Hall Philip Croft & James Campbell & Order to be Register

Let it be Registered.

Jno. Kelly Clk.

Registered February 7, 1828.

P-265.   Roswell Hall
         To Bill of Sale   For and in Consideration of the
       E. P. Hall   sum of Two hundred dollars to
                                   me in hand Paid the receipt
                                   Whereof is hereby Acknowledged
I have bargained and sold unto Enoch P. Hale one Negro girle Mary between nine and ten years old the right of said Negro I do Warrant and forever defend   I also Warrant her to be sound Negro so far as I know or believe

as Witness my hand this 10th day of August 1828.

Jas. H. Hog. Attest   Roswell Hall

P-265.   State of Tennessee
                                May term 1827
       Marion County Court

Then Was the Within Bill of Sale from Roswell Hall to Enoch P. Hall for Negro girl named Mary Proven in Open Court by the Oath of James H. Ory subscribing Witness thereto and ordered to be Certified for registration.

Given under my hand & Private seal not having a seal of office in Jasper this 25th day of January 1828.

JNO. KELLY Clk. (L.S.)

Registered Feb. 7, 1828.

P-266.   Roswell Hall
      To Bill of Sale
    Philip Kroft

For and in Consideration of one hundred and thirty dollars to Me in hand Paid the receipt Whereof is hereby Acknowledged I have bargained and sold unto Philip Kroft one Negro Girl named Delphia between five and six Years of Age the right of said I do Warrant and will forever defend   I also do Warrant her to be a sound Negro as far as I know or believe

    as Witness My hand this 10th day of August 1826

Jas. H. Hoey.) Attest   Roswell Hall

State of Tennessee

                       May term 1827

Marion County Court

    Then Was the Within Bill of Sale from Roswell Hall to Philipp Kroft for a Negro Girl named Delphia Was Proven in Open Court by the Oath of James H. Hoey Subscribing Witness thereto and Ordered to be Certified for registration.

    Given under My hand & Private Seal Not having a seal of office in Jasper this 25th January 1828.

                               Jno. Kelly Clk.

(L.S.) Registered Feby 7th 1828.

P-266.   Thomas Shirley
      To Deed
    John Bronson

This Indenture Made and entered this 20th day of November 1827 by and between Thomas Shirley Jr. of the County of Marion and State of Tennessee of the One Part and John Bronson of the County and state aforesaid of the other Part

    Witnesseth that for and in Consideration of the sum of three hundred dollars to me in hand Paid the receipt of Which is hereby Acknowledged. I the said Thomas Sherley Jr. hath and doth by these Presents Grant Bargain and sell unto the said John Bronson two Certain tracts or Parcel of land situated, lying and being in the County of Marion aforesaid on the North West side of Sequachie river and bounded as follows to Wit:

    The first of seventy five Acres Beginning at a stake the South boundary of a 12 Acres Survey of Coulters thence With the line of the 12 Acres tract West 10 Poles to a stake thence North forty Poles to a stake and Pointers; thence West 36 to an oak on Tenys line Cooksays Corner; thence With his line South Eighty four Poles to a Chestnut; thence West 136 Poles ton Pointers on t Bronson line; thence With the Sam south 57 Poles to a Maple to Beans; thence With his line in Part East 154 Poles to Pointers; thence North to the beginning of the Other tract of forty Acres situated as aforesaid Beginning at a stake and Pointers or Hendrix line; thence East 58 Poles to a buck gum and Black oak; thence south 86½ Poles to a Chestnut; thence West 84 Poles to a black oak, thence North 41½ to a white oak; thence East 17 Poles to a hickory & dogwood With said Hendrix line thence along the same north 15" East 26 Poles Balck Oak thence North 8" Poles to the beginning

To have and to hold the Aforesaid tract or Parcel of land With their Appurtnances to the said John Bronson and his heirs forever from the Claim of every Person or Persons Whatsoever I the said Thomas Sherley Will Warrant and forever defend.

In testimony Whereof I the said Thomas Shirley Jr. hath hereunto set My hand and seal first herein Written Acknowledged in our Presence this 21st Nov. 1827

Witness

Wm I. Standifer

Rolla Rain

Thomas Shirley Jr.

P-267. Marion County

State of Tennessee County Court

November Term 1827.

Then Was the Deed of Conveyance from Thomas Shirley Jr. to John Bronson for One hundred and fifty Acres of land was duly Acknowledged in Open Court by said Shirley and Ordered to be Certified for registration.

Given under My hand & Private seal not having a seal of office in Jasper the 18th day of January 1828.

(L.S.) Registered Feby 23th 1828.

Jno. Kelly Clk.

P-267. Thomas Cox
            To
        John Bronson

This Indenture Made the 2d day o f August in the Year of our Lord 1827 by and between Thomas Cox of the County of Marion and State of Tennessee of the one Part and John Bronson of the County and state aforesaid of the Other Part

Witnesseth, that for and in Consideration of the sum of one hundred dollars to me in hand Paid the receipt of Which is hereby Acknowledged I the said Thomas Cox hath and doth by these Presents Grant, bargain, sell convey and confirm unto the said John Bronson and his heirs a Certain tract or Parcel of land containing twenty five Acres more or less situated, lying and being in the County of Marion on the North West side of Sequachie river on the Waters of little Sequachie being a Part of a 50 acres tract granted by the State of Tennessee to the said Thomas Cox by Grant No. 12495 Which said 25 Acres is bounded as follows to Wit

Beginning at a stake and Pointers the South West Corner of said Bronson 12 acres survey thence S. 45 East 37½ Poles to the Corner of William Mathews 25 acres tract (bying Mority of said 50 acres) thence north 45 East With said Mathews Conditional line one hundred and seventy poles to said Mathews thence North 37½ Poles to Pointers on a line of 37½ acres survey of said Bronson thence a direct line to the beginning.

To have and to hold the aforesaid tract or Parcel of land With the appurtenances unto the said John Bronson and his heirs and Assigns forever from the lawful Claim and demand of all and every Person or Persons Claiming by through from or under me the said Thomas Cox and my heirs and from the Claim and demand of no other Person or Persons Whatsoever.

In Testimony Whereof I the said Thomas Cox hath hereunto set
my hand and seal the day and Year first herein Written

                                        Thomas Cox   seal.

P-267.   State of Tennessee   )
)   August Term 1827.
          Marion County Court   )

        Then Was the Within deed of conveyance from Thomas Cox to
John Bronson for twenty five Acres of land in Marion County duly Acknowledged in open Court by the said Thomas and Ordered to be Certified
for registration.
        Given under my hand (not having a seal of office) and Private
seal in Jasper this 23rd day of February, 1827.

                                        Jno. Kelly Clk.
                                        By G. W. Rice   D.C.

(L.S.)
Registered Feby. 23, 1828.

P-267.   Amos Griffith   )
                  To   Deed   )   This Indenture Made and enter-
          Thomas Shirley   )   ed into this day of _____
)   in the Year of our Lord Eight-
)   een hundred and twenty seven
between Amos Griffith of the County of Marion and State of Tennessee of
the one Part and Thomas Shirley Jr. of the County and State aforesaid
of the Other Part
        Witnesseth that for and in Consideration of the sum of
(P-268) Thirty dollars to me in hand Paid the receipt Whereof is hereby
Acknowledged I have this day bargained and sold and by these Present
doth bargain sell Alien enforce and convey unto the said Thomas Sherley
Jr. a Certain lot or Parcel of land in the town of Jasper containing one
quarter of an Acre of land and known and designated in the General Plan
of said town as lot No. 86.
        To have and to hold the said lot of land to him the said
Thomas Shirley and his heirs and assigns forever Against the title and
Claim of the said Amos Griffith his heirs and assigns With all and Singular the appurtenances thereunto belonging or in Any Wise appertaining.
        In Witness Whereof I have hereunto set my hand and seal the
date first above Written.   In Present of

Jno. Kelly   )
Chas Read.   )   Amos Griffith   (seal)

State of Tennessee   )
)   May Term 1827
Marion County Court   )

        Then was the Within Deed of Conveyance from Amos Griffith to
Thomas Shirley for lot No. 86 in the time of Jasper duly Acknowledged
in Open Court and Ordered to be Certified for registration.
        Given under My hand & Private seal not having an official
seal at office in Jasper this 23d January 1828.

P-268. Alexander Ferguson
        To Deed   This Deed of Conveyance, Wit-
    Howell Mitchell   nesseeth Alexander Ferguson of
                                   the County of Marion and State
                                   of Tennessee for and in Con-

sideration of three hundred and fifty dollars hath and by these Presents
doth Grant bargain sell and convey unto t Howell Mitchell of the County
of Marion and state aforesaid his heirs and assigns forever the following described eighty seven and a half acres of land be the same more or
less lying in the said County of Marion on the North side of Tennessee
River

       Beginning at a hickory Howells Mitchell Corner thence With
the line South 30" East 180 Poles to a Walnut on the bank of the Tennessee river thence down the same as it meanders south 33 West 76 Poles
south 58 West 28 poles to a Mulberry and Hackberry, thence North 28 "
West 216 Poles to a black oak in the line of the entire tract; thence
north 60" East 67 Poles to the beginning containing Eighty seven and a
half Acres more or less With all and singular the hereditaments and appurtenances Whatsoever thereunto belongingor in any wise appertaining
and all the estate right title interest Property Claim and demand of
him the said Alexander Ferguson and to the same either in law or equity;
       To have and to hold the same Eighty seven & a half Acres of
land unto the said Howell Mitchell and his heirs & against the lawful
title claim and demand of him the said Alexander Ferguson and all those
Claiming or to Claim under by or through him will forever Warrant the
same and should the title hereby Vested Proved insufficient to anable
the said Howell Mitchell and his heirs or assigns to hold said land
than he the said Alexander Ferguson is hereby bound to refund the aforesaid sum of three hundred and fifty dollars in such Payments as his
heirs has been received.
P-269. In Witness Whereof I have hereunto set My hand and seal the
20th day of January 1824.
       Signed sealed and delivered in Presents of

Lewis Campbell
Warren Mitchell   Alexander Ferguson   (seal)

State of Tennessee
                            February Term 1824
Marion County Court

       Then Was the Within Deed of Conveyance from Alexander Fer-
guson to Howell Mitchell duly Acknowledged in open Court by said Ferguson Ordered to be certified and admitted to Record.
       Given under my hand and private seal not having an official
seal at office this 24th March 1825.

(Seal)   Jno. Kelly   Clk.
Registered March 2d 1828.   By A. Kelly D. Clk.

P-269. Ruebin Stinett
        To
    Jesse Humble   This Indenture made this 15th
                                     day of November in the Year of
                                     our Lord 1827 By and between

Ruebin Stinett of the County of Marion and State of Tennessee of the one Part and Jesse Humble of the same County and State of the other Part

Witnesseth That for and in consideration of the sum of Four hundred Dollars to Me in hand Paid the receipt of Which is hereby Acknowledged I the said Ruebin Stinett hath and doth by these Presents Grant bargain sell convey and confirm unto the said Jesse Humble and his heirs and assigns forever two certain tracts or Parcels of land situated lying and being in the County of Marion on the north west side of sequachie River on the west side of little sequachie and being the same now in the Possession and occupation of Me the said Ruebin Stinett the one containing thirty six Acres and bounded as follows to Wit:

Beginning at Pointers at a Corner of Luke Hendrix survey and running West 12 Poles to Pointers thence With Polly Cox line South West 60 West 55 Poles to a stake said Cox's corner; thence west passing her Corner in all 32 poles to a poplar thence With a Mountain north 35 Poles to a gum thence north 11 west 28 poles to two white oak from one foot thence north 55" East 42 poles to a Poplar thence north five Poles to a Black oak thence East 58 poles to a stake on said Hendrix's line and With his line South fifty nine Poles to the beginning of the Other tract containing fifty acres and bounded as follows to Wit:

Beginning at a poplar near Amos Cox's line a corner of the said Stinett thirty six Acres survey (the one hereby conveyed) thence up the Mountain West 106 poles to Pointer thence down said Mountain North Sixty Poles to a stake thence North 77 East 131 poles to a Pointer at a corner of Luke Hendrix 50 acres survey thence With the same East 8 poles to a black oak said Stinnett corner thence With the line of the Same South 5 Poles to a poplar thence south 55" W 42 poles to two white oaks thence south 11" East 26 poles to a gum thence south thirty five poles to the beginning

To have and to hold the aforesaid tract or Parcels of land With all and singular the hereditaments and appurtenances to the said Jesse Humble and his heirs and assigns forever the Claim and demand of all and every Person or Persons Whatsoever I the Ruebin Stinnett Will Warrant and forever defend.

In testimony Whereof I the said Ruebin Stinnett hath hereunto set My hand & seal this day and Year first Written

P-270. Signed sealed delivered in our Presents

Stephen Hicks		his
G. W. Woods.		Rueben X Stinnett (seal)
		mark

State of Tennessee

Marion County Court

November Term 1827.

Then Was the Within Deed of Conveyance from Ruebin Stinnett to Jesse Humble for 86 Acres of land Was duly Proven in Open Court by the Oaths of Stephen Hicks and George W. Woods subscribing Witness thereto and ordered to be certified for.

Given under My hand & Private seal not having a Seal of office in Jasper the 18th January 1828.

(L.S.) Registered March 20, 1828.   Jno. Kelly   Clk.

P-270. Jesse Cozzart
       To
Ephraim Hixon

This Indenture Made this 11th day of Feb. in the Year of our Lord One thousand eight hundred and twenty six between Jesse Cozzart of the County of Marion and State of Tennessee of the one Part and Ephriam Hixon of the County and state aforesaid of the Other Part

Witnesseth that Said Jesse Cozzart for and in consideration of the Sum of three hundred dollars to Me in hand Paid the receipt Where-of is hereby Acknowledged hath and by these Presents doth grant bargain sell and confirm unto the said Ephriam Hixson's his heirs and Assigns forever a Certain tract or Parcel of land containing one hundred and sixty Acres be the same more or less lying and being in the County of Marion on the south east side of the Sequachie River

Beginning on a Red Oak and post oak on the top of a Ridge on a Conditional line; thence the same south thirty degrees West twenty three Poles to a stake and Pointers thence south fifty eight degrees thirty four poles to a Black oak thence fifty four degrees West twenty poles to Pointer Resshaw Thence south With Resshow, fifty seven poles to a mulberry tree on the bank of Condrass Creek on a Conditional line thence With said line south twenty twenty five degrees West sixty poles to a Spanish Oak, thence South fifty eight degrees, East seventy eight Poles With said Conditional to a White oak at the foot of the foot of the Mountain, thence With the meanders of the same West fifty Deg. East one hundred and eight Poles to Pointers thence West thirty three Deg. East twenty eight Poles to Pointers thence north fifty Deg. East thirty six poles to a White oak, thence East fifty four Poles to a beach of Lymns; thence sixty five deg. East forty poles to a Chestnut tree thence North Seventeen Poles to a White oak; thence West With the Mountain one hundred and thirty Poles to a Poplar and Chestnut oak at the foot of said Mountain; thence north seventy six Poles to an Ash tree and Pointers; thence West Eighty three Poles to a stake and spring Where F. McNatt formerly lived With all and singular the woods Water Water courses Profits Commodities hereditaments and Appurtanances Whatsoever to the said tract of land belonging or any wise appertaining and there version and reversion remainder and remainders rents and issue thereof and All the estate right title interest Profits Claim and demands of him the said Jesse Cozzart his heirs and Assigns forever or in and to the same and every Part or Parcel thereof either in law or equity.

to have and to hold the said one hundred and sixty

P-271. acres of land With Appurtenances unto the said Aphraim Hixson his heirs of all and every Person or Persons and Assigns forever against any lawful title Claim or demand Whomsoever Will Warrent and forever defend these Presents

In Witness Whereof the said Jesse Cozzart hath hereunto set his hand and affixed his seal the day and Year above Written.

Signed sealed and delivered in Presents of J. C. Everett

L. Everett
James McReynold

                              his
                    Jesse X Cozzart (Seal)
                         mark

P-271.   State of Tennessee   0
                                                       0   November Term 1827.
         Marion County Court   0
                                                       0

        Then Was the Within Deed of Conveyances from Jesse Cozzart
to Ephraim Hixson for one hundred and sixty Acres of land was duly Proven
in Open Court by the Oath of John C. Everett and Larken Everett subscribing Witness thereto and ordered to be Certified for registration.
        Given under my hands & Private seal not having a seal of of-
fice in Jasper the 18th day of January 1828.

(L.S.)   Registered March 21st 1828.   Jno. Kelly Clk.

P-271.   Scott Teny   0
            To   Deed   0   This Indenture Made the twen-
         John Woodley   0   tieth day of February in the
                                           0   Year of our Lord one thousand
                                                  eight hundred and twenty seven
between Scott Teny, of the County of Bledsoe and State of Tennessee of
the one Part and John Woodley of the County of Warren and State aforesaid
of the Other Part
        Witnesseth that the said Scott Teny hath for and in consider-
ation of the sum of two hundred dollars to him in hand Paid by the Said
John Woodley the receipt Whereof Acknowledged bargained sold aliened
conveyed and confirmed and by these Presents doth grant bargain sell alei
convey and confirm unto the said John Woodley his heirs and assigns forever a Certain tract or Parcel of land containing twenty five Acres lying
and being in the County of Marion on the south east side of Sequachie
River bounded and described as follows to Wit:
        Beginning at an Ironwood near a branch at the foot of the
Mountain below a sulphur gum spring thence north thirty three Poles to
Pointers thence east eighty nine Poles to a post oak thence south fifty
nine Poles to a black oak thence West twenty poles to a stake at the foot
of said Mountain thence along the same north 64° West fifty poles; thence
a direct line to the beginning With the hereditaments and Appurtenances
thereunto belonging or in any wise appertaining.
        To have and to hold the said tract or Parcel of land With its
Appurtenances to the said John Woodley and his heirs forever. I will forever defend against my self my heirs or assigns and no further.
        In Witness Whereof I have hereunto set my hand and seal the
day and Year first herein Written.
        Sealed and signed in Presence of

David Oats   Attest   0
John Hail   0   Scott Teny   (seal)
                                           0
State of Tennessee   0
                                           0   Term 1827.
Marion County Court   0

        Then Was the Within Deed of conveyance from Scott Teny to John
Woodley for 25 Acres of land, Was this day duly Acknowledged in Open Court
by the said Teny and ordered to be Certified for registration.
        Given under My hand and Private seal not having an official
seal at office in Jasper this 18th January 1828.

(L.S.) Registered March 20, 1828   Jno. Kelly   Clk.

P-272.   John Newman
              To
         Rachel McDaniel

This Indenture Made this 5th day of November in the Year of Our Lord one thousand eight hundred and twenty six between John Newman of the one Part and Rachel McDaniel of the Other Part of the County of Marion and State of Tennessee

Witnesseth as follows that said John Newman for and in consideration of two hundred Dollars to him in hand Paid the receipt is hereby Acknowledged and hath granted bargained sold assigned and by these Presents grant bargain sell assign and Convey all and singular My right title interest Claim of a Certain tract of land containing fifty Acres unto Rachel McDaniel and her heirs and assigns & bounded and lying in the County and State aforesd in Blevens cove adjoining the land of John King.

Beginning at a white oak near the foot of Cumberland Mountain then north forty Poles to a stake then east eighty eight Poles to Pointers on Kings line then north with the same twenty two Poles to a black gum near the south fork of the dry branch on Conditional line then up sd branch With the same north Seventy five West one hundred and fifty Poles to Pointers at the foot of the Mountain; thence east With the same fifty Poles to the beginning including and improvements and its appurtenances Which land I do Warrant and forever defend from any Person or Persons Claim or Claims except the Claim of Danforth or Whereby I do bind myself my heirs jointly and severally by these Presents

as Witness My hand and seal this 3rd day of Dec. 1826.

Ewin Clayton
John McDaniel   John Newman   (seal)

State of Tennessee
                                    November Term 1827.
Marion County Court

Then Was the Within Deed of Conveyance from John Newman to Rachel McDaniel for fifty Acres of land Was this day duly Proven in Open Court by the Oaths of Ewin Clayton and John McDaniel subscribing Witness thereto and ordered to be Certified for registration.

Given under my hand and Private seal not having a seal of office in Jasper this 18th of January 1828.

                                    Jno. Kelly   Clk.

(L.S.)   Registered March 22nd 1828.

P-272.   John Newman
              To   Deed
         Rachel McDaniel

This Indenture Made the 15th day of November in the Year of our Lord One thousand Eight hundred and twenty six between John Newman of the one Part and Rachel McDaniel of the other Part Both of the County of Marion and State of Tennessee

Witnesseth as follows, that the said John Newman for and in consideration of two hundred dollars to him in hand paid the receipt is

P-272. John Newman
  To Deed
  Rachel McDaniel

This Indenture Made the 15th day of November in the year of our Lord One thousand Eight hundred and twenty six between John Newman of the One Part and Rachel McDaniel of the other Part Both of the County of Marion and State of Tennessee.

  Witnesseth as follows, that the said John Newman for and in Consideration of two hundred dollars to him in hand Paid the receipt of which is hereby Acknowledged and hath granted bargained sold Assigned and by these Presents doth grant sel Assign and convey all My right title interest and Claim of a Certain tract of land Containing twenty five acres unto Rachel McDaniel and her heirs and Assigns & bounded as follows

  lying and being in the State and County Aforesaid Containing twenty five Acres lying on the Waters the south fork of dry Creek in Blevins Cove adjoining Newman fifty Acres survey

  Beginning at the North West Corner of said survey near said Creek then West up the same fifty five Poles to a dogwood near the foot of the Mountain then south With the same eighty eight poles to a stake and Pointers at the foot of the Mountain; then East fifty five Poles to a dogwood on the line of the fifty acres survey then North eighty eight Poles to beginning.

P-273. Which land I do Warrant and forever defend from any Person or Persons Claim or Claims except severally by these Presents

  as Witness my hand and seal this 3rd day of Dec. 1826.

Ewin Clayton
John McDaniel. Attest   John Newman (seal)

P-273. State of Tennessee   November Term 1837.

  Marion County Court

  Then Was the Within deed of conveyance from John Newman to Rachel McDaniel for 25 acres of land was duly Proven in open Court by the Oath of Ewin Clayton and John McDaniel the subscribing Witness thereto and Ordered to be Certified for registration.

  Given under My hand & Private seal not having a seal of office in Jasper This 18th day of January 1828.

(L.S.) Registered March 22nd, 1828.   Jno. Kelly Clk.

P-273. David Martin
  To Deed
  Conrod Huley

This Indenture Made the 17th January in the Year of Our Lord One thousand eight hundred and twenty seven between David Martin of Warren County and State of Tennessee the one Part and Conrod Huley of Marion County and State aforesaid of the Other Part

  Witnesseth that the said Martin for and in Consideration of the sum of five hundred dollars to him in hand Paid by the sd Huley before the sealing and delivering of these Presents the receipt of Which is hereby Acknowledged hath Granted bargained and sold and by the Presents doth

P-273. grant bargain and sell unto the sd Huley his heirs and Assigns a Certain Piece or Parcel or tract of land situated lying and being in the County of Marion on the Piery Gizzard containing forthy nine Acres and bounded as follows to Wit:

by John Bibles line and John Gala Line and John Conghorns line together With All in singular the tenements appurtenances and hereditaments ther to or belonging or belonging

To have and to hold the said Piece Parcel or tract of land hereby granted bargained and sold and every part and Parcel thereof With all and singular the tenements appurtenances and hereditaments unto and for the only Proper use and behoof of him the sd Huley his heirs and assigns forever and the sd Martin for himself and his heirs all and Singular the promise hereby granted bargained and sold With the tenements hereditaments and appurtenances unto the sd Hulney his heirs and assigns Against him the sd Martin and his heirs and every and all other Person or Persons Whatsoever shall and Will forever Warrant and defend by these Presents and the sd Martin for himself his heirs executors Administrators doth covenant and Promise that he is now seized and Possessed of a good perfect Indefeacable estate of inheritance in fee Simple of and in the promise hereby Granted bargained and sold that he has lawful Proven and absolute authority to rent and sell the same in Manner and form aforesaid that the sd Premises now are and forever hereafter Shall be and remain free and Clear of and from all form of gifts granted bargained sales, judgments executions Incumbrances Whatever.

In Witness Whereof the sd Martin hath hereunto set his hands and affixed his seal the day and Year first Afore Written.

David Martin   (seal)

signed Sealed in the Presents of Sam Jackson Jr.

David Miller.

P-274.   State of Tennessee   May Term 1827.

Marion County Court

Then Was the Within Deed of Conveyance from David Martin to Conrod Huley for forth nine Acres of land was proven in open court by the Oaths of Saml Jackson Jr. and David Miller subscribing Witness thereto and ordered to be Certified for registration.

Let it be registered.

Jno. Kelly   Clk.

Registered March 22nd, 1828.

P-274.   Anderson Check
            To
         John Lane

This Indenture Made and entered into between Anderson Check of the State of Tennessee and the County of Marion of the One Part and John Lain Sr. of the other Part

Witnesseth that the said Anderson Check for and in consideration of Seventy Dollars to him in hand Paid the receipt of Which is hereby Acknowledged doth grant bargain sell alien and confirm unto the said John Lane his heirs executors Administrators and doth grant bargain sell alien and confirm a Certain tract or Parcel of land lying and being in the Countyof Marion a beginning on the south line at the branch: thence south to the Corner thence East to the corner thence North to the Corner thence West to the Stephen A. Blevins line thence East to the thence With said branch to the beginning With all and severall the appurtenances contained thereto Warrant and defend to the said John Lane his heirs executors and Administrators against all Claims or claims Claiming through or by him the said Anderson Cheek.

In Witness our hands and seals this 20th day of November 1826.

Anderson Cheek   (seal)

Amos Griffith, Attest
Steven A. Blevins

State of Tennessee   }
                                          } November Term 1826
Marion County Court   }

Then Was the execution of the Within Deed of Conveyance from Anderson Cheek to John Lane for fifty Acres of land duly Acknowledged in Open Court by the said Cheek and ordered to be Certified for registration. Test

Jno. Kelly Clk.

Registered March 25, 1826.

P-274. John Hopkins   }
           To   }   This Indenture Made the 20th day
        Isaac W. Price   }   of November 1827 Between John
                              }   Hopkins of the County of Marion
                              }   and State of Tennessee of the
one Part and Isaac W. Price of the County and State Aforesaid of the Other Part

Witnesseth that the said John Hopkins for and in Consideration of the sum of one hundred and thirty dollars to him in hand Paid by said Isaac W. Price before the sealing and delivering of these Presents the receipt of Which is hereby Acknowledged hath Granted bargained and sold and by these Presents doth grant bargain and sell unto the said Isaac W. Price his heirs and assigns a Certain Parcel or tract of land situate lying and being in the County of Marion on the North West side of Sequachie River Containing Thirty Seven Acres adjoining land of Luke Hendrix Asans of Hasett Bronson an Occupant Polly Cox and John Bronson and bounded as follows to Wit.

Beginning at two Black Oaks the Most southwardly Corner of said Hendrix survey as asans of said

P-275. Bronson thence With his line north 71 West Seventy Poles to a black Oak South 41 West two Poles to a dogwood south forty Poles to a stake & hickory on said Hendrix line as a. of Polly Cox & John Bronson: thence along the same south forty east thirty two Poles to a hickory: thence East eighty eight Poles to an White Oak, thence North fifty four Poles to a stake & black gum thence West to the beginning including the Place Whereon the said John Hopkins now lives together with the hereditaments and appurtenances to have and to hold the said tract or Parcel of land with its appurtenances to the said Isaac W. Price and his heirs forever and the said John Hopkins for himself and his heirs all and singular the Premise hereby granted bargained sold With the tenements hereditaments

P-274. and agrath warrant to the said Isaac W. Price his heirs and assigns
against him self and his heirs but not Against any other Person & Persons.

In Witness Whereof the said John Hopkin hath hereunto set his
hand and seal affixed his seal the day and date first above Written
Signed sealed and delivered in presence of

Stephon Ricke   )
Fountain Esquire   )   John Hopkins   seal.

P-275.   State of Tennessee   )
)   November Term 1827.
         Marion County Court   )

Then Was the Within deed of conveyance from John Hopkin to
Isaac W. Price for thirty seven Acres of land was duly Acknowledged in
open Court by the said Hopkins and ordered to be Certified for Registration.

Given under my hand & Private seal not having a seal of office in Jasper this 10th day of January 1828.

(L.S.) Registered March 24th, 1828.   Jno. Kelly Clk.

P-275.   Isaac W. Price   )
              To   )   This Indenture Made this 22nd
         Anderson Cheek   )   day of May in the Year of Our
)   Lord 1827 by and between Isaac
                                                          W. Price of the county of Marion
and State of Tennessee of the one Part and Anderson Cheek of the County
and State aforesaid of the Other Part

Witnesseth that for and in Consideration of the sum of Two
hundred Dollars to me in hand paid the receipt of Which is hereby Acknowledged I the said Isaac W. Price, hath and doth by these Presents
grant bargain sell alien enooff and confirm unto the said Anderson Cheek
his heirs and assigns forever a Certain tract or Parcel of land containing sixty acres situated lying and being in the county of Marion on the
West side of Sequache River adjoining lands of Jesse Smith A. Cheek &
Green H. Pryor.

Beginning at a sycamore and Pointers said Smith's Corner;
thence With a Conditional line south nine east forty eight Poles crossing a branch to two Pointers; thence North seventy one East eighteen
Poles to a Red oak on Pryor line thence Along the same north sixty Two
East thirty six Poles to Pointers; thence North eighty seven East forty
six Poles to two post oaks; thence north fifty one East forty six poles
to a sweet gum thence north seventy four poles to Pointers on the top of
a ridge; thence West eighty poles to Pointers on Smith line; thence south
eighty poles to Pointers Smith Corners; thence West With his line to the
beginning including the house and improvement made by Charles Price it
being a

P-276. tract of land granted by the State of Tennessee to the said Isaac
W. Price by Grant No. 9209 bearing date the 11th of September 1824 and
conveyed by me the said Price to Anderson Cheek With all and singular
the Wood Water course Profits Commodities hereditments and appurtenances
Whatsoever to the said tract or Parcel of land belonging or in any wise

P-275. A...t...l...

To... ... to hold the said tract of land and appurtenances to the said Anderson Cheek & his heirs to the sole use of him the said Anderson Cheek and his

P-275 heirs forever ... the said Isaac W. Price for himself and his heirs that the said Price Will Warrant and defend the title of the said tract of land to the said Cheek and his heirs against the Claim of himself only an those Claiming under him but against the Claims of nobody else.

In Witness Whereof the said Isaac W. PRice has herein set his hand and seal the Day and Date above Written.

Signed sealed an Delivered in our Presents

E. Hornbeck
Isaac Hick   Attest   Isaac W. Price   (Seal)

State of Tennessee
)
) May Term 1827.
Marion County Court   )

Then Came the Within deed of Conveyance from Isaac W. Price and Anderson Cheek for sixty acres of land Acknowledged in Open Court by the said Price and Ordered to be Certified for Registration.

Given under My hand and Private seal not having a seal of office in Jasper the 25th of January, 1828.

(L.S.) Registered March 24th, 1828.   Jno. Kelly   Clk.

P-276. Obediah Deane
              To   ) This Indenture Made the twenty
        Levi Womack.   ) first day of January in the Year
) of our Lord one thousand eight
) hundred and twenty three between
Obediah Bean of the State of Tennessee and County of Marion of the One Part an Levi Womack of the State and County aforesaid of the Other Part

Witnesseth That for and in consideration of the Sum of Seventy Five Dollars to him in hand Paid at or before the sealing and delivering of these Presents hath given granted sold and conveyed unto the said Levi Womack a Certain tract or Parcel of land situated lying and being in Marion County aforesaid on the Water of Battle Creek in Sweeten Cove

Beginning at the foot of the Mountain on the north boundary line of a twenty three Acres survey granted to the said Obediah Bean by the said State of Tennessee, thence running southwardly so as to range With a large Poplar and Elm established as a boundary between the said Bean and the said Womack to the foot of the Mountain on the south boundary line of said tract thence Westwardly and northwardly and eastwardly round agreeable to the calls of the grant to the beginning supose to contain twelve Acres more or less

To have and to hold the aforesaid land With all and singular the hereditaments and appurtenances gr, In and to the same belonging or in any wise appertaining to the only Proper use benefit and behoof of him the said Levi Womack his heirs and assigns forever and the said Obediah Bean for himself his heirs executors and administrators doth convey and agree

P-277 to and with the said Levi Womack his heirs and assigns forever that the before recited land and bargain Premises he will Warrant and forever defend against the right title interest or Claim of all and every Person or Persons Whatever

In Witness Whereof the said Obediah Bean hath unto set his hand and affixed his seal the day and Year first Written.

Signed sealed and delivery in Presentae of

Abner C. Womack	
Robert McDowell	Obediah Bean (seal)
P-277. State of Tennessee	
	November Term, 1823.
Martion County Court	

Then Was the Within deed of conveyance from Obediah Bean to Levi Womack duly acknowledged in Open Court by the said Bean and Ordered to be Certified and admitted to record.

Given under my hand & Private seal not having an official seal at office this 25 day of March 1825.

(L.S.) Registered March 25th, 1828.   Jno. Kelly Clk.
                                                       By A. Kelly D. Clk.

P-277 Obediah Bean	
To	This Indenture Made this sixty
John Patton	day of September in the year of
	our Lord one thousand eight hun-
	dred and twenty three between

Obediah Bean of the State of Tennessee and County of Marion of the one Part and John Patton of the State and County Aforesaid of the Other Part

Witnesseth that for and in consideration of the sum of three hundred Dollars and fifteen dollars to him in hand paid the receipt Whereof is hereby Acknowledged hath Given granted sold and Conveyed unto the said John Patton a certain tract or Parcel of land situated lying and being in Marion County Aforesaid on the Waters of Battle Creek in Sweetens cove

Beginning on a sweet gum thence West one hundred and two Poles to a hornbean thence south six degrees east twenty six Poles to Pointers thence south nine degrees east twenty Poles to a Black eye. Thence south sixty five degrees east sixteen Poles to a dogwood; thence south fourteen degrees West thirty six Poles to a White Walnut; thence North Seventy eight degrees East twenty Poles to alym; thence south sixty four degrees East twenty two Poles to a Poplar thence north 78 degrees East fourteen Poles to a dogwood; thence south 49 degrees East twenty Poles to Pointers; then North 40 degrees East twenty Poles to a stake, then Ninety six Poles to the beginning, Containing fifty Acres more or less

To have and to hold the Aforesaid land With all and singular the hereditaments and appurtenances of in and to the same belonging or in any wise appertaining to the only Purpose or benefit and behoof of him the said John Patton or his heirs and assigns forever that the before recited land and bargained Premises he Will Warrant and forever defend against the right title interest or claim of all and every Person or Persons Whatever

P-277.   In Witness Whereof the said Obediah Bean hath hereunto set his
hand and affixed his seal the day and Year first above Written in Presence
of

Robert Bean Jr.
Isham Womack   Obediah Bean   seal

P-277.   State of Tennessee

                                              November Term, 1823
         Marion County Court

         Then Was the Within deed of Conveyance from Obediah Bean to
John Patton

P-278 duly Acknowledged in Open Court by said Bean and Ordered to be
Certified and admitted to record.
         Given under My hand and Private seal not having an official
seal at office this 24 March 1825.

(L.S.) Registered March 25 1828.   Jno. Kelly   Clk.
                                                   By A. Kelly D. C.

P-278.   Isham Womack
            To   This Indenture Made the Eleventh
         Abner C. Womack   day of April in the Year of Our
                                            Lord one thousand eight hundred
                                            and twenty between Isham Womack
of the State of Tennessee and County of Marion of the One Part and Abner
C. Womack of state and County Aforesaid of the other Part
         Witnesseth, that the said Isham Womack for and in consideration
of the sum of two hundred dollars Paid at or before the sealing and delivery of these Presents, the receipt Whereof is hereby Acknowledged hath
given bargain and sold and conveyed unto the sd Abner C. Womack his heirs
and assigns forever a Certain tract or Parcel of land situated lying and
being in the Marion County Aforesaid on the Waters of Battle Creek in Sweetens Cove, it being an equal Mority of an one hundred and eight acres tract
Originally granted to the said Isham Womack by the State of Tennessee, it
being the East half of said tract
         To have and to hold the aforesaid land With all and singular
the hereditaments and Appurtenances of in and to the same belonging or
in Any wise appertaining to the Only Proper use benefits and behoof of
him the said Abner C. Womack, his heirs and assigns forever and the Said
Isham Womack for himself his heirs executors and Administrators doth
Covenant and agree to and With the said Abner C. Womack that the before
recited land and bargained Premises he Will Warrant and forever defend
Against the right title Claim and interest of him and his heirs forever.
         In Witness Whereof the said Isham Womack have hereunto set
his hand and affixed his sealed the day and Year first above Written.
         Signed sealed and delivered in Presence of

Obediah Bean
Arthur X Long   Isham Womack   Seal.
      mark

P-278.   State of Tennessee   0
                                      0   August Term 1825.
          Marion County Court   0

          Then Was the Within deed of Conveyance from Isham Womack to
Abner C. Womack for fifty four Acres of land duly Acknowledged in Open
Court by the said Isham and ordered to be Certified for record.
          Given under My hand and Private seal not having an official
seal of office in Jasper this 15th day of August 1825.

                                               Jno. Kelly Clk.

(L.S.)   Registered March 25, 1828

P-278.   Obediah Bean |
            To | This Indenture Made the twenty
         William Eaves | third day of February in the Year
                                      | of Our Lord One thousand eight
                                      hundred and twenty seven be-
tween Obediah Bean of the State of Tennessee and County of Marion of the
one Part and William Eaves Sr. of the County and State aforesaid of the
Other Part
          Witnesseth that the said Obediah Bean for and in Consideration
of the sum of fifty dollars to him in hand paid at or Acknowledged hath
given

(P-279) granted to Jothan Eaves
          Beginning on a beech on said Eaves line at the foot of the
Mountain and Near the bank of a dry creek thence West seventy Nine Poles
to a beech at the foot of the Mountain; thence South Fourteen West With
the Mountain eighty Poles to a stake and Pointers; thence south twenty
four West With the Mountain sixty Poles to a stake and Pointers at the
foot of the Mountain; thence east across the cove eighteen Poles to a
small Spanish Oak thence N. Thirty eight East With the Mountain one hundred and seventy Nine Poles to the beginning containing forty acres more
or less.
          To have and to hold the aforesaid land With all and Singular
the hereditaments and appurtenances of in and to the same belonging or
in any Wise appertaining to these only Proper use benefits and behoof of
him the said William Eaves his heirs and assigns forever and the said
Obediah Bean for himself his heirs executors and Administrators doth
Covenant and agree to and With said William Eaves his heirs and assigns
that the before recited land and bargained Premises he Will Warrant and
forever defend against the right title interest or Claim of all and every
Person or Persons Whatever
          Witness Whereof the Said Obediah Bean has set his hand and
affixed his seal the day and year first above Written.
          Signed sealed and delivered in Presence of us.

Robert McDowell |
William Eaves Jr. | Obediah Bean   (Seal)

P-279.   William Eaves Sr. |
            To | This Indenture Made the twenty
         Obediah McBee | third day of March in the Year
                                      | of Our Lord One thousand eight

hundred and twenty seven between William Eaves Sr. of the County of Marion
and State of Tennessee of the one Part and Obediah McBee of the County and
State Aforesaid of the Other Part.

Witnesseth that the said William Eaves Sr. for and in consideration of the sum of sixty dollars Paid at or before the sealing & delivery
of these Presents the receipt Whereof is hereby Acknowledged hath given
granted bargained sold and conveyed and confirmed unto the said Obediah
McBee his heirs and assigns forever a Certain tract or Parcel of land
situated lying and being in the county of Marion aforesaid on the Waters
of Battle Creek in Sweetens Cove A Part of a forty Acre tract Which was
granted to Obediah Beane

Beginning on a stake on the East boundary line of said tract;
thence West Across a little cove into a small Lym on the West boundary;
thence south fourteen West With the Mountain ten Poles to a Stake and
Pointers; thence south twenty fourteen West With the Mountain ten Poles
to a stake and Pointers; thence south twenty

(P-280). With the Mountain eight Poles to a stake and Pointers at the
foot of the Mountain; thence East Across the cove eighteen Poles to a small
Spanish Oak or bluff of Mountains; thence north thirty eight East With
the Mountain to the beginning containing fifteen acres more or less

To have and to hold the same above said land With all and Singular the hereditaments and appurtenances in and to the same belonging or
in any wise appertaining to the Only Proper use benefits and behoof of
him the said Obediah McBee his heirs and Assigns forever the said William
Eaves for himself his heirs executors and Administrators doth Covenant
and agree to and With the said Obediah McBee his heirs and assigns that
the before recited land and bargained Premises he Will Warrant and forever defend against the right title interest and claim of all and every
Person or Persons Whatever.

In Witness Whereof the said William Eaves set his hand and
affixed his seal the day and year first above Written.
Signed sealed and delivered in Presence of

Obediah Beene
William Eaves   William Eaves   Sr. (seal)

P-280.   State of Tennessee
                                                 November Term 1827.
         Marion County Court

Then Was the Within Deed of Conveyance from William Eaves to
Obediah McBee for fifteen Acres of land Was duly Proven in open Court by
the Oath of Obediah Beene and William Eaves Jr. subscribing Witnesses
thereto and ordered to be Certified for registration.
Given under my hand and seal not having a seal of office at
Jasper This 18th day of January 1828.

                              Jno. Kelly Clk.

(L.S.) Registered March 25, 1828.

P-280.   Lemuel Beene & Others
              To   This Indenture Made the 15th day
         Robert Beene   of January In the Year of Our
                                              Lord One thousand eight hundred
                                              and twenty five between Lemuel
Beene, John Owens, Obediah Beene, John Beene John Patton William Beene
Benjamin Beene Jesse Selman Levi Womack heirs of Robert Beene deceased
of the first Part and Robert Beene of the second Part

        Witnesseth that the Party of the first Part and in consider-
ation of the Sum of two hundred and forty dollars to them in hand paid
by the said Party of the second Part the receipt Whereof is hereby Acknowledged hath bargained sold and conveyed by these Presents doth bargain, sell and convey unto the said Party of the second Part the receipt
Whereof is hereby Acknowledged hath bargained sold and conveyed by these
Presents unto the said Party of the Second Part and his heirs and assigns forever all that tract or Parcel of land Whereon the Robert Beene
formerly resided bounded as follows to Wit

        Beginning on a sugar tree Near the foot of the Mountain being
the south West running North one hundred and fifty six Poles to a White
Oak on the West by Robert Beene Jr. thence Eastwardly With the Mountain
Benjamine Selman North West Corner thence With said Selman to a Walnut
it being said Selmans South West Corner thence Westwardly With said Mountain to the beginning

        To have and to hold the aforesaid lands to the only Proper use
benefits and behoff of him the second his heirs and assigns forever end
the Ppartey of the first Part for ourselves our heirs and assigns ourselves
firmly by these Presents that the before recited land We Will Warrant and
forever defend from the lawful Claim of all and every Person & Persons
Whatever.

        In Witness Whereof We have hereunto set our hand and affixed
our seals the day above Written.

Attest.   Lemuel Beene   (Seal)
                                                his
                                         John X Owen   (Seal)
                                               mark
                                         Obediah Beene   (Seal)
                    Lemual Neene agent for John Beene   (Seal)
                                                his
William Womack   John X Patton   (Seal)
Robert McDowell   mark
                                         William Beene   (Seal)
                                         Benjamine Selman (Seal)
                                         Jesse Beene   (Seal)
                                         Levi Womack   (Seal)

P-281.   State of Tennessee
                                         November Term 1827.
         Marion County Court

        Then Was the Within Deed of Conveyance from Lemanuel Beene and
Others to Robert Beene Was this day Proven in Open Court by the Oath of
William Womack and Robert McDowell as subscribing Witness thereto attest
the same as a concerning Witness With himself and that said McDowell is
Without the limits of the State Whereupon it is ordered that said deed
be Certified for registration.

Given under my hand & Private Seal not having a seal of office
in Jasper this 18th day of January 1828.

Jno. Kelly Clk. (L.S.)

Registered March 26, 1828.

P-281.   The State of Tennessee
                    To   State of Tennessee
James Simms   assignee of Luke Hendrix   No. 16081

        To all to Whom these Presents shall come greeting. Known ye
that by virture of the of the Part of Certificate No. 1391 dated the 26th
day of February 1818 issued by the Register of East Tennessee to Luke Hendrix for 25 acres and entered on the 22nd day of May 1820 by No. 5881 on
occupant claim under the Act of 1819 there is granted by the State of Tennessee (Great seal) unto James Simms assignee of the said Luke Hendrix a
certain tract or Parcel of land containing eighty two Acres by Survey bearing date the 29th day of October lying in the third district in Marion
County on Battle Creek adjoining Nathan Crockett, James Standifer and
Mc Lemons Reservation and bounded as follows to Wit:
        Beginning at a stake on the North bank of said Creek opposite
a corner Poplar of said Standifer and runs down North Seventy eight West
twenty four Poles to a beech, thence With the Mountain North thirty two
West thirty five Poles to a Walnut thence North fifty eight West sixty
nine Poles to Pointers; thence North fifty three Poles to a gum thence
With said Mc Lemons reservation East one hundred and seventy two Poles
to a gum thence With said Mc Lemons reservation East one hundred and seventy two Poles to a hickory on the bank of said creek thence down With
said Crockett and Standifer South nineteen West thirty Poles thence South
sixty West eighty Poles thence south thirty nine East seventy six Poles
thence South sixty four West sixteen Poles thence North fifty eight West
thirty Poles to the beginin With the hereditaments and appurtenances.
        To have and to hold the said tract or Parcel of land With
its Appurtenances to the said James Simms and his heirs forever.
        In Witness Whereof William Carroll Governor of the State oof
Tennessee hath hereunto set his hand and caused the grate seal of the
state to be affixed at Murfreesborough on the 30th day of October in the
Year of our Lord one thousand eight hundred and twenty one and of the
Independence of the United States the forty sixth.

                                        By the Governor
                                        Wm. Carroll.

David Graham Secretary.

        James Simms is entitled to the Within Mentioned tract of land.

                                        D. McGavock
                                        Register of West Tennessee
                                        by H. Mc. Gavoch D. R.
        Recorded in the Register's office of West tennessee 9th No-
vember 18__

Registered April 14, 1828.   T. Mc. Gavock D. R.

P-282. State of Tennessee
　　　　To
James Standifer
Assignee of Luke Hendrix

State of Tennessee
No. 16080

　　　To all to Whom these Presents Shall come Greeting. Know ye
that by Virtue of Part of Certificate No. 1391 dated 26th day of Feby
1818 issued by the registered of East Tennessee to Luke Hendrix for 250
Acres and entered on the 22nd day of May 1820 as an Occupant Claim under
the act of 1817 by No. 5834.
　　　Then is granted by the said State of Tennessee unto James
Standifer assignee of Luke Hendrix a Certain tract or Parcel of land
Containing one hundred and fifty Acres by Survey bearing date the 15th
day of November 1820 lying in the third of Marion County on Battle Creek
adjoining Geo. Lowreys reservation Wm. Dunaway, Jonathan Crockett and
James Simms, and bounded as follows to Wit:
　　　Beginning at an Elm and Horn briar Corner of said reservation
and running East With it One hundred and forty one Poles to a Hickory
Thence West With Said Dunaway North One hundred and ten Poles to a dogwood, Thence with said Crockett, North eight West Ninety five Poles to
a stake thence North sixty seven West fortey Poles to an ash thence With
said Simms south twenty eight Poles to Plumb thence West six Poles to a
Horn beam; thence south five West thirteen Poles south sixty West twenty
Poles, thence North sixty Eight West forty four Poles to a Poplar on the
bank of Battle Creek having come down said creek thence West seventy Poles
to a stake on the West bank, thence With said Creek and Mountain South
sixteen East ten Poles thence Crossing the Creek East five Poles to a
beach on the East bank, thence on down South twenty seven East twenty
Poles south eight East sixty Poles, South twelve' East forty six Poles
south twenty East forty Poles to Pointers on bank, thence East twenty
Poles to Pointers on the reservation thence North fifty eight Poles to
the Beginning, With the hereitament and appurtenances
　　　To have and to hold the said tract or Parcel of land With its
appurtenances to the said James Standifer and his heirs forever
　　　In Witness Whereof William Carroll Governor of the State of
Tennessee hath hereunto set his hand and Caise the great seal of the state
to be affixed at Murfreesborough on the 30th day of October in the Year
of Our Lord one thousand eight hundred and twenty one and of the Independence of the United States of forty sixth.

　　　　　　　　　　　　　　By the Governor
　　　　　　　　　　　　　　William Carroll
　　　　　　　　　　　　　　　(GReat seal　)

Daniel G.Rahom Secretary

　　　James Stanifer is Intitled to the Within Mentioned tract of
land.

　　　　　　　　　　　　　　D. McDowell
　　　　　　　　　　　　　　Register of West Tennessee
　　　　　　　　　　　　　　By F. Mc Gavock D. R.
　　　Recorded in the Register's office of West Tennessee 9th No-
vember 18__

　　　　　　　　　　　　　　F. Mc Gavock　D. R.

Registered April 15, 1828.

P-283.   William Arnett
　　　　　To
　　　James Elledge

This Indenture Made the 23rd day of May
in the Year of our Lord one Thousand
eight hundred and twenty five between
William Arnett of the County of Marion
and State of Tennessee of the one Part
and James Elledge of the county and state aforesaid of the other Part

Witnesseth that for and in consideration of the sum of two hundred dollars to him the said William Arnett in hand Paid by said James Elledge the receipt Whereof is hereby Acknowledged hath any by these Presents doth grant bargain sell Alien enfross and Confirm unto him the said James Elledge his heirs & Assigns forever a certain tract or Parcel of land Containing fifty acres situated lying in the county of Marion Aforesaid on the north West side of Sequachie on the head Waters of Warmers and bounded as follow to wit

Beginning at an Ash above the head of a spring now Made use of by the said Elledge it being the beginning Corner of the said Arnett Survey of one hundred and sixty Acres then running down the branch of said Sering the Center of the same being the lines S. 81 East 18th Poles S. 2' E. 17 Poles S. 49' E. 6th Poles to a stake in the branch and Pointers thence along Standifers line Again W. 47' E. 84 Poles to Pointers then N. 30 Poles to Post Oak on the north boundary of said Arnett Survey of thirty eight Acres, then With his line West 52 Poles to Chestnut, then S. 52 Poles to stake on the line of the said 160 Acres Survey and With the ssame West 23 poles to Pointers at the foot of the Mountain & With the Same S. 18' W. 24 Poles then S. 40 poles to the beginning including fifty Acres and the place Where the said Elledge now lives be the same more or less it being Part of two tracts of land Granted by the State of Tennessee to the said Arnett by Granted No. 18750-18753.

To have and to hold the said tract or Parcel of land With the appurtenances to the said James Elledge and his heirs forever from the landed Claim of him the said William Arnett & his heirs and from the lawful Claims of every Person & Persons Whatever Claiming or through from or under the Claim of him the said William Arnett or his heirs so far as the title from the State of Tennessee has Vested in him Will forever Warrant and defend by these Presents.

In testimony whereof the said William Arnett hath hereunto set his hand and seal the day & Year dated above Written.

Signed sealed & Acknowledged.

　　　　　　　　　　　　　　　　　Wm. Arnett   (seal)

In Presence of Wm. Jones

　　　　　　　　　　　　　　　　　Jno. Kelly

P-283.   Andrew Still
　　　　　To
　　　Geo. T. Gillespie

This Indenture Made and entered
into this 15th day of April in the
Year 1828 between Andrew Still of
the County of Marion and State of
Tennessee of the one Part and Geo. T. Gillespie of the County of Green and State aforesaid of the other Part

Witnesseth that the said Andrew Still for and in consideration of the sum of five hundred dollars to him in hand paid the receipt Whereof is hereby Acknowledged by the said Geo. T. Gillespie hath Granted bargained and sold and by these Presents doth grant bargain sell & Convey to the said Geo. T. Gillespie his heirs & assigns a Certain tract or Parcel of land situated lying and being in Marion county & State of Tennessee both side of Creek running above & near Genl. William Stones it being all of that

P-284 Part of a tract of land granted by the State of Tennessee for two two hundred Acres, to the said Andrew Still on the first day of Dec. 1820 by Grrant 9793 Which hiss Within a tract of land by the State of No. Caroline to Jno. Sevier for ten thousand and five hundred Acres and by him conveyed to Southgate and London Carter as heretofore run out by Jno. McIver Agent for Southgate and the heirs of London Carter and Within the boundary Claimed by said heirs of London Carter, It being fully understood between the said Andrew Still & Said Geo. T. Gillespie that the said Still hereby conveyed to said Geo. T. Gillespie, his heirs & the Whole of two hundred Acres as before recited Which lies Within the said boundary of said tract of ten thousand five hundred Acres as heretofore surveyed by Jno Kelly & Marked for the said Southgate & the heirs of London Carter including the Improvements Whereon said Andrew Still formerly lived suppose to contain one hundred & fifty Acres more or less Which said tract of land With the hereditments & Appurtenances thereto belonging or in any Wise appertaining.

I will Warrant & defend to the said Geo. T. Gillespie his heirs & as an estate in fee simple Against me or My heirs or any Person or Persons Whatever Claiming by through or Under me.

In testimony Whereof I have hereto set My hand & seal the day and date first Written.

Andrew Still   (seal)

P-284.   State of Tennessee
                                        Circuit Court April term 1828
              Marion County

        then was the Within deed of conveyance from Andrew Still to Geo. T. Gillespie duly acknowledged in court by the Said Andrew Still ordered to be Certified and Admitted to record.

        Given under my hand & Private seal not having an official seal at office in Jasper this 15th day of April 1828.

                                        S. Hicks Clk.

(L.S.)   registered April 16 1828

P-284.   James Mayo
                   To   This Indenture Made this 28th day
              Absolum Deakins   of May in the Year of our Lord one
                                         thousand eight hundred and twenty
                                         seven between James Mayo of the
County of Marion and State of Tennessee of the one Part & Absolum S. Deakins of the County & State forsaid of the other Part

        Witnesseth that for and in consideration of the sum of one dollar to me in hand Paid by the said Absolum Deakins the receipt Whereof is hereby Acknowledged hath granted, bargained and sold and by these Presents doth bargain sell alien enforse and confirmed unto the said Absuplun

Deakins his heirs and assigns forever a Certain tract or Parcel of land situated lying and being in the said County of Marion in the south east side of S quachia In adjoining lands of Sam Gardner Containing trhree hundred Acres

Beginning at a stake and elm on the bank of the River the upper Corner of the Gardner 100 Acres tract then east With the same one hundred Poles to a small black Walnut corner to Gardner 200 Acres Survey then With the line of the same one hundred and nine Poles to Pointers then east Ninety three Poles crossing The Wagon road to a stake on Gardner line in Fountain Rogers field. then North one hundred and Ninety Poles crossing said road to a black gum then one hundred two Poles to a chincenpine Oak on the bank of the river then With the same as it Meanders to the beginning including the land Property

P-285 Wherein the said Absolum Deakins George Stewart and William Williams Now lives, it being a tract of land granted by the State of Tennessee to the said James Mayo for 200 Acres by Grant No. 12657 bearing date the 13th day of Feby. 1826 together With all and singular the appurtenances Whatsoever to the before mentioned tracts of three hundred of land belonging or in any Wise appertaining.

To have and to hold the said tract ad lands herein before described rath the appurtenances unto the said Absolum Deakins, his heirs executors admrs, and assigns forever free and clear of the lawful title Claim and demand of him the said James Mayo his heirs executors admrs. or any other Persons Claiming from by or Under then so far as the title is Vested in the said Mayo by the Grant Above recited.

In testimony Whereof I have hereunto set my hand and seal the day and date above Written.

Signed and sealed in Presence of

James May (seal)

G. W. Brown and William Brown.

P-285. State of Tennessee

Marion County Court

February Term 1828.

Then Was the Within deed of conveyance from James Mayo to Absolum Deakins for 200 acres of land in Marion county duly Acknowledged in Open Court by the said Mayo and ordered to be Certified for Registration.

Given under my hand and Private seal (not having a seal of office) at office in Jasper this 28th day of February 1828.

Jno. Kelly Clk.
By G. W. Rice D. C.

(L.S.) Registered April 16 1828.

P-285. Absolum Deakins
To
Geo. T. Gillespie

This Indenture Made and entered entered into this 16th day of April 1828 between Absolum Deakins of the county of Marion & State of Tennessee of the One Part and Geo T. Gillespie of the County of Greene and State aforesaid of the other Part.

P-285.   Witnesseth that the said Absolum Deakins for and in consideration of the sum of forty one dollars to him in hand paid by the said Geo. T. Gillespie, hath granted bargained & sold & by these Present doth grant bargain & sell to the said Geo. T. Gillespies his heirs & assigns a Certain tract or Parcel of land situated lying and being in the County of Marion and State of Tennessee on the south East side of Sequachie river adjoining lands of James Gardnerm Containing three hundred Acres beginning at a stake and Elm on the river the upper Corner of Gardner 100 Acres tract then East With the same one hundred and forty Poles to a small black Walnut Corner to Gardiner's 200 Acres survey, then With the lines of the same north one hundred and nine Poles to Pointers then East Ninety three Poles Crossing the Wagon Road to a stake on Gardner line in Fountain Rogers field then North one hundred & Ninety Poles crossing said Road to a black Gum then West forty two Poles to a chingnepine Oak on the bank of the River; then down the same as it Manders to the beginning, including the lands & Premises Whereon the said Absolum Deakins, George Stewart and William Williams line it being a tract of land Granted by the State of Tennessee to James Mayo for 300 Acres Grant No. 12457 bearing date the 13th February 1826 and conveyed by the same James Mayo to the said Deakins by deed dated the 28th of May 1827 together With all and singular the Appurtenances Whatever to the before Mentioned tract of three hundred Acres of land belonging or in any Wise Appertaining

P-286   To have and to hold said tract of land herein before described With the Appurtenances unto said Geo. T. Gillespie his heirs & forever free and clear of the lawful title Claim & demand of him the said Absolum Deakins his heirs or any Person Claiming by through or under him so far as the title is Vested in him the said Absolum Deakins by the before described title under said Mayo by Virtue of said Grant.

        In testimony Whereof I have hereunto set my hand & seal the day first Written.

James Davis

                                    his
                        Absolum X Deakins (seal)
                                    mark

P-286. State of Tennessee   ⟩
                                ⟩ Circuit Court
        Marion County   ⟩ April Term 1828.
                                ⟩

        Then Was the Within Deed of Conveyance from Absolum Deakins to Geo. T. Gillespie duly Acknowledged in Open Court by the said Absolum Deakins and ordered to be Certified and admitted to Record.
        Given under My hand & Private seal having no seal at office in Jasper this 16th day of April 1828.

                                    Stephens Hicks Clk.

Registered April 16, 1828.

P-286. George Foster   ⟩
            To P. of Atty.   ⟩   Known all men by these Presents
        John McGowen   ⟩   that I George Forster late of
                                 ⟩   Marion now of Franklin County
                                     State of Tennessee, do Authorize
& empower Col. John McGowan of the County of Franklin & State Aforesaid to sell rent or dispose of any lots or land I may have in said County of Marion & to Make all the right title & Claim that I have or Permit A.

P-286 Foster or Charlie John Foster hereby to entry or entries Made in My Name or theirs as the Case May be) as fully & Ample as we could do ourselves for ready & Monies & give receipt for the Same in Our name & to all Other Acts and things of necessary to be done.

Given under my hand & Seal this 13th day of August, 1828.

Henry Gotcher   Jurat
Jas. Deakins   Jurat.

George Forster   (seal)
J. A. Forster
C. T. Forster   (seal)

P-286.   State of Tennessee
      Franklin County

February Term 1828.

Then Was the Within Power of Atty from George Foster & C. G. Foster, to John McGowen Was duly Proven in opn Court by the Oaths of Henry Gotcher and Joseph Deakins Witness thereto and Ordered to be registered, let it be registered.

E. Russell Clk.

Registered April 16th, 1828.

P-286.   Henry Long
     To
William Morrow

This Indenture Made the 13th day of September in the Year of our Lord one thousand eight hundred and twenty six between Henry Long of the County of Marion and State of Tennessee of the One Part and William Morrow of the state and county aforesaid of the Second Part,

Witnesseth that for and in consideration of the sum of one thousand dollars to him the said Henry Long in hand Paid the receipt Whereof is hereby Acknowledged hath by these Presents bargained sold unto the said William Morrow a Certain tract or Parcel of land Containing one hundred Acres situated lying and being in the Said County of Marion

P-287 on the north bank of Tennessee river adjoining lands of the said Long in What is known by the name Mullins Cove it being Part of a tract of land Granted by the State of Tennessee to the said Henry Long for one hundred and fifty five Acres by Grant No. 24934 bearing date the 19th day of May 1826, beginning at an ash tree on the bank of said river it being the beginning Corner of the Original tract of 145 Acres thus running With Said river as it Meanders south twenty four degrees East twenty four Poles South seven degrees East eighty eight Poles South three degrees West twenty Poles to the Mouth of a Creek or branch known by the Name of the dry Creek or branch a Conditional line With George Harris then up the same South seventy East twenty four Poles south thirty eight East twelve Poles South fifty four, East seventeen Poles to Maple and White oak on the north bank of said Creek or branch on What is called the Mountain line of the original survey then along the out lines of the same North twenty six degrees eighty eight Poles to black Gum then North fifty four degrees East thirty Poles to a Poplar and hickory near the head of the Spring now Made use by the Said Morrow, then north thirteen degrees East fifty eight Poles then North thirty three, East forty four Poles to Pointers on the Said Longs line of a survey of 180 Acres then along the same West one hundred and thirty Poles

P-287. to strike and black Walnut Pointers at or near the said Longs Fence thence along the same S. 15 W. 11 Poles S. 16' W. 4½ Poles S. 50' W. 16 Poles then S. 65' W. to the Beginning including the aforesaid one hundred acres of land be the same more or less With all and Singular the Water Courses, Woods, Profits Commodities hereditaments and Appurtenances thereunto belonging in any wise appertaining either in law or equity.

To have and to Hold the Aforesaid tract of land With its Appurtenances to the Aforesaid William Morrow and his heirs and Assigns forever free and clear of the lawful title Claim and demand of all manner of Parsons Whatever, I the said Henry Long do bind myself, my heirs & assigns to Warrant and forever defend the title of the Aforesaid tract of land and Premises by Virtue of these Presents.

In Witness Whereof I have hereunto set my hand and seal this day and date first above written.

Signed sealed and Acknowledged in Presence of

Jno. Kelly   ◊
A. Kelly   ◊   Henry Long   (seal)

P-287.   State of Tennessee   ◊
                                    ◊   November Term 1827.
         Marion County Court   ◊
                                    ▌

Then Was the Within Deed of Conveyances from Henry Long to William Morrow for one hundred Acres of land Was duly Proven in Open Court by the oaths of John Kelley and Alexander Kelly Jr. the subscribing Witness thereunto and ordered to be Certified for registration.

Given under My hand at office in Jasper the 18th day of April 1828.

Registered April 18th, 1828.

P-287.   James Standifer   ◊
            To   ▌   This Indenture Made this fourth
         Michal L. Stinson   ◊   day of April in the Year of Our
                                   ▌   Lord one thousand eight hundred
                                             and twenty six between James
Standifer of the County of Bledsoe and State of tennessee of the one Part and Michal L. Stevens of the County of Marion and State Aforesaid of the Other Part,

Witnesseth that the said James Standifer for and in consideration

P-288 of the sum of one Dollar to him in hand Paid the receipt Whereof is hereby Acknowledged granted bargained and sold and by these Presents doth grant bargain and sell unto the said Michal L. Stinson his heirs and assigns All that tract or Parcel of land situated and being in the County of Marion on the Waters of Sequachie River or Creek Containing Seventy two Acres and bounded as follows to wit:

Beginning at a White Oak and beech on the Southeast bank of the river Where the lower line of Standifers 89 Acres tract Crosses the river, thence down the river as it Meanders West fourty four Poles, South twelve West eighteen Poles to a beech on the bank of the river, thence East one hundred and twenty three Poles to Pointers thence North one hundred and thirty eight to the beginning. Also one other tract of fifty Acres adjoining to the twelve Acres tract Beginning at a black gum on the North east bank of the river Corner to Standifer for 12 Acres tract thence up the river as it Meanders North eight " East twenty four Poles North thirty Nine e st twenty three Poles to a black Oak on the bank of the River thence West one hundred and twenty Seven Poles Crossing the Wagon road to a Post oak thence South eighty Nine Poles to a Small elm near Standifer corner thence east With his line sixty nine Poles to a corner of his 12 Acres tract thence North With the same forty six Poles to its Corner thence East With the same Crossing the Road thirty eight Poles to the beginning together With all and singular the Premises With its appurtenances thereunto belonging or in any Wise Appertaining.

To have and to hold the said hereby Conveyed With the Appurtenances unto the Said Michal Stinson heirs and assigns forever and the said James Standifer for himself his heirs executors and Administrators the Aforesaid tract of land and Premises unto the said Michal L. Stinson, his heirs and assigns Against the Claim of all Person Whatsoever Claiming from by or under him or his heirs, doth and Will Warrant and forever defend these Presents.

In Witness Whereof the said James Standifer hath hereunto set his hand and seal the day and date first Written. (The Words hundred - and the Word - Claiming from by or under him or his heirs - enterlines before signed)

Signed and Acknowledged in the Presence of

Jno. Kelly
Burgess Mathews

James Standifer   (seal)

P-288. State of Tennessee

Marion County

Circuit Court
April Term, 1828.

Then Was the Within deed of Conveyance from James Standifer to Michal L. Stinson for 122 Acres of land in Marion County duly Proven in Open Court by the Said James Standifer Ordered to be Certified and admitted to record.

Given under hand and Private seal (not having and official seal at office in Jasper this 24 day of April 1828.

(L.S.) Registered April 30th, 1828.

Stephen Hicks, Clk.
Jno. Kelly D. Register.

P-288. Michal L. Stinson
        To Deed of Convey.
        Enoch P. Hale

This Indenture Made this 19th day of January in the Year of our Lord one thousand eight hundred and twenty eight between Michal L. Stinson, of the County of Marion & State of Tennessee of the one Part and Enoch P. Hale of the County & state aforesaid of the Other Part

P-289.   Witnesseth that the said Michal L. Stinson for and in consideration of the sum of one thousand Dollars to him in hand Paid the receipt

Whereof is hereby Acknowledged hath granted bargained and sold and by
these Presents doth grant bargain and sell unto the said Enoch F. Hale his
h irs and Assigns all that tract or Parcel of land lying and beingih the
County of Marion and on the Waters of Sequachie river. Containing eighty
8 Acres and bounded as follows to wit:

Beginning at a White Oak on the South West side of said river
and running with a Mountain knob South 33° W One hundred and thirty Poles
to a stake thence West one hundred Poles to a sweet gum thence North one
hundred and two to a White Oak on the North West side of said River having
Crossed said River thence East one hundred and S venty four Poles Crossing
said river again to the beginning including the fish trap ford on the
Georgia road - Also one other Tract containing twelve Acres adjoining
lands of the Aforesaid Stinson and bounded as follows to Wit:

Beginning at a beech on the North bank of said river on said
Stinson line thence running up said river, thence as it Meanders N. 34° W
twenty seven Poles to a black gum thence West thirty seven and a half Poles
to two black Gums, Thence South forty four Poles to pointers on the said
Stinson line With the same to the beginning together with All and Singular the Premises With Appurtenances thereunto belonging or any Wise appertaining.

To have and to hold the said land hereby Conveyed With the appurtenances unto the said Enoch P. Hale, his heirs and assigns forever,
the said Michal L. Stinson for himself his heirs executors and Administrators the Aforesaid tract of land and Premises Unto the said E. P. Hale his
heirs and Assigns against the Claim or Claims of all Persons Whatsoever
doth and Will Warrant and forever defend by these Presents.

In Witness Whereof the said M. L. Stinson hath hereunto set
his hand and seal the day and date first Above Written.

Signed sealed and delivered in Presence of

G. W. Wood
Philip Kroft   Michal L. Stinson   (Seal)

P-289. State of Tennessee
                                    Circuit Court
        Marion County   April Term, 1828.

Then Was the Within deed of Conveyance from Michal L. Stinson
to Enoch P. Hale duly Proven in Open Court by the Oath of George W. Woos
and Phillip Kroft subscribing Witness thereto and ordered to be Certified
and admitted to record.

Given under My hand & Private seal (not having an official
seal) at office in Jasper this 24 day of April 1828.

Registered April 30th, 1828.

                                    Stephen Hicks   (seal)

P-289. Commissioners &C.
        To   This Indenture Made the 3rd
        James Chaudoin   day of October in the Year of
                                Our Lord one thousand eight
                                hundred and twenty seven be-
tween William Stone David Oats, Burgess Mathew, Alexander Kelly, William King, William Stephen and David Miller, Commissioners in trust for
the County of Marion and town of Jasper and their successors in office
of the one Part and James Chaudoin of the Aforesaid county and state

P-289 of the Other Part,

      Witnesseth that for and in consideration of the sum of forty three dollars to us in and paid the receipt Whereof is hereby Acknowledged hath and by these Presents Doth grant bargain Alien enfores and confirm Unto the

P-290 said James Chaudoin his heirs and administrators a Certain lot of land in the town of Jasper known and designated in the Original Plan of said town by lot No. 79 Containing one Quarter of an Acre sold at Public auction as the law directs,

      To have and to hold the Aforesaid lot of land With all and singular the rights and Profits emoluments and Appurtenances belonging or in any Wise appertaining or in any wise Appertaining to the same to the same to the only means behoff of him the said James Chaudoin his heirs &C and the said Commissioners in trust as aforesaid and Will as far as they are Authorized as Commissioners forever Warrant and defend to the said James Chaudoin his heirs ect. the Above recited lot Against the right title interest Claim and demand of all and every Person & Persons Whatever.

S. Hicks Attest　　　　　　　　　　Wm Stone　　　　　(seal)
Jno. Kelly　　　　　　　　　　　　　Burgess Mathew　　(seal)
　　　　　　　　　　　　　　　　　　David Oates,　　　(seal)
　　　　　　　　　　　　　　　　　　Alexander Kelly　(seal)
　　　　　　　　　　　　　　　　　　William Stiphen　(seal)
　　　　　　　　　　　　　　　　　　David Miller　　　(seal)

P-290.　State of Tennessee

　　　　　　　　　　　　　　　　　　February Session, 1828.

　　　Marion County Court
　　　　　 Then Was the Within Deed of Conveyance from the Commissioners in trust for the County of Marion and town of Jasper To James Chaudion for lot No. 79 in the town of Jasper duly Proven in Open Court by the Oath of John Kelly and Stephen Hicks subscribing Witnesses thereto and ordered to be Certified for registration.
　　　　　 Given under My hand & Private seal not having a seal of office this 27th of February 1828.

　　　　　　　　　　　　　　　　　　Jno. Kelly Clk.
　　　　　　　　　　　　　　　　　　By. G. W. Rice D. Clk.

Regist red May 13th 1828.

P-290.　State of Tennesee

　　　　　 To all to whom these Presents Shall Come Greeting. Know ye that by Virtue of the residence of Certificate No. 1459 dated the 11th day of August 1818, issued by the Register of East tennessee to Will H. Ragdale for 100 Acres and entries on the 28 day of March 1821 by No. 6222, then is granted by (seal) a Certain tract or Parcel of land Containing eighty eight Acres by Survey bearing date the 30th day of March 1821 lying in the third district in Marion County on Sequichie River including the fish trap ford on the Georgia line and bounded as follows to Wit
　　　　　 Beginning at a White oak on the south east side of said river

P-290. and running With a Mountain knob South 33' W. one hundred Poles
to a sweet gum, thence north one hundred and two poles to a White oak on
the Northwest side of said river, having crossed said river thence east
one hundred and twenty four Poles Crossing said river again to the beginning With the Hereditament and Appurtenances.

To have and to hold the said piece or Parcel of land With its
Appurtenances to the said Imes St nuifer and his heirs forever.

In Witness Whereof William Carroll Governor of the State of
Tennessee hath hereunto set is hand and Caused the Great seal of the
State to be affixed at Murfreesborough on the 19 day of Oct. in the Year
of Our Lord one thousand eight hundred and twenty one and of the Independence of

P-291 the United States the forty sixth.

By the Governor
Wm. Carroll

Danial Graham Secretary
Record in the Registers office of West Tennessee 8th November
1821.

T. McGavoch Register of
West Tennessee
T. McGavock, D. R.

Registered June 1828.

P-291. State of Tennessee)
            To Grant   (The State of Tennessee
     John Bridgeman   (No. 10622
                            (

To All to Whom these Presents Shall Come Greeting, know ye
that In consideration of an entry Made in the entry taker Office of
Marion County of No. 212 dated the 6th day of July 1824 at the rate of
twelve and a half cent per Acre by John Bridgeman, there is granted by
the State of Tennessee unto the Said John Bridgeman and his heirs a certain tract or Parcel of land Containing three hundred Acres lying in the
County Aforesaid on the Northwest side of Sequachie river adjoining the
land of T. Hopkins, Beginning at a stake on the bank of said River at the
Corner most Eastwardly of Hopkins tract, thence up said river as it Meanders North eighty seven East thirty two Poles south eighty five East
forty eight Poles North fifty seven East thirty two Poles North twenty
one East twenty Poles North Sixty Nine West thirty six poles; North thirty Poles North Eighteen! West twenty six; North sixty Seven West twenty
nine West forty six Poles, North thirteen east; Eighteen Poles North
thirty three East sixty Poles; North twenty two West twenty Nine Poles to
a stake on the bank of said river; thence West one hundred and sixty three
Poles to a stake; thence south two hundred and thirty Poles to a stake on
Hopkins line; thence south fifty East With the same one hundred and
fifty eight Poles to the beginning; including lands occupied by Seian
of the Kellys — Survey the 20th November 1824, With its Appurtenances.

P-291   To have and to hold the said tract or Parcel of land With its
appurtenances to the said John Bridgeman and his heirs forever.

In Witness Whereof William Carroll Governor of the State of
Tennessee his hereunto set his hand and caused the Great seal of the State
to be affixed at Murfreesboro on the 1st day of March in the Year of Our
Lord One thousand eight hundred and twenty five and of America Independence the forty ninth.

(Seal)

By the Governor,
Wm. Carroll
Daniel Graham Secretary.

John Brigeman hath the title to the Within described tract of
land.

Dury P. Armstrong
Reg. of East Tennessee

Registered June 3d, 1828.

F-292.   State of Tennessee
            To Grant
       Scott Terry & Adam Lamb.

State of Tennessee
No. 10620

To all to Whom these Presents shall come Greeting Know ye
that in Consideration of an entry Made in the entry Takers office of
Marion County of No. 202 dated on the 6th day of July 1824 at the rate
of twelve and a half cents per acre by Scott Terry and Adam Lamb there
is granted by the State of Tennessee unto the said Terry and Lamb and
their heirs a Certain tract or Parcel of land, Containing six hundred
and forty Acres lying in the county Aforesaid or the South east side of
Sequachie river adjoining lands of W. Kelly, I Mayo, J. B. Brumby,

Beginning at a stake on the bank of said River Where the north
boundary line of Kelly, J. Mayo Survey intered the Same thence up the
river as it Meanders North Eighty seven; East thirty two Poles; South
eighty five ' East forty eight Poles, north fifty seven East twenty two
Poles North one'East twenty Poles North sixty nine ' West thirty six Poles,
North thirty Poles, North Eighteen West twenty six Poles; North sixty
Seven ' West thirty Poles North fifteen East fifty six Poles North twenty East twenty six Poles; north twenty Nine ' West forty Six poles North
eighteen Poles to a Pointers; thence east one hundred and forty Poles
Crossing the Public road to a stake and Pointers, thence south one hundred and forty three Poles to a sugar tree at the foot of the Mountain
thence West With the same as it Meanders south twenty three West sixty two
poles south fifty six West fifty two Poles; South thirty Seven and a half
West thirty Seven and a half West thirty six; south seventeen West one
hundred Poles; South thirty six West eighty four Poles; to an ash at the
foot of said Mountain on the line of B. Brumby; thence North fifty West
two hundred and Seventy two Poles Crossing said Public Road to the beginning surveyed the 19th day of November 1824 With its appurtenances.

To have and to hold the said tract or parcel of land, with
the appurtenances to the said Terry and Lamb and thir heirs forever.

In Witness Whereof William Carroll Governor of the State of
Tennessee have hereunto set his hand and caused the Great seal of the
State to be affixed at Murfreesboro on the first day of March in the Year

P-292. of our Lord one thousand eight hundred and twenty five and of
American Independence the forty.

> By the Governor
> Wm Carroll
> Daniel Graham Secretary

Scots Perry Jr. Adam Lamb have title to the Within described
tract of land.

> Drury P. Armstrong
> Reg. of E. T.

15th June 1825

Then Was this Grant recorded in My Office

> Dury P. Armstrong
> Reg. of East Tennessee

Registered Jane 30th 1828.

P-292. State of Tennessee		State of tennessee
To		No. 28816.
James Jones		

Know ye that by resdue of Certificate No. 1468 dated the 11th
day of August 1818 issued by the Registered of East Tennessee to William
H. Ragsdale for 200 Acres and entered on the 21st day of July 1821 by
No. 6247 then is Granted by the State of Tennessee unto James Jones Assignee of William H. Ragsdale, a Certain tract or Parcel of land Containing

P-293. one hundred Acres by survey bearing date the 20th day of March
1822 lying in the third District in Marion County on the North West of
Sequachie river adjoining lands of John Hail Jr. David Nichols and bounded as follows to Wit:
(State seal) Beginning at Pointers the North east Corner of said Hail
survey of 100 Acres thence South along the same twenty Poles to a Post
Oak & Pointers poplar; thence east seventy six Poles to Pointers thence
North one hundred and twenty three Poles to two black gums on said Nichols
line; thence along the same West sixteen Poles to Pointers thence North
fifty five Poles to a stake & Pointers in said Hails line and With same
East to the beginning With its appurtenances to the said James Jones and
his heirs forever.
In Witness Whereof William Carroll Governor of the State of
Tennessee hath hereunto set his hand and Caused the Great seal of the
State to be affixed at Murfreesboro on the 1st day of December in the Year
of Our Lord one thousand eight hundred and twenty four and of the Independence of the United States the forty ninth.

> by the Governor
> Wm. Carroll
> Daniel Graham Secretary

James Jones is entitled to the Within Mentioned tract of Land.

P-293.

T. McGovock, D. Reg.
of West Tennessee

Recorded in the Register office of West Tennessee 25th February 1825.

H. W. McGovock, D. Register

Registered June 30th 1828.

P-293.   State of Tennessee   State of Tennessee
              To   No. 19052
       John Cunningham

To all to Whom these Presents shall Come Greeting. Know ye that by Virtue of Part of Certificate No. 765 dated the 2nd day of November 1814, issued by the Register of East Tennessee to George Gordon for 500 Acres and entered on the 6th day of June 1821 by No. 6302 there is granted by the State of Tennessee Unto John Cunningham Assignee of the said George Gordon a Certain tract or Parcel land Containing one hundred and fourteen acres by survey bearing date the 7th of June 1821 lying in the third district on Marion County on Battle Creek Adjoining Robert C. Gordon and Mathew Barbee and Bounded as follows to Wit

Beginning at a White Oak at the foot of the Mountain on the road side Corned to said Barbee; thence With the Meanders of the Mountain N. 56½' West forty Poles S. 76' West forty eight Poles N. 25' West thirty for Poles N. 76' W. Thirty Poles N. 37' W. twenty eight Poles N. 28' to one hundred and ten Poles to a hickory at the foot of the Mountain thence West fifty six Poles to a hickory on George Lowrey reservation line thence south With the same sixty eight Poles to a Stake on the same thence East twenty four Poles to a stake; thence South twenty four Poles to a Poplar on Robert C. Gordon line of his entry; thence With the same East thirteen Poles to a beech on the Bank of Battle creek Corner to said Gordon; thence S. 40'; east one hundred and sixty five Poles along ad Gordon line, crossing said Creek several time to a stake on said line; thence eight six Poles to a stake on said Barbee line thence With the same N. 27' E. fifty one Poles to the beginning, Including his Improvements & spring With the hereditaments and Appurtenances.

To have and to hold the said tract or Parcel of land With its appurtenances to the said John Cunningham and his heirs forever.

In Witness Whereof William Carroll Governor of the State of Tennessee hath hereunto set his hand and Caused the great

P-294   seal of the State of Tennessee to be affixed at Murfreesboro of the 28th day of April in the Year of Our Lord one thousand eight hundred and twenty and of the Independent of the United State the forty Seventh.

By the Governor
Wm Carroll

Daniel Graham Secretary.

John Cunningham is entitled to the Within Mentioned tract of land

D. McGavock Register of
West Tennessee
By Brice F. Martin D. Register.

P-294. Recorded in the Registers office of East Tennessee 13th October 1828 in Book K.

H. W. McKeveck, D. Register

Registered June 30th 1828.

P-294. Samuel McBee
      To Deed of Con.   This Indenture Made this day of
   George E. Brock   January one thousand and eight
hundred and twenty three between
Samuel McBee of the State of Tennessee and County of Marion of the one
Part and George E. Brock of the County of Franklin and State aforesaid
of the other Part,

Witnesseth that for and in consideration of the sum of fifty
dollars to him in hand Paid the receipt Whereof is hereby Acknowledged
hath Given G. Rented sold and conveyed unto the said George E. Brock a
Certain tract or Parcel of land situated lying and being in Marion County aforesaid on Sweetens Creek of Battle in Sweetens cove

Beginning on a sugar tree said McBee south East Corner; thence
North forty four Poles to a Holly; thence West four Poles to a Holly;
thence North Seventy West fifteen Poles to a beech; thence thirty five
West ten Poles to a Poplar; thence south thirty six West seventy four
Poles to poles on said McBee south boundary line thence East to the Be-
ginning Containing twenty Acres.

To have and to hold the aforesaid land With all and Singular
the hereditaments and Appurtenances of in and to the same belonging or
in any wise appertaining to the Only proper use benefits and behoof of
him the said George A. Brock, his heirs and assigns forever and the said
Samuel McBee for himself his heirs Administrators and executors doth
Covenant and Agree and With the said George A. Brock his heirs and assigns forever that the before described land and bargained Premises he
Will Warrant and forever defend Against the right title interest Claim
of him and is heirs.

In testimony whereof the said Samuel McBee hath hereunto set
his hand and affixed this seal the day & Year first Above Written.

      Signed in Presence of

                                 his
Obadiah Beene   Samuel X McBee
Thomas Maxwell   mark

State of Tennessee Marion County Court February Session 1820.

Then Was the within Deed of Conveyance from Samuel McBee to
George Brock for twenty Acres of land in Marion County duly acknowledged
in Open Court by the said McBee and ordered to be Certified for register-
ation.

Given under my hand and Private seal, Not have a seal of of-
foce in Jasper this 28 day of February 1828.

                             Jno. Kelly Clk.
                             By G. W. Rice D. C.

(Seal)
Registered July 1st 1828.

P-294. Urias Martin
       To Deed

John Wynn

    This Indenture Made this second day
of January in the Year of our Lord
one thousand eight hundred and twenty eight

P-295. Between Urias Martin of the State of Tennessee and County of
Marion of the one Part and John Wynn of the State and county aforesaid of
the Other Part,
        Witnesseth that the said Urias Martin for and in Considera-
tion of the Sum of three hundred dollars to him in hand Paid the receipt
Whereof is hereby Acknowledged hath Given Granted bargained sold and
Conveyed unto the said John Wynn a certain tract or Parcel of land situated lying and being in Marion County aforesaid on the Waters of Battle
Creek in Sweetens Cove, beginning on a horn beam; thence south to a
sycamore at the foot of the Mountain; thence With the Mountain South
eighty two degrees East to a buckeye; thence With John McGovans line
North to a stake and Pointers thence with West to the beginning Containing forty Acres More or less, it being of a one hundred and thirty eight
Acres tract of land originally Granted to Robert Beene Sr. by the State
of Tennessee.
        To have and to hold the aforesaid land With all and Singular
the hereditaments of in and to the same belonging or in any Wise appertaining the Only Proper use and behoof of him the said John Wynn, his
heirs and assigns forever and the said Urias Martin for himself his heirs
executors and administrators doth covenant and agree to and With the said
John Wynn his heirs and assigns forever that the before recited land and
bargained Premises he Will forever Warrant and forever defend Against
the right title Claim interest of all and every Person or Persons Whatever.
        In Witness Whereof the said Urias Martin hath hereunto set
his hand and affixed his seal the day and Year first Above Written.
        Signed in Presence of

Obediah Beene
     his

Thomas X Wynn
    mark

             his
Urias X Martin Seal
      mark

P-295. State of Tennessee

    Marion County Court

February Session 1828.

        Then Was the foregoing deed of conveyance from Uriad Martin to
John Wynn, for forty Acres of land in Marion County duly Acknowledged in
Open Court by the said Martin and ordered to be Certified for Registration
        Given under my hand and Private seal not having a seal of of-
fice the 28th day of February 1828.

                  Jno. Kelly Clk.
                  by G. W. Rice D. C.

Registered July 1st 1828.

their heirs and assigns a Certain piece or Parcel or tract of land situated lying and being in the County of Marion and State of Tennessee on the Waters of Battle Creek containing One hundred and six Acres and bounded as follows to Wit;

here ingunted the bounderes and reference to the Grant of known beginning at a beech on Hollys line thence With the Meanders of the Mountain to a Chesnut; thence With Wootens lines Crossing the Public road to a beech at the foot of the Mountain; thence With the Said Mountain to a Pointers on Holbys line thence with the same to the beginning Corner.

To have and to hold the said piece Parcel or tract of land hereby granted bargained and sold and every Part and Parcel thereofall and Singular the tenements appurtenances and hereditamnts unto and for the only Proper use and behoof of the said James and John Clipper their heirs and assigns forever and the said Roberts and McMurray for themselves and their heirs all and singular the Premises hereby granted bargained and sold With the tenements appurtenances and hereditaments unto the said Clipper there heirs and assigns Against them the said Roberts and McMuray and their heirs and every and all Others Person or Persons Whatever shall and Will forever Warrant and defent by these Presents and the Said Roberts and McMurray for themselves their heirs executors and Administrators doth covenant and Promises that they now are seized and Possessed of a good, Perfect and indefeasable estate of inhirtance in fee simple of and in the Premises hereby granted bargained and sold and that they have lawful Power and absolute Authority to grant bargain and sell the same in Manner and for me aforesaid that the sd Premises now are and forever shall be and remain free and clear of and from all former gifts granted bargain sales Judgements execution and incumberance Whatever.

In Witness Whereof the sd J. H. Roberts and John McMurray hath hereunto set our hands and affixed our seals the day and date above Written

Signed seale. and delivered in Presence of

Usaac H. Roberts (seal)
John McMurray (seal)

P-297. Ias McCain
David Miller

State of Tennessee   Court May Term 1827.

Marion County Court

Then Was the Within Deed of Conveyance Proven in Open Court by the Oaths of David Miller and James McClain subscribing Witness thereto and Ordered to be Certified for Registration.

Given under my hand & Private seal not having a seal of office in Jasper this 25th day of January 1828.

Jno. Kelly Clk.

Registered July 3rd 1828.

P-297. John Hatfield
     To Deed
Elisha Kerplin

This Indenture Made and entered into this 19th day of Feby 1827 between John Hatfield of the County of Marion and State of Tennessee of the one Part and Elisha Kerlen of the County of

P-298 Bledsoe and Allen Kerplin of the County of Marion, both of the State
of Tennessee of the Other Part,

Witnesseth that the said John Hatfield hath sold unto the said
Elisha Kerplin and Allen Kerplin a Certain tract or Parcel of land in
Marion County bounded and described as follow viz;

Beginning at a small Walnut tree Corner of John Herde and Alexander Kelly on the lower line of the sixteenth lot thence along the
line of the said Herd, North 70 west sixty Poles to a black Oak Corner
to Roger tract then Along said line south 38° West one Hundred and fifty
poles to a beech and Elum thence along Isaac Stovars line the same Corner
fourteen Poles to a White oak; thence South 39° East Seventy two Poles
to a White oak; thence south 26° West one hundred and thirty five Poles
to a Pointer on Spring line; thence along the same south 50° East thirty
three Poles to a hickory; thence along With the line of William Cooper
North 40° East forty Poles to black oak thence South 54° East sixty two
Poles to a dogwood thence along the line With George Reece and Samuel
Vale, north 40° East One hundred and fifty three Poles to a black gum
thence 27° West fifty eight Poles to a Poplar, thence North 30° East
eighty Poles to Pointers on the line of lot No. thence along the same
North fifty ° West seventy one poles to the beginning Containing two hundred and sixty six Acres for the sum of thirty five dollars and fifty cents
the receipt of Which is hereby Acknowledged before the sealing of these
Presents Which Above named tract of land Was granted unto the said Hatfield by the State of Tennessee No. of Grant 11634 bearing date the 23rd
of August 1828 With its Appurtenances,

To have and to hold the said tract of land and the said Hatfield doth forever relinquish and quit Claim unto the said Elisha & Allen
Kerplen to the Above described tract of land and now it is plaining understood by both the Parties that the said Hatfield doth Convey all the Virtue
that there Maybe in the State title and no other

Signed sealed and delivered in Presence of Witness-

| James Loyd | Wurat | | |
| David Cornett | Wurat | 0 | John Hatfield (seal) |

State of Tennessee

Marion County Court

February Session 1828.

Then Was the Within Deed of Conveyance from John Hatfield to
Elisha Kirplin for two hundred and sixty Acres of land in Marion County
Which Was on Monday of this term Proven by the oath of James Loyd and by
the oath of David Cornett subscribing Witness thereto and admitted for
registration.

Given under my hand and Private seal not having an official seal
this 20th day of Gebruary 1828.

Jno. Kelly Clk.
By G. W. Rice D. Clk.

Registered July 5th, 1828.

P-298. Luke Standifer
To Deed
Alexander Coulter

P-295.   John Doss
             To   Deed
         Jonathan Blevins

This Indenture Made and entered into in the Year of Our Lord
One thousand eight hundred and
twenty seven between Doss of the
State of Tennessee Marion County of the One Part and Jonathan Blevins of
the County and State Aforesaid of the Other Part

Witnesseth that for and in consideration of the sum of fifteen
dollars to me in hand Paid the receipt is hereby Acknoledged hath bargained granted and sold alien and Confirm Unto Johnathan Blevins a Certain tract
or Parcel of land Containing three Acres lying and being in the State of
Tennessee Marion County in the third District it being a Part of a 100 Acres
tract granted by the State of Tennessee to John Doss and being the South
Corner of said tract,

Beginning and running as follows to Wit:

Beginning on a black oak running West 36½ Poles to a stake;
thence North to a stake; thence East for Compliments With hereditaments

To have and to hold to sd Jonathan Blevins his heirs and assigns
for ever the said John Doss Will Forever Warrant and defend the rite of
said land from himself his heirs and other Person or Persons Whatever to
the sd Blevins heirs and Assigns forever.

In Witness Whereof I have here unto set my hand and seal the
Year and date first above Written,

Signed sealed and delivered in Presence of us.

W. D. L. Renfro   John Doss   (seal)
Stephen A. Blevins Witness

P-296.   State of Tennessee

         Marion County Court

February Term 1827.

Then Was the Within deed of conveyance from John Doss to Jonathan
Blevins for three Acres of land Proven in Open Court by the Oaths of
Stephens A. Blevines and W. H. L. Rentfro subscribing Witness thereto and
Ordered to be Certified for registration

Given under my hand and Private seal not having and official
seal at My office at office in Jasper the 18th day of January 1828.

                                    Jno. Kelly Clk.

(L.S.) Registered July 1st 1828.

P-296.   Henry Box
             To Power Atty.
         Mathew Barbee

State of Alabama
St. Clair County
March 28th 1824.

Know all men by these Presents that I Henry Box of the County
of St. Clair of the State of Alabama have and do by these Presents nomi-
nate Constitute and appoint My Certain friend Mathew Barbee my lawful
agent to Act as an Agent in all Manner of things as he the said Mathew
Barbee May deem fit to institute surety in law all the said Premises the
same as if I were Personally Present to Institute a suit in law or equity
as the case may be for the Purpose of recovering two Certain Negroes of
Which I have been robbed in the Indian Nation at Lowry Fernya by George

Gray, William Gray, James Lewis Richard Sharp and Esq. Sharp and Others in the Year Eighteen hun red and sixteen the name of one of the said Negros One Was a boy named Brown then a out ten Years Old, the other a girl the age about sixteen, this is therefore to Authorize the said Mathew Barbee to Pursue and take the said Negroes Wheresoever he May find in My name or should it be Necessary the further Authorize the said Mathew Barbee to sued and be sued Plead are be impleaded or in any Manner to do or Act in the recovery of the Aforesaid Property in all things the same as if I were Myself Personally Present.

In Witness Whereof I have hereunto set my hand and seal, In Presence of

John Box
Jesse O. Roberts   Henry Box   (seal)

Be it known that on the 20th day of Mach 1824 before Me Hugh Callahan Acting Justice of the Peace for the County aforesaid Personally appeared Henry Box Within named and Acknowledged the above letter of Attorney to be his Act and Deed.

In testimony Whereof I have hereunto set my hand and seal the day and Year last aforesaid.

                                 Hugh Callahan   (Seal)
                                 Justice of the Peace of the
                                 County of St. Clair, Alabama.

P-296.   State of Alabama

        St. Clair County

I Christopher A. Green, Clerk of the County Court of the County of State Aforesaid do hereby Certify that Hugh Callahan the Justice of the Peace to the Aforesaid Power of Attorney is and Was an Acting Justice of the Pece at the time of his official Attestations to the said instruments and the said instrument and that faith and credit should and might and ought to have to all his official act as such.

In witness whereof — Given under my hand and Private seal there being no official seal at Present in office.

        Test C. A. Green Ck. CC.

Registered July 2nd, 1828.
March 28th 1824.

P-297. Isaaac H. Roberts & John McMurray
           Too   Deed
      James Clipper Jr.
      John Clipper

This Indenture Made the 15th day of July in the Year of Our Lord one thousand eight hundred and twenty six between I. H. Roberts and John McMurray both of the State of Tennessee and County of Marion of the One Part and James Clipper and John Clipper of the State and County Aforesaid of the other Part

Witnesseth that the said Roberts and McMurray for and in consideration of the sum of seven hundred dollars to him Paid by the said Clipper at or before the Sealing and delivery of these Presents the receipt of Which is hereby Acknowledged hath granted, bargained and sold by these Presents doth grant, bargained sold unto the said John Clipper

This Indenture Made this eighteen day of June in the Year of our Lord Eighteen hundred and twenty seven between Luke Standifer of the County of Bledsoe and State of Tennessee of the One Part and Alexander Coulter of the County of Marion and State Aforesaid of the Other Part,

Witnesseth that for and in Consideration of the sum of twenty One dollars to him the Said Luke Standifer Paid the receipt Whereof is hereby Acknowledged hath and by these Presents doth grant bargain sell Alien enfroff and Confirm unto the said Alexander Coulter his heirs and assigns forever a Certain tract or Parcel of land containing four Acres situated in Marion County of the North West side of Sequachie P-299. Joining lands of the said Coulter and Roswell Hall,

Beginning at a stake on the second line Called for in a deed of Conveyance from the said Standifer to the said Coulter for sixteen Acres fifteen Poles N. 86 W. from Bitsey Pechs reservation then North fifteen degrees East eight and half Poles to a stake then North Seventeen West ten Poles to a stake then North eight Poles to a stake then North twelve degrees East twenty nine Poles to a hickory on the Point of the ridge Eastwardly of the head of the Spring or Mill Pond then North five West eighteen Poles to a stake on the line of Standifer five Acre Survey at the foot of the Mountain; thence along the same south forty four West sixteen Poles to a stake then south twenty Poles to a stake and Pointers at a Corner of the said Coulter sixteen acre tract above the head of the Spring; then along his line S. 3 W. 20 Poles running through the Mill Pond then S. 7 E. 5½ Poles to a stake then S. 6 Poles to a stake Near a hickory then S. 17 E. 10 Poles to a stake thence S. 15 W. 8½ Poles to a stake; then S. 86 E. 2 poles to beginning including the aforesaid four acres be the same More or less being Part of Two Grants issued from the State of Tennessee the said Luke Standifer by Grant 15388 for 160 Acres & No. 13148 for 5 Acres together With all and singular the Woods Water Watercourses Profits Commodities hereditaments and Appurtenances Whatsoever to the said tract of land belonging or in any Wise appertaining and the reversion and reversions remainder and remainders rents and issus and all the estate right title interests Property Claim and demand of him the said Luke Standifer his heirs and assigns forever of in and to the same and every Part and Parcel thereof either in law or equity:

To have and to hold the aforesaid four Acres of land With its appurtenances under the said Alexander Coulter his heirs and Assigns forever against the lawful title Claim and demand of every Person or Persons Whatever Will Warrant and forever defend by these Presents.

In Witness Whereof I hereunto set my hand and seal this day and date first above Written.

Signed sealed and delivered in Presence of

Samuel Standifer	
Thos. Griffith	Luke Standifer (seal)

P-299   State of Tennessee

Marion County Court

February Session 1828.

Then Was the Within deed of Conveyance from Luke Standifer to Alexander Coulter Which Was on Monday of the term Proven by the Oaths of Samuel Standifer the Subscribing Witness thereto for four Acres of land in Marion County this day duly Acknowledged by the said Luke Standifer and

P-299 ordered to be Certified for registration.

Jno. Kelly Clk.
By G. W. Rice D.C.

Attest.
Registered July 5th. 1828.

P-300. Morgan Jones
            To   Deed
        James Clipper

This Indenture made the 19th of July in the Year of Our Lord one thousand eight hundred and twenty six between Morgan Jones of the State of Tennessee and of Marion County of the one Part and James Clipper of the State and County aforesaid of the Other Part,

Witnesseth that the sd Jones for and in Consideration of the sum of fifty dollars & five dollars to him in hand Paid by the said Clipper at or before the sealing and delivering of these Presents the receipts of Which is hereby Acknowledged hath granted bargained and sold and With these Presents doth grant bargain and sell unto the P. Jas. Clipper his heirs and Assigns a xertain Parcel or tract of land situated lying on the Water of Battle Creek Containing ten Acres and bounded as follows to Wit:

Adjoining Said Tompkins and S. Simimings lands beginning at a stake on Tompkins Northeast 8 Poles to a beach Corner of said Tompkins thence southeast 22 Poles to a stake thence North With Conditional line twenty two to a stake and Pointers at the foot of the Mountain then With the Meanders of it North West fifty one Poles to a stake; thence south West Nine Poles to a stake on Simimings line thence Southeast thirty two Poles thence south West eighteen Poles to W. Trossell line thence southeast forthy six Poles to beginning together With all and singular the tenements Appurtenances and hereditaments there unto appertaining or belonging.

To have and to hold the said piece P rcel or tract of land hereby granted bargained and every Part and Parcel thereof With all and singular tenements and appurtenances and hereditaments unto and forever the only Proper use and behoof of the said James Clipper his heirs and assigns forever and the said M. Jones for himself and his heirs and all Singular the Premises hereby granted bargained and Sold With the tenements hereditaments and appurtenances unto the said James Clipper his heirs and assigns Against him the Jones his heirs every and all Other Person or Persons Whatever shall and Will forever Warrant and defend by tese Presents and P. Jones for himself his heirs executors and administrators doth covenant and Promise that he now is seized and possessed of a good perfect and indefeasible state of inheritance in fee simple of all Premises hereby granted bargained and sold and that he has lawful and Authority to grand bargain and sell the same and from the aforesaid Premises now and forever hereafter Shall be and remain free and clear of and from All former gifts granted bargained sales judgments, executions and incumbrances Whatsoever.

In Witness Whereof the said M. Jones hath hereunto set his hand and fixed his seal the day and Year first above Written.

Signed sealed and delivered in Presence of

David Miller
John Clipper

Morgan Jones   (seal)

P-300. State of Tennessee   ◊

Marion County Court   ◊   May Term 1827.

         Then Was the Within Deed of Conveyance from Morgan Jones to James Clipper for ten Acres of land duly Proven in open Court by the Oaths of Miller and John Clipper subscribing Witnesses thereto and ordered to be Certified for registration.

         Given under my hand and Private seal not having a seal of office in Jasper this 25th day of January 1828.

         Registered July 7th 1828.

                         Jno. Kelly Clk.

P-301   Elijah Hicks   ◊

      To   Deed   ◊   This Indenture Made the 19th day

   Houston Hixon   ◊   of March in the Year of Our Lord

                     ◊   One thousand eight hundred and twenty Seven between Elijah Hicks of the County of Marion and State of Tennessee of the one Part and Houston Hixon of the County and State aforesaid of the Other Part

         Witnesseth that the said Elijah Hicks for and in consideration of the sum of one hundred dollars to him in hand Paid by the Houston Hixson at or before the sealing and delivering of these Presents the receipt of Which is hereby Acknowledged hath granted bargained and sold and by these Presents doth grant bargain grant and sell unto the said Houston Hixson his heirs and assigns forever a Certain or Parcel tract of land granted by the State of Tennessee to the said Elijah Hicks for sixty Acres by grant No. 21275 bearing date the twenty eight day of January 1824 Situated lying and being in the sd Cty of Marion on the Southeast side of Sequatchee River adjoining lands of Epriam Hixson sd Hicks and William House and bound as follows: (to Wit)

         Beginning at a Poplar & dogwood at the head of a spring it being the beginning Corner of said Hixsons Survey thence along his line running through the head of said Spring West twenty three Poles to a White oak thence south 72° West forty Poles to Pointers thence along said Hicks line south fifty six Poles to a White Oak thence along said House line south 75° degrees East one hundred and Seventeen Poles to Pointers thence West fifty three Poles to a sweet gum on said Hixsons line & With the same a direct line to the beginning including sixty acres be the same More or less together with all the singular and Woods water water Courses Profits and Commodities, hereditaments and appurtenances thereto belonging or in any wise appertaining to the Aforesaid tract of land.

         To have and to hold to the said Houston Hixson his heirs and assigns forever free and clear of the lawful title Claim and demand of him the said Elijah Hicks or any Person Claiming from by or under him or his heirs forever Will Warrant and forever defend the aforesaid tract of land to the said Houston Hixson sofar as the right of the same is vested in him the Said Elijah Hicks by the Grant from the State of Tennessee as Above specified.

         In Witness Whereof I the Elijah Hicks hath hereunto set my hand and seal the day and date first above Written.

         Signed delivered and acknowledged in Presence of

P-301.

Amos Griffith
Isaac Hicks   Elijah   (Seal)

P-301. State of Tennessee   )
)   May Term 1827.
        Marion County Court   )

      Then Was the Within deed of Conveyance from Elijah Hicks to
Houston Hixson for sixty Acres of land Proven in Open Court by the oaths
of Isaac Hicks and Amos Griffith subscribing Witnesses thereto and ordered to be Certified for registration.
      Given under my hand and Private seal not having a seal of
office in Jasper the 25th day of January 1828.

                Jno. Kelly Clk.

Registered July 7th, 1828.

P-301. Roswell Hall   )
            To. Deed   )   This Indenture Made and enter-
        Hopkins S. Swinsy   )   ed this the twelveth day of
                                    February in the Year of Our
                                    Lord one thousand eight hun-
dred twenty seven between Roswell Hall of the County of Marion and State
of Tennessee of the One Part and Hopkins S. Turney of the County and
State aforesaid of the other Part
      Witnesseth that the said Roswell Hall for and in considera-
tion of the Sum of Thirty Five Dollars to him in hand paid the receipt
Whereof is hereby Acknowledged hath bargained and sold and by these
Presents doth grant bargain and Convey to the

P-302 said Hopkins S. Turney a Certain Parcel or tract of land Containing fifteen Acres situated lying and being in the County of Marion and
state of Tennessee on the Northeast side of Sequachie River granted by
the State of Tennessee to said Roswell Hall by Grant No. 22818 and bounded as follows to Wit;
      Adjoining lands of Luke Standifer and James Standifer begin-
ning at a Mulberry Corner to the said Standifer thence along Luke Standifers line North 25° East sixty three Poles to Pointers thence south sixty Poles to a stake; thence East thirty five Poles to Pointers on James
Standifer's line and With the same North to the beginning together With
all and singular the hereditaments and appurtenances thereunto belonging
or in any wise appertaining All so all the rights title claim interest
or demand Whatsoever of him the said Roswell Hall of in and to the above
bargained Premises
      To have and to hold to the said Hopkins L. Turney his heirs and
assigns forever.
      In Witness Whereof the said Roswell Hall hath hereunto set his
hand and seal the first day and Year afore Written.

                Roswell Hall (Seal)

P-303. State of Tennessee

May Term 1827.

Marion County Court

Then Was the Within deed of Conveyance from Roswell Hall to Hopkins L. Turney fifteen Acres of land Acknowledged in Open Court by the said Hall and ordered to be Certified for registration.

Given under my hand & Private seal not having a seal of office in Jasper the 25th. day of January 1828.

(LS) Registered July 8th 1828.

Jno. Kelly Clk.

P-302. William Hendrix
       To. Deed.
       Hiram Stinnett

This Indenture Made the 20th day of November in the Year of our Lord 1827 by and between William Hendrix of the County of Marion and State of Tennessee of the one Part and Hiram Stinnett of the same County and State of the Other Part

Witnesseth that for and in consideration of the Sum of three dollars to me in hand Paid the receipt of Which is hereby Acknowledged, I the said William Hendrix hath and by these Presents doth grant bargain and sell Convey and Confirm unto the said Hiram Stinnett and his heirs forever a Certain tract or Parcel of land situated lying and being in the County of Marion aforesaid on the little Sequachee River Adjoining land of Jess Stinnett Containing 36 Acres bounded as follows to Wit:

Beginning at a beech on the bank of little Sequachee thence along a line With Jess Stinnett S. 49 Poles to an Ironwood at the foot of the Mountain; then along the same as it Meanders S 29° E. 81 Poles to a Walnut then S. 41° East 31 Poles to a Wamut on Hendrix line then along the Same N. 44 E. 24 P to a Sugar tree an ironwood on the bank of a beech or logwood then up the same 55 poles to a beech on bank of the same thence N. 49° E. 56 poles to a stake on the South bank of said Sequachee then up the same as it Meanders north 48° W. 8½ Poles N. 18° W. 30 Poles thence north 45° W. 19 poles to the beginning including 38 Acres be the same more or less.

To have and to hold the Aforesaid tract or Parcel of land With the appurtenances unto the said Hiram Stinnett and his heirs from the Claim and demands of all and every person or Persons I the said William Hendrix Will Warrant and forever defend.

In Testimony Whereof I have hereunto set my hand and seal the day and Year first herein Written.

Signed Sealed and Acknowledged in our Presence

Jno. Kelly.
Geo. W. Rice.

William Hendrix

P-303   State of Tennessee

November Term, 1827.

Marion County Court

Then Was the Within deed of Conveyance from William Hendrix

P-303. to Hirman Stinnett for 386 Acres of land in Marion County Was
duly Acknowledged in Open Court by the said Hendrix and Ordered to be
Certified for registration.

Given Under my hand and Private Seal not having a seal of
office in Jasper the 18th day of January 1828.

(L.S.)   Jno. Kelly Clk.

Registered July 8th, 1828.

P-303.   Jonathan Eaves   )
             To   Deed   )   This Indenture Made the second
         Joel Cross   )   day of February in the Year of
                                         Our Lord Eighteen hundred and
                                         twenty seven between Jonathan
Eaves of the State of Tennessee and the County of Marion of the one
Part and Joel Cross of the State and County aforesaid of the other Part
        Witnesseth that the said Jonathan Eaves hath for and in Con-
sideration of the sum of two hundred dollars to him in hand Paid at or
before the sealing & delivering of these Presents the receipt Whereof
is hereby Acknowledged hath given granted sold and Conveyed unto the
said Joel CRoss a Certain tract or Parcel of land situated lying and being in Marion County aforesaid on the Waters of Battle Creek in Sweetens
Cove on a spur of the Mountain.
        Beginning at a stake & White oak; thence South thirty two
Poles to Pointers thence East twenty Poles to a hackberry thence north
thirty two Poles to Pointers West to the beginning, Containing four Acres
more or less.
        To have and to holf the aforesaid land With all & Singular
the hereditaments & appurtenances of in and to the same belonging or in
any wise appertaining to the Only Proper use benefit and behoof of him
the said Joel Cross his heirs and assigns forever & the said Jonathan
Eaves for him self his heirs executors & Administrators doth Covenant
and agree to and With the said Joel Cross his heirs & assigns that the
before recited land and bargained Premises he Will Warrant & forever
defend Against the rights titles Claim or interest of all and every Person or Persons Whatever.
        In Witness Whereof the said Honathan Eaves hath hereto set
his hand & affixed his seal the day and date first above Written.
        In the Presence of

Henry Gocher   )
Mathew Wynn   )   Jonathan Eaves   (seal)
Izihier Cross   )

P-303.   State of Tennessee   )
)   February Term, 1827.
         Marion County Court   )

        Then Was the deed of Conveyance from Jonathan Eaves to Joel
Cross for four Acres of land duly Acknowledged in Open Court by the
said Eaves and ordered to be Certified for registration.
        Given under my hand & Private seal not having an official

seal of office at office in Jasper, this the 18th. day of January, 1____

Jno. Kelly Clk.

(L.S.) 1828.
Registered July 8th. 1828.

P-303.   Joh. Overturf
              To   Deed
         David Stanfield

This Indenture Made the 13th day of January in the Year of Our Lord One thousand eight hundred and twenty ssvn between John Overturf of the County of Marion and State of Tennessee of the one Part and David Stanfield of the County aforesaid of the Other Part

Witnesseth for and in consideration of fifty dollars to me in hand Paid the said John hath bargained and sold and by the Present do bargain

P-304   sell lien remiss & Convey unto the Said David a Certain tract or Parcel of land containing eight Acres lying and being in Marion County on Waters of Battle Creek,

Beginning on a White oak one the bank of the creek near Tussell Corner thence West With his line fifty six Poles to a stake at the foot of the Mountain With the same North forty five Poles to a stake on Doolys line; thence With the same scut fifty three east seventy two Poles to the beginning said land lying on Battle Creek.

To have and to hold said tract or Parcel of land together With all and singular the rights remainder appurtenances the same belonging or in any wise appertaining to the said David Stanfield his heirs and assigns forever and the said John Overturf for himself his heirs executors & Administrators doth covenant and agree to the said David Stanfield the said bargained Premises Will Warrant and forever defend from him his heirs and assigns and all person or Persons lawfully Claiming or to Claim.

in Witness Whereof the said John doth Put his hand and seal the day and date above Written.

G. W. Salmon
Thom. A. Smith, Witness

                                                   his
                        John   X   Overturf   (seal)
                                  mark

P-304. State of Tennessee

        Marion County Court

November Term, 1827.

Then was the Within deed of Conveyance from John Overturf to David Stanfield for eight acres of land duly Acknowledged in Open Court by the said Overturf and ordered to be Certified for registration.

Given under my hand & Private seal (not having a seal of office in Jasper this (LS); 8th January 1828.

Jno. Kelly Clk.

Registered July 8th, 1828.

1-304.   John Overturf
        To   Deed.
     David Stanfield

This Indenture Made the 13th day of January in the Year of Our Lord One thousand eight hundred twenty Seven between John Overturf of the County of Marion and State of Tennessee of the one Part & David Standfield of the County Aforesaid of the Other Part,

Witnesseth for and in consideration of Two Hundred and fifty dollars to me in hand Paid by said David hath bargained & sold and by these Presents do bar ain sell Alien remise and Convey to said David a Certain tract or Parcel of land lying and being in Marion County of the Waters of Battle Creek containing twenty two Acres,

Beginning on an elm Trussell Corner; thence With the Mountain south eighty West nineteen Poles to a dogwood; thence South sixty five twenty eight Poles to a sugar tree thence North eighty Seven West twenty to a stake thence eighty two West fifteen six Poles to Pointers thence Seventy three West twenty two Poles to an horn beam thence thirteen Poles to a thence twenty six Poles to a Sugar tree thence North thirty three East one hundred and twenty four Poles to a gum; then With said Tussell line thirty two to the beginning said land lays on Battle Creek.

To have and to hold said tract or Parcel of land together With all and Singular rights remainders and appurtenances the same belonging or in any wise appertaining to the said David Stanfield his heirs and assigns forever and the said John Overturf for himself his heirs executors & Administraters doth covenant and agree unto the said David Stanfield that the said Bargained Premises he Will Warrant and forever defend from him his heirs and assigns and other Person or Persons lawfully Claiming or to Claim.

In Witness Whereof the said John doth Put his hand and seal the day and date above Written

                                    his
P-305.   John Overturf X (Seal)
J. W. Salmon   mark
Thos. A. Smith

       State of Tennessee
                            November Term 1827.
       Marion County Court

Then was the Within deed from John Overturf for twenty two Acres of land duly Acknowledged in Open Court by said Overturf and ordered to be Certified for registration.

Given under my hand & Private seal (not having a seal of office in Jasper this the 13th day of (LS) 1823.

                                Jno. Kelly Clk.

Registered July 8th, 1823.

P-305   Henry Long
         To   Deed.
     Pleasant McBride

This Indenture Made & entered into this 23rd day of September in the Year of Our Lord 1826 between Henry Long of the County of Marion and State of Tennessee of the one Part and

P-305. Pleasent McBride of the County and State aforesaid of the Other Part

Witnesseth that for and in consideration of the sum of one hundred and sixty dollars to John Sapp and as in hand paid the receipt whereof is acknowledged by the said John Sapp, and as the Original title is vested in me the said Henry Long I do therefore by these Presents relinquish Quit Claim & Convey unto the said Pleasent McBride a Certain tract or Parcel of land containing thirty Acres situated lying and being in the said county of Marion on the North bank of Tennessee river adjoining lands of William Hail & George Harris, b

beginning at an Ash tree on bank of said River it being the upper Corner on the river of the Original Survey on Which the grant is founded a Part of Which is about to be Conveyed by Virtue of these Presents and also it being a Corner to said Hail then along said Hail line North eighty one degrees East forty eight Poles to an elm near the head of a Spring at the foot of the Mountain then along the Various Course of said Mountain Northwestwardly to the second hollow below Where Jasper McInturff now lives Where there is a wooden bridge or causeway then down said hollow to the Mouth and up With the meanders of said river to the beginning including the aforesaid thirty Acres be the same more or less and the Premises Claimd by said McBride, That is to say the Place himself and McInturf now lives it being Part of a tract of land granted by the State of Tennessee to the said Henry Long for one hundred and forty five Acres by grant No. 24934 bearing date the 9th day of May 1826, With all and singular the woods water water courses profits, commodities hereditaments and appurtenances thereunto belonging or in any wise appertaining to have and to hold to him the said Pleasent McBride his heirs and assigns forever against the lawful title Claim and demand of any Person Claiming from by or under me or my heirs I will warrent and forever defend the title of the Aforesaid Tracts of land and Premises to the said McBride and his heirs forever sofar as the title of the same is vested in me by Grant from the State of Tennessee as herein before specified and no farther.

In testimony whereof I hereunto set my hand and seal this day and date above Written.

Signed sealed and ack'd in Presence of

Ignatius Hall   Henry Long   (seal)
Jno. Kelly

P-305 State of Tennessee |
                               | May Term 1827.
       Marion County Court |

Then Was the Within deed of conveyance from Henry Long to Pleasent McBride

P-306 for thirty Acres of land Acknowledgee in open court by the said Long and ordered to be Certified for registration.

Given under My hand & Private seal not having a seal of office in Jasper this the 25th day of January 1828

(L S)   Jno. Kelly Clk.
Registered July 9th, 1828.

P-306. Henry Long
     To Deed
George Harris Jr.

This Indenture Made and entered
into this 23rd day of September
in the Year of Our Lord 1826 between Henry Long of the County
of Marion and State of Tennessee of the One Part and George Harris Jr.
of the County and State aforesaid of the Other Part

    Witnesseth that for and in consideration of the Sum of eighty
dollars to John Sapp in hand Paid the receipt Whereof is hereby Acknowledged by him the said John Sapp and as the Orginal is Vested in
Me the said Henry Long I therefore do by these Presents relinguish quite
Claim and Convey unto the said George Harris Jr. a Certain tract or Parcel of land Containing fifteen Acres (It being that Part of a tract of
land granted to me by the State of Tennessee for One hundred and forty
five Acres by Grant No. 24934 bearing date the 9th day of May 1826 that
lives between that Part I conveyed to Pleasent McBride and the Part I
sold to William Morrow beginning on the bank of Tennessee River at the
Mouth of the Rocky Dry branch known by the name between Ware the Said
Harris now livs and William Morrow then up the Said Channel of the said
branch it being a former Condition to the Mountain line of the original
survey of said 145 Acres and With said Mountain line to said McBride's
Corner and With his line to the River at the Mouth of second hallow below Where McIntues now livs Where there is a Wooden bridge or Crossaway
then down the river as it Maunders to the beginning Including the Premises
Where the said Harris now livs the aforesaid fifteen Acres be the same
More or less With all and singular the Woods Water Water course Profits
Commodities hereditaments and appurtenances thereunto belonging or in
any Wise appertaining either in law or equity.

    To have and to hold the aforesaid tract of land and Premises
unto the said George Harris Jr. his heirs and assigns forever against the
lawful title Claims and demand of any Person or Persons Claiming from
or under me or my heirs. I Warrant and forever defend the aforesaid
tract of land to the said George Harris Jr. and his heirs sofar as the
title of the same is in My the Grant from the State of Tennessee as above
Specified and as full.

    In Witness Whereof I have hereunto set my hand and seal the
day and date above Written.

    Signed and ack's in Presence of Ignatius Hall Jno. Kelly.

                     Henry Long   seal.

P-306. State of Tennessee

          May Term 1827

Marion County Court

    Then Was the Within deed of conveyance from Henry Long to
George Harris Jr. for fifteen Acres of land was acknowledged in Open
Court by the said Long and Ordered to be Certified for registration.

    Given under my hand and Private seal (not having a seal of
office) in Jasper this 25th day of January 1828.

                     Jno. Kelly Clk.

(L S) Registered July 9th 1828.

P-306. Elijah Hicks Jr.   §
        Isaac Hicks   §   This Indenture Made the 13th day
              To   Deed   §   of June in the Year of Our Lord One
        James Mayo   §   thousand and eight hundred twenty
                            eight between Elijah and Isaac Hicks

both

P-307. of Marion and State of Tennessee of the One Part and James Mayo of the County and State aforesaid of the Other Part,

      Witnesseth that for & in consideration of the Sum of three hundred and sixty dollars to him the said Isaac Hicks in hand Paid by the said Mayo the receipt Whereof is hereby Acknowledged hath granted bargained & sold and by these Presents do grant bargain sell alien enfross and Convey unto the Said James Mayo a Certain tract or Part of an tract or Parcel of land granted by the State of Tennessee to Elijah Hicks for One hundred and forty Acres Grant No. 21274 being date the 28th day of January 1824, it being one half of said tract of 140 Acres agreeable to the Vision heretofore Made by John Kelly between Isaac Hicks and Jushua A. Ashburn bounded and described as follows.

      Beginning at a White Oak the Most southwardly Corner of Eprian Hixson Survey of one hundred Acres near a branch then along said Hixson line N. 41 W 94 Poles to a black oak then along said Mayo's line of a tract 134 Acres N. 49 W. 22 Poles to a black oak; then S. 30 W. 44 Poles to a stake and Pointers Poplar & bee Gum then along the division between Isaac Hicks and said Ashburn as run and Marked S. 52 E. 96 Poles to a stake near a branch then S. 25 E. 78 Poles on the South boundary of said Survey then E. 53 Poles to dogwood S. E. Corner then N. 116 Poles in Part along Houston Hinson Survey to Pointers then a direct line to the beginning including seventy Acres of land be the same more or less With all and singular the Woods Water Water courses Profits Commodities hereditaments and Appurtenances.

      To have and to hold the said James Mayo his heirs and assigns forever the aforesaid seventy Acres of land as above free Clear of the lawful title Claim and demand of him the said Elijah Hicks (Who the title Afore is veted in or his heirs or assigns or any Persons Whatsoever Claiming from by or under or either of them Will Warrant and forever defend by those Presents either in law or equity as the Purchased was Made from and With the said Isaac Hicks and a Payment Made him he doth further Covenant and agree to and With the said James Mayo that if the before recited tract or Parcel of land and Premises should at any time hereafter be taken from him or his assigns by Virtue of any older or better title then the one by those Presents Conveyed then and in that Case the said Hicks is to be referred to the said Mayo or his assigns to the Value of three hundred dollars two hundred of that in Money and one hundred in Cotton the Amount received by him for said land inclusive of an allowance for the Warrant With legal interest on the same from the time the said Mayo or any Person Under him should or might be legally disposed by due cause of law.

      In Witness Whereof we the said Elijah Hicks & Isaac Hicks hereunto set our hand and Seal this day and date above Written.

      Signed Ack's in Presence of

Jno. Frack   Elijah Hicks   (seal)
Jno. Kelly   Isaac Hicks   (seal)

P-307. State of Tennessee

Marion County Court

February Tenn 1827.

Then Was the Within deed of Conveyance from Elijah and Isaac Hicks to James Mayo for Seventy Acres of land Was duly Proven in Opun Court by the Oaths of John Hicks and John Kelly the Subscribing Witness s. thereto and Ordered to be Certified for registration.

Given under My hand and Private seal Not having affixed seal at office in Jasper this 18th day of January 1828.

(L S) Registered July 9th 1828.   Jno. Kelly   Clk.

P-308   Samuel McReynolds
        And Stephen Hicks Admars
            To Bill of Sale
        Alexander Coulter

We Stephen Hicks and Samuel McReynolds Administrators of all And Singular the goods and Chattels rights and Credits of Joseph McReynolds deceased do hereby assign and transfer unto Alexander Coulter all the rights Claims or demands that We have either in law or equity as Administrators as aforesaid of the said Joseph McReynolds to a Certain Negro Man slave by the name of Edmond Which was by the said Joseph McReynolds in his life time Mortgaged to a Certain Martin Miller of Madison County in the State of Alabama on the 20th day of January 1819, We believe the equity of redemption is in us and therefore do assign the same or Value received to the said Alexander Coulter.

Given under our hands this the 12th day of October in the Year 1822.
Witness
Daniel Riggle and
Sololon Piggle   Ack'd.

                            Samuel McReynolds   (seal)
                            Stephen Hicks   (seal)
                            Administrators of the Estate
                            of James McReynolds

P-388.   State of Tennessee

         Marion County Court

February Term 1826

Then Was the Within form Samuel McReynolds & Stephen Hicks to Alexander Coulter for a Negro boy Edmond duly Proven in Open Court by the oaths of Solomon Riggle and Daniel Riggle the subscribing Witnesses thereto and ordered to be Certified for registration.

Given under my hand and Private seal not a seal of office in Jasper the 18th day of January 1828.

(L S L) Registered July 9th 1828   Jno. Kelly   Clk.

P-388.   Joel D. Mitchell
            To   Deed
         William C. Mitchell

This Indenture Made this 23rd day January in the Year of our Lord one thousand eight hundred and twenty seven between

Joel D. Mitchell of the County of Marion and the State of Tennessee of the one Part and William C. Mitchell of the County of White and State aforesaid of the Other Part,

Witnesseth that for and in consideration of the sum of four hundred dollars the said Joel D. Mitchell in hand paid the receipt Whereof is hereby Acknowledged hath sold Conveyed and confirmed by these Presents to the said William C. Mitchell his heirs and assigns forever a Certain tract or Parcel of land Containing sixty two Acres being in the County of Marion and State of Tennessee below the Mouth of Battle Creek bounded to Wit;

Adjoining the land John Kelly and Others beginning at a White oak near the foot of the Mountain on said John Kellys line running West forty six poles to Pointers then South ten " West until it strikes the Southern boundary line of the tract of land that Alexander Kelly sold to James G. Gunter then east With said line to a black oak at corner; Then east ten ° north ninety five Poles to a hickory thence With said John Kelly line to the beginning including sixty two Acres be the same More or less it being a Part of a tract of land of one hundred and fifty Acres that Alexander Kelly sold to James G. Gunter, With all and singular the hereditaments and Appurtenances.

To have and to hold unto him the said William C. Mitchell his heirs & assigns forever the said tract or Parcel of land from him the Joe D. Mitchell his heirs and assigns or any other Person or Persons Claiming under by or through him Will forever Warrant and it is expressly understood by the Parties that if the said tract of land should hereafter be taken by any older or better title than the one by these Presence conveyed that said J. D. Mitchell not being Accountable for any Part of these considerations of Money.

In Witness Whereof I have hereunto set my hand and seal the day and date above Written.

Thomas W. King
Laikln Bathel. Attest   Joe D. Mitchell (seal)

P-209. State of Tennessee
                                                          May Term 1828.
        Marion County Court

Then Was the Within deed of Conveyance from Joel D. Mitchell to William C. Mitchell for sixty two acres of land of Marion County Acknowledged in Open Court by the said Joel D. Mitchell and ordered to be Certified for registration. Let it be registered.

Registered July 9th 1828.   Jno. Kelly   Clk.

P-309. Alix Basham and
        Nancy Basham   Know all Men by these Presents
             To P. of Atty.   that Nereus James Carnett late
        James Carnett   of Virginia deceased, left a
                                          considerable Personal estate to
be divided and distributed among his heirs and legally representative and Whereas Nancy Basham Wife of Alexander Basham and grandaughter of the said James Cornett deceased, being desirous to obtain her Portion

P-309. of said estate now know ye that We Alexander Basham and Nancy
Basham his Wife of the County of Marion and state of Tennessee have made
ordaned Constituted and appointed James Garnett of Said County of Marion
and State of Tennessee one true and lawful attorney for us in our names
and for our own Proper use and benefit to ask demand and receive of and
from the executors or Administrators if any there be or from any Other
Person that have our Part of said estate and upon receipt thereof to our
Said Attorney a general release or discharge for the Same to Make executor and deliver hereby ratifying Confirming and allowing Whatsoever for
the same to Make executor and deliver hereby ratifying Confirming and
allowing Whatsoever our said Attorney shall lawfully do in the Premises.

In Witness We have hereunto set our hand and seal the 22nd
day of February A. D. 1828.
Sealed and delivered

William I. Standifer   his
W. M. Arnette   Alexander X Basham
                                         her mark
                                       Nancy X Basham
                                         mark

P-309.   State of Tennessee
                                       February Session, 1828.
         Marion County Court

Then Was the Within Power of Attorney from Alexander Basham
and Nancy Basham Wife to James Garnett duly Acknowledged in Open Court
by the said Alexander & Nancy his wife and ordered to be Certified for
registration.

Given Under my hand and Private seal not having a seal of
office at office in Jasper the 26th day of February 1828.

(L S) Registered July 26th 1828.   Jno. Kelly Clk.
                                        By G. W. Rice D. C.

P-309.   Dixon M. L.
            To   Deed   This Indenture Made this twen-
         Dickards Ben   ty third day of January in the
                                        Year of Our Lord one thousand
                                        eight hundred and twenty eight
between Mathew L. Dixson of Franklin County and State of Tennessee of
the one part and Benjamin Deckard of the County aforesaid of the other
Part

Witnesseth that the said Mathew L. Dixson for and in consideration of four hundred dollars hath bargained sold and conveyed and
confirmed & by these Presents doth bargain sell Convey and confirm unto
the said Benjamin Deckard his heirs and assigns forever a Certain tract
or Parcel of land in the County of Marion on the Fiery Gizzard Creek,

Beginning at the south west Corner of Conrods Hulneys 150
Acres on William Andersons line; thence With Anderson line to the Mountain and With the same southwardly to John Cohorns line & with his lines
& David Martin line to the Mountain & With the same northwardly to Hul-
seys southeast Corner then With his south boundary line West to the beginning, Containing one hundred and eighteen Acres be the same More or

into being Part of 135½ Acres granted to said Mathew L. Dixson.
P-310.   To have and to hold the before recited lands & bargained Premises With all and singular the rights profits rents issues hereditaments & Appurtenances of in and to the same belonging to the only Proper use benefit & behoof of him the said Benjamin Deckard his heirs and assigns forever and the said Mathew D. Dixson his heirs & assigns doth further Covenant & agree to & With the said Benjamin Deckard his heirs and assigns that the before recited land & bargained Premises Will Warrant & forever defend against the rights title interest Claim & demand of all and every Person or Persons Whatever.

In Witness Whereof the said Mathew L. Dixson hath hereunto set his hand & affixed his seal the day & year above Written.

Signed sealed & delivered in Presence of

P. S. Deckard
Mathew Deckard   M. L. Dixson   seal.

P-310.   I hereby relinquish all rights I have ever heretofore gave either in law or equity to the Within described lands.

Witness My hand & seal this the 16th day of July 1828.

Nathel Hunt   (seal)

P-310.   State of Tennessee   July Term 1828.

Franklin County Circuit Court

Then Was the Within deed of Conveyance from Mathew L. Dixson to Benjamin Deckard for one hundred and eighteen Acres of land lying in the County of Marion in this State was this day duly Acknowledged in Open Court by the said Mathew P. Dixson to be his act and deed for the Purpose therein Mentioned and also a relinquishment from Nathaniel Hunt to the same land to the said Benjamin Deckard was duly Acknowledged by the said Nathaniel Hunt to be his act and deed for the purpose therein Mentioned Wherefore it ids ordered by the Court that said deed and relinquishments be Certified to the County of Marion for registration. Let this be registered.

In testimony I Jonathan Spyker Clerk of said Court have hereunto set My hand this the 7th day of July 1828

Jonathan Spyker Clk.
Registered July 28th 1828.

P-310.   Dixson, Mathew   L.
            To   This Indenture Made the twenty
       Benjamin Deckard   third day of January between
                                      Mathew L. Dixson and Benjamin
                                      Deckard both of the County of

Franklin & State of Tennessee,

Witnesseth that the said Mathew L. Dixson for & in consideration of the sum of one dollar to him in hand Paid hath given granted bargained sold conveyed & confirmed unto the said Benjamin Deckard his heirs & assigns forever a Certain tract or Parcel of land in the County of Marion on the Fiery Gizzard Creek

P-310   Beginning at the head of Conrad Mulseys thence With his north
boundary line West to the beginning containing one hundred acres be the
same more or less which tract of land the said Mathew L. Dixson doth Warrant & forever defend Against the right title Claim & demand of himself
his heirs and assigns or any other person or persons Claiming under him
or them.

In Witness Whereof the Mathew L. Dixson hath hereto set his
hand and affixed his seal the day and Year above Written.
Signed sealed & delivered in Presence of

P. S. Deckard and
Jonathan Deckard   M. L. Dixson   seal

I hereby relinquish all rights I have ever heretofore had
either in law or equity to the Within described lands.
Witness My hand & seal this 16th July 1823.

Nath Hunt   seal.

P-310.   State of Tennessee
                                              July Term 1828.
Franklin County Circuit Court

Then Was the Within deed of Conveyance from Mathew L. Dixson

P-311.   To Benjamin Deckard for one hundred acres of land lying in the
County of Marion in the State of Tennessee Was this day duly Acknowledged
in Open Court by the said Mathew L. Dixson to be his act and deed for the
Purpose st herein Mentioned And also a relinquishments from Nathaniel
Hunt to the same land to the said Benjamin Deckard was duly acknowledged
in Open Court by the said Nathaniel Hunt to be his act and deed for the
Purpose therein Mentioned.
Witness it was ordered by the Court that the said deed and
relinquishments be Certified to the County of Marion for registration
that them be registered.
In testimony Whereof I Jonathan Spyker Clerk of said County
Court have hereunto set my hand this the 17th of July 1828.
Registered July 25th, 1828.

Jonathan Spyker Clerk.

P-311.   Morgan Jones
            To   Deed
         James Clipper

This Indenture Made this nineteenth
day of July in the Year of Our Lord
one thousand eight hundred and twenty six between Morgan Jones of the
State of Tennessee and the County of Marion and James Clipper of the State
and County aforesaid of the other Part,
Witnesseth that the said Jones for and in consideration of
the sum of one hundred to him in hand Paid by the said Clipper at or before the sealing and delivery of these Presents the receipt of Which is
hereby Acknowledged hath granted bargained and sold and by these Presents doth grant bargain and sell unto the said Clipper his heirs and assigns a Certain piece Parcel or tract of land situated lying and being
in the County aforesaid on Battle Creek containing ten Acres bounded as

follows to Wit;

P-311.   bounded on the south side by Nathan Durhams line William Payne
line on the north side and Natural boundary

Beginning on a beech stump near the foot of the Mountain on the
bank of s'd creek ad Durham's Corner running thence northeast 39 Poles to
a stake on Paynes line thence southwest 26 Poles to a sasomore on the
bank of sd Creek and down With its meanders south east 62 Poles to the beginning together With all and singular the tenements Appurtenances and
hereditaments thereto Appertaining or belonging,

To have and to hold the sd piece or Parcel or tract of land
hereby granted bargained and sold and every Part and Parcel thereof With
all and singular the tenements and appurtenances and hereditaments unto
and for the only Proper use and behoof of him the sd James Clipper his
heirs and assigns forever and the sd Jones for himself and his heirs all
and singular the Premises hereby granted bargained and sold With the tenements hereditaments and Premises unto the said Jas. Clipper his heirs and
assigns against him the said Jones and his heirs and every all and other
Person or Persons Whatever shall and Will forever and Will forever WaRrant
and defend by these Presents and the said Jones for himself his heirs executors and administrators doth covenant and Premises that he is now is
seized and Possessed of a good and Perfect and Indefeasable estate of in-
heritences in fee simple of and in the Premises hereby granted bargained
and sold and that has lawful Power and absolute authority to grant bargain and sell the same in Manner and form aforesaid that the sd Premises
now are and forever hereafter shall be and remain free and Clear of and
from all former gifts grants bargained sale Judgements executors and
incumbrances Whatever.

in Witness Whereof the said Jones hath hereunto set his hand and
affixed his seal the day and Year first above Written.

Signed sealed and delivered in Presence of

David Miller
John Clipper   Morgan Jones   (seal)

P-311.   State of Tennessee
                                          May Session 1827
          Marion County Court

Then Was the Within deed of Conveyance from Morgan Jones to
James Clipper for Ten Acres Was duly Proven in Open Court by the Oaths
of David Miller and James Clipper, the Subscribing Witnesses thereto and
ordered to be Certified for registration. Let it be Registered. A Copy
test.
P-312   Jno. Kelly   Clk.
Registered August 16th 1828.   By G. W. Rice D. Clk.

P-312 Isaac Standifer
          To   Deed   This Indenture Made the 16th
       William Standifer   day of March in the Year of
                                          Our Lord one thousand eight
                                          hundred and twenty five be-
tween Isaac Standifer of the County of Marion and State of Tennessee of
the Other Part of the on Part and William Standifer of the County and
State aforesaid

P-312   Witnesseth that the said Isaac Standifer for and in consideration of the sum of sixty dollars to him in hand paid the receipt Whereof is her by Acknowledged hath and by these Presents doth grant bargain sell alien enfross and Confirmed to the said William Standifer his heirs and assigns forever a Certain tract or Parcel of land Containing six Acres and one half lying and being in the County of Marion on the northwest side of Sequachie River adjoining lands of William Standifer and bounded as follows

Beginning on the West boundary of a survey of one hundred acres When the same Crosses William Standifer's spring branch then down the branch N. 44 East 60 Poles then South 45 degrees East 22 Poles then south twenty five degrees East twenty Poles to a small white walnut then south thirty five degrees West forty eight Poles to a small black Walnut near a large Poplar Stump on the said West boundary and With the same north to the beginning including six acres and one half be the same more or less it being Part of a one hundred tract granted by the State of Tennessee to Alexander B. Bradford by Grant No. 15953 bearing date the 11th of October 1821 With all and singular the Woods Water Water course Profits Commodities hereditaments and appurtenances Whatsoever to the said tract or Parcel of land belonging or appertaining and the reversion and reversions rents and remainders rents and issus thereof and all the estate right title interest Property Claim and demand of him the said Isaac Standifer for his heirs and assigns forever of in and to the same and every Part and Parcel thereof either in law or equity.

To have and to hold the said six acres and one half of land the appurtenances unto the said William Standifer his heirs and assigns against the lawful title Claim and demand of all Manner of Persons Will Warrant and forever defend by these Presents.

In Witness Whereof the said William Standifer has hereunto set his hand and seal this day and date first above Written.

Signed and acknowledged in Presence of

Luk Standifer   Ø
Amos Griffith,   Attest   Ø   Isaac Standifer.
                                                 Ø

P-312.   State of Tennessee   Ø
                                                 Ø   May Session 18825
         Marion County Court   Ø

Then Was the Within deed of conveyance from Isaac Standifer to William Standifer for Acres of land duly Acknowledged in Open Court by the said Isaac & Ordered to be Certified for registration. Let it be registered.
         Attest

                                          Jno. Kelly   Clk.
                                          By G. W. Rice   D.C.

P-312.   Samuel Standifer   Ø
            To   Bill of Sale   Ø   Know all Men by these Pres-
         Jemima Standifer   Ø   ents that I Samuel Standifer
                                                  Ø   of the County of Marion and
                                                         State of Tennessee and in
consideration of the sum of five hundred dollars to me in hand paid the receipt Whereof is hereby Acknowledged hath bargained & sold by these

P-312. Presents doth bargain & sell unto Jemina Standifer of the

(P-313). State aforesaid two Negro boys names Jefferson & Abraham age about nine year and Jefferson about five Years.

   To have and to hold the said two Negro boys to the only Proper use & benefit of the said Jemina Standifer her heirs executors administrators & assigns forever.

   I do hereby Warant the title of said Negro Against Myself My heirs executors administrators & assigns & all other Persons Whatsoever.

   In Witness Whereof I do hereby set my hand and seal this the twenty first day of April in the Year of A. D. 1828.

   Signed sealed & delivered in Presence of

Wm I Standifer	
Jesse Humble	Samuel Standifer (seal)

P-313. State of Tennessee

            May Term 1828.

  Marion County Court

   Then Was the Within bill of sale from Samuel Standifer to Jemina for two Negro boys named Jefferson & Abram duly Proven in Open Court by the oath of William I. Standifer a subscribing Witness thereto and ordered to be Certified and admitted to record. Let it be registered.

Registered August 17th 1828.

             Attest
             Jno. Kelly Clk.
             By G. W. Rice D.C.

P-313 William Wood

  George W. Wood
    To
  Hopkins L. Turney

         This Indenture Made and entered into this the 25th day of January in the Year of Our Lord one thousand eight hundred twenty six between William Wood and George W. Wood of the County of Marion and State of Tennessee of the one Part and Hopkins L. Turney of the County and State aforesaid of the other Part,

   Witnesseth that for and in consideration of the sum of forty dollars to us in hand Paid the receipt Whereof is hereby Acknowledged we have this day bargained and sold and doth by these Presents bargain sell alien enfross and confirm unto the said Hopkins L. Turney a Certain town lot or lot of ground in the town of Jasper Containing one quarter of an Acre of land adjoining the lot now occupied by said Turney known and designated in the plan of said town by Lot No. 69.

   To have and to hold the said lot of land to him the said Hopkins L. Turney and his heirs forever Against the title and Claim of all Persons Whatsoever With all and singular the appurtenances thereto appertaining or in any Wise belonging.

   In testimony Whereof we have hereunto set our hands and seal the day and Year first above written.

   Signed sealed and delivered in the Presence of

Enoch P. Hale	William Wood (seal)
Thos. J. Hasting	G. W. Wood (seal)

P-313   State of Tennessee

Marion County Court   May Term 1827.

Then Was the Within deed of Conveyance from George W. and
William Wood to Hopkins L. Turney for Lot No. 69 in the town of Jasper
Proven in open Court by the Oaths of Enoch P. Hale and Thomas J. Hasting,
subscribing Witness thereto and ordered to be Certified for registration
this the 25th day of January 1828.

A. Griffith Register
(L S) Registered September 25th 1828   By Jno Kelly D. R.
                                          Jno. Kelly Clk.

P-313. George Lane

   To   This Indenture Made this thirteenth
        John Barker   day of September in the Year of Our
                         Lord one thousand eight hundred and
                         twenty seven between George Lane of
Warren County and John Barker of Marion County both of the State of Tennessee,

        Witnesseth the said George Lane for and in consideration of the
sum of three hundred and sixty dollars to him Paid the receipt Whereof is
hereby Acknowledged hath

(P-314.) bargained and sold and by these Presents doth bargain sell enfross and confirm the sd John Barker his heirs and assigns forever a Certain tract or Parcel of land Containing one hundred and twenty Acres lying and being in the County of Marion of the Southeast side of Sequachie
River and bounded as follows to Wit;
        Beginning on a black oak and hickory the southeastwardly from
where John Barker now lives thence running south one Poles to a stake
thence West ninety eight Poles to a sweet gum thence North one hundred
and ninety six Poles to a stake thence east ninety eight Poles to a black
oak and White oak thence south to the beginning
        To have and to hold the aforesaid tract or Parcel of land to
the said John Barker his heirs and assigns forever With all the Privileges
and appurtenances thereunto belonging or in any Wise appertaining and the
said George for himself his heirs &c shall and Will Warrant and forever
defend by these Presents.
        In Witness Whereof the George Lane hath hereunto set his hand
and seal the day and date first afore Written.

John Townsen   Jurst
Thomas Smith   Jurst. Attest   George Lane   (seal)

P-314. State of Tennessee
                                        February Session 18281
        Marion County Court

        Then Was the Within deed of Conveyance from George Lane to John
Barker for one hundred and twenty acres of land in Marion County duly
Proven in Open Court by the oahts of John Townson and Thomas Smith subscrib-
ing Witnesses thereto and ordered to be Certified for registration.

P-314.   Given under my hand and Private seal not having a seal of office in Jasper this 28th day of February 1828

L. S.
Registered September 25th, 1828.   Register, Amos Griffith
                                                    Jno. Kelly   Clk.
Registered by John Kelly, D. C.   By G. W. Rice D. C.

P-314   George Land   §   This Indenture Made this the seven-
           To   §   teenth day of Feb. one thousand
           William Hawkins   §   eight hundred and twenty five be-
                                     §   tween George Land of Warren County
of the one Part and William Hawkins of Marion County of the Other Part
both of the State of Tennessee,

            Witnesseth that the said George Lane for and in consideration
of the saum of Two hundred dollars in hand Paid at or before the sealing
and delivering of these Presents the receipt is hereby Acknowledged have
Given granted bargained and sold & by these Presents doth give grant bargain and sell unto William Hawkins his heirs and assigns forever a Certain
tract or Parcel of land containing sixty acres, lying and being in Marion
County and bounded as follows to Wit:

            Beginning at a Conditional Corner made by William Hawkins and
Thos. Maxwell thence East to a white oak a conditional corner With John
Burgess N. 38 E. 84 Poles to a White oak thence one hundred Poles to a
white Oak & Dogwood thence West to a Pointer, it being a Conditional Corner Made between William Hawkins & Thomas Maxwell south course on a Conditional line Made by sd Hawkins & sd Maxwell to the beginning Corner,
together With all and singular the receipts remainders appurtenances thereof or in any Wise appertaining thereunto.

            To have and to hold the said tract or Parcel of land unto
William Hawkins his heirs and assigns forever, and the said George Lane
do Warrant & forever defend the rights & titles of said Land from himself
his heirs and executors administrators & assigns and from no Other Prson
to the said

(P-315) William Hawkins his heirs & Assigns for their own Proper use benefit & behoof.

            In Witness Whereof I the said George Layne have set My hand
& affixed My seal this day and date first above Written.
            In Presence of

                                                    his
Thomas Maxwell   Jurat   §   George   X   Layne   seal
John Maxwell   Jurat.   §   mark

P-315. State of Tennessee   §
                                   §   February Session, 1828.
        Marion County Court   §

        Then Was the Within deed of conveyance from George Layne to
William Hawkins for sixty Acres in Marion County duly Proven in Open Court
by the Oaths of Thomas Maxwell and John Maxwell subscribing Witnesses thereto and ordered to be Certified for registration.

P-315.   Given Under my hand and Private seal not having a seal of office this 28th day of February 1828

(Seal)   Jno. Kelly Clk.
Registered Sept. 26th 1828.   By G. W. Rice D. C.

P-315.   George Brock   }
              To   }   This Indenture the Nineteenth
         Valentine Bronson   }   dat of November in the Year of
                                         }   Our Lord one thousand and eight
                                         }   hundred and twenty six between
George A. Brock in the County of Franklin State of Tennessee of the one
Part and Valentine Brandson of the County of Marion and State of Tennessee
aforesaid of the other Part,
        Witnesseth that the said George A. Brock for and in consideration of the sum of Two Hundred and twenty dollars to him in hand Paid
at or before the sealing and delivery of these Presents the receipt Whereof is hereby Acknowledged hath Given granted bargained sold and conveyed
and confirmed unto the said Valentine Bronson his heirs and assigns forever a Certain tract or Parcel of land situated lying and being in Marion
County aforesaid on the West side of Big Sequachee River
        Beginning at two White Oaks it being the beginning of a Corner
of a two hundred Acres tract granted to said Brock. Thence south two hundred and twenty Poles to Pointers thence West to Green H. Pryor line one
hundred and sixty five Poles to Pointers thence east to a conditional line
Established between Col. Bronson and Green H. Pryor thence With said conditional line to the beginning Containing one hundred Acres more or less.
        To have and to hold the aforesaid land With all and singular
the hereditaments and appurtenances of in and to the same belonging or in
any Wise appertaining to the only Proper use benefit and behoof of him
the Valentine Bronson his heirs and assigns forever and the said George
A. Brock himself his heirs executors and administrators doth Covenant and
agree to and With the said Valentine Bronson his heirs and assigns that
the before recited land and bargained Premises he Will Warrant and forever defend Against the right title Claim or interest of all and every
Person or Persons Whatever
        In Witness Whereof the said George A. Brock have set his hand
and affixed his seal the day and Year first above Written.

                                        George A. Brock   (seal)

State of Tennessee   }
                              }   November Term 1827.
Marion County Court   }

        Then Was the Within deed of Conveyance from George A. Brock
to Valentine Bronson for one hundred Acres of land duly Acknowledged in
Open Court by the said Brock and ordered to be Certified for registration.
        Given under My hand and Private seal not having a seal of office in Jasper this the 18th day of January 1828.

(L.S.)Registered Sept. 26th 1828.   Jno. Kelly   Clk.

P-305. William H. McLaughlin
To
John Smith T.

This Indenture Made the second day of July in the Year of Our Lord one thousand eight hundred and twenty five between William H. Mc-

Laughlin of Davidson

P-316. County and State of Tennessee the one Part and John Smith T. of the County & State of Missouri of the other Part,

Witnesseth that the said William H. McLaughlin for and in consideration of the sum of two thousand dollars to him in hand Paid by said John Smith the receipt Whereof is hereby Acknowledged hath given granted sold alien Convey and Confirmed and by these Presents doth give grant bargain sell alien convey and confirm unto the said John Smith T. his heirs and assigns forever a Certain tract or piece of land situated lying and being in the County aforesaid and State of Tennessee on the Tennessee River including Clark's ferry containing one thousand acres being the tract of 1000 Acres granted by the State of Tennessee to John Smith T. and by him heretofore conveyed to said William H. McLaughlin,

To have and to hold the said aforesaid land With all and Singular the rights Profits, emolents hereditaments and appertaining of in and to the same belonging or in any Way appertaining to the Only Proper use benefit and behoof of him the said John Smith T. his heirs and assigns forever and the said William H. McLaughlin for himself his heirs executors or administrators do covenant and agree to and With the said John Smith T. his heirs and assigns that the behoof recited land and bargained Premises he Will Warrant and forever defend against the right title interest or Claim of all and every Person or Persons Whatsoever Claiming by his or under him.

Signed sealed and delivered in Presence of

James McLaughlin &)
W. M. Vaulx) Witness

Ack. W. M. H. McLaughlin

P-316 State of Tennessee

Davidson County Court

July Session 1827.

This Indenture of bargain and sale between Wm. McLaughlin of the One Part and John Smith T. of the Other Part Was Acknowledged in Open Court by the oaths of W. M. McLaughlin to be his act and deed and ordered to be Certified for registration.
Attest

Nathan Erving Clerk of said County

Registered October 14th 1828.

P-316. Wiley Belsher Commis.
To
Benjamin F. Harris &
Wm. C. Harris

This is Indenture Made this the 14th day of October 1828 between Wiley Belsher Commissioner under a decree of the Circuit Court of

Marion County of the one Part and Benjamin Franklin Harris and Wm. Charles

P-316   Cole Claiborn Harris of the Other Part,

Witnesseth that Whereas at the last June Special Term held
for Marion County Tennessee a decree was Pronounced in the Case Wherein
John McGowan Complainant and Samuel Harris and Roswell Hale were defts
Whereby among things the said Wiley Belzsher Was directed to Make sale of
the tract of land (Wiley Belsher) decree Mentioned for Current bank nots
to the higest bidder before the Cour House in Jasper after giving forty
days notice of the time and Place of sale & Proceeds of such sale to pay
to Complainant $521. with interest from February also the Cost of Psuit
in equity & the Plus to be paid to said Harris and Whereas the Wiley Belsher Pursuant to decree aforesaid from the 13th. 1828 dec Proceed to tract
of land before the Court House in Jasper Pursuant to the Terms of said
decree & his Autority as Commissioner When Benjamin Harris & Wm Charles
Cole Harris became the Purchaser for seven hundred and eighty dollars
they being best and highest bidder Which ad tract of land lies in Marion
County Nine Miles from Jasper on both sides of the Main road leading
from Jasper to Winchester on Battle Creek being the same tract granted
to James Standifer Jr. Containing one hundred and sixty Acres More or
less & on Which James Harris now lives

Whereas Commissioners after selling said tract of land received the Consideration of Money Made his report to Court at Oct. Term,
1828 of the Circuit Court at Jasper that he

(P-317) sold sd land by Virtue of sd decree and his Authority aforesaid
hath received the consideration of Money and applied it as said decree
directed & thereupon said report Was Confirmed & the said Wiley Belsher
was directed to convey said tract of land to the Purchaser in fee simple
all of Which Will More fully appear by reference to the record of said
suit in equity between John McGowan complainant & Samuel Harris & Roswell
Hall defendants the decree therein Pronounced the repor of said Commissioner & the Confirmation thereof among the record of the Circuit Court
of Marion County now Indenture

Witnesseth that the said Wiley Belsher Commissioner as aforesaid for and in Consideration of the Premises and the Authority Vested
in him as aforesaid & for & in consideration of the said sum of seven
hundred & eighty dollars to him in hand Paid the receipt Whereof is hereby
Acknowledged hath bargained & sold & by these Presents doth bargain and
sell under the said Benjamin Franklin Harris & Wm Charles Cole Claiborn
Harris & their heirs the tract of land aforesaid With all its appurtenances.

To have and to hold the sd. tract or Parcel of land With all
its appurtenances to the said B. F. Harris & Wm C. C. C. Harris & their
heirs to the Sole use & benefit of them the said B. F. & Wm. C. C. C.
Harris & their heirs forever,

Witnesseth Whereof the said Wiley Belsher Commissioner as aforesaid hath hereunto set his hands and seal the day and Year first Above
Written.

Signed sealed and delivered in Presence of Wiley B.

                                        Wiley Belsher   seal.

P-317.   State of Tennessee

          Marion County Circuit Term 1828

          Then Was the Within executors of the Within deed from Wiley

P-317 Belcher to as Benjamin F. Harris & Wm C. C. C. Harris duly Acknowledged in Open Court by the said Wiley Belcher and ordered to be Certified for registration.

Given under my hand & Private seal (not having an official seal) at office in Jasper this the 14th day of October, 1828.

Stephen Hicks Clk.

(L.S.) Registered Oct. 14th, 1828.

P-317. Larken Bethel
                To Deed.
        William Orear

This Indenture Made this thirty first day of November in the Year of Our Lord one thousand eight hundred and twenty three between Larken Bethel of the County of Franklin and State of Tennessee of the one Part & William Orear of the County aforesaid of the Other Part,

Witnesseth that the said Larken Bethel for and in consideration of the sum of one hundred and forty eight dollars & fifty Cents to him in hand Paid by the said William Orear the receipt Whereof is hereby Acknowledged hath Given granted bargained sold conveyed and confirmed & by these Presents doth give grant bargain sell convey & confirm unto the said William Orear his heirs & assigns forever a Certain tract or Parcel of land in the County of Marion & State aforesaid on the head waters of Battle Creek on the road leading from Georgia to Caldwell Bridge including the Hurt Store b

beginning at a black oak near the head of a Spring Mark L.B. thence north forty nine Poles to a black oak thence east sixty six poles to four sourwoods thence south then south forty nine Poles to a stake; then West to beginning Containing twenty Acres be the same more or less,

To have and to hold the before recited land and bargained Premises With all & singular the right profits rents issues hereditaments & appurtenances of in and to the same belonging or in any wise appertaining to the Only Proper Use benefits and behoof of him the said William Orear his heirs & assigns forever and the said Larken Bethel doth further Covenant and agree to and With the said William Orear his heirs & assigns that the before recited lands & bargained Premises he Will Warrant and forever defend Against the right title interest Claim & demand of all and every Person or Persons Whatever.

In Witness

(P-318) Whereof the said Larken Bethel hath hereunto set his hand & affixed his seal the day and Year first Above Written.

Signed sealed and delivered in Presence of

Leroy May   Proven
James Petty   Proven

                                     Larken Bethel   seal

P-318. State of Tennessee

        Marion County Court

August Session, 1828.

Then Was the Within deed of Conveyance from Larken Bethel to William Orear for twenty five acres of land in Marion County was proven in Open Court by the oaths of Leroy May and James Petty subscribing Witnesses thereto and ordered to be Certified for registration. Let it

P-318   be registered.

Jno. Kelly Clk.
By G. W. AGe D. Clk.

Registered Oct. 21st 1828.

P-318.   George Lane
       To Deed
      Thomas Maxwell

This Indenture Made the eighteenth of February in the Year of Our Lord One thousand & twenty five between George Lane of Warren County of the one Part and Thomas Maxwell of Marion County of the Other Part both of the State of Tennessee,

Witnesseth that the said George Lane for and in consideration of the Sum of five hundred dollars to him in hand Paid at or before the sealing & delivery of these Presents the receipt Whereof is hereby Acknowledged hath given granted bargained sold & by these Presents doth give grant and bargain & sell unto Thomas Maxwell his heirs & Assigns forever a Part of a tract of land surveyed and granted to himself Warrant No. 22180 surveyed on the 2nd day of June 1821 sd. tract or Parcel of land Containing Ninety four Acres & quarter more or less situated lying and being in the third District in Marion County on the South east side of Sequachee River adjoining lands of said Sanes; and bounded as follows to Wit

Beginning at a Poplar on said Lanes line & also a Corner; thence south along the same Passing his Corner in all one hundred and twenty two Poles to a Poplar thence east to a White oak it being the Conditional Corner Made between Thos. Maxwell and Wm. Hawkins Thence North course it being a conditional line Made by sd. Hawkins & Maxwell to a stake and Pointers on the old Original line thence West to Pointers on said Lane line and With same a direct line to the beginning together With all and singular the receipts remainders Appurtenances thereof or in any wise appertaining thereto.

To have and to hold the said tract or Parcel of land unto Thomas Maxwell his heirs & Assigns forever & the said George Lane do Warra & forever defend the rights & titles of said land from himself his heirs executors and administrators & Assigns or from no Other Person Whatsoever to the sd Maxwell his heirs or assigns for their own Proper use benefit & behoof.

In Witness Whereof I the sd George Lane have set my hand & fixed my seal this day and date first above Written.

in Presence of

Wm. Hawkins   Jurat   Attest   his
John Maxwell   Jurat   George   X   Lane   seal
                                                mark

P-318.   State of Tennessee
                               February Session 1828.
      Marion County Court

Then Was the Within deed of Conveyance from George Lane to

1-315 Thomas Maxwell for Ninety four acres and a Quarter of land duly Proven in Open Court by the Oaths William Hawkins and John Maxwell, Subscribing Witness thereto and ordered to be Certified for registration.

Given under my hand and Private seal Not having a seal of office this eighth day of February 1828.

Jno Kelly Clk.
G. W. Rice D. C.

Registered October 1st, 1828.

P-319. Joseph Jones
        To. Deed
        Isaac Cooper

This Indenture Made the 23rd day of August in the Year of Our Lord one thousand eight hundred and twenty six between Joseph Jones of the County of Marion and State of Tennessee of the One Part and Isaac Cooper of the County aforesaid of the Other Part,

Witnesseth that for and in consideration of the sum of Fourteen dollars to me In hand paid the receipt Whereof is hereby Acknowledged I Joseph Jones hath and by these Presents doth grant bargain sell alien enfeoff and Confirm unto the sd Isaac Cooper his heirs and Assigns forever a Certain tract or Parcel of land Containing six Acres lying and being in the County of Marion on the North West of Sequachee River on Halls branch:

Beginning on a White Oak on the bank of said branch on the south boundary of sd Bronsons survey of one hundred Acres then along the same East forty one Poles to a stake the South West Corner of sd. Survey then North forty four Poles to a stake on the bank on fork of sd branch then down the Channel of sd branch to the beginning.

Also one othe tract adjoining a tract of twenty Acres that Adjoins said six Acre tract bounded as follows

Beginning at a hickory and White Oak a corner of sd Jones and Blevins thence south forty three degrees West thirty four Poles to a Post Oak thence With a Conditional line North forty degrees West forty Poles to a Post Oak thence north twenty eight degrees east forty four Poles to a dogwood thence fifty three poles to Pointers east twenty four Poles to the beginning it being eighty four Acres granted by the State of Tennessee to the said Jones by Grant No. 8925 dated the 2nd day of August 1824 in all including fourteen Acres be the same More or less With all and singular the Wood and Water and Water courses Profits Commodities hereditaments and appurtenances Whatsoever to the said tract of land belonging to or in any way appertaining and reversion and reversions and remainder and remainders rents and issus thereof and all the Actual rights titles Interest Property Claim and demand of him the sd Joseph Jones his heirs and Assigns forever of in and to the Same and every Part and Parcel thereof either in law or equity.

To have and to hold the sd fourteen Acres With the appurtenances unto the sd Isaac Cooper his heirs and Assigns forever against the lawful title Claim summons of all and every Person or Persons Claiming by from or under me Will Warrant and forever defend by these Presents sofar the State of Tennessee is concerned.

In Witness Whereof the s'd Joseph Jones hath hereunto set his hand and seal this day and date first Above Written.

Signed sealed and delivered in Presence of

P-319
A. Kelly Jr.

Joseph Jones   (seal)

P-319.   State of Tennessee

Marion County Court

August Term 1826.

        Then Was the foregoing deed of conveyance from Joseph Jones
to Isaac Cooper for fourteen Acres of land duly Acknowledged in Open
Court by the said Jones ordered to be Certified for registration. Let
it be registered.

                       Jno. Kelly Clk.
                       By G. W. Rice D. Clk.

Registered October 22nd 1828.

P-319 Mitchell J. C.
      To   Release
James Stewart

This Indenture Made and entered
into this the 4th day of March
One Thousand Eight Hundred and
Twenty Five between J. C. Mitchell
of the County of McMinn and State of Tennessee of the One Part and James
Stewart of the County of Marion and state aforesaid of the Other Part,
        Witnesseth that for and in consideration of the relinguishment
of the right and title that J. C. Mitchell have of in and to a piece of
land Claimed by him by Virtue of a grant from the State of Tennessee to
the said J. C. Mitchell, Which lies North and east of a branch called
and known by the Name of Allison Spring branch to James Stewart his heirs
and assigns forever, the James C. Mitchell doth by these Presents remise
release and forever Quit Claim all the rights title

(P-320) interest Claim and demand that he has of in and to the land in-
cluded Within the K lines of the survey or interest that the said James
C. Mitchell may Claim south of the spring branch aforesaid and South of
the said Mitchell state Grant lines including and adjoining the lands
where the said Mitchell now lives by Virtue of a title derived to him by
Mense conveyance from a twenty thousand acre survey and Grant from the
State of North Carolina dated the 20th July 1795 from him his heirs and
all other Persons Claiming or to Claim in this or by him the said Mitchell
or from or under him to the said James Steward his heirs assigns forever,
Will Warrant and defend.
        Witness the hand & seal of the said James C. Mitchell the
4th day of March 1825, of the American Independence the forty Ninth

John Mitchell and
Archbald Lewis
Thos. A. Ramsey and
Ezekial McAllister, Attest

        J. C. Mitchell

P-320.   State of Tennessee

Marion County Court

May Session, 1825

        Then Was the executors of the foregoing of Conveyance from

James Mitchell to James Stewart for Acres of land in Marion County duly
Proven in Open Court by the Oaths of Thomas A. Ramsey & Ezekial McAllister
two of the Subscribing Witnesses thereto and ordered to be Certified for
registration. Let it be Registered.

                                        Test.
                                        Jno. Kelly Clk.
                                        By G. W. Rice D. C.

Registered October 22nd, 1828.

P-320. James Stewart
            To   Release   )   This Indenture made and entered
        J. C. Mitchell   )   into this the 4th day of March
)   1825 by and between James Stewart
                                        of the County of Marion and State
of Tennessee of the one Part and James Mitchell of the County of McMinn
of the other Part,

        Witnesseth that the said James Stewart for and in considera-
tion of a deed of religuishment and Quit-Claim of even date of this instrument Made by the said Mitchell to the said Stewart for all the land
Claimed by the said Stewart Within the lines of his said Stewart State
grant or entry Made in Marion County Where he now lives and Adjoining
thereto lying south and east of a spring branch and the said spring branch
is to be the dividing line from the Mulberry Corner in the old road down
the ___to Mouth thereof to the said James C. Mitchell his heirs and assigns
forever but if the title to the same shall fail yet the said Stewart nor
his heirs &C be in any Wise liable for the consideration or damage of any
kind.

        In Witness Whereof the said Stewart hath hereunto set his hand
and seal this date above Written,

Exekial McAllister   )   his
Thos. A. Ramsey   Witness   )   James   X   Stewart
)   mark

State of Tennessee   )
)   May Session 1825.
Marion County Court   )

        Then Was the execution of the Within deed of Conveyance from
James Stewart to James C. Mitchell for _____ Acres of land in Marion
County duly Proven in Open Court by the oaths of Thomas A. Ramsey & Exekial McAllister the subscribing Witness thereto and ordered to be Certified for registration. Let it be registered.

                                        John Kelly Clk.
                                        By G. W. Rice D. Clk.

Registered October 22nd. 1828.

P-321. Williamson Standifer
            To   Deed   )   This Indenture Made this the 18th
        Jane & Clarissa Standifer)   day of July in the Year of Our
)   Lord one thousand eight and twen-
ty five between William Standifer of the County of Marion and State of Tennessee of the One Part and Jane Standifer & Clarissa Harlow Standifer of

P-321.   the County and State aforesaid of the Other Part,

Witnesseth that for and in consideration of the sum of one
hundred to him the said William Standifer in hand Paid the receipt Whereof is hereby Acknowledged hath by these Presents bargained sold and delivered unto the said Jane & Clarissa a Certain tract or Parcel of land
Containing one hundred and four Acres, It being a Part of a tract of
land granted by the State of Tennessee to the said William Standifer
for one hundred eighty Acres by Grant No. 17684 bearing date the 29th
day of July 1822 Situated lying and being in the said County of Marion
on the north West side of Sequachee River and bounded as follows,

Beginning at a black gum near the center of the North boundary line of the afore Mentioned tract of 180 Acres then running South
one hundred and thirty five Poles to a stake and Pointers then West twenty Poles to Pointers; thence south forty two Poles to a stake and Pointers then east one hundred and nine Poles to a black oak and White oak;
then North one hundred and Seventy Seven Poles to a Post oak then West
Nienty Poles to the beginning, including the improvements formerly occupied by Sheltion Standifer and the aforesaid one hundred and four
Acres of land to be the same More or less With all and singular the Woods
Water Water Courses Profits Commodities hereditaments and appurtenances
to the said tract of land belonging or in any Wise appertaining and the
remainder and remainders rents and issus and all the estate right titles
interest Property Claim and demand of him the sd William Standifer and
every part and Parcel thereof either in la or equity.

To have and to hold unto the said Jane Standifer and Clarissa
Harlow Standifer and their heirs forever reserving to the said Jane Standifer the full use and benefit of the afore Mentioned land and Premises
until the said Clarissa becomes of lawful age or should Marry and I the
Said William Standifer do hereby bind Myself My heirs &c to forever Warrant and defend the aforesaid Tract of land to the Said Jane and Clarissa
their heirs &c Against the lawful title Claim and demand of all and every
Person or Persons Claiming from by or Under me or My heirs forever.

In Witness Whereof I have hereunto set my hand and seal this
day and date first above Written,

Signed sealed and acknowledged in Presence of

Jno. Kelly
Isaac Standifer   William Standifer   (seal)

P-321.   State of Tennessee
                                             February Session, 1827.
         Marion County Court

Then was the Within deed of conveyance from William Standifer
to Jane and Clarissa H. Standifer for 104 Acres of land duly Proven in
Open Court by the Oaths of Jno Kelly & Isaac Standifer subscribing Witnesses thereto and ordered to be Certified for registration. Let it be
registered.

                                        Jno. Kelly   Clk.
                                        By G. W. Rice D. Clk.

Registered October 22nd 1828.

P-321. William Pryor
    To   Deed
    William Williams

This Indenture Made this twenty Ninth of January in the Year of Our Lord one thousand eight hundred twenty five between William Pryor of the County of Marion and State of Tennessee of the one Part and Williams of the County and State aforesaid of the Other Part,

    Witnesseth that the said William Pryor for and

(P-322) in consideration of the sum of seventy five dollars to him in hand Paid the receipt of Which is hereby Acknowledged hath given grant-ed bargained and sold and by these Presents doth give grant bargain and sold unto the said William Williams his heirs and assigns forever one tract of land lying in Marion County aforesaid and on the North West side of Sequatchie River containing fifteen Acres be the same More or less and bounded as follows to Wit

    Beginning on a Walnut tree a Corner of Amos Griffith Survey; thence running With his line south thirty five east seventy Poles to a Hickory thence south twenty four With his line South thirty five east seventy Poles to a hickory thence south twenty four and half west thirty Poles to a Poplar; thence north fifty five West seventy five Poles to a hickory thence North thirty nine east fifty three Poles to the beginning.

    To have hold and enjoy the afore Mentioned granted and bargain-ed Premises to the said William Williams his heirs and assigns and the said William Pryor his heirs &c do and Will Warrant and forever defend the title of the said land to the said William Williams his heirs and as-signs forever Against the Claims of any Person or Persons Whatsoever.

    In Witness Whereof he hath hereunto set his hand and affixed his seal this day and Year first above Written.

    Signed sealed and delivered in Presence of

John Williams   William Pryor
Paul M. Williams

P-322.   State of Tennessee   1825

    Marion County Court

    Then Was the Within deed of conveyance from William Pryor to William Williams for fifteen Acres of land Was duly Acknowledged in Court by the Alien and the same is admitted to registration. Let it be register-ed.

                                    Jno. Kelly Clk.
                                      By G. W. Rice D. Clk.

Registered October 22nd, 1828.

P-322.   Commissioner &c
      To Deed.
      Phillip Maybre

This Indenture Made the fourth day of April in the Year of our Lord one thousand eight hundred and twenty one between William Stone, David Oats, Burgess Mathews, Alx Kelly, Wm. King, Wm. Stephen, David Miller, Commissioners in trust for the County of Marion and town of Jasper and their successors of the One Part

P-322.   and Phillip Mabre of the County of White and State of Tennessee
of the Other Part

Witnesseth that for and in consideration of the sum of three
hundred and forty six dollars to us in hand Paid the receipt Whereof is
hereby Acknowledged hath and by these Presents doth grant bargain alien
enfroff and Confirm unto the said Phillip Maybre his executors and administrators two Certain lots of land in the town of Jasper Known and
designated in the Original Plan of Said town by lots 54 and 55 Containing
one Quarter of an Acre each sold at public auction as the law directs.

To have and to hold the aforesaid lots of land With all and
Singular rights and Profits emoluments and appurtenances belonging or
in any Wise appertaining to the same to the only use and behoof of the
said Phillip Mabre his heirs &c and the said Commissioners in trust as
aforesaid and Will as far as are authorized as Commissioners forever Warrant and defend to the said Phillip Mabre his heirs &c the above recited
lots Against the rights titles interest Claim and demand of every Person or Persons Whatever.

In Testimony Whereof we hereunto set our hands and seals this
day and date first above Written.

David Oats   Wm. Stone
Burgess Mathews   Alex Kelly
Wm. King   Wm. Stephen
David Miller

P-323. State of Tennessee   August Term 1822.

        Marion County Court

Then Was the Within deed of conveyance for lots Nos. 53 and
55 was this day acknowledged in Court by David Oats one of the Commissioners and ordered to be Certified and admitted to record.

Given under my hand and Private seal not having an official
seal at office this the 1st day of August 1822.

                                    Jno. Kelly Clk.
Registered October 22, 1828.

P-323.   The Last Will and Testament
              of   In the Name of God Amen.
         William Standifer Decd.

I, William Standifer of the County of Marion and State of Tennessee, being sick and weak of body but of sound Mind and disposing Memory for Which I thank God and Calling to Mind the Uncertainty of human
life and being desirous do dispose of all such Worldly substance as it
hath pleased God to bless me With I do hereby Make my last Will and Testament.

I give and bequeath the same in Manner and form following
that is to say I give and bequeath to My loving Wife Jemina Standifer all
the household furniture and stock With four Negroes that is Sarah Calvin
Moses Becky. To have and to hold the same until her decease or marriage,
at her death I give and bequeath Sara Calvin and Moses to My Son Alford
Standifer and Becky she May dispose of as she thinks Proper And I give
My Wife Jemina Standifer all land north and east of the Cross fence now

P-323. running through My farm except one half of the Apple Orchard for
My son Alford Standifer and two Acres of land for him too so as not to
interfer with Said Jemina Standifer building. In Case the above named
Negro Sarah Should have another child I give said Calvin to My two grandsons Samuel Terry Standifer and William Scott Standifer and not Other
wise.

I give to my son Alford Standfer all the tract of land Where
I now live containing about one hundred and Seventy seven Acres at my
Wife deceased or marrige I give a Negro Man named B Lackburn to my Wife
Jemina Standifer and my son Alford Standifer Jointly between them until
her decease then said Negro Blackburn is to be sold and the Money divided
between My four sons James Standifer Luke Standifer Isaac Standifer &
Samuel Standifer.

I give and bequeath to my son James Standifer Negro man named
Mennel.

I give and bequeath to my son Standifer a Negro Woman and her
name Salle and her Child named Levi.

I Give and bequeath to My son Isaac Standifer 2 Negro boys
named Abraham & Jefferson.

I give and bequeath to My daughter Fannie Hendrix a Negro boy
named Grace.a Negro man named John I want sold. Out of the Price of said
Negro I want my three daughters to have fifty dollars each that is Polly
Griffith Naomi & Sausannah Yarnell.

I give to my to grand sons twenty five dollars each that is
Luke O. Standifer and Jess H. Standifer. the balance of the piece of
said Negro I give to My Wife Jamina Standifer and My son that is Jane
Standifer Luke Standifer Isaac Standifer Samuel Standifer & Alford Standifer I want executors thereinafter named to sell a fifty Acre tract Part
of a one hundred and eighty Acre tract granted to me by the State and I
want all my debts paid out of the price of said land.

I give and bequeath to Clarissa Harlow Standifer my grand
daughter a negro girl named Dice. Said Clarisa H. Standifer is to have
said Negro in the tenth year of her age.if said Clarissa

(P-324) H. Standifer should deceased before she should Marry I want said
division equally divided between My hairs herein above named.

I give and bequeath to Jane Standifer five dollars and lastly
I duly Contubute add appoint My friend Luke Hendrix and Isaac Standifer
executors of this My last Will and Testament.

In Witness Whereof I have hereunto set my hand and seal the
the thirteenth day of April in the Year of Our Lord 1826.

Signed sealed published and declared to be the last Will and
testament of the above named William Standifer in Presence of us who at
his request and in his Presence have hereunto subscribed our names as
Witnesses to the same.

Jasse Humble
James Chaudoin   William Standifer

P-324. State of Tennessee

       Marion County Court   August Session, 1826.

       Then Was the last Will & Testament of William Standifer de-

P-324. ceased, this day Produced in Open Court and that James Chadoin
& Jesse Humble the subscribing Witnesses thereto Appeared in Open Court
being the examinee on oath seprate Sequeth that the executors thereof
Was the last Will and testament of William Standifer deceased, and that
he signed and subscribed the same in their Presence Without hestitation
and that they believed the said deceased was at the same time in Possession of his mental facalities Whereupon the same was Ordered to be
Certified and admitted to record.

     Registered October 23rd 1828.

                                  Test
                                  Jno. Kelly   Clk.
                                  By G. W. Rice D. Clk.

P-324.   The last Will and Testament
            of   Be it remembered that on the
    David Hendric Decd.   6th day of April 1825 that I
                             David Hendrix of the State of
Tennessee and the County of Marion being in a consideration of body but
of sound mind - thank God for it - being desirous to Make known how my
desirous is respectively My Wordly afore I now Proceed to Make it known.

     I give to my two sons Fethoric Hendrix and Duglas David Hen-
drix the tract or Parcel of land that I now live on to be divided as
follows

     running a straight line Across the said tract half way between
the field Fetheric now lives and my field giving the upper Part to my
son David Duglas give to my wife the benefit of David Part of said land
and dividing her Widow for the Purpose of raising & schooling the Children
and also for the same I give My daughter Jennie Gardner $10.00.

     I give to my daughter Phebe Gibson $10.00.
     I give My daughter Margret Richardson $10.00
     I give to my daughter Nicey $10.00.
     I give to my daughter Nahaley $10.00.
     I give My daughter Malinda $10.00.
     I give My daughter Miletha $10.00

     further desirous that if my wife lives till David D. become of
age that she shall live With him if Yet a Widow undivided Widowhood. It
is further My desire that if my stepson Dacer shall Continue With his
Mother to help With the Children that he shall be entitled to a horse
saddle and briddle With one hundred dollars and I further desire that
after all debts that is Just are satisfied If anything remain it shall
be equally divided amongst the legatees and I am desirous and hereby
Authorize and empower Robert Green and Amos

(P-325) Richardson as my executors to attend to my business as Witness
to the foregoing Writing, I hereunto set my hand & seal this the 6th
day of April 1825.

Ruben Richardson   Attest his
W. M. Gibson   David X Hendrix (seal)
                                         mark

P-325.   State of Tennessee
                                    I John Kelley Clerk of the
    Marion County Court   Court of Pleas and Quarter

P-325 Session of said County do Certify that the last Will and Testament of David Hendrix deceased the execution of Which Was this day duly Proven in Open Court by the Oaths of Rubben Richardson and William Gibson subscribing Witness thereto Whereupon it was ordered to be Certified and Omitted to record.

    Given under My hand and Private seal not having an official seal at office in Jasper this the 15th day of May 1825.

(L.S.)   Jno. Kelly   Clk.
Registered October 23rd 1828.

P-325. Andrew R. Johnson
        To   Deed of Con.   This Indenture Made this Nineteenth
  William Barnes   day of February in the Year of Our Lord one thousand eight hundred and twenty seven between Andrew R. Johnson of the County of Marion and State of Tennessee of the one Cart and William Barnes of the County and State Aforesaid

    Witnesseth that the said Andrew R. Johnson for the Consideration of four hundred dollars in hand Paid and secured to be Paid by the said William Barnes hath bargained and sold to the said William Barnes a Certain Piece or Parcel of land on Battle Creek in the Aforesaid County Containing fifty eight Acres More or less,

    Beginning at a White Oak a Corner of said Johnsons Grant near the foot of the Mountain; thence north twenty one Poles to a large Poplar; thence north Seven and one half degrees, east eighty four Poles to a Stake on the edge of a road along the line of John Barnes; thence South eighty east along William Barnes fence eighty Poles to a large White Oak in the bottom; thence south eleven east to the foot of the Mountain on the line of the Original Grant; thence With the Various lines of the same to the beginning, together With all Woods Way a Water Water course Profit Commodities and Appurtenances to said land belonging.

    To have and to hold to the said William Barns and his heirs and assigns forever Against the Claim of the said Johnson and his heirs & all Persons Claiming under him and no farther.

    In Witness Whereof the said Andrew R. Johnson hath set V his hand & seal the date above Written.

    Signed sealed & delivered in Presence of
                                    his
Geo. Gordon   Andrew R X Johnson
John Barnes   Attest.   mark

P-325. State of Tennessee
                          February Term 1827.
    Marion County Court

    Then Was the Within Deed of Conveyance from Andrew R. Johnson to William Barnes for 58 Acres of land duly Proven in Open Court by the Oaths of George Gordon and John Barnes subscribing Witnesses thereto Ordered to be Certified for registration.

    Given in under my hand and Private seal not having an official seal of office in Jasper the 18th day of January 1828.

(L.S.) Registered October 23rd 1828.   Jno. Kelly Clk.

P-325.　Alexander Fancher
　　　　　　To
　　　Thomas Brantly.

This Indenture Made this 19th day
of February in the Year of Our Lord
1827 by and between Alexander Fancher of the County of Marion and
State of Tennessee of the One Part and Thos. Brantly of the aforesaid State
of the Other Part,

　　　　Witnesseth that for and in consideration of the sum of sixty
dollars to

(P-326) me in hand Paid the receipt of which is hereby Acknowledged I
the said Alexander Fancher hath by these Presents granted bargained sold
conveyed and Confirmed and do bye these Presents grant bargain sell Convey and confirm unto the said Thomas Brantly his heirs executors administrators and assigns forever a Certain lot or Parcel of Ground situated
lying and being in the town of Jasper Containing one quarter Acre Which
said lot of or Piece of Ground is known and designated in the general
Plan of said town as lot No. 99.

　　　　To have and to hold the aforesaid lot or Piece of ground With
the Appurtenances to the said Thos. Brantley his heirs &c forever from
under the said Alexander Fancher from the lawful Claims and demand of
all other Person or Persons Whatsoever I the said Alexander Fancher Will
Warrant and forever defend.

　　　　In Testimony Whereof I have hereunto set my hand and seal this
day and Year first herein Written.

　　　　Signed sealed in Presence of Chas. Reeds　Alexander F.

　　　　　　　　　　　　　　　　　　　　Alexander Francher

P-326.　State of Tennessee

　　　Marion County Court

February Term, 1827.

　　　　Then Was the Within deed of Conveyance from Alexander Fancher
to Thomas Brantly No. 99 Duly Acknowledged in Open Court by said Fancher
and Ordered to be Certified for Registration.　Given under my hand and
Private seal not having an official seal at office in Jasper the 18th of
October 1828.

　　　　Registered October 23rd, 1829　　　Jno. Kelly Clk.
　　　　　　　　　　　　　　　　　　　By G. W. Rice　D. Clk.

P-326.　John Stone
　　　　　To　Deed
　　　John Pickett

This Indenture Made this 21st
day of May in the Year of Our
Lord eighteen hundred and twenty seven between John Stone of
the County of Marion and State of Tennessee of the One Part and of the
County and State Aforesaid of the Other Part

　　　　Witnesseth that the said John Stone for and in consideration
of the sum of Two hundred dollars the receipt Whereof is hereby Acknowledged hath Granted bargained and sold and do by these Presents Grant bargain sell alien and Confirm unto the said John Pickett his heirs and assigns forever a Certain tract or Parcel of land containing sixty Acres by

P-326. Grant No. 12519 bearing date the _____ of February 1826 Situated
in the said County of Marion on the southeast side of Sequachie River adjoining lands of Scott Terry.

Beginning at a dogwood on southeast bank of said Sequachie
River Where Terrys line Crossies the river then down the river as its
Meanders S. 40° E. 46 Poles S. 60° E. 52 Poles S. 65° E. 455 38½° E. 24
Poles to a boxelder at the foot of a large ridge then With said ridge
65 Poles to a stake & Pointers then N. 24 W. 100 Poles then N. 49 W. 30
Poles to a dogwood and Pointers on said Terrys line then With the same
S. 52 poles to beginning including the foresaid sixty Acres be the same
More or less as Pr the aforesaid grant Iss. for State of Tennessee With
all and singular the appurtenances to the said tract or Parcel of land
belonging or in any wise appertaining either in law or equity.

To have and to hold the said tract of sixty acres of land
as herein before described With all and singular the appurtenances to the
said John Pickett his heirs and assigns forever free and Clear of the
lawful title Claim and demand of him the said John Stone his executors
Administrators or Assigns Will Warrant and forever defend the title of
Aforesaid tract of land by Virtue of these Presents.

In Witness Whereof I have hereunto set My hand and seal this
day and Year first Above Written

(P-327)   Signed and sealed in Presence of

D. Rankin
Houston Hixson   John Stone   seal.

P-327.   State of Tennessee
                                         May Term, 1827.
         Marion County Court

Then Was the Within deed of Conveyance from John Stone to John
Pickett for Sixty Acres of land Was Acknowledged in Open Court by the said
Stone and ordered to be certofied for registration.

Attest   Jno. Kelly   Clk.
                                         G. W. Rice   D. C.

Registration October 23rd 1828.

P-327. Roswell Hall
            To.   Deed   This Indenture Made this 21st
        Joshua Cox   day of May in the Year of Our
                                         Lord one thousand eight hundred
                                         And twenty seven between Ros-
well Hall of the County of Marion and State of Tennessee for the one
Part and Joshua Cox of the county and State aforesaid of the Other
Part.

Witnesseth that the said Roswell Hall for and in consideration of the sum of four Hundred dollars to him in hand Paid by the
said Joshua Cox at or before the sealing & delivering of these Presents
the receipt Whereof is hereby Acknowledged hath granted bargained alien
released and confirmed and by these Presents doth grant bargain sell Alien
enfross and Confirm Unto the said Joshua Cox his heirs and assigns forever
a Certain tract or Parcel of land situated lying and being in the said

1-327. County of Marion on the northeast side of Sequachee river Containing one hundred and sixty Acres in three different Grants bounded and described as follows to Wit:

Beginning Near the foot of the Mountain at a dogwood it being the north west Corner of William Standifers survey of 150 acres then south along his line 54 poles to a White Oak then West 24 Poles to a white oak at the foot of the Mountain then along the same as it Meanders S. 34 E. 30 poles to a White Oak then N. 18 W. 30 Poles to a white oak then N. 70 W. 16 Poles to a Chesnut then N. 15 E. 60 Poles to a balch gum then West crossing a cove 38 Poles to a stake and beech at the foot of the ountain again then along the same S. 27 E. 16 poles to a gum then S. 50 E. 19 Pol s then S. 58 W. 28 Poles then S. 58 E. 22 poles to a hickory then S. 12 Poles to the beginning Including fifty Acres it being grant 15948 and Grant 11620 bounded as follows:

Beginning at a White oak south east Corner of the Aforesaid 50 acres on said Standifer line then West With a line of sd fifty Acres 28 Poles to Pointers at the foot of the Mountain then With the same S. 44 W. 100 Poles then S. 84 Poles N. 68 E. 110 poles to a stake at the foot of the Mountain then Along William Arnnetts line N. 32 Poles to a Maple then E. 58 poles to Pointers on Standifers line, and With the same North to the beginning including 50 Acres The Third and last Grant as above spiken of No. 11619 containing sixteen Acres Making in all one hundred and sixteen Acres bounded as follows,

Beginning at a stake and pointers on the line of the first Mentioned 50 acres at the foot of the Mountain then With the same as it Meanders up the cove at 58 Poles N. 33 W. 8 Poles to a stake at the foot of the Mountain again then With the same S. 37 E. 111 poles to a stake then West 30 Poles to the beginning to-gether With all and singular the appurtenances to the said tract or Parcel of land belonging or in any Wise Appertaining.

To have and to hold the said tract of one hundred and sixteen acres of land as herein before separately described with the Appurtenances to Joshua Cox his heirs and Assigns forever (P-328) in fee simple and clear of the lawful title claim and demand of him the said Roswell Hall or any Person Claiming from by or under him or his heirs or assigns forever Will Warrant and defend as far as the rights of the same is Vested by the before Numbered granted from the State of Tennessee and no further.

In Testimony Whereof I have hereunto set my hand and seal day and date first Above Written.
Signed and Ack. in Presence of

Jno. Kelly

E. P. Hale   Roswell Hall

P-328.   State of Tennessee

                                               May Term 1827

      Marion County Court

Then Was the Within deed of conveyance from Roswell Hall to Joshua Cox for one hundred and sixteen Acres acknowledged in Open Court by the said Hall and ordered to be Certif ied for registration.

Given under my hand and Private seal of office Not having an official seal this 25th day of September 1828.

P-328.

L. S. Registered October 23rd, 1828.

P-328. Thomas Cox
    To   Deed.
  William Mathews

This Indenture Made the 20th day of August in the Year of Our Lord 1827 by and between Thomas Cox of the County of Marion State of Tennessee of the One Part and William Mathews of the County and State aforesaid of the Other Part,

    Witnesseth, that for and in consideration of the sum of one hundred dollars to me in hand paid the receipt of Which is hereby Acknowledged I the said Thomas Cox doth by these Presents grant bargain sell Convey and con Firm unto the said William Mathews a Certain trot or Parcel of land situated lying and being in the county of Marion aforesaid on the Northwest side of Sequachie River on the Waters of Little Sequachie River and bounded as follows to Wit;

    Beginning at a stake the beginning of the division Made With John Bronson of a 50 acres Survey Made in the Entry Takers office Pf Marion County in the name of said Thomas Cox running thence south forty five degrees east thirty seven and a half Poles to a black oak then north 45 east one hundred and seven Poles to a red oak and White oak thence North 45 West thirty seven Poles to a Conditional With said Bronson thence a direct course to the beginning including the dwelling house and spring now Made use of by the said Thomas Cox

    To have and to hold Aforesaid tract or Parcel of land With all and singular the hereditaments and appurtenances thereunto belonging or in any Wise appertaining unto the said William Mathews his heirs forever from the lawful Claim and demand of all and every Person or Persons Claiming by through from or under me the said Thomas Cox and from the lawful demand of no other Person or Persons Whatsoever and further the said Thomas Cox doth covenant and agree that Should the said Wm. Mathews be ejected and from said tract or Parcel of land by Virtue of an older and better title than the one Thomas Cox is to refund the Consideration Mentioned in these Presents With all he received.

    In Witness Whereof I the said Thomas Cox have hereunto set my hand the day and date herein Written.

                        Thomas Cox   (seal)

P-328. State of Tennessee

       Marion County Court

                August Session 1827.

    Then Was the Within deed of conveyance from Thomas Cox to William Mathews for twenty five (25) Acres of land in Marion County Was duly Acknowledged in Open Court and Ordered to be Certified for registration. Let it be registered.

                      Jno. Kelly Clk.
                      By G. W. Rice D. Clk.

Registered October 23rd 1828.

P-329.   John McIver
          To   Deed
     Joel Hilliard

This Indenture made this the eleventh day of April in the Year of Our Lord one thousand eight hundred and twenty seven between John McIver of the County of Rutherford and State of Tennessee of the one Part,

Witnesseth that the said John McIver for and in Consideration of the sum of four hundred and eighty dollars to him in hand Paid by the said Joel Hilliard at or before the sealing and delivery of these Presents the receipt Whereof is hereby Acknowledged hath Granted bargained and sold alien released and Confirmed and by these Presents doth grant bargain and sell Alien release and Confirm unto the said Joel Hilliard his heirs and assigns forever, a Certain tract or Parcel of land situated lying and being in the said County of Marion Containing One hundred and sixty Acres on the southeast side of Sequachie River adjoining lands of the Said McIver as assignee of Andrew McCallie and James Anderson and bounded as follows;

Beginning at a black oak Near a spur of the Mountain on the Conditional line With said Anderson running thence along the same north sixty seven degrees West one hundred And eighty six Poles to a Post Oak thence north one hundred and twelve Poles to a black oak then east one hundred And seventy two to Pointers; thence south to the beginning including the farm and improvements on Which said Hilliard now lives, Which said tract of land was Originally surveyed as an occupant Claim and granted by the State of Tennessee Under the said John McIver as Assignee of Jessee Blackburn by Parent No. 48565 bearing the first day of January one thousand eight hundred and twenty three as by the same Will fully appear to-gether With all and singular the appurtenances Whatsoever to the said tract of land be-longing or any Wise Appertaining and the reversion and reversions remainder and remainders grants issues and Profits thereof and every Part and Parcel thereof and all the state right title interest Property Claim and demand Whatsoever of him the said John McIver either in law or equity.

To have and to hold the said tract of one hundred and sixty acres land herein before described With the Appurtenances Unto the said Joel Hilliard his heirs and assigns forever free and clear of all claim and demand of him the said John McIver his heirs executors and Administrators doth hereby covenant Promises and agrees to and With the said Joel Hilliard his heirs and assigns that if the said Joel Hilliard his heirs or assigns shall at any time hereafter be evicted from the said bargained Premises or any Part thereof in Virtue of these Premises or any Part thereof in Virtue or title Whatever more value in law than the title now Conveyed to him in Virtue of these Premises that then and in that Case he the said John McIver shall pay and refund unto the said Joel Hilliard his heirs and assigns at the rate of three dollars per acre for each and every Acre f om Which he or they Shall be evicted by due Course of law With interest thereon from the time of such eviction.

In Witness Where of the said John McIver hereunto set his hand and seal the day and Year first herein Written.

Signed and delivered in Presence of John Leoney Cannon Cooper.

                         John McIver   (seal)

P-329.   State of Tennessee   )
)
         Marion County Court   )   August Session 1827.
)

         Then Was the Within deed of conveyance from John McIver to
Joel Hilliard   (P-330)   for one hundred and sixty Acres of land in
Marion County was duly Proven in Open Court by the oath of John Looney
& Common Cooper the subscribing Witnesses thereto and Ordered to be
Certified for registration.

                                      Jno. Kelly Clk.
                                      By G. W. Rice D. Clk.

Registered Oct. 24, 1828.

P-330-   James Condra   )
            To   Deed   )   This Indenture this 12th day
         Mary Barker   )   of August in the Year of Our
)   Lord one thousand eight hun-
dred and twenty six by and between James Condra of the County of Marion
and State of Tennessee of the one Part and Mary Barker of the same county and state of the other Part,
         Witnesseth that for and in consideration of the sum of two
hundred and fifty dollars to him in hand paid the receipt Whereof is
hereby Acknowledged, I the said James Condra hath and do by these Presents grant bargain sell Convey and Confirm unto the said Mary Barker and
her heirs forever a Certain tract or Parcel of land containing fifty
Acres situated lying and being in the County of Marion Aforesaid on the
Northwest side of Sequachie River adjoining the lands of William Kelly
and bounded as follows to Wit:
         Beginning at a dogwood at sd Kelleys Corner thence south
With his line eight Poles to Pointers thence east one hundred Poles
Crossing the road to a hickory thence North eighty Poles to Pointers
thence West one hundred Poles Crossing road to the beginning including
house and improvements Where Henry Watson formerly lived,
         To have and to hold the aforesaid tract or Parcel of land
With the Appurtenances to the sd Mary Barker and her heirs forever from
the Claim and demand of all and every Person Whatsoever Claiming by
through from or under me the sd James Condra and from the lawful Claims
and demands of all any every Person or Persons Whatsoever I the sd.
James Condra Will Warrant and forever defend but it is expressly understood by the Contracting Parties that should the aforesaid or Parcel of
land by Virtue of an older or better title then the one by these Presents conveyed to the said Mary Barker shall or may be ejected or ex-
pelled from the enjoiments of the Aforesaid Piece or Parcel of land
then and in that Case then and the said James Condra Covenant and agrees
to refund unto the said Mary Barker her heirs the said Consideration of
two hundred and forty dollars bearing interest from date hereof.
         In testimony Whereof I the said James Condra have hereunto
set My hand and seal the day and Year first herein Written.
         Signed sealed and delivered in Our Presence.

Isaac Hicks   )
Howell Barker.   )   James Condra   (seal)

P-330. State of Tennessee
                                    | August Session 1827.
        Marion County Court |

        Then Was the Within deed of conveyance from James Condra to
Mary Barker for fifty Acres of land in Marion County was Proven in Open
Court by the oaths of Isaac Hicks and Roswell Barker Subscribing Witnesses thereto and ordered to be Certified for registration. Let it be
registered.

                                    Jno. Kelly   Clk.
                                    By G. W. Rice   D.C.

Registered October 24th 1828.

P-330. Mathew L. Dixson |
            To Deed. | This Indenture this 6th day of
        David Oats | September in the Year of Our
                                   (Lord one thousand eight hundred
& twenty Seven between Mathew L. Dixson of the County of Franklin and
State of Tennessee of the (P-331) one Part David Oats of the County
of Marion & State aforesaid of the other Part,
        Witnesseth that the said Mathew L. Dixon for & in Consider-
ation of the sum of 400. dollars to him in hand Paid the receipt Whereof
if hereby Acknowledged hath given granted bargained sold conveyed &
Confirmed & by these Presents doth give grant bargain sell Convey &
Confirm unto the said David Oats his heirs & Assigns forever a Certain
tract of land in the County of Marion Aforesaid on the East side of
Sequatchie river
        Bigining at a Post in the South boundary line of Hickson
& Prigmoresland that includes the Old Deer Head Town then With their line
south west 59 W. Ninety six Poles to two Post oak their Corner then
east forty five Poles to a black Oak; N. 50 E. fofty four Poles to a
White Oak north 20 east thirty eight poles to a White oak north 59 east
thirty six Poles to two hickories in Lassons line & With the same North
one hundred & four Poles to the beginning Containing one hundred Acres
be the same More or less.
        To have & to hold the before recited land & bargained Prem-
ises With all & singular the rights Profits rents issues hereditaments
& Appurtenances or in & to the same belonging or any wise Appertaining
to the Only Proper use benefit & behoof of thim the said David Oats his
heirs & Assigns forever and the said Mathew L. Dixson for himself & his
heirs doth further Covenant & agree to & With said David Oats that the
before recited land & bargained Premises he Will Warrant & forever defend Aginst the right title interest Claim & demand of all & every Person or Persons Whatsoever.
        In Witness Whereof the said Mathew L. Dixson hath hereunto
set his hand & affixed his seal the day & Year above Written.
        Signed sealed and delivered in Presence of Leroy May A. Kelly
Jr. John Goodwin.

                                    M. L. Dixson   (Seal)

P-331. State of Tennessee

Marion County Court   November Term 1827.

   Then Was the Within deed of conveyance from Mathew L. Dixson
to David Oats for one hundred Acres of land in Marion County Was Proven
in Open Court by the Oaths of Alexander Kelly & John Goodwin subscribing Witness thereto and Ordered to be Certified for registration.
   Given under My hand and Private seal (not having a seal of
office in Jasper this 18th day of October 1828.

            Jno. Kelly Clk.
            By G. W. Rice D. Clk.

(L.S) Registered October 24th. 1828.

P-331. The last Will and Testament
       of   I Samuel Merritt of the County
   Samuel Merritt, Deceased. of Marion and State of Tennessee
               being Very sick and Weak of body
but of sound Mind and Memory and knowing that if it is the lot of all to
die do Make this My last Will and testament as to What Property I have
   I do give and bequeath in the following Manner.
   I do give and bequeath unto my beloved wife Barbary one bed
and furniture Cupboard shefware except two Puter dishes and also do give
her one Cow and one eight gallon pot and urn two Churns and one table
   as to My daughter Sarah I do give one cow and Yearling one
bed and furniture a Certain black Mare
   I give unto My Son Jim and Joseph Merritts and the Colt that
she is now with.
   I do Give unto Samuel Woffanbarger and Also one Plow Chains
froe and ax.
   I do give Joseph Merritt one cow
   as to My daughter Thersa one heirfer and bed and furniture.
   as to My son Samuel Merritt (P-332) I do give him one
sorrel Mare Until he raises a Colt and it is Old enough to Wine and then
equally divided Amongst My sons.
   as to my stock of hogs after there is a Sufficiency of Meat for
My family killed out of them the Young hogs and Cattle that is Not disposed of and Crops of cotton and Corn I want equally divided Among my
Wife and Children that now lives With me After all my just debts is Paid
out of it and Chest and two Puter dishes tea kettle I want equally divided between Betsy Conder Early Houston Roberts Condren and Nancy
Merritt and Note of hand on Isham Miles for thirty five dollars I give
unto Thomas and Benedict Merritt.
   I want What sheep I have equally divided Amongst My Children
that I have not all ready gone some to by My Will.
   Signed in Presence of the Witness this 13th of October 1827.
              his
James Loyd Jurat   Samuel X Merritt (Seal)
   his   mark
Thomas X T. Kill Attest
   mark

P-331. State of Tennessee   )
) February Session 1828.

      Marion County Court   )

        Then Was the foregoing last Will and Testament of Samuel Merritt decd, duly Proven in Open Court by the Oaths of James Loyd a subscribing Witness thereto and ordered to be Certified for registration.
        Given under My hand and Private seal not having a seal of office in Jasper the 28th day of February 1828.

                             Jno. Kelly Clk.
                             By G. W. Rice D. Clk.

(Seal) Registered October 25th. 1828.

P-332. Hercilus Jones.   )
        To Gifts   ) Known All Men by these Presents
      Thomas Jones.   ) that Hercilus Jones of the County of Marion and State of Tennessee for and in Consideration of the sum of five hundred dollars to me in hand Paid hath bargained sold and delivered unto Thos. Jones of the County and State aforesaid All my crops of the Present Years to gether With my household and kitchen furniture and also My perishable Property.
        Given under My hand and seal this 29th of Sept. 1827.

J. B. Minor
Anthony W. Moore   Attest   Hercilus Jones   (seal)

P-332. State of Tennessee   )
) February Session 1828.

      Marion County Court   )

        Then Was the Within Bill of Sale from Hercilus Jones to Thos. Jones for the Crops of the Present Year With the household and Kitchen furniture and all the perishable Property of Hercilus Jones Acknowledged in Open Court and ordered to be Certified for registration.
        Given (Seal) under my hand and Private seal not having a seal of office this day of February 1828.

                             Jno. Kelly Clk.
                             By G. W. Rice D. Clk.

Registered Oct. 25th. 1828.

P-333. Thomas Jones   )
        To his Bond   ) Know All Men by these Presents
      Brothers & Sisters   ) that I Thomas Jones of the County of Marion and State of Tennessee hold and firmly bound unto all my lawful Brothers and Sisters under my own age in the sum of one hundred dollars each to be discharged in a horse saddle and briddle the boys to have their share at the age of eighteen and exclusive of that the boys is to have eighteen Months schooling except Abraham and he is to have twelve Months and the girls to have their Property at the age of sixteen, Also a bed and furniture also six Months schooling. I the said (P-333) Thomas Jones am also bound to

P-333. Keep My Father & Mother in Peaceable Possession of the Place Where they now reside during their Natural lives I said Thomas held and bound in the sum of Two thousand dollars to perform Agreeable to the Above obligations to be Void Otherwise remain in full force and Virtue in law.
Given Under My hand and seal 29th Sept. 1827.

J. B. Minor
Anthony Z. Moore   Test.   Thomas Jones (seal)

P-333. State of Tennessee
                                     February Session 1828.
        Marion County

        Then Was the Within bond from Thomas Jones to his Natural brothers and sisters duly Acknowledged in Open Court and Ordered to be Certified for registration.
        Given Under My hand and Private seal not having a seal of Office in Jasper this the 28th day of February 1828.

                            Jno. Kelly Clk.
                            By G. W. Rice D. Clk.

(Seal)
Registered October 25th. 1828.

P-333. Elizabeth Trussell
            To   Deed of Gift   Known All Men by these Pres-
        Elizabeth A. Spangler   ents that I Elizabeth Trussell
                                        of the County of Marion and
State of Tennessee for and in consideration of the Natural love and affection Which I have and bear unto My beloved Grand-daughter Elizabeth Annie Spangler infant daughter of Bennett Spangler of the County and State aforesaid I have given granted and confirmed and by these Presents do give grant & Confirm unto the said Elizabeth Ann Spangler one Cow and Calf and two feather beds & furniture.
        To have and to hold & enjoy the said Personal estate afore sd to herself her heirs &c forever to the Only Proper use and behoof of the said Elizabeth Ann and her heirs as aforesaid and I the sid Elizabeth Trussell do hereby warrant and defend the right of the said Personal estate to the said Elizabeth Ann from me and My heirs forever or any Other Person or Persons All of Which Personal estate I have Put into the Possession of the said Elizabeth Ann Spangler at a sealing & delivering of these Presents.
        In testimony Whereof I have hereunto set My hand and seal this 21st day of February in the Year of Our Lord 1828.
                                        her
Joseph Rice   Elizabeth X Trussell (seal)
Stephen M robes   Attest.   mark

P-333. State of Tennessee
                                     February Session 1828.
        Marion County Court

        Then Was the Within deed of gift from Elizabeth Trussell to Elizabeth A. Spangler infant daughter Bona Spangler Was this day duly

P-333. Proven in Open Court by the oaths of Joseph Rice and Stephen Marbes subscribing witness th reto and ordered to be Certified for Registration.

Given under My hand and Private seal this 28th day of February 1828.

Jno. Kelly Clk.
By G. W. Rice D. Clk.

Registered Oct. 25th. 1828.

P-333. Moses Easterly
            To Deed
        William Stone

This Indenture Made this the 30th day of Nov. in the Year of Our Lord One thousand eight hundred and twenty six between Moses Easterly of the County of Marion and State of Tennessee of the one Part and William Stone of the County and State aforesaid of the Other Part,

Witnesseth that the said Moses Easterly for and in Consideration of the said sum of one dollar to him the said Moses Easterly in hand Paid the receipt of Which is hereby Acknowledged hath and by these Presents doth grant bargain sell and Confirm unto the said William Stone and his heirs forever a Certain tract or (P-334) Parcel of land Containing three Acres be the same More or less being Part of Grant No. 12-466 Containing 50 acres Granted to the said Easterly by the State of Tennessee on the 16th day of February 1826 lying on the North West side of Sequachie River

Beginning at V. Pointers on the North boundary of 160 Acres Survey of William Stone Where a 100 Acre Survey of the said Stone interest the same thence east With the line of the 160 Acres Survey seven Poles to the bank of a small creek thence up the said Creek including its Meanders Until it intersects With a line of Said Wm Stone 100 Acres Survey thence south With the Same to the beginning

To have and to hold the said William Stone his heirs and assigns forever Against the lawful title Claim and demand of every Person or Persons Will Warrant and forever defend.

In Witness Where the said Moses Easterly hath hereunto set his hand and Seal the day and date above Written.

Bird Farmer
Thomas Payne. Test.

Moses Easterly

P-334. State of Tennessee

Marion County Court

February Session 1828

Then Was the Within deed of Conveyance from Moses to William Stone for three Acres of land in Marion County duly Acknowledged in Open Court by the said Easterly and ordered to be Certified for registration.

Given under my hand and Private seal not having an official seal of office in Jasper the 28th day of February 1828.

Jno. Kelly Clk.
By G. W. Rice D. Clk.

(seal)
Registered October.

P-334. Samuel Jackson
      To   Deed.
Hannah Ray.

This Indenture Made the 16th day of February in the Year of Our Lord one thousand & eight hundred twenty eight between Samuel Jackson Sr. of the County of Marion & State of Tennessee of the one Part and H annah Ray of the other Part of the State and County Aforesaid,

Witnesseth that for and in consideration of the Sum of one hundred and forty dollars to the said Samuel in hand Paid by the said Hannah the said Samuel hath bargained & sold and by these Presents do bargain sell alien remise and Convey unto the said Hannah a Certain Piece or Parcel of land situated lying and being in the County of Marion State of Tennessee on the Waters of Battle Creek Containing twenty five Acres More or less

Beginning the <u>son</u> Rit on a Conditional Corner on a stake at Wilsons Corner running East_____ Poles thence North 58 east fifty Poles to a Conditional Corner on a Spanish oak and hickory thence eastwardly With said Conditional line by a large poplar at the fork of a Path and the dry Creek; thence down said dry Creek to Hays line thence With said Hays line to his Walnut Corner thence up the hollow to the beginning A Conditional line.

To have and to hold the aforesaid tract of land together With all and singular the rights Members and Appurtenances to the same belonging or Any Wise Appertaining to the said Hannah Ray her heirs & Assigns forever and the said Samuel Jackson Senior for himself his executors administrators doth covenant and agree to and With the said Hannah Ray her heirs and executors and administrators that the said bargained Premises he Will Warrant and forever defend Against the Claim or Claims of all Person or Persons Whatsoever Pretending to Claim or hold the same by Virtue of deed of Conveyance from the said Samuel his heirs or Assigns.

In Witness Whereof the said Samuel <u>Sit</u> his hand and seal day and date Above Written.

Thomas Ray   Jurat
John Overturf Jurat.

P-335. State of Tennessee

    Marion County Court

February Session 1828

Then Was the Within deed of conveyance from Samuel Jackson to Hannah Ray for twenty Acres of land in Marion County Was duly Proven by the Oaths of Thomas Ray and John Overturf subscribing Witnesses thereto and to be Certified for registration.

Given Under My hand and Private seal <u>nt</u> having an official seal at office in Jasper the 28th day of February 1828.

Jno. Kelly Clk.
By G. W. Rice D. Clk.

(Seal)
Registered October 27th 1828.

P-335. Rober McDowell
      To   Deed.
George A. Brock

This Indenture Made this the 20th day of January in the Year of Our Lord One thousand eight

123

P-335. hundred & twenty three betwixt Robert McDowell of the State of Tennessee Marion County of the One Part & George A. Brock of sd. State & Franklin County of the other Part,

Witnesseth that the sd Robert McDowell for and in consideration of the sum of one hundred dollars to him in hand Paid by the said Brock at or before the sealing & delivering of these Presents the receipt Whereof is hereby Acknowledged hath given granted bargained & sold aliened Conveyed & Confirmed unto the said George A. Brock his heirs and Assigns forever a Certain tract or Parcel of land containing forty seven Acres & two third more or less it being a Part of a tract of eighty seven Acres & two thirds Made and granted to the said Robert McDowell situated lying & being in the State of Tennessee Marion County on Sweetens Creek Waters of Battle in Sweeten Cove,

Beginning at Pointers at the foot of the Mountain thence aS 8 Poles to Robert Bean Snr. N. W. holly Corner thence South on sd Beans 66 Poles to Pointers thence W. 82 Poles to Pointers on sd McDowell W. Boundary line thence N. 99 Poles to a Holly thence along Samuel McBees line 24 Poles to a holly thence N. 67 degrees West fifteen Poles to a beech thence N. 35 W. ten Poles to a Poplar thence N. 8 Poles to Pointers at the foot of the Mountain thence With the Mountain South 69 E. one hundred and thirty five Poles to Pointers it being the beginning.

To have and to hold the aforesaid land With all & Singular the rights Profits and Appurtenances of into the same belonging or any Wise Appertaining to the only Proper use & behoof of him the said George A. Brock his heirs & assigns that the before recited land & bargained Premises he the said Robert McDowell Will Warrant & forever defend the right & title of sd land from himself his heirs executors administrators and assigns & from no Other Person Whatever.

In Witness Whereof I the said Robert McDowell have hereunto set my hand & affixed my seal the day and date first above Written.

Signed sealed & delivered in Presence of

Obediah Bean
Abner C. Warmack.   Robert McDowell   (seal)

P-335. State of Tennessee
                                     May Session 1828.
        Marion County Court

Then Was the forgoing deed of Conveyance from Robert McDowell to George A. Brock for 47-2/3 Acres of land Was duly Proven by Obediah Bean a subscribing Witness thereto Who Sworn that he saw Abner C. Warmack a Concurring Witness attest the same and that the said Warmack is a non-resident of the State Which is ordered to be Certified & admitted to record. Let it be registered.

                              Jno. Kelly Clk.
                              by G. W. Rice D. Clk.

Registered Oct. 27th. 1828.

P-336. Hall   Roswell   This Indenture Made the 28th day
          To   Deed   of November in the year of Our
        Thomas Sherley Jr.   Lord 1825 by and between Roswell

P-336. Hall of the County of Marion and State of Tennessee of the one part and Thomas Shirley Jr. of the County and State aforesaid

Witnesseth that for and in consideration of the sum of Two Thousand dollars to me in hand Paid the receipt of Which is hereby Acknowledged I the said Roswell Hall hath this day bargained sold granted conveyed and confirmed unto the said Thomas Shirley Jr. and do by these Presents grant bargain sell and confirm unto the said Thomas Shirley Jr. his heirs executors &c forever a certain lot or Piece of land in the town of Jasper known and designated in the original Plan of said town as lot No. 65 With the appurtenances it being the same on Which the brick house now stands Occupied by David Rankin as a store.

To have and to hold to the aforesaid lot or pieces of land With the Appurtenances to the said Thomas Shirley Jr. his heirs and &c forever from the Claims and demands of all Person or Persons Whatsoever I the said Roswell Hall Will Warrant and defend.

In testimony Whereof I the said Roswell Hall have hereunto set my hand seal day and date first above Written.

Signed sealed and delivered in our Presence.

S. Hicks   Roswell Hall
Wm. Rice.

P-336.   State of Tennessee   )
)   May Session 1828.
          Marion County Court   )

Then Was the Within deed of conveyance from Roswell Hall to Thomas Shirley Jr. for Lot No. 65 in the town of Jasper Was Acknowledged in Open Court by said Hall and Ordered to be Certified and admitted to record. Let it be registered.

                                    Jno. Kelly Clerk
                                    By G. W. Rice D. Clk.

Registered October 28th. 1828.

P-336.   Hopkins L. Turney. |
            To   Deed. | This Indenture Male and entered
          Thomas Shirley Jr. | into this the 28th day of Jan-
                                         | uary in the Year of Our Lord one
                                         | thousand Eight hundred and twen-
ty eight between Hopkins L. Turney of the County of Marion and State of Tennessee of the one Part and Thomas Shirley Jr. of the County and State aforesaid of the other Part,

Witnesseth That the said Hopkins L. Turney for the consideration of five hundred dollars to him in hand paid by the said Shirley the receipt Whereof is hereby Acknowledged hath bargained & sold by these Presents doth bargain sell Alien enfross and Convey to the said Shirley his heirs and assigns forever three lots of land Containing one quarter of an Acre each situated lying and being in the town of Jasper known and designated in the Plan of said town by lots No. 70 6(& 40.

To have and to hold the said lot of land unto the said Shirley & his heirs forever and the said Turney Will forever Warrant and defend the title of said lots from all lawful Claims of any Person or Persons Whatever.

In testimony Whereof I have hereunto set My hand and seal the day and Year above Written.

Hopkins L. Turney   (seal)

Wiley Belcher
Wm. I. Standifer   Attest.

P-336.   Marion County Circuit Court   }
                                          }   June Term 1828.
            State of Tennessee   }

        Then Was the Within deed of conveyance from Hopkins L. Turney
to Thomas Shirley Jr. for lots No. 70 69 & 40 in the town of Jasper duly
Acknowledged in Open Court by the said Hopkins L. Turney and ordered to
be Certified for registration.
(P-337)   Given under my hand and Private seal not having official seal
at office in Jasper this the 2nd day of June 1828.

(seal)
Registered Oct. 27th 1828.

P-337.   Green H. Pryor   }
              To   }   This Indenture Made this the
        Henry H. Conatser   }   twenty second day of December
                                }   one thousand and eight hundred
and twenty seven between Green H. Pryor of the County of Marion and State
of Tennessee of the one Part and Henry H. Conatser of the County and
State aforesaid of the other Part
        Witnesseth that the said Pryor for And in Consideration of
the sum of Four hundred and twenty five dollars in Property to him in
hand Paid the receipt Whereof is hereby Acknowledged hath and by these
Presents doth grant bargain and sell unto the said Conatser his heirs
and assigns forever a Certain tract or Parcel of land Containing one
hundred Acres in the County Aforesaid on the Southeast side of Sequachie
River adjoining land of the said Pryor and a tract of land entered in the
name of Elisha Mayfield
        Beginning at a stake and Pointers on bank of said River near
a place Called the Island Ford then down the river as it Meanders to the
said Mayfield Entery then east one hundred and thirty Poles to a White
oak then North one hundred and Seven Poles to said river then With the
Same northwardly to the beginning with its Appurtenances
        To have and to hold the said tract With its appurtenances to
the said Conatser and his heirs forever Against the lawful Claim and demand of all and every Persons or Person Whatsoever shall and Will Warrant and forever defend by these Presents.
        In testimony Whereof the said Pryor hath hereunto set his hands
and seal this day and date first above Written.
        Signed sealed and delivered in Presence of H. Hatfield.
                                          Thomas Smith
                                          James Barker
                                          Green H. Pryor (seal)

P-337.   State of Tennessee   }
                                  }   August Session, 1829.
          Marion County Court   }

Ordered by the Court that a deed of Conveyance for 100 Acres of land from Green H. Pryor to Henry H. Conatser Which Was Proven in at May Session 1829 by Thomas Smith and James Barker the subscribing Witness thereto by the name of John Barker be Altered to said James Barker.

Jno. Kelly Clk.
By G. W. Rice D. Clk.

P-338. Anderson Cheek
       To Deed
Stephen A. Blevins

This Indenture Made and entered into this the 27th day of April and Year of Our Lord 1828 between Anderson Cheek of the one Part of the County of Marion & State of Tennessee and Stephen Blevins of the County and State Aforesaid of the other Part.

Witnesseth for and in consideration of the sum of one hundred dollars to him the said Anderson Cheek in hand Paid by the said Stephen Blevins the receipt Whereof is hereby Acknowledged that the said Anderson Cheek hath bargained and sold unto him the said Stephens Blevins a Certain tract or Parcel of land lying and being in the County of Marion and on the Waters of Hall branch Containing 26 acres be the same more or less adjoining David Nichols and bounded as follows, Viz;

Beginning on the top of the hill at a stake thence running With a conditional line between said Blevins & Nichols to a Corner Made between them thence running south to a brach on said Nichols land thence With the branch to said Blevins; then running With said line of said Blevins Corner then to top of a hill; thence to the top of a hill to the beginning. The said Cheek doth forever defend the right title Claim or Claims from all Other Persons Whatsoever in law or equity unto him the said Blevins With the Appurtenances benefit effects & the said Anderson Cheek and his heirs doth relinquish their rights title unto him the said Blevins and his heirs forever in Confirmation and in the Presence of these Witness we set our hand and affix our seal the day and date above Written

Anderson Cheek   (seal)

P-338. State of Tennessee

Marion County Court

May Session 1828.

Then was the forgoing deed of conveyance from Anderson Cheek to Stephen A. Blevins for 26 acres of land Was Acknowledged in Court by said Cheek and ordered to be Certified and admitted to record. Let it be registered.

Jno. Kelly Clk.
By G. W. Rice D. Clk.

Registered Oct. 30th. 1828.

P-338. James Standifer
       To Deed.
Andrew Bronson

This Indenture Made this 18th day of April in the Year of Our Lord one thousand eight hundred and twenty eight between James Standifer in County of Marion and State of

P-338. Tennessee of the one Part and Andrew Bronson of the County of Marion and State aforesaid of the other Part

Witnesseth that for and in consideration of the sum of three hundred dollars to him the said Standifer in hand Paid the receipt Whereof is hereby Acknowledged hath by these Presents bargained sold and Conveyed unto the said Andrew Bronson a Certain tract or Parcel of land situated in the County of Marion Aforesaid on the southeast Side of Sequachie river described & bounded as follows to Wit.

Beginning at a stake on bank of said Sequachie River in an Old field Where the road leading from Kellys Bridge runs square out from the river an at a Point Opposite thereto then running up sd. river as it Meanders to a stake it being the upper Corner on said river Specified in Grant No. 12450 then south along a line sd. survey Another Survey in the name of sd. Standifer to the road leading from sd. bridge then along said road as Now established until near the beginning so as to Make a square line to the beginning agreeable to the directions of said read including Ninety Acres be the Same More or less it being the Whole of a tract of land for eight Acres Granted by the State of Tennessee to the sd. Standifer by Grant No. 12450 and Part of a tract granted by said State to the Said Standifer for eighty five by Grant No. 12450 With all and singular the Woods Water Water Courses Profits Commodities and hereditaments and Appurtenances to the Said tract or Parcel of land.
(P-339)   To have And to hold to the said Andrew Bronson his heirs and Assigns forever I will Warrant and forever defend the title of same from All Manner of Persons Whatever.

In Witness Whereof I hereunte set my hand and seal this day and date first Above Written.

Signed and acknowledged in Presence

John Kelly John Burgess	James Standifer (seal)
P-339. State of Tennessee	May Session 1828.
Marion County Court	

Then Was the Within deed of Conveyance from James Standifer to Andrew Bronson for 90 Acres of land Was duly Proven in Open Court by the Oaths of John Kelly and John Burgess the subscribing Witnesses thereto and Ordered to be Certified and Admitted to record. Let it be registered.

Jno. Kelly Clk.
By G. W. Rice D. Clk.

Registered Oct. 31st 1829.

P-339. John Wooten and Mathew Trussell
            To   Deed of Conveyance.
       James Clipper & John Clipper

This Indenture Made this the twenty fifth day of January in the Year of Our Lord One thousand eight hundred and twenty seven between John Wooten of Marion County and State of Tennessee and Mathew Trussell of sd. State and County of Lincoln of the one Part and James Clipper & John Clipper of the County of Marion & State aforesaid of the Other Part

Witnesseth that for & in consideration of the sum of one hun-

P-338. dred and fifty dollars to the said Mathew Trussell in hand Paid of the said John & James Clipper the receipt hereof is hereby Acknowledged we the said John & Mathew has bargained and sold & by these Presents doth bargain and sell, Alien remise and Convey unto the said James & John one Certain Piece or Parcel of land of forty seven Acres More or less bounded as follows

Beginning at a Maple on said Clipper's line to the beginning situated lying and being in the County of Marion on the Waters of Battle Creek adjoining lands of said Clipper & Jesse Wooten & John Wooten the same being Part of sixty Acres tract And a hundred Acre entry Granted by the State of Tennessee to sd John Wooten

To have and to hold the sd. Piece or Parcel of land to-gether With all and singular the rights Members hereditaments to the said Part belonging or any wise Appertaining unto them the said James Clipper & John Clipper their heirs and Assigns forever and the said John & Mathew doth Covenant & agree to & With the said James & John their heirs executors and Administrators that the said bargained Premises they Will Warrant and forever defend free from the rights title & interest or Claim of all and every Person or Persons Whatever Claiming or Pretending to Claim the same.

In Witness Whereof We the said John & Mathew has hereunto set our hand and seal on the day & Year first Above Written.

Signed sealed and delivered in Presence of

William T Trussell	Jurat		John Wooten (seal)
Bedford Bethel	Jurat		Mathew X Trussell (seal)
			his mark

P-339.   State of Tennessee

Marion County Court

Session 1828.

(P-340)   Then Was the Within deed of Conveyance from John Wooten & Mathew Trussell To James Clipper & John Clipper for forty sum Acres of land in Marion County Which Was heretofore Proven in Open Court by the Oaths of William TRussell and Bluford Bethel subscribing Witness thereto Which Was failed to be entered on the Minute Book. Now Ordered to be Certified for registration upon the Oaths of George W. Rice Who Proved to the satisfaction of the Court that the same Was heretofore Proven by the Witnesses to the same. Let it be registered.

Jno. Kelly   Clk.
By G. W. Rice D. Clk.

Registered Oct. 31st. 1828.

P-340.   George Carroll et al
         To.   Deed
     John Hall

This Indenture Made this the 17th day of August eight hundred & twenty eight by & between George Carroll Jacob Carroll William Carroll Jr. and Luster Harris heirs of William Carroll Sr. Dec'd all of the County of Marion and State of Tennessee of the one Part & John Hall of the County and State aforesaid of the Other Part,

Witnesseth that for and in Consideration of a title bond Given by sd. William Carroll dec'd for five Acres of land now in Compliance with said bond We the said heirs as aforesaid doth convey to said Hall the said tract of land containing the five Acres beginning on a holly tree then

Westward to Little Sequatchie thence down Sequachie to the line of a tract of land A. Coulter then Eastwardly from Coupts.

To have and to hold the same tract or Parcel of land With its appurtenance to the said Hale his heirs & Assigns forever from the Claim and demand of all and every Person or Persons Whatever Claiming by through or Under us this this the said heirs as aforesaid.

In Witness Whereof We have her Unto set our hands & seal the day & Year first herein Written.

Signed sealed in Presence of

D. Rankin
Sam W. Roberson

George Carroll   (seal)
Jacob Carroll   (seal)
William Carroll   (seal)
Laster   X Harris   (seal)
            his mark

P-340.   State of Tennessee

Marion County Court

August Session 1828.

Then Was the Within deed of Conveyance from George Carroll, Jacob, Carroll, William Carroll & Laster Haynes to John Hale for five Acres of land Was this day Proven in Open Court and executed thereof acknowledged by the Conveyance and ordered to be Certified for registration. Let it be registered.

                                    Jno. Kelly Clk.
Registered Oct. 31st. 1828   By G. W. Rice D. Clk.

P-340.   John Kelly
              To   Deed.
         Henry Grayson

This Indenture Made this the 28th day of June in the Year of Our Lord one thousand eight hundred and twenty eight between John Kelly of the County of Marion and State of Tennessee of the one Part and Henry Grayson of the County and State Aforesaid of the Other Part,

Witnesseth that for and in consideration of the sum of three hundred and seventy five dollars to him the said Kelly in hand Paid by the said Grayson the receipt Whereof is hereby Acknowledged hath by these Presents sold bargained and Conveyed to the said Henry Grayson his heirs and Assigns forever Certain tract or Parcel of land Containing seventy seven Acres situated lying and being in the County of Marion and State of Tennessee on both side of Sequachee River it being a Part of a tract granted by the State of Tennessee to the said John Kelly for one hundred & forty Acres bearing date the 30th day of July 1822 No. 17694 bounded and described as follows

Beginning at a beech on the north West bank of Sequachee River at the Mouth of the first branch Above D'd. Griffith It being the beginning Corner of the Original Grant or Survey then running up said branch along said Griffiths line south 5 W. 50 Poles to a White oak then S. 45 W. About two Poles to a stake and beech & sweet gum Pointers then running through said tract along a line With Joshua T. Ashburn N. 77 W. 95 Poles to a stake and Pointers on Tatums line & With the same N. 13 E. 53 Poles to a stake & Pointers known by Roberts Corner in the Grant and With his line N. 23

P-341. E. Poles to a suger tree Pryors Corner then With his line down the Channel on the branch With his line to the bank of Sequachee then up the Various Meanders of the Same Agreeable to the Grant thereto interfering to a Sycamore on the south east side of said Sequachie it being the upper coner on the river of said Grant Also a Corner of said Griffith or Terrys Survey aluded to said Grant then along their line S. 58 W. 106 Poles to a White oak on the ed S. E. bank of sd. river then a direct line Crosseing the sd river to the beginning (including seventy seven Acres as by Survey to be the same More or less) With All and singular the Woods Water Water courses Profits Commodities hereditaments and Appurtenances to him the said Henry Grayson his heirs and assigns forever.

To have And to hold the said Tract or Parcel of land as above described either in law or equity from the lawful title Claim and demand of all Manner of Persons Whatever for Which I the Said John Kelly My heirs &c do Warrant and forever defend by Virtue of these Presents.

In testimony Whereof I hereunto set My hand and seal the day and date Above Written.

Signed and Ack. in the Presence of

Jesse Rodgers
Mathew Williams

Ack.   John Kelly   (seal)

P-341.   State of Tennessee

August Term 1828.

Marion County Court

Then Was the Within deed of Conveyance from John Kelly to Henry Grayson for Seventy seven Acres of land in Marion County duly Acknowledged in Open Court and ordered to be Certified for registration. Let it be registered.

Jno. Kelly Clk.
By C. W. Rice D. Clk.

Registered Oct. 31st 1828.

P-341. George Lane
        To   Deed
    Joseph Jones

This Indenture Made and entered into this the twenty eight day of February in the Year of Our Lord one thousand eight hundred and twenty seven between George Lane of the County of Marion and State of Tennessee of the one Part and Joseph Jones of the County of Marion and State of Tennessee

Witnesseth that the said George Lane hath this day for and in Consideration of the sum of three hundred dollars to him in hand paid by the said Joseph Jones his heirs &c Certain tract or Parcel of land situated lying and being in thee County of Marion and State of Tennessee on the Waters of Sequachie river containing one hundred and fifteen Acres Which is bounded as follows to Wit;

Beginning at a White oak the northwestwardly Corner of Hixson & Prigmore's Entry of 136 Acres thence down a branch along line of sd Hixson and Prigmore Entry 100 Acres N. 5° E. 26 Poles to an elm and Poplar on bank of Sequachie River at the Mouth of said branch and down the river as it Meanders West 31 Poles N. 70 W. one hundred and seven Poles N. 60 W. thirty eight Poles N. 46° W. 13 Poles North 3d West 15 Poles to a Wal-

P-341. mit thence West 21 Poles to a horbern thence south 136 Poles to a
2 post oak Pointers on said Hixsons and Prigmores line and With the same
to the beginning With all and severally the Appurtenances Pertaining thereto the said tract of land.

(P-342)   To have and to hold the same Which I warrant and defend
Against all Claims or Claim of Persons holding or Claiming in or through
me from the title Made by me by the State of Tennessee

as Witness My hand and seal this 12th day of August 1828.
Signed in the Presence of us.

E. Hornbeak   his
Jas. H. Hornbeak   George Lane   X   (seal)
                                                      mark

P-342. State of Tennessee   .
                                         August Session, 1828.
        Marion County Court

        Then Was the Within deed of Conveyance from George Lane to
Joseph Jones 115 Acres of land in Marion County Was Proven in Open Court
by the oaths of Elijah Hornbeak and James Hornbeak subscribing Witness
thereto and Ordered to be Certified for registration.   Let it be registered.

                                         Jno. Kelly Clk.
                                         By G. W. Rice   D. Clk.

Registered Oct. 31st. 1828.

P-342. William Barnes
           To   Deed.   This Indenture Made this the
        Daniel Hafner   fifteenth day of September eighteen
                                         hundred and twenty seven between
William Barnes of the State of Tennessee and County of Marion and Daniel
Haner of the State and County aforesaid of the Other Part,

        Witnesseth that the said William Barnes for and in consider-
ation of the sum of one hundred And fifty dollars Paid at on before the
sealing and delivering of these Presence thereceipt Whereof is hereby
Acknowledged hath given granted bargained sold and conveyed unto the
Daniel Hafner his heirs and assigns forever a Certain tract or Parcel of
land situated lying and being in the County of Marion Aforesaid on the
West side of Battle Creek

        beginning at a stake Near the head of a spring at the foot of
the Mountain then With the same North sixty one east thirty three Poles
to a Battle Creek thence up the Same as it Meanders North fifty West twenty
Poles thence North ten West twenty Poles to a Stake and Pointers thence
West seventy Nine Poles to Pointers thence South forty two Poles to Pointers at the foot of the Mountain; thence a direct line to the beginning,
Containing fifty acres More or less.

        To have and to hold the aforesaid land With all and singular the
hereditaments and Appurtenances of in and to the same belonging or any
wise appertaining to the only use benefit and behoof of him the said Daniel Hafner his heirs and assigns forever and the said William Barnes for
himself his heirs executors and Administrators doth covenant and agree to
and With the said Daniel Hafner his heirs and assigns that the before recited land and bargained Premises he Will Warrant and forever defend

P-342. against the right title inter t or Claim of him and his heirs or Assigns forever.

In Witness Whereof the said William Barnes have set his hand and affixed his seal the day and Year first Above Written.

Signed sealed and delivered in Presence of us.

his
Obediah X Bean
    mark his
Samuel Bean X
      mark

William Barnes   (seal)

P-342. State of Tennessee

Marion County Court

August Session 1828.

Then Was the forgoing deed of Conveyance from William Barnes to Daniel Hafner for fifty Acres of land in Marion County Duly Proven in Open Court by the Oaths of Obediah Beane and Samuel Beane subscribing Witnesses and ordered to be Certified for registration. Let it be registered.

Jno. Kelly   Clk.
By G. W. Rice   D. Clk.

Registered Oct. 31st 1828.

P-343. Henry M. Ruthledge
       To   Deed of Con.
   Flut Manuel

This Indenture Made this day of August in the Year of Our Lord one thousand & eight & twenty three between Henry M. Ruthledge of the one Part of the County of Franklin & State of Tennessee and Flut Manuel of the County of Marion & State aforesaid of the Other Part

Witnesseth that for & in consideration of the sum of one dollar in hand Paid to the said Henry by the said Flut the said Henry hath bargained & sold & by these Presents doth bargain sell alien remise release & Convey unto the said Flut all that Certain tract of land Containing twenty Acres & thirty five Poles situated lying and being in the County of Marion Aforesaid on Battle Creek near the Mouth of the Fiery Gizzard Commencing & running as follows Viz;

On a stake in David Martin South boundary line running Due east to With said boundary line fifty three Poles to a White oak thence due south along the foot of the Cumberland Mountain seventy five Poles to a White Oak thence due south along the Cumberland Mountain seventy five Poles to a White Oak then due West on the Conditional line between Daniel Hill and the said Flut Manuel fifty three Poles to a White Walnut. Susan Lowreys east boundary reservation line thence due north along line to the beginning.

To have and to hold the said tract of land together With all and singular the rights Members & Appurtenances to the same belonging unto him the said Flut his heirs & Assigns forever free from the Claim or Claims of all and every Persons Whatsoever Claiming or Pertending to Claim in behalf of or under color of title from the said Henry.

In Witness Whereof the said Henry hath hereunto set his hand & seal on the day & Year first Above Written in Presence of

Jas. McCain
John Cochrane

H. M. Rutledge   (seal)

P-343.   State of Tennessee

Marion County Court

August Session 1825.

      Then Was the execution of the foregoing deed of conveyance from
Henry M. Rutledge for twenty Acres of land and thirty five Ppoles duly
Proven in Open Court by the Oaths of James McCain and John Cochrane and
ordered to be Certified for registration.
      Given Under my hand & Private seal not having official seal
at office in Jasper this the 15th day of August 1825.

                                        Jno. Kelly Clk.

(L.S.)
Registered Nov. 11th, 1828.

P-343.   The State of Tennessee
          To   Deed.   State of Tennessee
      James Johnson.   No. 24355.

      To All to Whom these Presents shall come greeting. Know Ye
that by Virtue by Part of Certificate No. 1175 dated this the 30th day
of March 1816 and Certificate No. 1037 dated the 1st day of August 1815
both issued by the Register of East Tennessee the Power to the heirs of
the Wm. Marshall for 50 Acres and the latter to Jacob Peck for 100 Acres
and entered on the 6th day of December 1820 by No. 5988 there is granted
by the State of Tennessee unto Jams Johnson the Assignee of the heirs of
the said Wm. Marshall & Jacobs Peck a Certain tract or Parcel of land
Containing one hundred thirty two Acres by survey bearing date the 20th
day of January 1821 lying in the Third district in Marion County on the
Waters of Tennessee River adjoining Westley Glazier Johnathan Newman
James Drain & John Evans and bounded as follows to Wit
      Beginning at a stake at the head of a Spring and running
Across With said Glazier North twenty Nine West eighteen Poles to
Pointers thence seventy seven West fifty two Poles to Pointers ; thence
North sixty seven West six Poles to a black oak. Said Glaziers Corner
(P-344) also said Newman and With his line north Four East fifteen Poles
to a post oak thence North sixty one West twenty Poles to an Ash thence
With the Mountain south fifteen east Ninety five Poles to a Poplar thence
With said Drain south sixty east sixty two Poles to a black oak north 34
east sixty three Poles to an ash thence South 43 east Fofty six Poles to
Pointers thence With said Evans south 34 east one hundred and four Poles
to a hornbean, thence With the Mountain south seventy West thirty seven
Poles to a hornbean south 30 West 56 Poles to a black oak thence West
eighteen Poles to a gum South 54 West fourteen Poles to a black oak said
Glazier Corner and With his line to the beginning With the hereditaments
and Appurtenances.
      To have and to hold the said tract or Parcel of land With its
Appurtenances to the Said James Johnson and his heirs forever.
      In Witness Whereof William Carroll Governor of the State of
Tennessee hath hereunto set his hand and Caused the Great Seal of the State
to be affixed at Murfreesboro on the twenty fifth day of November in the
Year of Our Lord one thousand eight hundred and twenty five and on the
Independence of the United States the fifteenth.

P-344.   By the Governor
Daniel Graham   William Carroll
Secretary

          Recorded in the Registers Office of West Tennessee May the
6th. 1826.

                                          E. McGavock. D. Reg.

          James Johnson is entitled to the Within Mentioned tract of
land.

                                          D. McGavock Register of
                                          West Tennessee

                                          By H. W. McGavock
                                          D. Register
Registered Dec. 22nd. 1828.   Jno. Kelly Register.

P-344.   State of Tennessee   )
)   The Undersigned Commissioners
)   and surveyors (duly Authorized)
)   have agreeably to the terms of
the late Cherokee Treaty Concluded hath the City of Washington on the
twenty Seventh day of February one thousand eight hundred and Nineteen
surveyed and laid Off to George Lowrey six hundred and forty Acres of
land on the North Side of Tennessee river on Battle Creek,
          Beginning at two elms and a hornbean on the East side of Bat-
tle Creek thence east two hundred and twelve Poles to a stake at the
foot of a rocky Mountain (crossing the Public road at one hundred and
eight Poles) south crossing a rocky spur of said Mountain) one hundred
and sixty Poles to sugar tree thence south sixty four degrees east twenty eight Poles (along the foot of said Mountain) to a stake thence east
Ninety Poles to a hickory sourwood and forked beech on the Side of Mountain thence South two hundred and twelve Poles to a beech and elm thence
West three hundred and twenty Poles to a hornbean Crossing said Creek
three times thence North three hundred and seventy Poles to the beginning
Crossing the Creek at one hundred and Ninety four including his improvements as the Center thereof as Possible Surveyed the 13st day of January
1820.

                                          R. Hudson

Horace B. Houston
Drury Armstrong C. C.
Registered December 31st 1828.

                                          Robert Armstrong, Surveyor
                                          Jno. Kelly D. Register

P-345.   State of Tennessee   )
)   The Undersigned Commissioners and
)   Surveyors (duly authorized) have
)   agreeably to the terms of the late
                                          Cherokee One thousand eight hun-

P-345. dred and Nineteen Surveyed and laid off to Elizabeth Peck six hundred and forty (640) Acres of land on the North side of Tennessee.

Beginning at a sweet gum sapling and a bunch of White Oaks (about twenty Poles on the east side of a large spring) thence east three hundred and twenty Poles to a double White Oak (Crossing the Valley road at two hundred and forty eight Poles) thence south three hundred and twenty Poles to a small hickery (Crossing the branch at one hundred and eighty two Poles and the Georgia road at two hundred Poles thence West three hundred and twenty Ples to the beginning Crossing the road and Creek including her improvements as near the Center thereof as Possible.

Surveyed the 28th day of January 1828.

Drury P. Armstrong
Horce B. Houston D.C.

R. Hudson
Robert Armstrong
Surveyor

Registered January 17th 1829.

Jno. Kelly D. Register.

P-345. William Standifer
    To Deed.
   Samuel Standifer

This Indenture Made this 26th day of April in the Year of Our Lord one thousand eight hundred and Twenty five between William Standifer of the County of Marion and State of Tennessee of the one Part and Samuel Standifer of the County and State Aforesaid of the Other Part

Witnesseth that for and in consideration of the sum of one hundred and fifty dollars to him the said William Standifer in hand Paid the (P-346) receipt Whereof is hereby Acknowledged hath and by these Presents doth grant bargain sell alien enfross and confirm unto the said William Standifer his heirs and assigns forever a Certain tract or Parcel of land Containing one hundred and twenty five Acres be the Same More or less lying and being in the County of Marion on the North West side of Sequachee River,

Beginning at a black gum northwest Corner of James Standifer Survey thence along a line of Luke Standifer's forty five Acres N. 56 W. 98 Poles to Pointers on the West boundary line of the Original Survey thence along the same North 26 Poles to a dogwood thence east 16 Poles to an ash & Ironwood at the foot of the Mountain thence Along the same as it Meanders S. 77° E. 64 Poles thence North 77° E. 54 Poles thence North 52° E. 68 Poles S. 30° E. 40 Poles thence south 58° East to a branch Wash that runs out of the Mountain and With the same down as it Meanders and the Main dry Creek to the south boundary of said tract on sd James Standifers line and With his lines West to the beginning it being Part of a tract of land granted by the State of Tennessee to the said William Standifer for one hundred and eighty Acres by Grant No. 16093 With all and singular the Woods Water Water courses Profits Commodities hereditaments & Appurtenances Whatsoever to the said tract or Parcel of land belonging or Any Wise appertaining and the reversion and reversions remainder and remainders units rents and issues thereof and All the estate right title interest Property Claim and demand of him the said William Standifer his heirs and Assigns forever of in and to the Same and any Part or Parcel thereof either in

P-345. law or equity.

     To have and to hold the said one hundred and twenty five
Acres of land With the Appurtenances unto the said Samuel Standifer
his heirs and Assigns forever against the lawful title Claim and demand
of All and evry Person or Persons Claiming by from or Under Me Will Warrant and defend by these Presents.

     In Witness Whereof the said William Standifer hath hereunto
set his hand and seal the day and Year first Above Written.

Isaac Standifer   Attest   William Standifer
Luke Standifer

P-346. State of Tennessee

                        May Session 1825.

    Marion County Court

     Then Was the Within deed of Conveyance Proven in Open Court
by the Oaths of Luke Standifer and Isaac Standifer subscribing Witnesses
thereto ordered to be Certified for registration. Let it be registered.

                        Jno. Kelly Clk.
                        By G. W. Rice D. Clk.
                        Jno. Kelly D. R.

Registered January 21st 1829.

P-346. Commissioners & C.
            To   Deed. Lot No. 74   This Indenture Made this 21st
    Jesse Humble   day of February in the Year of
                                Our Lord one thousand eight Hun-
dred and twenty Seven between William Stone David Oats Burgess Mathews
Alexander Kelly William King William Stevens and David Miller Commis-
sioners in trust for the County of Marion and town of Jasper and their
Successors in Office of the one Part and Jesse Humble of the County of
Marion and State of Tennessee of the Other Part

     Witnesseth that for and in consideration of the sum of one hun-
dred and fifteen dollars to me in hand Paid the receipt of Which is hereby Acknowledged hath and by these Presents doth Grant bargain sell alien
enfroff and Confirm unto the said Jesse Humble his heirs executors and
Administrators a Certain lot of land in the town of Jasper known and designated in the original Plan of said town by lot No. Seventy four Containing one quarter of an Acre sold to Public Auction as the law directs

     To have and to hold the aforesaid lot of land With all and sing-
ular the rights and profits Omoluments and Appurtenances belonging or
any Wise Appertaining to the same to the Only use and behoof of him the
said Jesse Humble his heirs &c and the said Commissioners in trust as
aforesaid and Will as far as they are Authorized as Commissioners forever
Warrant and defend to the said Jesse Humble his heirs &c the above recited lot against the rights titles interest Claim and demand of all and
every Person or Persons Whatever.

     In Testimony Whereof We hereunto set our hands and seals this
day and date first Above Written.

S. Hicks   Wm. Stone   (seal)
Jno. Kelly   Attest   David Oats   (seal)
                                 Burgess Mathews)seal)
                                 Alex Kelly   (seal)
                                   Wm. Stiphens (seal)
                                   David Miller (seal)

P-347.   State of Tennessee

Marion County Court

February Session 1827.

Then Was the Within deed of Conveyance from the Commissioners in trust for the town of Jasper to Jessee Humble for Lot No. 74 in said town Was Acknowledged in Open Court by said Commissioners and Ordered to be Certified for registration.

Given under My hand and Private seal not having an official seal at office in Jasper This the 19th day of January 1829.

Jno. Kelly Clk.
By G. W. Rice   D.C.

(L.S.)
Registered Jan. 21st 1829

Jno. Kelly   D. Register

P-347.   Thomas Maxwell
          To   Deed
       John Wynn.

This Indenture Made this the sixteenth day of February in the Year of Our Lord one thousand eight hundred & twenty four between Thomas Maxwell & John Maxwell of the State of Tennessee and County of Marion of the Other Part & John Wynn of the same Place of the Other Part,

Witnesseth that the sd. Thomas & John Maxwell for and in consideration of the sum of one hundred dollars to him in hand Paid at or before the sealing & delivery of these Presents the receipt Whereof is hereby Acknowledged hath given Granted bargained & sold & release a Certain tract or Parcel of land Containing sixteen Acres More or less it being a Part of a Survey Made & granted Samuel McBee by the sd State of Tennessee situated lying and being in the said State & County Aforesaid on Sweetens Creek Water of Battle Creek in Sweetens Cove buting and bounding as follows,

beginning at Pointers on Jonathan Eves north boundary line N. 35° E. Seventy four Poles to a Poplar on said McBees North boundary line thence N. eight Poles to Pointers at the foot of the Mountain it being Robert McDowell North West Corner thence With the Mountain south sixty nine east to a Spring branch that runs from the Mountain between Where John Maxwell & Henry Cotcher now lives it being the Conditional line Made between Thomas Maxwell & John Maxwell thence south course on said line to a hornbean on the bank of the dry Creek leading from Samuel McBee down the Cove thence down sd creek with all its Meanders to the Main Creek At the sd Eves & McBee line Thence West on said line to the beginning

To have and to hold the aforesaid land with all and singular the rights Properties & Appurtenances thereof & unto the same being or any Wise Appertaining With the only Proper use and behoof of him the said John Wynn his heirs and assigns that before released land and bargained Premises then the sd Thomas & John Maxwell Will Warrant and forever de-
(P-348)   fend the rights & title of the said land from themselves their heirs executors Administrators & Assigns & all other Person Whatever.

In Witness Whereof We the sd Thos. & John Maxwell have hereunto set our hands and affixed our Seals the day And Year first Above Written.

In Presence of

Robert Beene Jr.   Thos. Maxwell   (seal)
A. R. Johnson.   John Maxwell   (seal)

P-348. State of Tennessee
                                         February Term 1824
        Marion County Court

        Then Was the Within deed of Conveyance from Thomas Maxwell to
John Wynn duly Acknowledged in Open Court by the said Maxwell and ordered
to be Certified and Admitted to record.
        Given under My hand and Private seal not having an official
seal at office this the 21st day of January 1829.

                                         Jno. Kelly   Clk.
                                         By G. W. Rice   D. C.
(L.S.)   Jno. Kelly D. Register
Registered January 21st. 1829.

P-348. Hercules Jones
             To   Deed   This Indenture Made this the twen-
        Thomas Jones   ty Nineth day of Dec. in the Year
                                           of our Lord one thousand eight hun-
dred and twenty seven between Hercules Jones for in and in consideration
of the Sum of fifteen hundred dollars to him in hand Paid the receipt
Whereof is hereby Acknowledged hath and by these Presents doth grant bargain and sell alien enfross and Confirm unto the said Thomas Jones his
heirs and assigns forever a Certain tract or Parcel of land Containing
one hundred and eighty three Acres be the same More or less lying on
the northwest side of Sequachie adjoining lands of Adam Clemons bounded
as follows to Wit
        Beginning at a Post Oak on a Conditional With said Clemons
thence With said line 59 W. 46 poles to a double red oak thence _____
poles to a black Oak thence N. 29 E. one hundred and six Poles to a dogwood thence east Ninety Poles To Pointers thence S. two hundred and Nineteen Poles to two Post Oaks thence West to the beginning Then beginning
at a stake and Pointers on the North West of the branch Which Passs by
Jones to the West boundary of his one hundred and sixty Acre tract thence
West forty six Poles to a Stake and Pointers at the foot of the Mountain
With the same south twenty nine West eighty Poles to a Post Oak thence
forty six Poles to a black gum thence North Nine east With the line of a
tract eighty Poles to the beginning With all and singular the Woods Water
Water courses Profits Commodities hereditaments and appurtenances to the
said tract of land belonging or appertaining and the reversion and reversions remainder and remainders rents and issus thereof and all the estate
rights title interest Property Claim and demand of the said Hercules Jones
his heirs and Assigns forever of in and to the same and every Part or Parcel thereof either in law or equity
        To have and to hold the sd one hundred and eighty three acres
of land With the Appurtenances to the said Thomas Jones his heirs assigns forever Against the lawful title Claim and demand of all and every
Person or Persons Whatsoever I shall and Will forever Warrant and forever
defend by these Presents.

P-348.   In Witness Whereof the said Hercules Jones hereunto set his hand and Seal the day and Year Above Written.
Signed sealed and delivered in Presence of us

Joseph D. Minor   Hercules Jones.
Anthony B. Minor

P-349.   State of Tennessee   }
                                       }   February Session 1828.
         Marion County Court   }

Then Was the Within deed of Conveyance from Hercules Jones for 183 Acres of land in Marion County duly Acknowledged in Open Court by the said Hercules Jones and ordered to be Certified for registration.
Given under My hand and Private seal (Not having a seal of office) this the 28th day of February 1828.

                                       Jno. Kelly Clk.
                                       By G. W. Rice D.C.

(L.S.) Registered January 22nd 1829.

                                       Jno. Kelly Clk.

P-349.   Isaac Standifer   }
             To   Deed   }
         David Rankin   }   This Indenture Made and entered into this the 4 day of September one thousand eight hundred & twenty eight between Isaac Standifer of the County of Marion & State of Tennessee of the one Part and David Rankin of the County and State aforesaid of the other Part,

Witnesseth that for and in consideration of the sum of eleven hundred & fifty dollars to me in hand Paid the receipt Whereof is hereby Acknowledged that I the said Isaac Standifer have and doth by these Presents grant bargain sell Alien and Confirm unto the said David Rankin a Certain tract or parcel of land Containing two hundred and twenty Nine Acres situated lying and being in the County of Marion & State of Tennessee on the north West of Sequachie River adjoining lands Farrell Belsher Alford Standifer and Jemina Standifer Andrew Bronson and a fifty Acre tract belonging to the estate of William Standifer deceased and Alexander Fancher bounded and distinguished as follows,

Beginning at Pointers it being the S. W. Corner of the tract of land originally granted to illiam Standifer as Assigns of John Mill Sapp then along Belsher and the said Standifer's line North 140 Poles to a small black Walnut near a large Poplar stump then north 35 E. 48 Poles to a White Walnut on sd. Standifers branch then up the Same N. 25 W. 20 poles N. 45 W. 22 Poles S. 44 W. 6 Poles to a stake on the said Standifer line again then along the same N. 104 Poles to a stake and Pointers then E. 89½ Poles to Poles to Pointers then S. 179 Poles to a hickory S. E. Corner of a survey originally in the name of A. B. Bradford then east 20 poles to a black oak a Corner to William Standifer 180 Acres then along a line of the same north 124 Poles to Pointers then S. 44 E. 60 Poles to a Chestnut then down a hollow S. 11½ W. 54 Poles to a White oak then south 55 E. 48 Poles to Pointers thence N. E. Corner of the said Mill Sapp tract

P-349. then along the same and a Condition With Mill Sapp. W. 40 Poles
then S. 16 W. 140 poles to the beginning including two hundred and twenty
Nine Acres be the same More or less it being a Part of three tracts of
land two of Which Was granted by the State of Tennessee by William Standifer by grant No. 15386 & 17686 and one to Alex. B. Bradfprd by No. 15955
With the hereditaments and appurtenances

 To have and to hold the said tract or Parcel of land With its
Appurtenances to the said David Rankin his heirs and assigns forever from
the Claim and demand of all and every Person & Persons Whatsoever Claiming by through or under Me the said Isaac Standifer from the Claim and
demand of all and every Person or Persons Whatsoever.

 In Witness Whereof I have hereunto set my hand and seal this
day

 Signed sealed and delivered in Presence of James Chandoin
Burgess Mathews

       Isaac Standifer

P-350. State of Tennessee   }
         } November Session 1828.
 Marion County Court   }

 Then Was the Within deed of Conveyance from Isaac Standifer
to David Rankin for 229 Acres of land in Marion County this day duly Proven in the Court by the Oaths of Burgess Mathews and Isaac Chandionasubscribing Witness thereto and ordered to be Certified and admitted to
record. Let it be Registered .

       Jno. Kelly Clk.
       By G. W. Rice D. Clk.

Registered January 29th. 1819

       Jno. Kelly D. Register

P-350. Thomas Lackey   }
  To Bill of Sale } Known all men by these Presents
 Obediah Bean   } that I, Thomas Lackey of the State
           of Tennessee and County of Marion
for and in Consideration for the sum of five hundred dollars Paid the receipt Whereof is hereby Acknowledged hath bargained and sold delivered
unto Obediah Beens of the State and County Aforesaid for a Certain Negro
boy named Hiram about twenty years of Age Which said Negro boy I do Warrant and forever defend Against the right title Claim or interest of all
and every Person or Persons Whatever further I do Warrant said Negro boy
to be sound and free from any disorder or impedement Whatever.

 In Witness Wh ereof I have hereunto set My hand and seal this
the eleventh day of October one thousand eight hundred and twenty four.
 In Presence of us.

Isaac H. Roberts
Robert Been.   Attest   Thomas Lackey.

P-350. State of Tennessee   }
         } February Session 1825.
 Marion County Court   }

 Then Was the Within Bill of Sale from Thomas Lacksy to Obediah

P-350. Beene for one Negro Man Proven in Open Court by the Oaths of
Isaac H. Roberts and ordered to be Certified for Registration. Let it
be registered.

Jno. Kelly   Clk.
By G. W. Rice D. Clk.

Registered January 29th. 1829.

Jno. Kelly D. Register

P-350.   Jonathan Eves
   To   Deed
   Obediah Bean

This Indenture Made this the
eighteenth day of January in
the Year of Our Lord one thou-
sand eight hundred and twenty three between Jonathan Eves of the State
of Tennessee and County of Marion of the one Part and Obediah Beene of
the State and County aforesaid of the Other Part.
   Witnesseth that for and in Consideration of the sum of two
hundred dollars to him in hand Paid the receipt Whereof is hereby Acknowledged hath given Granted sold and Conveyed unto the said Obediah
Beene a Certain tract or Parcel of land situated lying and being in the
County of Marion Aforesaid on the Waters of Battle Creek in Sweetens Cove
   Beginning at a stake and Pointers West of said Eves Plantation
thence West six Poles to a sugar tree a Corner of said Eves Survey thence
West Ninety nine Poles to a beech and holly at the foot of the Mountain
thence With the same North six West eighteen Poles. Thence north Seventy
West forty six Poles to a black Oak thence North eight Poles to a hornbean thence with (North) forty one West thirty thence North sixty one
Poles to Pointers at the foot of the Mountain thence as it Meanders south
59 east sixteen Poles thence South thirty five east twenty four thence
south eighty eight east thirty six Poles to Samuel McBee thence south to
the said McBee line one hundred and thirty five Poles to Pointers on a
Conditional line between said Eves and McBee and With the same one hundred and fifty seven Poles to pointers thence south to the beginning.
Containing eighty four Acres More or less.
(P-351)   To have and to hold the Aforesaid land With All and Singular
the hereditaments and Appurtenances of in and to the same belonging or
my Wise Appertaining to the Only Proper use benefit and behoof of him
the said Robert Beene his heirs and Assigns forever And the said Jonathan
Eves for himself his heirs executors and administrators doth Covenent
and agree to and With the said Obediah Beene his heirs and Assigns forever that the before recited land and bargained Premises he Will Warrant
and forever defend Against the right title interest or Claim of him and
his heirs forever.
   In Witness Whereof the said Jonathan Eves hath hereunto set
his hand and affixed his seal the day and Year first Above Writen.
   Signed in Presence of

William Eves
John Maxwell

Jonathan Eves

P-351.   State of Tennessee

   Marion County Court

November Term 1823.

Then Was the foregoing Deed of Conveyance from Jonathan Eves to Obediah Beens for eighty four Acres of land Was this day Acknowledged in Court by the said Eves and Ordered to be Certified and Admitted to record. Let it be registered.

Jno. Kelly   Clk.
By G. W. Rice D. Clk.

Registered January 29th 1829.

Jno. Kelly Reg.

P-351.   George A. Brock
         To   Deed
         Thomas Maxwell

This Indenture Made this the 25th day of January in the Year of Our Lord one thousand eight hundred and twenty three betwixt George A. Brock of the State of Tennessee and County of Franklin of the one Part and Thomas Maxwell of the sd State and County of Marion of the Other Part,

Witnesseth that the said George A. Brock for and in Consideration of the sum of three hundred dollars to him in hand Paid by the said Thomas Maxwell at or before the sealing & delivering of these Presents the receipt Whereof is hereby Acknowledged hath given Granted bargained sold and released and by these Presents doth give grant bargain sell & release a Certain quanity of land Containing sixty Seven Acres land & two thirds More or less it being a Part of two Surveys forty Seven Acres and two thirds Surveyed & granted to Robert McDowell & twenty Acres Surveyed and granted to Samuel McBee situated lying and being in the said State & County of Marion on Sweetens Creek or Battle in Sweetens Creek butting and bounding as follows

Beginning at Pointers at the foot of the Mountain thence S. eight Poles to a holly it being Robert Beenes Jon N. W. Corner thence on sd Beenes line South sixty six Poles to Pointers thence W. eight two Poles to Robert McDowells West boundary line Pointers N. fifty five Poles to a sugar tree it being Samuel McBee Southeast Corner thence west eighty six Poles on sd McBees line to Pointers thence North thirty six east Seventy four Poles to a Poplar on said McBees North boundary line thence North eight Poles to Pointers at foot of the Mountain it being Robert McDowells North West Corner thence With the Mountain south sixty nine east one hundred and thirty five Poles to the beginning.

To have and to hold the aforesaid land With all and singular the rights Profits & Appurtenances thereof unto the same belonging or any Wise appertaining to the only Proper use & behoof of him the said Thomas Maxwell his heirs and assigns that the before recited land and bargained Premises the said George A. Brock Will Warrant & forever defend the rights & titles of said land from himself his heirs executors Administrators & Assigns & from all other Persons Whatever.
(P-352)   In Witness Whereof I the said George A. Brock have hereunto set my hand & affixed My seal this day & Year first above Written.
In Presence of

Obediah Beene
Levi Wamack

George A. Brock.

P-352.   State of Tennessee

         Marion County Court

November Session 1823.

P-352.   Then Was the Within deed of Conveyance from George A. Brock to
Thomas Maxwell for 67-2/3 Acres of land was duly Proven in Court by the
Oaths of Obediah Beene and Levi Wonnck, subscribing Witness thereto and
ordered to be Certified and Admitted to record.   Let it be registered.

                                        Jno. Kelly   Clk.
                                        By G. W. Rice D. Clk.

Registered Febry. 10th. 1829.

P-352.   Ruth Oglesby   {
              To   Bill of Sale   {   State of South Carolina
         John Morris   {   Pendliton District
                                       {

        Known all Men by these Presents that I Ruth Oglesby of the
State and District Aforesaid for and in consideration of the sum of Two
Hundred Dollars to Me in hand Paid by John Morris have bargained and
sold one Negro Man named Peter to said John Morris of the State of Ten-
nessee Which Negro I forever Warrant and defend to said Morris as good
Property and as lawful sale.
        Given under My hand & seal this 15th day of September 1815.
                                             her
Rigen Sprigg, Witness.   Ruth X Oglesby (Seal)
                                             mark

P-352.   The State of South Carolina {
                                      {
                                      { I Daniel E. Huger Presiding
                                      { Judge of Court of Common Pleas
                                         & General session of the Peace
in and for the State of South Carolina do hereby certify that John T.
Lewis Esquire Whose Certificate and signature Appears on the Book of
the bill of Sale hereto annexed from Wm. Ruth Oglesby to John Morris is
now and Was at the time the said Certificate bears date Clerk of the
Courts of Common PLeas and Registered of Marion County in and for the
District of Pendletof in the State of South Carolina and that in full
faith and credit is due and ought to be given to His his Certificate
and Signature as such and that the same is in due form or law.
        In testimony Whereof I have Caused the Public seal of the
Common Courts of Pleas for Granville District and State of South Caroline to be affixed to this (Seal) Granville Court house this the 16th
day of March A. D. 1829.
        Given under my hand.

                                        Daniel Huger

P-352.   The State of South Carolina {
                                      { I John H. Goodlett Clerk of the
         Granville District   { County Court of Common Pleas and
                                      { General Session of the Peace in
and for the District of Granville and State Aforesaid do hereby Certify
that Daniel E. Huger the Esquire Whose signature appears to the foregoing
Conveyance on this shett of Paper is Presiding Judge of the Court of Com-

P-352. mon Pleas and quarter Session of the Peace In the State of South
Carolina duly Commissioned Sworn and Acting as such and that due faith
and Credit is due and ought to be given to all his Certificates and official Acts as such.

In Tistement Whereof I have hereunto set My hand and affixed
the Public Seal of the said Courts at Granville Courthouse.
This the 16th day of March A. D. 1829
(Seal)

Jno. Kelly D. Register

J. H. Goodlett C.

Registered April 1 th 1829.

P-352. David Miller
        To   This Indenture Made and entered
    William C. Walker.   into this the 25th day of Sept-
                                    ember in the Year of Our Lord
one thousand eight hundred and twenty eight between David Miller of the
County of Marion State of Tennessee of the one Part and Wm. C. Walker of
(P-352) the County and State aforesaid of the Other Part,
        Witnesseth that the said David Miller for and in Consider-
ation of the sum of three hundred and fifty dollars to him in hand Paid by
the Wm. C. Walker the receipt Whereof is hereby Acknowledged bargained
sold and released and by these Presents doth bargain release and Convey
unto the sd Wm. C. Walker a Certain tract or Parcel of land situated lying and being in the County of Marion and State of Tennessee it being the
same Place Where the sd David Miller now lives a Grant No. 12433 and
bounded as follows, to Wit;
        Beginning at an ash on a line of James Lowery Reservation thence
With Rutledge line North sixteen to a box elder thence North fifty eight
West sixty two Poles to a Stake thence North 16° West sixty eight Poles
to a hackberry thence North firty Poles to a sugar tree at the foot of the
Mountain thence With the Meanderings of the same South 45° east thirty
seven Poles, South 5° East twenty Poles thence south eighty east ten
Poles south forty five ° east one hundred and five Poles thence forty
to a Stake on Lowerys line thence With same West to the beginning, together With all and singular the hereditaments and Appurtenances thereto
belonging or any Wise Appertaining and all the estate right title Claim
interest Claim or demand Whatsoever of him the sd David Miller either
in law or equity of in and to the above described Premises.
        To have and to hold unto the sd. Walker his heirs and assigns
forever .
        In Witness Whereof I have hereunto set my hand and seal the
day and Year above Written.

Samuel Jackson, Jnr.
Jermiah Ninty   X his   Attest   David Miller
                 mark

P-353. State of Tennessee
                                      November Session 1828.
        Marion County Court

        Then Was the Within deed of Conveyance from David Miller to

P-353. William C. Walker for fifty Acres of l nd Was this day Produced in Court and executed then and Proven by the Oaths of Samuel Jackson and Meamiah Ninty and ordered to be Certified for registration. Let it be registered.

Jno. Kelly   Clk.
By G. W. Rice   D. C.

Registered April 17th. 1829.

Jno. Kelly D. Reg.

P-353.   Thomas Davenport
         To   Deed
   William Shelton

This Indenture Made the 18th day of April in the Year of Our Lord eighteen hundred and twenty eight betwixt Thomas Davenport of the State of Tennessee and County of Marion of the one Part & William Shelton of the same Place of the other Part,

Witnesseth that the said Thomas Davenport for and in Consideration of the sum of one hundred dollars to him in hand Paid at or before the sealing and delivery of these Presence the receipt Whereof is hereby Acknowledged hath given granted bargained & sold & by these Presents doth give grant bargain & sell unto William Shelton his heirs and assigns forever a Certain tract or Parcel of land Containing seven Acres More or less situated lying & being in the sd. State & County Aforesaid on the N. W. Side of Sequatchee River hutting & bounding & follows

Beginning on a dogwood & ironwood Corner it being the said Sheltons Northeast Corner of his handred and fifty Acre survey running from thence North Wardly by a straight line to the northermost Corner of the sd. Shelton Survey on the Point of ridge to the sd. line supposed to be something Near one hundred & forty & fifty Poles in length thence east Wardly on the said Sheltons line With all its Meanders to the beginning to-gether With all and singular the receipt Members & Appurtenances thereof or any Wise appertaining thereunto the sd. tract or Parcel of land unto William Shelton his heirs & assigns forever & the sd Thomas Daven-(P-354)   port do Warrant & forever defend the rights and titles of sd. tract or Parcel of land from himself his heirs & assigns & from no other Person Whatever to the Shelton his heirs & assigns for their own Proper use benefit & Behoof.

In Witness Whereof I the   sd. Thomas hath hereunto set my hand & affixed My seal this day and date first Above Written in the Presence of

Thomas Maxwell
Joseph H. Francis,   Witness

Thomas Davenport.

P-354.   State of Tennessee

         Marion County Court

May Session 1828.

Then Was the forgoing deed of Conveyance from Thomas Davenport to William Shelton for Seven Acres of land Was Acknowledged in Open Court and ordered to be Certified and Admitted to record. Let it be Registered.

Jno. Kelly   Clk.
By G. W. Rice   D. Clk.

P-354.   Registered May 2nd. 1829. J.

Jno. Kelly   D. Register

P-354.   William Brumby
       To   Deed
    Abraham Coffelt

This Indenture Made the twenty Seventh day of January in the Year of Our Lord one thousand eight hundred and twenty

Seven between William Brumby of the County of Marion and State of Tennessee of the one Part and Abraham Coffelt of the State and County Aforesaid of the Other Part,

Witnesseth that the sd. William Brumby doth transfer his rights and titles of four Acres of land adjoining the said Coffelt and a Part in the Said Coffelts farm Which the said William Brumby Made and entered and has entered the sd. four Acres for sd Coffelt by his finding Money to Pay the entering of it for Which I said Brumby do transfer all my rights and title of the four Acres on the Southeast side of Big Sequachee River situated in said County

Beginning on a stake on Brannons line running West on sd. Coffelts line to a stake thence south two rods to a black Oak thence southeast to a stake thence With Goffs line to Brannons Corner thence to the beginning Which piece of land the said Brumby does Warrant and forever defend from him and his heirs to him the said Coffelt.

In Testimony Whereof the said William Brumby hath hereunto set his hand and affixed his seal this day and date first Above Written.

In Presence of

John Townson
Edmond Gouf

his
William   X   Brumby
mark

P-354.   State of Tennessee

    Marion County Court

November Session 1828.

Then Was the Within deed of Conveyance from William Brumby to Abraham Coffelt for four Acres of land Was this day Produced in Court and execution thereof Proven by the Oaths of Edmund Gauf a Subscribing Witness thereto and ordered to be further Proven.

Jno. Kelly   Clk.
By G. W. Rice   D. C.

P-354.   Abner Philips
       To   Deed.
    Richard Philips

This Indenture Made and entered into between Abner Philips and Richard Philips of the County

and State of Tennessee -

Witnesseth that for and in Consideration of the sum of one hundred dollars to him the said Abner Philips in hand Paid by the said Richard Philips Whereas this day the said Abner Philips hath in hand paid by the said Richard Philips Whereas this day the said Abner Philips hath acknowledged granted bragained and doth sell Certain tract or Parcel of land unto

P-355. him the said Richard Phillips lying and being in the County of Marion and on the North West side of Sequachee River

Beginning at a red bud on the bank of said River the South east Corner of Richard Philips 100 Acres survey thence up the river with its Meanders North Seventy Nine east fourteen Poles north Seventy east Ninety one Poles north eighty three east fifty Poles North sixty three east twenty four Poles North forty one West thirty four Poles North twenty Poles to Pointers Corner to Isabella Coopers Survey of 50 Acres thence With her line West thirty Poles to Pointers thence north forty two Poles to Pointers thence West fifty four Poles to Pointers thence south in Part With Richard Philips one hundred and fifteen Poles to the beginning With its appurtenances

To have and to hold said tract or Parcel of land With its Appurtenances to the said Richard Philips and his heirs forever.

In Witness Whereof I set my hand and affixed My seal May 25th 1828.

D. Rankin   Abner Philips   (seal)
S. A. Blevins

P-355.   State of Tennessee   }
                                               }   November Session 1828.
         Marion County Court   }

Then Was the Within deed of Conveyance from Abner Philips to Richard Philips for 50 Acres of land Was this day Produced in Open Court and executions thereof Acknowledged by the Conveyor and ordered to be Certified for registration. Let it be Registered.

                                               Jno. Kelly D. Register
Reg. May 4th. 1829.

                                               Jno. Kelly Clk.
                                               By C. W. Rice D. Clk.

P-355.   Isaac Roberts   }
              To   P. of Atty.   }   Known All Men by these Presents
         Isaac H. Roberts   }   that I Isaac Roberts of the Coun-
                                                   ty of Marion and State of Tennes-
see hereby Ordained Constitute and appoint Isaac H. Roberts of the County And State Aforesaid My true and lawful Attorney in My Name to act demand and receive in My name and instead a Certain legacy or estate coming to me of My Wife Susan Roberts (formally Susan Wynn) from the estate of Mathew Wynn (her father) of the State of South Carolina do hereby Authorize and empower in the Aforesaid Isaac H. Roberts in My name to sell or receipt or the name and to transact the same in every respect for Me as I Should or Could do Where I Myself Personally Present Now I do hereby ratify and Confirm all and every thing My said Attorney Shall or May do in and of the Premises herein before Mentioned in as full and Complete a Manner as if I Was Personally Present and transact the Same.

In Witness Whereof I the said Isaac Robert have hereunto set My hand and seal this the fifteenth day of November A. D. 1828.

P-355.   Signed and Delivered in Presence of

John Chilton   his
Wiley Belshar   Isaac X Roberts
                                         mark

P-355. State of Tennessee
                                     November S ssion 1828.
        Marion County Court

    Then Was the Within Power of Attorney from Isaac Roberts to Isaac H. Roberts this day Produced in Open Court and execution thereof Acknowledged by the said Isaac Roberts and ordered to be Certified and Admitted to Record. Let it be registered.

                                Jno. Kelly   Clk.

                                By G. W. Rice   D. Clk.

Registered May 4th. 1829.

                              Jno. Kelly D. Register.

P-356. Alexander Coulter
            To   Deed   This Indenture Made and entered
        George W. Rice   into this the thirty first day of
                              December in the Year of Our Lord
one thousand eight hundred and twenty eighty by and between Alexander Coulter of the County of Marion and State of Tennessee of the one Part and George W. Rice of the County and State Aforesaid of the other part,

    Witnesseth that for and in consideration of the sum of six hundred dollars to me in hand Paid by the said George W. Rice the receipt Whereof I do hereby Acknowledge have this day bargained sold aliened remise release Convey and Confirm and by these Presents doth grant bargain sell a Certain Piece or Parcel or lot of land lying and being in the town of Jasper and County Aforesaid Whereon Burgess A. Mathews now lives known and designated in the Original Plan of said town by Lot No. Sixty Six to-gether With all and singular the tenements hereditaments and Appurtenances thereunto belonging or any wise appertaining and the reversion and reversions remainder and remainders rents issues and Profits thereof and also all the estate right title interest Claim and demand to him the said George W. Rice his heirs and Assigns forever.

    To have and to hold the Aforesaid lot No. sixty six as aforesaid to him the said George W. Rice his heirs and assigns forever free and Clear of the lawful title Claim and demand of all and every Person or Persons Claiming by from through or under me or any other Person Will Warrant and forever defend the same to him either in law or equity.

    In Witness Whereof I the said Alexander Coulter have hereunto set My hand and affixed My seal the day and date Above Written.
    Signed and sealed and Acknowledged in Presence of

D. Rankin
    William   Alex. Coulter   (seal)

P-356. State of Tennessee
                                     February Session 1829.
        Marion County Court

P-355.   Then was the Within dee of Conveyance from Alexander Coulter to George W. Rice for lot No. sixty six in the town of Jasper This day Produced in Open Court And execution there of Duly Acknowledged by the Conveyance and Ordered to be Certified and Admitted to record. Let it be register.

                                    Jno. Kelly   Clk.
                                    By Geo. W. Rice   D. C.

Registered May 5th. 1829.

                                    Jno. Kelly D. Register

P-356.   William Brumby
                To   Deed.
         Edward Gauf .

This Indenture Made the twentieth day of November in the Year of Our Lord one thousand and eight hundred and twenty six between William Brumby of the County of Marion and State of Tennessee of the one Part and Edward Goff of the County and State aforesaid of the other Part,

        Witnesseth that the Said William Brumby for And in Consideration of the sum of three hundred dollars to him in hand paid at or before the sealing and Signing of these Presents the receipt Whereof is hereby Acknowledged hath Given Granted bargained and sold unto the said Edward Goff a Certain Piece or Parcel of land Containing eight five Acres More or less the beginning as such '-

        beginning on a black oak on the North Corner of Thomas Smith Near the bank of his Spring branch Thence running With his line South Ward to Townsens line then running West With said line to a black oak out side of Abraham Coffelt field then With the Conditional line to Ephriam Brannon West Corner and thence With Brannon To The Beginning Which I will (P-357) Warrant and forever defend from me or my heirs and if this covenant does not hold it is Plainly understood that I Will Not refund back.
        Given Under My hand and seal this

John Townsons
David Belcher   Test.

                                         his
                                William X Brumby
                                      mark

P-357.   State of Tennessee

                                    February Session 1829.

         Marion County Court

        Then Was the Within deed of Conveyance from William Brumby to Edmund Gauf for eighty five Acres of land in Marion County and execution thereof duly Proven by John Townson one of the subscribing Witness thereto Who Swears that he saw David Belcher attest the same as a Concurring Witness and that the said Belsher is a man resident of this State Ordered to be Certified for registeration.

                                    John Kelly   Clk.
                                    By G. W. Rice   D. Clk.

Registered May 6th. 1829.

                                    John Kelly D. Register

P-357   Edmund Gouff
          To   Deed.
        Ephriam Brannon

This Indenture Made the third day of November in the Year of one Thousand eight hundred And twenty eight between Edmund Goof of the County of Marion and State of Tennessee of one Part and Ephriam Brannon of the Other Part of said County and State,

Witnesseth that for and in Consideration of the sum of two hundred and eighty dollars to him in hand Paid the receipt Whereof is hereby Acknowledged hath and by these Presents doth bargain sell alien enfross and Confirm unto the said Ephriam Brannon his heirs and assigns forever a Certain tract or Parcel of land Containing eighty five Acres More or less lying and being in the County of Marion including the Place Whereon the said Edmund Gouf now lives

Beginning at a black oak on the North Corner of Thomas Smith line near the bank of his spring branch thence running With the said line one hundred Poles to a Stake and Pointers thence north With said line to a black oak Outside of Abraham Coffelts field thence With the Conditional to Ephriam Brannons West Corner And thence With brannons line to the beginning With All and singular the Woods Water Water Courses Profits Commodities hereditaments and Appurtenances to the said tract of land belonging or Appertaining And the reversion and reversions remainder and remainders rents And issue thereof And All the estate rights title interest Property Claim and demand of him the said Edmund Goff his heirs and assigns forever of in and to the Same and every Part or Parcel thereof either in law or equity.

To have and to hold the Said eighty five Acres of land With the Appurtenances unto the said Ephriam Brannon his heirs and assigns forever Against the lawful title Claim and demand of him the said Edmund Gauf his heirs assigns &c and all and every Person or Persons Whatsoever. Shall or Will Warrant And forever defend by these Presents.

In Witness Whereof the said Edmund Gauf hath hereunto set his hand and seal the day and Year Above Written.

Signed Sealed and delivered in Presence of

Peter Looney
Henry Young   Edmund Goof   (seal)

P-357.   State of Tennessee

                                         February Session 1829.
         Marion County

Then Was the Within deed of Conveyance from Edmund Gauf to Edmund Brannon for eighty five Acres of land in Marion County and exe-
(P-359) cution duly Acknowledged in Open Court by the said Edmund Gauf and Ordered to be Certified and Admitted to records.

                                   Jno. Kelly   Clk.

Registered May 5th. 1829.

                                   Jno. Kelly D. Register
                                   by G. W. Rice   D. Clk.

P-252. William Brumby   0
      To   Deed   0   This Indenture Made the 11th
     Lewis Johnson   0   day of October in the Year of
                   0   Our Lord one thousand eight

hundred and twenty five between William Brumby of the county of Marion and
State of Tennessee of the one Part and Lewis Johnson of the County and State
Aforesaid of the Other Part,

     Witnesseth that the aid Brumby for and in Consideration of
the sum of one hundred & 25 dollars to him in hand Paid the receipt is
hereby Acknowledged Hath and by these Presents bargained and sell alien
enfroas and Convey to the sd. Lewis Johnson his heirs and assigns forever said tract of land Containing fifty Acres lying and being in the
County of Marion on the South east side of Sequachie River adjoining the
lands of John Looney and Joel Hilliard b;

     beginning at a b..   orner thence South With
the same Seventy three Poles to   ointers sd. Looneys Corner thence West With his line sixty ...   ) Pointers on sd line
thence North Ninety Seven Poles to Pointers ... ice east one hundred forty
three Poles Passing the South west Corner of Turney & Rankin tract to
Pointers thence south twenty five Poles to a black oak on Hilliards line
the once West With the same eighty Poles to the beginning, Together
With all and Singular hereditaments and appurtenances to the sd tract of
land belonging.

     To have and to hold to the said Lewis Johnson his heirs and
assigns forever the fifty Acres of land With hereditaments and Appurtenances against the sd William Brumby and his heirs and Assigns and every
Person and Persons Whatever, Will Warrant and forever defend.

     In Witness Whereof the sd William Brumby have hereunto set
my hand and seel the day and date above Written. Now it is understood
that if the title Vested in Me by the tract of land I Will Not refund
the Purchase Money nor any Part of it and is released from any damages
Whatever.

     Signed sealed and Acknowledged in Presence of

W. R. Hickey   0   his
William Marcum   0   Wm.   X   Brumby   (seal)
John Looney   0   mark

P-358. State of Tennessee   0
                             0   February Session 1829.
     Marion County Court   0

     Then Was the Within deed of Conveyance from William Brumby to
Lewis Johnson for fifty Acres of land in Marion County and execution
thereof Proven in Open Court by the oaths of William Marcum and John
Looney two of the subscribing Witnesses thereto and ordered to be Certified and Admitted to record.
     Test

                                    J no. Kelly   Clk.
                                    By G. W. Rice   D. Clk.

Registered May 6th 1829.

                                    Jno. Kelly   D. Reg.

P-358. Erasmus Alley

      To   Bill of Sale

Alexander Coulter

Known all Men by these Presents that I Erasmus Alley Constable of Marion County in the State of Tennessee have this day sold to the higest bidder at in the (P-359) town of Jasper by Virtue of divers executions and one attachment two executions in favor of James Chaudoin for forty two Dollars and one in favor of Leeper and Chambers for thirty three dollars and forty three Cents One in favor of Saml Seay for Seven dollars and Seventy five Cents One in favor of Issac E. Price for ten dollars & Seventy five Cents and one in favor of John Webb for fifteen dollars; and one attachment in favor William P. Rice for four dollars and twelve and a half cents; and one execution in favor of Nichols Hands for thirty one dollars; and one in favor of Smith Panky for Nine dollars exclusive of Costs All of Which I have taken bond of indemnity to sell Agreeable to law (With the executions of John Webb and William P. Rice a Negro boy Named Abraham taken as the Property of Samuel Standifer by Virtue of the Aforesaid Presents and Whereas on this day I have sold by Virtue of the aforesaid of the Precepts to the highest bidder on the Public Square in the town of Jasper Aforesaid Negro boy named Abraham and Alexander Coulter became the highest bidder in consideration of the said sum of two hundred and one dollars to me in hand Paid as a Constable Aforesaid and in Consideration of said Precept together With the lawful Cost on the Same I the said Erasmus Alley do for Myself my heirs executers &C hereby Warrant and defend the rights and title to the Said Negro boy Abraham and to said Alexander Coulter from the lawful Claim And demand from the lawful Claim or demand of all and every Person or Persons Whatever.

    In testimony Whereof I have hereunto set My hand and seal this 10th day of 1829.

    Signed and Acknowledged in Presence of

Hopkins L. Turney

Thos. J. Haslerling

          Erasmus Alley   (seal)

P-359. State of Tennessee

Marion County Court

          February Session 1829.

    Then Was the Within bill of sale from Erasmus Alley to Alexander Coulter for a Negro boy named Abram and execution thereof duly Proven in Open Court by the oath of Hopkins L. Turney and Thomas J. Haserling the subscribing Witnesses thereto and ordered to be Certified and Admitted to record.

    Test

          John Kelly   Clk.

          By G. W. Rice   D. R.

Registered May 6th 1829.

          Jno. Kelley D. Register

P-359. Commissioners &C.

      To   Deed.

James Chaudoin

This Indenture Made this the 22nd day of August in the Year of Our Lord one thousand eight hundred and twenty eight between William Stone David Oats Burgess Mathews, Alexander Kelly and William King William Stevens and David Miller Commissioner in trust of the County of Marion in the town of Jasper and their suc-

P-359. cessors in office of the one Part and James Chaudoins of the
County of Marion and State of Tennessee of the Other Part,

Witnesseth that for and in consideration of the sum of three
hundred dollars to us in hand Paid the receipt Whereof is hereby Ack-
nowleaged hath and by these doth grant bargain alien enfcoff and Confirmed unto the said James Chaudoin his heirs executors and administrators two Certain lots of land in the town of Jasper known and designated
in the original Plan of said town by lots No. 87 and 88 Containing one
Quarter of an Acre each sold at Public Auction as the law directs.

To have and to hold the aforesaid lot of land With all and
singular the rights and Profits emaluments and appurtenances belonging
or any Wise Appertaining to the same to the Only use and behoof of him
the said James Chaudoins, his heirs etc. and the same to Commissioners
in trust as Aforesaid and Will as far as they are Authorized as Commissioners forever Warrant and defend to the said James Chaudoins, his
heirs etc. the above recited lots Against the right title interest Claim
and demand of all and every Person or Persons Whatever.

In Testimony Whereof we hereunto set our hand and seal this
day and date above Written.
        Test

S. Hicks
Jno. Kelly

Wm. Stone
Burgess Mathews
Alex. Kelly
David Oats

P-360. William Stevens
            to
        David Miller

February Session 1829.

Then Was the Within deed of Conveyance from the Commissioners
in trust for the County of Marion and town of Jasper to James Chaudoin
for lots 87 and 88 in Jasper and executions thereof duly Proven in Open
Court by the oaths of Stephens Hicks and John Kelly, subscribing Witnesses thereto and ordered to be Certified for registration.

Jno. Kelly Clk.
By G. W. Rice D. Clk.

Registered May 6th. 1829.

P-360. Luke Standifer
            To.   Deed
        William Campbell

This Indenture Made this 16th day
of December in the Year of our Lord
1828 by And between Luke Standifer
of the County of Bledsoe and State of Tennessee of the one Part and
William Campbell of the County of Marion and State aforesaid of the Other
Part

Witnesseth that the said Luke Standifer for and in consideration of the sum of five hundred dollars to him in hand Paid the right
of Which is hereby Acknowledged hath and doth by these Presents bargain
sell convey and confirm unto the said William Campbell a Certain tract
or Parcel of land situated lying and being in the County of Marion on the
Northwest side of Sequachie River containing eight Acres More or less being
a part of two sevral tracts or Parcels of land granted by the State of

Tennessee to William Arnett of the County of Marion and State aforesaid And Conveyed by said Arnett to said Standifer by Grant No. 18750 for one hundred and sixty Acres No. 18750 for thirty eight Acres Which said Tract of ninety eight Acres is bounded as follows to Wit

Beginning at an Ash above the head of a Spring it being the beginning Corner of the sid Arnett Survey of one hundred and sixty Acres then running down the branch of said Spring the Center of the Same being the line; South eighty one east eighteen Poles E. 17 Poles S. 49 E. 6 Poles to a stake in the branch and Pointers then along lane N. 47 E. 84 Poles to Pointers then North 80 Poles to a Post oak on the north boundary of said Arnett survey of thirty eight Acres then east along the same 57 Poles to Pointers; then South 85 Poles to a small hickory and Pointers then South 36° W. 52 Poles to a black oak then S. 40° W. 165 Poles to Pointers at the foot of the mountain, Then along the same N. 25° E. 9 Poles; N. 6° W. 22 Poles to the beginning.

(P-360) To have and to hold the aforesaid tract or Parcel of land With the appurtenances to the said William Campbell his heirs &c forever from the lawful Claims and demand of all others Claiming by through (P-361) from or under him the said Luke Standifer and from the Claim of all and every Person or Persons Whatever.

In testimony Whereof I the said Luke Standifer hath hereunto set My hand And seal the day and Year first herein Written.

Signed sealed And delivered in Presence of H. Montgomery.

J. B. Minor   Luke Standifer

P-361. State of Tennessee

                                          February Session 1829.

        Marion County Court

Then Was the foregoing deed of conveyance from Luke Standifer to William Campbell for Ninety eight Acres of land in Marion County Was this day Produced in Open Court and execution thereof Acknowledged by the Conveyance and ordered by the Court to be Certified for registration.

                                          Jno. Kelly D. Register

Registered May 28th. 1829

                                          Jno. Kelly Clk.
                                          By G. W. Rice D. Clk.

P-361. James Hickey, Admr.
            To   Deed.   This Indenture Made this the
        William Campbell   10th. day of December in the
                                    Year of Our Lord one thousand
eight hundred And twenty eight between James Hickey Administrator of the estate of John B. Griffith deceased of the County of Marion and State of Tennessee of the one Part and William Campbell of the County of Marion And State Aforesaid of the Other Part,

Witnesseth that for And in Consideration of the Part of entry Money paid by said Williams Campbell for entering the land from Which the title Above to be Conveyed Was founded the receipt of Which is hereby Acknowledged hath and by these Presents doth grant bargain sell Alien Enfcoff and Convey unto the said William Campbell his heirs & forever

P-361. a Certain Part of a tract of land Granted by the State of Tennessee
to John Griffith deceased for one hundred Acres by Grant No. 9818 bearing
date 2nd day of December 1824 situated lying and being in the said County
of Marion and bounded and described as follows.

Beginning at a Southwest Corner of an entry of one hundred
and sixty acrs entered by William Arnett thence West to the foot of Cumberland Mountain on said Griffith hs line thence With the Meanders of
said Mountain to the said entry of one hundred And sixty Acres Made by
said Arnett; thence With said line South Westwardly to the beginning including seventeen Acres be the same More or less to-gether With all Profits,
Commodities, hereditaments and appurtenances to the Aforesaid tract of
land;   To have and to hold to the said William Campbell his heirs
And Assigns forever free and clear of the lawful Claim and demand of him
the said James Hickey as Administrator of the said estate Above Mentioned
and no further.

In Witness Whereof I the said James Hickey Administrator hath
hereunto set my hand and seal the day and date first Above Written.

Signed Acknowledged in Presence of

Amos Griffith	James Hickey
Wm. S. Griffith, Attest	Administrator of estate of
	Jno. Griffith.

P-361. State of Tennessee

Marion County Court

February Session 1829.

Then Was the foregoing deed of Conveyance from James Hickey
Administrator of the estate of John Griffith decd. to William Campbell
for seventeen Acres of land and execution thereof duly Proven in Open
Court by the Oaths of Amos Griffith and William S. Griffith Subscribing
Witnesses thereto and admitted to be Certified for record.

Jno. Kelly   Clk.
By G. W. Rice   D. Clk.

Registered May 8th 1829.

Jno. Kelly D. Register.

P-362.   Thomas Shirley   Sr.
    To   Deed.
    Anderson Cheek

This Indenture Made this the
29th December 1828 by and between
Thomas Sherley Sr. of the County of Marion and State of Tennessee of the one Part and Anderson Cheek of
the County and State Aforesaid of the Other Part,

Witnesseth that for and in consideration of the sum of three
hundred And twelve and a half dollars to Me in hand Paid by the said Anderson Cheek I the said Thomas Shirley hath and Doth by these Presents grant,
bargain, sell and Confirm unto the Anderson Cheek a Certain tract or Parcel of land Containing sixty Acres situated lying and being in the County
of Marion on the north side of Sequachie River adjoining lands of John
Kelly and bounded as follows to Wit:

Beginning at a White oak Northwestwardly of a spring Made use
of by John Shropshire at the foot of the Mountain; thence south one hundred and six Poles to Pointers; thence east seventeen Poles to a Corner

of the said Kelly Survey of 140 Acres; thence the same course Continuing
along is line in all Seventy Seven Poles to a Stake Cherry and red bud
on the branch thence up the same N. 41° W. 28 poles North 17° east 20
poles to a White Oak and Sweet gum; thence North 1° east 31 Poles to a
black hau thence E. 11 Poles to Pointers thence North sixty Poles to
Pointers thence West to a Stake at the foot of the Mountain; thence
along the same a direct line to the beginning.

To have and to hold the Aforesaid tract or Parcel of land
With the appurtenances to the said Anderson Cheek and his heirs forever
from the lawful Claim and demand of all the every Person or Persons Whatsoever I the said Thomas Shirley Will Warrant and forever defend.

In testimony Whereof I have hereunto set my hand and seal the
day and Year first herein Written.

Signed sealed and delivered in Presence of

```
            his
Isaac   X   Steel
            mark
            his
Samuel  X   Brown
            mark
```

```
                        his
            Thomas   X   Shirley
                        mark
```

P-362.   State of Tennessee

Marion County

February Session 1829.

Then Was the Within deed of Conveyance from Thomas Shirley
to Anderson Cheek for sixty Acres of land in Marion County and execution
of Acknowledgement in Open Court by the Conveyor and Ordered to be Certified and Admitted to record.

Jno. Kelly   Clk.
By Geo. W. Rice D. Clk.

Registered May 8th. 1828

Jno. Kelly   D. Register

P-362.   Elizabeth Pack
    To   Deed
    Alexander Coulter

This Indenture Made And entered
this 17th day of January in the
Year of Our Lord one thousand
eight hundred and twenty Nine between Elizabeth Pack of the Cherekee
Nation of the One Part and Alexander Coulter of the County of Marion
and State of Tennessee of the Other Part,

Witnesseth at for and in Consideration of the sum of Seven
thousand five hundred to her the said Elizabeth Pack in hand Paid the
receipt Whereof is hereby Acknowledged hath and by these Presents doth
grant bargain sell and convey unto the said Alexander C. Coulter his
heirs and assigns forever a Certain tract or Parcel of land Containing
(P-363) six hundred Acres it being a reservation taken by the Said
Elizabeth Pack at on by Virtue of the Stipilation of a treaty Made and
entered into by John Calhoun Secretary of War and Certain Chief and herd-
men of the Cherekee Nation at the City of Washington on the 27th day of
February 1819 and Ratified by the President and With the Concent and ad-
vice of the Senate of the United States on the 10th day of March 1819

P-363. situated lying and being in said County of Marion and State aforesaid on the north West side of Sequachie River on Hudson Creek Surveyed
the 28th day of January 1820.

beginning at a small sweet gum sapling and a bunch of White
Oaks About twenty Poles on the east side of a large spring thence east
three hundred and twenty Poles to a double White oak thence South three
and twenty Poles to a hickory crossing the branch at one hundred and
eighty two Poles And the Georgia road and two hundred Poles; thence West
three hundred and twenty Poles to two Post Oaks, Crossing the Cheak at
one hundred thirty two Poles; thence North three hundred and twenty Poles
to the beginning With All and singular the Woods Water Water courses
Profits Commodities, hereditaments and Appurtenances Whatsoever to the
said tract or Parcel of land belonging or Any Wise Appertaining and the
reversion and reversions remainder and remainders rents and issues and
all the estate right title interest Property Claim and demand of her the
Said Elizabeth Pack her heirs and assigns forever of in and to the same
And every Part and Parcel thereof either in law or equity;

To have and to hold the Aforesaid six hundred acres of land
With its Appurtenances unto the said Alexander Coulter his heirs and
Assigns forever against the lawful title Claim and demand of all and
every Person or Persons Whatever Will Warrant and foever defend by these
Presents.

In Witness Whereof I hereunto set My hand and seal the day and
date first Above Written.

Signed sealed and delivered in Presence of

D. R. Rawling
Thos. J. Haserling   Elizabeth Pack   (seal)

P-363. State of Tennessee
                                            February Session 1829.
       Marion County Court

Then Was the foregoing Conveyance from Elizabeth Pack to
Alexander Coulter for six hundred acres of land in Marion County and
execution thereof duly Proven in Open Court by the Oaths of Daniel R.
Rawlings and Thomas J. Haserling, subscribing Witness thereto and ordered to be Certified and Admitted to record.

                                    Jno. Kelly Clerk.
                                    By Geo. W. Rice   D. C.

Registered May 12th. 1829.

                                    Jno. Kelly D. Register

P-363. Henry M. Rutledge
            To   Deed   This Indenture Made this the
        William Darwin   twentieth day of January in the
                                      Year of Our Lord one thousand
eight hundred and twenty between Henry M. Rutledge of the County of
Franklin and State of Tennessee of the one Part & William Darwin of the
County and State aforesaid of the Other Part

Witnesseth that for And in Consideration of the sum of one
hundred and sixty six dollars by the said William Darwin to the said
Henry M. Rutledge in hand Paid the receipt Whereof is hereby Acknowledged
he the said Henry M. Rutledge hath bargained & sold and by these Pres-

ents doth bargain sell alien, remise, convey & confirm unto the said William Darwin all that piece parcel or tract of land heretofore granted to the said Henry M. Rutledge by the State of Tennessee by Grant No. 16445 lying on the head waters of Battle Creek in the County of Marion (Tennessee)

(P-364)   Beginning on a Basin the lower corner of the tract sold to Benjamin Trussell and running With his Mountain South thirty Seven degrees east fifteen Poles to a stake the east thirty one Poles to a dogwood thence south sixty six degrees east four Poles to a White Oak thence With Dooley line North forty one degrees twenty eight Poles to Pointers; thence six degrees forty eight Poles to a hickory; thence North forty degrees east forty Poles to a hornbean thence North fourteen degrees east twenty three Poles to a White Oak thence With Brunnetts line West sixteen Poles to a dogwood thence North Seventy one degrees West forty two Poles to a Walnut thence With the Mountain south fifty degrees West fifty eight Poles to a box elder thence North sixty three degrees West thirty six Poles to a White Oak thence South thirty degrees West forty five Poles to a stake; thence With said Trussells line south twenty Poles to a hornbean thence south forty two degrees east forty Seven Poles to the beginning, Containing said Grant eighty three Acres.

To have and to hold the said tract of eighty three Acres be the same more or less to him the said William Darwin his heirs and assigns forever and the said Henry M. Rutledge for himself his heirs and executors doth Covenant to and With the said William Darwin his heirs and executors that he Will Warrant and defend the said bargained Premises the Claims or Claim of all Persons Claiming or Pretending to Claim through same under Color of title from the said Henry M. Rutledge.

In Witness Whereof he the said Henry M. Rutledge hath hereunto set his hand & seal the day & Year first Above Written.

Signed sealed and delivered in Presence of

P. H. Butler
Rollei P. Raines
John Goodwin

one hundred And sixty dollars interlines before signed.

H. M. Rutledge

P-364.   State of Tennessee   }
                                      }   February Session 1829.
         Marion County Court   }

Then Was the Within deed of Conveyance from Henry M. Rutledge to William Darwin for eighty three Acres of land in Marion Count. And execution thereof only Proven in Open Court by the Oaths of Rollie P. Raines and Pleasant H. Butler two of the subscribing Witnesses thereto and ordered to be Certified and admitted to record.

Jno. Kelly   Clk.
By Geo. W. Rice D. Clk.

Registered May 12th. 1829.

Jm. Kelly D. Register.

P-364. Jno. Bryant
  To Deed
David Oats.

  This Indenture Made this the 23rd day of February in the Year of Our Lord one thousand eight hundred and twenty eight between John Bryant of County of Marion and State of Tennessee of the one Part and David Oats of the County and State aforesaid of the Other Part.

  Witnesseth that for And in consideration of the sum of one thousand dollars to me in hand paid the receipt of which is hereby Acknowledged I the said John Bryant hath and doth by these Presents grant bargain sell Convey and Confirm unto the said David Oats his heirs and assigns forever a Certain tract or Parcel of land Containing Seventy two and one half acres situated lying and being in the County of Marion on the North bank of Tennessee River and bounded as follows to Wit

  Beginning at a Maple on the bank of said river at the Mouth of an inlet running thence North 9° W. 100 Poles to an ash West 98 Poles to a box elder thence South 75° West 42 Poles to a stake thence East one hundred sixty nine Poles (it being the line between the said John Bryant to a stake of the bank of the river; thence North 55° east 52 Poles to begin-
(P-365) ning including the house and improvements nnow occupied by said John Bryant

  To have and to hold the aforesaid tract or Parcel of land With all and Singular the Appurtenances &c to the said David Oats his heirs and assigns forever from the lawful Claim and demand of all and every Person or Persons Claiming by through from or under me the said John Bryant and Against the lawful Claim & demand of No other Person & Persons Whatever.

  In Witness Whereof I the said John Bryant hath hereunto set My hand and seal the day & Year first herein Written.
  Signed sealed & delivered in our Presence

        John Bryant

Wm. Rankin
A. Kelly Jr.

P-365. State of Tennessee

Marion County Court

  February Session 1829.

  Then Was the Within Deed of Conveyance from John Bryant to David Oats for seventy two and a half Acres of land in Marion County and execution thereof duly sworn in Open Court by the oaths of William Rankin And Alexander Kelly Jr., subscribing Witnesses thereto and ordered to be Certified and Admitted to record.

      Jno. Kelly Clerk
      By G. W. Rice D. C.

Registered May 18th 1829

      Jno. Kelly D. R.

P-365. Anderson Cheek
  To Deed
  Tarlton Blevins

  This Indenture Made this 6th February 1829 by and between Anderson Cheek of the County
of Marion and State of Tennessee of the one Part and Tarlton Blevins of

P-P-365.   the Other All of the County and State aforesaid,

Witnesseth that for and in Consideration of the sum of one hundred and fifty dollars to me in hand Paid by the said Blevins to the said Cheek I the said Cheek hath and doth by these Presents grant bargain sell and Convey and Confirm unto the said Blevins Certain tract or Parcel of land Containing fifty Acres situated lying and being in the County of Marion on the North West side of Sequachie River adjoining lands of sd. Creek and David Nichols,

Beginning at a stake in a field Corner to Nichols Corner thence With his line West forty two Poles to a stake in a field Corner to 10 acres Survey of said Nichols thence With the same and Passing the south east Corner of it south one hundred and Twenty two Poles to a dogwood thence east fifty five Poles to a Chesnut Near the foot of a ridge thence West one hundred and twenty six Poles to Pointers on Cheek line thence West twenty three (23) Poles to a Pointer on Nichols line thence with the same south to the beginning.

In testimony Whereof I have hereunto set my hand and affixed KMy seal the day and date above written.

signed sealed and delivered in Presence of

John Hail   ◊
Geo. W. Rice   ▌   Anderson Cheek

P-365.   State of Tennessee   ◊
                                             ◊   February Term 1829.
         Marion County Court   ◊

Then Was the Within deed of Conveyance from Anderson Cheek to Tarlton Blevins for fifty Acres of land in Marion County and execution thereof Acknowledged by the Conveyors and ordered to be Certified and Admitted to record.

                                         Jno. Kelly   Clk.
                                         By G. W. Rice   D. Clk.

Registered May 12th. 1829.

                                         John Kelly D. Register

P-365.   Samuel N. Pryn   ◊
             To   Deed   ▌   This Indenture Made this the
         John R. Nelms   ◊   sixth day of February 1829 from
                                      ◊   Samuel N. Pryor of the County
of Marion and State of Tennessee of the one Part and John Nelms of the
(P-366)   County and State Aforesaid of the Other Part,

Witnesseth that the said Samuel N. Pryor for and in consideration of the sum of one hundred And thirty dollars to him in hand Paid the receipt of Which is hereby Acknowledged hath bargained and sold unto the said John B Nelms through Cannon Cooper his heirs and Assigns a Certain Piece or Parcel of land situated in the County of Marion in the State of Tennessee on the south east side of Sequachie River Containing fifty Acres more or less adjoining the land of Heiziah Ward Andrew & Charlie Read, Scott Terry, and David Rankins,

Begginning at black oak the Northeast Corner of a 10 Acre Survey

(P-366) of said Rankin then With his line North Seventy Four Poles to a Stake & Pointers on the south boundary of said Ward 100 Acres survey then With the line of the same West twelve Poles to Pointers then North Nineteen Poles to Pointers said Wilson & Reads Corner of their 160 Acres Survey then West With the line of the same one hundred And forty Poles Crossing the Wagon road to Pointers on the east Boundary of said Terrys and Rankin three hundred And fifteen Acre Survey. Thence With the line of the same South ten degrees east Ninety five Poles to Pointers on the line of 16 Acres Survey of the said Rankin then With the line of the same east thirty six Poles Crossing said road Pointers on the West boundary of 50 Acres survey of the said Rankin then With the line then With the line of the same North sixty six Poles to a red oak thence east Seventy four Poles to Pointers then south sixty six Poles to a Spanish oak on the line of sd 10 acres survey then With the same East to the beginning including the Place Where the same Nelms now lives together With its appurtenances to the same.

  To have and to hold the said tract or Parcel of land hereby Conveyed With its Appurtenances to the said John B. Nelms And his heirs or assigns forever & the said Samuel N. Pryor Will forever Warrant and defend the title hereby Conveyed against the legal Claim of himself and his heirs assigns but not Against the Claim or Claims of any other Person & Persons Whatever.

  In Witness Whereof I the said Samuel N. Pryor doth hereunto set my hand and seal the day and date first hereinWritten.

  Signed and delivered in Presence of

Lewis Johnson
Claiborn Gott

     Samuel N. Pryor

P-366. State of Tennessee

  Marion County Court

     February Session 1829.

  Then Was the foregoing deed of conveyance from Samuel N. Pryor to B. Nelms for fifty Acres of land in Marion County and execution hereto duly Acknowledged in Open Court by the Conveyor and ordered to be Certified and Admitted to record.

     Jno. Kelly D. Register

Registered May 12 1829.

     Jno. Kelly   Clk.
     By Geo. W. Rice   D. C.

P-366. Pryor Samuel N.
    To   Deed   Page 222
  Wm. H. R. Shelton

     This Indenture Made this the sixteenth day of February A. D. 1829 between Samuel N. Pryor of the County of Marion and State of Tennessee of the one Part and William H. R. Shelton of the County And State aforesaid of the Other Part,

  Witnesseth that the said Samuel N. Pryor for and in consideration of the sum of eighteen dollars to him in hand paid the receipt of which is hereby Acknowledged hath bargained and sold unto the said Wil-

P-366.   liam H. R. Shelton his heirs and assigns a Certain tract or Parcel of land Containing twelve Acres be the same More or less situated in the County of Marion and State aforesaid on the South east Side of Sequachie River adjoining lands of Thomas Hopkins and Lane and bounded as follows to Wit

        Beginning at a stake & Pointers on the south boundary of said
(P-367)   Hopkins thirty five Acre Survey two Poles West of the Southeast Corner Where the West boundary line of his fifty Acre Survey intersects the same then South With the line of said fifty acres Survey forty one Poles to a stake and Pointer said Lanes Corner then With his line North sixty five degrees West Ninety five Poles to a stake & Pointers on Lanes line; then east With the line of said Hopkins thirty five Acres eighty six Poles to the beginning to-gether With its Appurtenances,

        To have and to hold the sd. tract or Parcel of land hereby Conveyed With its Appurtenances to the said William H. R. Shelton and his heirs or assigns forever and the said Samuel N. Pryor Will forever defend the title hereby Conveyed Against the legal Claims or Claim of himself and his heirs or Assigns but Not Against the Claim or Claims of Any other Person or Persons Whatever.

        In Witness Whereof I the said Samuel N. Pryor doth hereunto set My hand & seal the day & date first Written.
        Signed in Presence of us

D. Rankin   Samuel N. Pryor
   his
Wm   X Blevins
   mark

P-367.   State of Tennessee

                                    February Session 1829.

   Marion County Court

        Then Was the Within deed of Conveyance from Samuel N. Pryor to William H. R. Shelton for twelve Acres of land in Marion County and execution thereof duly Acknowledged in Open Court by the said Samuel N. Pryor and ordered to be Certified And Admitted to record. Let it be registered.

                                Jno. Kelly   Clk.
                                  By Geo. W. Rice D. Clk.

Registered July 24th. 1829.

                                Jno. Kelly D. Register.

P-367.   William Arnett
        To   Deed   This Indenture Made the 17th day
   Richard W. Stone   of February in the Year of Our
                                Lord one thousand eight hundred
and twenty Nine between William Arnett of the County of Marion and State of Tennessee of the one Part and Richard W. Stone of the County and State aforesaid of the Other Part;

        Witnesseth that for And in Consideration of three hundred dollars to me in hand Paid the receipt of Which is hereby Acknowledged hath and by these Presents doth grant bargain sell alien enfeoff And Convey

P-367. unto the Said Richard W. Stone his heirs and assigns a Certain tract or Parcel of land Containing fifty Acres situated lying and being in the said County of Marion on the Northwest Side of Sequachie River on Farmers Creek and bounded as follows to Wit.

Beginning at a black oak on the south side of said Creek near the big road thence N. 33° E. 86 Poles to a sweet gum on the bank of said Creek thence North 31° W. 60 Poles to a black Oak thence S. 40° W. 165 Poles to Pointers the south line of the Original Survey then along said line to the beginning Containing Said fifty Acres of land it being Part of land granted by the State of Tennessee to William Arnett for 160 Acres by Grant No. 18750 With All and singular the hereditaments and appurtenances thereto belonging or any Wise Appertaining.

To have and to hold the Aforesaid tract or Parcel of land With its Appurtenances unto the said Rich'd W. Stone his heirs or assigns forever free and Clear of the lawful title Claim and demand of all Manner of Person or Persons Whatever, I Will forever Warrant and defend so far as the title of the same is Vested in Me by the Grant from the State of Tennessee aforesaid.

In Witness Whereof I hereto set my hand & seal the day and date first above Written.

Amos Griffith	
John Rice Attest	Wm. Arnett.

P-368.   State of Tennessee

Marion County Court

February Session 1829.

Then Was the Within deed of Conveyance from William Arnett to Richard W. Stone for fifty Acres of land in Marin County and execution thereof duly Proven by the Oaths of John Rice and Amos Griffith the subscribing Witnesses thereto and Ordered to be Certified and Admitted to record.

Jno. Kelly   Clk.
By G. W. Rice D. Clk.

Registered July 25 1829.

Jno. Kelly D. Register.

P-368. Isaac Keys & Wife
        To   Deed
        John Cornett

This Indenture Made the 18th day of Feby 1829 between Isaac Keys & Elizabeth his Wife of the Cherokee Nation of the one Part and John Cornett of Jackson County Alabama of the Other Part,

Witnesseth that the said Isaac Keys & Elizabeth his Wife for And in Consideration of the sum of One Thousand dollars agreed to be Paid to the Said Keys & Wife by Said Cornett have bargained & Sold & by these Presents do bargain & sell to Said John Cornett his heirs all the right title interest Which they the said Keys & Wife have in or to the reservation of 640 acres of land lying in Jackson County Alabama on the Waters of Mud Creek being the same reserved to Said Keys & Wife Under the

P-363. treaty Made between the United States & the Cherokee Nation ratified at the City of Washington on the 27th day of Feby 1819.

To have and to hold the said reservation of 640 Acres to the
said John Cornett & his heirs in as full & ample a Manner as the said
Keys & Wife are Authorized to bargain and sell by Virtue of the treaty
Aforesaid & the Interest Vested in Under it and Whereas there is Contract relative to the Purchase of said Reservation the Conveyance to
Which is to be Made said Coornett on his Compliance With sd. Contract and
this deed is to be Acknowledged by us in the form & delivered to Samuel
B. Mead as an escrow until said Cornett Shall Comply With said contract
in the event he Complies the Conveyance to be delivered him & to take
effect absolute & in the event he fail or refuses then We Authorized
said Mead to receive Said Contract said Mead to be the Judge Whether this
deed is to be delivered & When or Whether the cotract is to be rescinded.

In Witness Whereof the said Isaac Keys & Wife have hereunto
set their hand & seal the day & Year first Above Written.

his
Isaac Keys   X
mark
her
Elizabeth X Keys
mark

P-368.   State of Tennessee   Feby Term 1829.

     Marion County Court

Then Was the foregoing deed of conveyance from Isaac Keys &
Elizabeth Keys his Wife to John Cornett for 640 Acres of land in Jackson
County Alabama Was duly Acknowledged in Open Court by the said Keys &
Wife and the said Elizabeth being examined by the Court separately &
apart from her husband says that she freely and Voluntarily Acknowledged
the same Without the Pursussion or threatening of her husband Whereupon
the said Deed is Ordered to be Certified for registration.

Jno. Kelly   Clk.
By Geo. W. Rice   D. Clk.

Registered July 28th. 1829.

Jno. Kelly   D. Register

P-368.   Isaac Keys & Wife
       To Power of Atty
       Samuel B. Mead

Known all Men by these Presents
that We Isaac Keys and Elizabeth his Wife of the Cherokee
Nation divers causes of good
Causes & Consideration has herewith Moved have Made consitited & Appointed & by these Presents do Make Constitue & appoint Samuel B. Mead of
Jasper Tennessee our true and lawful Attorney for us & in our Names to
receive & sue for & take Possession of Reservation of 640 Acres of land
lying on the Waters of Mud Creek in Jackson County Alabama between the
same reservation reserved to us in a treaty between the United States &
the Cherokee Nation ratified on the 27th day of Feby. 1819 Which Possession
(P-369) our said Attorney is to take for us & in Our Manner we Authorize

P-369.   our Said Attorney to ask demand sue for & receive all rents &
Profits that May Accrue or that have Accrued to us or either of us & due
& Owning from thire Now In Possession thereof or that May hereafter be in
Possession thereof & upon receipt of such rents & Profits to execute all
necessary receipts & Acquittance & to Comply With all contracts Which We
have or May have Made relative to said reservation & the Profits thereof
hereby ratifying & Confirming Whatsoever our said Attorney May do in the
Premises we further Authorize our said Attorney to receive any Contract
we May have Made relative to said reservation or the rents thereof if he
Shall think it expedient to do so Upon such terms as he May think fit &
to do all things touching the Premises either in law or equity or Otherwise
that We are ourselves could do Were we Personally Present.

        In testimony Whereof we have hereunto set our hands & seals
this 18th day of Feby. 1829.

                                          his
                              Isaac   X   Keys
                                          mark
                                          her
                              Elizabeth X Keys
                                          mark

P-369.   State of Tennessee
                                          }   February Session 1829.
   —   Marion County Court

        Then Was the foregoing Power of Attorney from Isaac Keys &
Elizabeth Keys his wife to Samuel B. Mead this day Produced in Open Court
and execution thereof duly Acknowledged by the said Isaac Keys and the
said Elizabeth Keys being examined separately and apart from her said
husband Acknowledged the same to be her Act and deed for the Purpose
Therein Contained and that She freely and Voluntarily signed the same
Without any threat or Compulsion from her said husband and the same is
Ordered to be Certified for registration.

                                   Jno. Kelly   Clk.
Registered July 28th 1829.   By Geo. W. Rice D. Clk.

                                   Jno. Kelly   D. R.

P-369.   Erasmus Alley
              To Bill of   Know all Men by these Presents
          Rolla Raines   }   that I Erasmus Alley Constable
                                          of Marion County Tennessee have
this day by Virtue of an execution to me directed by Dniel R. Rollins a
Justice of the Peace for the County aforesaid bearing date the third day
of February 1829 for Ninety dollars besides interests and costs Which
James Campbell Assignee of Hall and Kroft obtained against G. W. Wood &
Others and proceeded to sell the personal Property of Said Wood to Satisfy said execution this day after given ten days legal notice of the time
and Place have sold the following Species of Personalty to Wit

              One bed and Stead and furniture
              one Cupboard
              one Bureau
              one Sguar Chest

P-368.   three tables one of them dining
                                one Clock and Bed and furniture and
                                six Chairs b

being the Property of the said Wood further Consideration of eighty five
dollars and eighty one Cents to me in hand Paid by the said Rains he being
the last and higest bidder beama the Purchaser of all the Propertys Same
Not named in the face and Afore in this bond but have sold all the Property of the said Wood to the said Rains for the Consideration aforesaid and
by Virtue of My Warrant office doth Warrant the same to Rains Rolla P.
and his heirs.

            In Witness My hand and seal this the 20th day of February 1829.

                                                E. Alley   Constable

P-369.   State of Tennessee   }
                                         }   Febry Session 1829.
         Marion County Court   }

        Then Was the Within Bill of Sale from Erasmus Alley to Rolla
P. Rains for Personal Property this day Produced in Open Court and Acknowledged by the said Alley and ordered to be Certified for registration.

                                        Jon. Kelly Clk.
                                        By Geo. W. Rice   D. Clk.

Registered July 28th. 1829.

                                        Jno. Kelly, D. Reg.

P-370.   Commissioner   }
                    To   Deed.   } This Indenture Made the 28th day
                Burgess A. Mathews   } of August in the Year of Our Lord
                                          } one thousand eight hundred and
twenty eight between William Stone David Oats Burgess Mathews Alexander
Kelly William King William Stephens and David iller Commissioners
in trust for the County of Marion and town of Jasper and their Successors
in Office of the one Part and Burgess A. Mathews of the County of Marion
and State of Tennessee of the Other Part,

            Witnesseth that for and in consideration of the sum of one hun-
dred & seventy five dollars to us in hand Paid the receipt Whereof is hereby Acknowledged hath and by these Presents doth grant bargain alien enfeoff
and Confirm unto the Said Burgess A. Mathews his heirs executors and Administrators two Certain lots of land in the town of Jasper known and designated in Original Plan of said town by lots No. 45 and 46 Containing one
Quarter of an Acre each sold at Public Auction as the law directs.

            To have and to hold the aforesaid lot of land With all and sing-
ular the rights and Profits emoluments And Appurtenances belonging or any
wise Appertaining to the Same to the only use and behoof of him the said
Burgess A. Mathews his heirs &c And Said Commissioners in trust as of him
the said Burgess A. Mathews his and said Commissioners forever Warrant
and defend to the said Burgess A. Mathews his heirs etc. the above recited lots Against the rights title interest Claim and demand of al and every

P-370. Person or Persons Whatever.

In testimony Whereof We hereunto set our hands and seals this day and date first above Written

S. Hicks   Wm. Stone
Jno. Kelly   David Oats
                                                  Burgess Mathews
                                                  Alex. Kelley
                                                  William Stevens
                                                  David Miller

P-370.   State of Tennessee M   April Term 1829.

         Marion County Court

        Then Was the Within deed of Conveyance from William Stone David
Oats Burgess Mathes Alex. Kelly William Stephens & David Miller Commissioners in trust for the County of Marion & town of Jasper for lots No.
45 and 46 in the town of Jasper Proven in Open Court by the Oaths of Stevens Hicks and John Kelly subscribing Witness thereto & Ordered to be Certified for registration.
        Given Under My hand & Private Seal Not having Official seal of
office at office in Jasper this the 25th day of July 1829.

                                          J. P. Standifer Clk.
L. S.
Registered July 28th. 1829.

                                          Jno. Kelly D. Register.

P-370.   Thomas Maxwell
    To   Deed.   This Indenture Made the thirteenth
James H. Hornbeak   day of May in the Year of Our
                                  Lord One thousand eight hundred
And twenty Nine betwixt Thomas Maxwell of the State of Tennessee & County of Marion of the one Part & James Hornbeak of the Same Place of the
Other Part,
        Witnesseth that the sd Thos. Maxwell for and in considera-
tion of the sum of thirty dollars to him in hand Paid at or before the
sealing & delivering of these Presence the receipt Whereof is hereby Acknowledged have given granted bargained & sold & by these Presents doth
give grant bargain & Sell unto James H. Hornbeak his heirs & Assigns forever that tract or Parcel of land containing four Acres Surveyed & Granted to himself it being an entry Made by Said Maxwell in the entry Takers
office of Marion County of No. 384 dated the 31st day of December at
the rate of twelve & a half cent Per Acre by the sd Thomas Maxwell situated lying and being in the State & County aforesaid on Sequachie River
(P-371)   David McCord and Burgess A. Mathews Jr.
        Beginning on the northwest bank of said river on sd. Mathews
Line thence South Crossing the river Eighteen Poles to a Stake and ash
thence enters in Part With McCord line thirty six Poles to Stake on
top of the bluff; then North eighteen Poles to a White oak on the Southeast bank of sd. river thence West Crossing the river thirty Six Poles
to the beginning including enardian coal Shoal known by the Name of
Sloans Old Fish Trap Surveyed the 9th day of July, 1823 together With

P-371. all and singular the receipt Members & Appurtenances thereof And Any Wise Appertaining thereunto the sd. tract or Parcel of land unto James H. Hornbeck his heirs & Assigns forever & the Said Thos. Maxwell Do Warrant And forever defend the rights & titles of Sd. land from himself his heirs executors Administrators & Assigns & from No Other Person Whatever & if the sd land is ever taken by any Older right the Sd. James H. Hornbeck Shall lose it & I the said Maxwell Deed sd land to Sd. Hornbeck his heirs & Assigns for their own Proper use benefits & behoof.

In Witness Whereof I have hereunto set My hand & Seal this day & date first Above Written in Presence of

E. Horbeak
John Bryant

Thomas Maxwell

P-371.   State of Tennessee

Marion County Court

May Session 1829.

P-371.   Then Was the Within deed of conveyance from Thomas Maxwell & James H. Hornbeak for Acres of land in Marion County Was this day Produced in Open Court and exeation thereof Acknowledged by the Conveyor and Ordered to be Certified and Admitted to record. Let it be registered.

Jno. Kelly Clk.
By Geo. W. Rice D. Clk.

Registered July 30th. 1829.

Jno. Kelly   D. R.

P-371.   William R. Jones
              To.   Deed.
         John Jones

This Indenture Made this the 16th day of August in the Year of Our Lord one thousand eight hundred and twenty Seven between Wm. R. Jones of the County of Marion and State of Tennessee of the one Part and John Jones of the County and State aforesaid of the other Part,

Witnesseth that the said William Jones for and in Consideration of the sum of One hundred dollars to him in hand Paid the receipt Whereof is hereby Acknowledged doth and by these Presents doth grant, bargain Sell Alien encoff and Confirm unto the said John Jones his heirs and Assigns forever a Certain tract or Parcel of land Containing about one hundred Acres lying and being in the County of Marion on the North west side of Sequachie River adjoining the lands of John Hall beginning on a Poplar the Southwest Corner of a 100 Acre Survey belonging to J. Jones thence South Ninety Poles With Halls line to Pointers thence east one hundred and eight Poles to Pointers having Crossed Halls branch; thence North Ninety Poles to Pointers thence One hundred and eight Poles to the beginning With all its Appurtenances.

To have and to hold the said one hundred Acres of land With Appurtenances unto the said John Jones his heirs and Assigns forever Against the lawful title Claim and demand of all Manner of Persons Whatever Will Warrant and forever defend by these Presents.

In Witness Whereof the said Wm. R. Jones hath hereunto set his hand and seal the day and date first Above Written.

Signed and Acknowledged in Presence of us.

P-371.
Mark Hendrix
John Hall

Wm. R. Jones

P-371.   State of Tennessee

May Session 1829.

Marion County Court

Then was the foregoing Deed of Conveyance from Wm. R. Jones to John Jones for one hundred Acres of land in Marion County Was this day Produced in Open Court and execution thereof Proven by the Oaths of Mark Hendrix and John Hall Sworn Witnesses thereto and Ordered to be Certified and Admitted to record

Jno. Kelly   Clk.
By Geo. W. Rice   Clk.

Registered August 1st 1829

Jno. Kelly D. Register.

P-372.   Kelly John
        To   Deed
     Joshua T. Asburn

This Indenture Made this the 2rd day of July in the Year of Our Lord 1826 between John Kelly of the County of Marion and State of Tennessee of the one Part and Joshua T. Asburn of the County of Marion and State of Tennessee of the Other Part.

Witnesseth that for and in Consideration of the sum of two hundred and fifty dollars to him the said Kelly in hand Paid by the said Asburn the receipt of Which is hereby Acknowledged by these Presents bargained and Sold unto the said Joshua T. Ashburn his heirs and Assigns a Certain tract of land Containing fifty five Acres in two Parcels Situated lying and being in the said County of Marion on the North West side of Sequachie River adjoining lands of Tatum, Henry GRayson and Scott Terry,

Beginning on Stake and Pointers on the Southeast Corner of Said Taytoms Survey of One hundred then Along same North thirteen degrees east 107 Poles to a stake and Pointers said Grayson Corner then Along his line 77° E. 95 Poles to a stake and Beech and sweet Gum Pointers on Said Terrys line and With the Same Up a Branch South 45° West 39 Poles to a White oak then S. 45 Poles to a sweet gum & Elm then S. 54° W. 24 Poles to a White Oak And Beech then West of land Granted to the Said John Kelly for 140 Acres by Grant No. 17694 And One Other Parcel adjoining the same on the South and said Taytum & Rec Fredrick A. Ross

Beginning at a Stake In the Center of a branch on th east boundary of Said Ross Survey of 15 acres then Along his line North 16 Poles to Stake and Pointers on Said Taytums line and With same And a line of the Above described tract; East 92 Poles to a stake in the Center of Said Branch and up the Center of the Same as it Meanders to the beginning including five and one half Acres it being Part of a tract of land Granted by the State of Tennessee to Thomas Boily for 50 Acres by Grant No. 11610 and by him Conveyed the said Kelly Which said tract of land With all and igular its hereditaments and Appurtenances I the said John Kelly for Myself and My heirs forever do covenant & agree by these Presents to Warrant and forever defend to the said Joshua T. Asburn his heirs

P-373. &c free And Clear of the lawful title Claim & demand of all Manner of Persons Whatever.

In Witness Whereof I have hereunto set My hand & Seal the day & date Above Written.

Signed and Ack. in Presence of
his

Thomas X Bailey   )
        mark   )   John Kelly   Seal.
)
Samuel Walker   )

P-373. State of Tennessee   )
)   May Session 1829.
        Marion County Court   )

Then Was the Within deed of Conveyance from John Kelly to Joshua T. Ashburn for fifty five Acres of land in Marion County Was this day Produced in Open Court and execution thereof Registered August 4th 1829.

                                Jno. Kelly   D. Register
                                Jno. Kelly   Clk.
                                By Geo. W. Rice   D. C.

P-373. Hezikiah Austin   )
            To   Deed.   )   This Indenture Made this the twen-
        Luke Hendrix and Admrs   )   tieth day of May in the Year of Our
        Burgess Mathews   )   Lord 1828 between Hezikiah Austin
of the County of Marion and State of Tennessee of the one Part and Luke Hendrix and Burgess Mathews Administrator of the estate of Micajah Hendrix deceased of the County and State aforesaid of the Other Part,

Witnesseth that the said Hezekiah Austin for and in Considera-tion of the sum of twenty seven dollars and twenty cents to him in hand Paid by sd Hendrix And Mathews the receipt Whereof is hereby Acknowledged hath given granted sold Alien Conveyed and Confirmed unto the sd. Hendrix & Mathews their heir and assigns forever a Certain tract or Parcel of land situated lying being in the County Aforesaid on the North West side Sequachie River

Beginning at a stake and black Gum in Stevens A. Blevins 54 Acres Survey thence With his line South 88° east 88 Poles to Pointers on the line A. Cheeks 76 Acres Survey thence With this line of the same West 22 Poles to Pointers thence south 43 Poles to Pointers on D. Nichols line thence With his line West 33 Poles to a Post Oak; thence North; thence North thence east 78 Poles thence 7° east 38 Poles to a stake; thence North 16° West 24 Poles to a Stake & Pointers; Blevins line thence along the same to the beginning Surveyed the 29th day of Jan. 1823.

(P-374)   To have and to hold the aforesaid land With all and singular the rights profits emoluments hereditaments and appurtenances of in and to the same belong_ or any Wise appurtaining to the Only Proper use and behoof of him the sd. Hendrix Burgess Mathews their heirs and assigns and the sd. Austin for himself his executors and Administrators dth Covenant and Agree to and With sd Mathews and Hendrix their heirs and assigns that the before recited land and bargained premises he Will Warrant and forever de-fend Against the right title interest or Claim of all and every Person or

P-374. Persons Whatever.

In Witness Whereof the sd. Hezekiah Austin hath hereunto set his hand and affixed his seal the day and date above Written.

Signed Sealed and delivered in the Presence of

Henry H. Havron

Elizabeth M. Blovins
        her
Nancy X Blovins   Attest.
     mark

Hezekiah Austin

The Above Named deed is to be returned to the said Austin if he Pays the twenty Seven dollars and twenty five Cents With the lawful Interest.

Witness our hand and seal this day and date above Written.

Luke Hendrix
Burgess Mathews

P-374.   State of Tennessee

Marion County Court

May Session 1839

Then Was the foregoing Conveyance from Hezekiah Austin to Luke Hendrix for thirty five Acres of land in Marion County was this day Produced in Open Court and execution thereof Acknowledged by the Conveyor and Ordered to be Certified And Admitted to record.

Jno. Kelly   Clk.
By Geo. W. Rice   D. Clk.

Registered 3rd. 1829.

Jno. Kelly D. Register

P-374.   David Oats and
           Nathaniel Danil
              To   Deed for 70 Acres of land
        William H. Standifer

This Indenture Made the 10th day of _____ in the Year of Our Lord one thousand eight hundred And twenty eight by and between David Oats and Nathaniel Danil Ser. both of the County of Marion and State of Tennessee of the one Part and William H. Standifer of the County And State aforesaid of the Other Part:

Witnesseth that for And in Consideration of the Sum of four hundred & fifty Dollars to us in hand Paid the receipt of Which is hereby Acknowledged We the said Oats and Davy hath A doth by these Presents bargain, sell, convey and confirm unto the said William H. Standifer, his heirs and assigns forever a Certain tract or Parcel of land Containing Seventy five Acres situated lying and being in the County of Marion on the east bank of Sequachie River and bounded as follows to Wit:

On the South by the School land lot No. 2 on the West by Sequachie river on the North Woodson M. White line on the east by said Oats & Danil two hundred and two Acres tract it being the Undivided Part of

P-374. Said deed Made by Said _____ to the Said Oats and Daniel to the beginning, including the house Where Edwards now lives and the improvements above the branch.

To have and to hold the aforesaid tract or Parcel of land With All And Singular the Appurtenances &c to the Said W. H. Standifer his heirs and Assigns forever from the lawful Claim and demand of all and every Person or Persons Claiming by from or under us the said Oats and Daniel Will forever Warrant and defend there Presents.

In Witness thereof We the said Oats and Danil have bargained and set our hand and seal the day And Year above Written.
(P-375)   Signed sealed and Acknowledged in Presence of A. Kelly.

A. Kelly
David Kenton   David Oats
John Ball.   Nathaniel Davis

P-375.   State of Tennessee

          Marion County Court   May Session 1829.

        Then Was the Within deed of Conveyance from David Oats and Nathaniel Davis to William H. Standifer for Seventy Acres of land in Marion County Was this day Produced in Open Court And execution thereof Proven by the Oaths of David Kenton and John Ball subscribing Witnesses thereto and Ordered to be Certified And Admitted to record.

                              Jno. Kelly
                              By Geo. W. Rice   D. Clk.

Registered January 21st 1830.

                              John Kelly D. R.

P-375.   Samuel Standifer
              To   Deed   Known All Men by these Presents
          Jerima Standifer   that I Samuel Standifer of the
                                     County of Marion and State of Ten-
                                     nessee for And in Consideration of
the Sum of five hundred dollars to Me in hand Paid the receipt Whereof is hereby Acknowledged hath bargained & Sold & by these Presents doth bargain & sell unto Jernina Standifer of the County & State aforesaid two Negro boys named Jefferson and Abram about Nine Years & Jefferson Age about 5 Years.

To have & to hold the said Negroes boys to the Only Proper use & benefits of the said Jernina Standifer his heirs executors Administrators & Assigns forever.

I do hereby Warrant the title of said Negroes Against Myself My heirs executors Administrators and Assigns & all Other Persons Whatever.

In Witness Whereof I do hereby set My hand & seal this 21st day of April in the Year of Our Lord 188

Signed sealed and delivered in Presence of Wm. I. Standifer Jesse Rumble.

                              Samuel Standifer.

P-375. State of Tennessee

Marion County Court

May Session 1828.

      Then Was the Within Bill of Sale from Samuel Standifer to Jernima Standifer for two Negro boys named Jefferson and Abram duly Proven in Open Court by the Oaths of William I Standifer a subscribing Witnessthereto and Ordered to be Certified and Admitted to Record. Let it be registered.

Jno. Kelly Clerk
By Geo. W. Rice D. Clk.

P-375. State of Tennessee

Marion County

I Amos Griffith of the County aforesaid do hereby Certify the within Bill of Sale and fore-going Clerk Certificate was Registered in My Office in Book B, Page 135 and 136, Aug. 17th - 1818.

P-375. State of Tennessee

Marion County Circuit Court

October Term 1829.

      Then Was the Within Bill of Sale from Samuel Standifer to Jernima Standifer for two Negro boys named Jefferson and Abram duly Proven in Open Court by the Oaths of Jesse Humble subscribing Witnesses thereto and Ordered to be Certified and Admitted to record. Let it be registered.
      Test

Wm. I. Standifer Clerk.

Registered October 13th. 1829.

Jno Kelly D. Register.

P-375. John Southgate
      To   Deed.
    John Bridgeman

This Indenture Made this twenty seventh day of March in the Year of Our Lord one thousand eight hundred And twenty eight between John Southgate of the City of Norfolk and the Commonwealth of Virginia by John McIver his Attorney in Fact of the one Part And John Bridgeman of Bledsoe and State of Tennessee of the Other Part,
(P-376) Witnesseth that the said John Southgate for And in Consideration of the sum of four hundred and eighty dollars to him in hand Paid by the Said John Bridgeman at or before the sealing and delivery of these Presents the receipt Whereof is hereby Acknowledged hath granted bargained and sold alien released and confirmed and by these Presents doth grant, bargain and sell Alien release and Confirm unto the said John Bridgeman his heirs Assigns forever a Certain Piece or Parcel of land, situate, lying and being in the County of Marion Containing sixty six acres on the North West side of Sequachie River Creek or river including the farm and Improvements on Which Clisha Cha latly lived and being Within the bounds of said Southgate upper half of a Certain 10500 Acre tract on said Cheek Originally Patented in the Name of John Sevier bounded and describ-ed as follows to Wit:

P-376.   Beginning at a point in the Center of said Creek opposite to a box elder on the North West bank About sixteen Poles below the lower Corner of James Tract on the Opposite side of the Creek running thence North twenty five degrees West twenty Seven Poles to a Walnut sapling at the foot of a ridge thence South sixty six degrees West one hundred and five Poles to a black oak and dogwood thence South fifty four degrees West fifty one Poles to a Post oak in a flat hollow, thence South twenty degrees West thirty Poles to a Point in said Center of said Creek Opposite to a spruce Pine and Ardar on the Northwest bank; thence up the Center of Said Creek as it Meanders South degrees east Sixty five Poles; North Sixty four degrees East sixty Poles north twenty five degrees East twenty two Poles; thence North thirty five degrees east eighty five Poles to the beginning the Consideration being for Said tract being a hundred And thirty dollars

        Also one other tract Containing fifty four Acres Above and adjoining the Above aforesaid tract,

        Beginning at a Walnut sapling one of the upper Corner of said Above described tract running thence North fifty degrees West fourteen Poles to Pointers; thence North twenty Seven degrees East One hundred degrees and sixteen Poles to a hickory; thence North fifteen degrees East fifteen Poles to a Point in the Center of Creek Opposite to a beech on the north West bank Marked in the Center of said Creek Opposite to a boxelder on the Northwest bank Corners of the first Above described tract line of said tract North twenty five degrees West twenty seven Poles to the beginning, the Consideration for the last described tract being One hundred and fifty dollars together With and singular the appurtenances to the said tract of land belong or in any Wise Appertaining and the reversion or reversions remainder and remainders Rents issues and Profits thereof and every Part and Parcel thereof and all the estate rights demand interest; Property Claim and demand Whatsoever of him the said John Southgate his heirs and Assigns forever of in and to Same and every Part and Parcel thereof either in law at equity.

        To have and to hold the said tracts of sixty six and fourty four Acres of land herein before described With the Appurtenances unto the Said John Bridgeman his heirs And assigns to the Only Proper use and behoof of him the said John Bridgeman his heirs and assigns forever in (P-377)   fee and Clear of all Claims and Demands of him the said John Southgate his heirs executors and Administrators and of all and every Person and Persons Whatsoever Claiming by from or under him them or either of them and the said John Southgate for himself his heirs executors and Administrators both hereby Covenant the Premises and agree to and With the said John Bridgeman his heirs and assigns that if the said John Bri geman his heirs and Assigns Shall at any time hereafter be ejected from the Said bargained Premises or any Part thereof in Virtue of any title or titles Whatever More Valid in Same than the title Now Conveyed to him in Virtue of these Presents that then and in that Case he the said John Southgate Shall Pay and refund unto the Said Bridgeman his heirs or assigns at the rate of five dollars for the first tract and three dollars and fifty cents for the last tract per acre for each and every Acre from Which he or they Shall be so evicted by une Course of law With interest thereon from the time of such eviction.

        In Witness Whereof the said John Southgate his Attorney in

P-377. fact the aforesaid John McIver hath hereunto set his hand and seal the day and Year first herein Written.

Sealed and delivered in Presence of

A. Skillen   John Southgate
Samuel Cathy   By his Attorney in Fact
N. Young   John Iver

P-377. State of Tennessee

               May Session 1828.
  Bledsoe County

    Thn Was the Within deed of Conveyance from John Southgate to John Bridgeman for one Hundred and ten Acres of land in Marion County duly Proven in Court by the Oaths of Samuel Cathy and Nathaniel Young Witness thereto and Ordered to be Certified to the Proper County for registration.

    In Witness Whereof I Scott Terry Clerk of the Court of Please and Quarter Session for said County have hereunto set My hand and Private Seal Not having a seal of office at office in Pikeville the 12th. day of May 1828.

              Scott Terry Clk.

(L.S.)
Registered January 30th. 1830.

P-377. State of Tennessee
        To   State of Tennessee
     Pllatiah Chilton   No. 25534.
     Asabel Rawlings

    To All to Whom these Presents Shall Come greeting know Ye that by Virtue of Part of Certificate No. 1770 dated the 11th day of October 1820 issued by the Board of Commissioners for West Tennessee to Joseph Rogers for two hundred Acres and entered on the 5th day of December 1820 by No. 6569 as an Occupant (L.S.) Claim Under the Act of 1819 t here there is granted by the said State of Tennessee Unto Palatiah Chilton and Asable Rawlings assigns of the Said Joseph Rogers a Certain tract or Parcel of land Containing one hundred and sixty Acres by Survey bearing date the 27th day of March 1821 lying in the third district in Marion County on the north side of Tennessee River adjoining Eliza Bruce and bounded as follows to Wit;

    Beginning at an elm on the north bank of said river on a Conditional line between said Bruce and Eliphus Roberson thence along said Condition North fifty degrees east two hundred and sixteen Poles to a stake nd Pointers then South two hundred and one Poles to a Stake and Pointers on the North bank of said river thence down the Various Meanders of the same North Seventy four degrees West forty four Poles north eighty four degrees West forty Poles North eighty one degrees West forty Poles Seventy degrees West one hundred Poles to the beginning With the hereditaments.

(P-378) To have and to hold the said tract or Parcel of land With its Appurtenances to the said Palatiah Chilton and Asable Rawlings and their heirs forever.

P-378.   In Witness Whereof Samuel Houston Governor of the State of
Tennessee hath hereunto set his hand and Caused the Great seal of the
State to be affixed at Nashville on the 3rd day of November in the Year
of Our Lord one thousand eighty hundred and twenty Seven and of the Independence of the United States the fifty second.

Daniel Graham   By the Governor
Secretary   Samuel Houston

        Palatiah Chilton And Agable Rawling Are entitled to the Within
Mentioned tract of land.

                                    D. McGavock Register of
                                    West Tennessee

        By Hillt Harrison D. R.   Recorded in the Registers office
of West Tennessee December 4th 1827.

                                    I. I. Summer D. R.

P-378. Palatiah Chilton
            To   Conveyance Deed.   This Deed of Conveyance Made
        Asabel Rawling   this sixty day of May in the
                                          Year of Our Lord One thou-
sand eight hundred And twenty eight And fifty second Year of the Independence of the United States of North America between Palatiah Chilton
of the County of Rhea of the one part and Asbel Rawlings of the State
of Tennessee that the said Palatiah Chilton for and in Consideration for
the Sum of five hundred dollars to him in hand Paid the receipt Whereof
is hereby Acknowledged hath by these Presents doth grant bargain sell Alien
Encoff and Confirm unto the said Asbel Rawlings his heirs and Assigns
forever Undivided half of two Certain tracts or Parcels of land one
tract of forty acres the Other one hundred and sixty Acres (160) the
title thereunto derived from the State of Tennessee by Patent Grants
No. 25533 and 25534 and dated the third day of November eighteen hundred And twenty Seven recorded in the Registers Office of West Tennessee
the 4th. day of December 1827. Founded on entries Made by the Pricipal
Surveyors office of the third district by No. 6063 and 60 dated the fifth
day of December 1820 in the Name of Palatiah Chilton and Asbel Rawling
as locaters on Perference of rights Occupants in Elizah and Eliphy Roberson and by their Assigns and transferred to the said Asbel Rawlings to
Which said entries Were apllied Certificate No. 1770 on this the 11th
day of October 1820 issued from the Board of Commissions of West Tennessee to Joseph Rogers for two hundred Acres and Assigns by Elisha
Rogers Administrators of the Joseph deceased to said and Rawlings Surveyed the 27th day of March 1821 Which said Grants of land situated lying
and being in the County of Marion on the North bank of Tennessee River About
one Mile above the Mouth of the Sequachie Creek and bounded as follows,
to Wit;
        Beginning at an elm on the North side of said river the be-
ginning Corner of the said Chiton and Rawlings 160 acres surveyed running with the same East Ninety eight Poles to Stake and Pointers thence
North sixty eight degrees West one hundred and twenty three Poles along
a Conditional line With McCarity to a Maple; thence south sixty four
Poles to a stake and Pointers on a Conditional line With the Elija Bruce

P-378. and said McCarty thence South sixty degrees east twenty Poles
and Pointers on said Conditions thence With the same South thirty degrees West thirty Poles to a Stake and Pointer on the bank of the said
river thence a direct line up the beginning Containing forty Acres the
Other tract by Grant No. 20534, thus beginning at an elm on the North
bank of the said river on a Conditional line said Bruce and Eliphy Roberson thence along said Conditional North 50° West two hundred and sixteen Poles to a Stake and Pointers thence East forty Nine Poles to a
stake and Pointers thence South two hundred and One Pole to a stake and
(P-379) Pointers on the North bank of said river thence Down the Various
Meanders of the same North 81 West forty Poles North 81 West forty Polles
North 70 West one hundred Poles to the beginning Containing one hundred
and sixty Acres With the hereditaments and Appurtenances.

To have and to hold the said tract of land With its Appurtenances to the said Asbeal Rawlings and his heirs forever Against the title and demand of said Chilton his heirs and assigns forever he the said
Palatiah Chilton Will by these Present Warrant and defend to the said
Rawlings his heirs and assigns Against him the said Rawlings his heirs
and Assigns Against him the said Palatiah Chilton his heirs and assigns and
all and every Person or Persons Whatever as an underfeasable estate and
Whatever in fee Simple.

In testimony Whereof I the said Palatiah Chilton have hereto
set My hand and seal the day and date first herein Written lines before
signing the Word one Undivided half of to the 27th day of March 1831.

Signed sealed and delivered in the Presence of

Thos. I. Campbell
James Berry   P. Chilton

P- 379. State of Tennessee   May Session 1828.

Rhea County Court

Then Was the foregoing deed of Conveyance duly Acknowledged
in Open Court by Palatiah Chilton the bargainor therein named Whereof
said deed Was Ordered by the Court Do be Certified for registration to
the County of Marion in the State of Tennessee the State tax having been
Paid.

Given under My hand and Private seal not having an official
seal at office in Washington the 7th day of May 1828.

(L.S.)   James Berry Clerk.

P-379. Morriss John
          To   Bill of Sale   Received of J John W. Salmon
        John W. Salmon   Four Hundred dollars to a cer-
                                      tain Negro Man named Peter aged
twenty five Years Which Negro Peter I Warrant to the said Salmon his heirs
and assigns from me Mr. heirs and assigns and all ther Persons lawfully
Claiming or to Claim I also Warrant him to be sound healthy.

In Witness Whereof I do hereunto se my hand seal this the
15th day of January 1816.

Signed Sealed and delivered in Presence of

P-770.
Samuel Stewart   John Morriss

P-379. State of Tennessee   )
)   October Term 1829.
        Marion County Circuit Court   )

        Then was the Within Bill of sale from John Morriss to John W.
Salmon for one Negro named Peter duly Acknowledged in Open Court by the
Said John Morris and Ordered to be Certified for registration. Let it
be registered.

                                          Wm. I. Standifer   Clerk.

P-379.   Thomas Davenport   )
     To   Deed.   )   This Indenture Made this 14th day
     Alex. Perry   )   of October in the Year of Our Lord
)   one thousand eight hundred and twen-
ty eight between Thomas Davenport of the County of Marion and State of
Tennessee of the one Part and Alexander Perry of the County and State
aforesaid of the other Part,

        Witnesseth that the sd. Thomas Davenport for and in Consider-
ation of the sum of one hundred and twenty five dollars to him in hand
Paid the receipt Thereof is hereby Acknowledged, hath granted bargained
and sold unto the said Alexander Perry his heirs and assigns a Certain
tract or Parcel of land Containing one hundred and twenty eight Acres
More or less a Part of Which was granted by the State of Tennessee and
a Part of a deed of conveyance to sd. Davenport lying and being in County and State aforesaid and on Sequachie River adjoining the lands of Wm.
Sheltons and Harvey Hamilton,
(P-380)   Beginning at a stake and Pointers it being said Sheltons upper
Corner Nearest to the river of his hundred and fifty Acre Srvy thence
east twenty two and a half Poles to a hornbean on the said river thence up
the same as it Meanders North twenty one and a half east twenty six Poles
North thirteen east fourteen Poles North twenty four West twenty eight
Poles North Seven and a half West sixteen Poles North nineteen east
eighteen Poles North six and a half east twenty Poles North eleven and a
half West twenty Poles North Sixteen West twenty Seven Poles North eighty
two West eighteen Poles to a stake and Pointers on the bank of Said river;
thence North Crossing the Same twenty Poles to a stake and Pointers on
the Southeast bank of said river on said Hamiltons Lline thence West
thirteen Poles to a Stake on the river banks of said River on Said Hamiltons Corner Thence West thirteen Poles to a stake onthe river bank thence
With the same south Seventy four degrees West twenty Poles to an Iron Wood
Pointer on the river bank thence South four Poles to a stake in the river
then West thirty one Poles to a stake in the Same thence South six Poles
to a Pine on the North West bank of sd river; thence up said river North
twenty six West sixteen Poles to a Post oak on the bank of Said river;
thence West twenty Poles to Pointers thence With the Meanders of the
ridge South twenty West thirty eight Poles to Pointers thence South eighty
Nine West sixteen Poles to a White oak thence south sixteen degrees West
twenty eight Poles to a Stake nd Pointers thence south twenty three Poles
to Pointers Sheltons line thence With the same to the beginning to-gether
With all and some the Premises With appurtenances thereunto belonging or
in any Wise Appurtaining.

P-380.   To have and to hold the sd. land hereby Conveyed With the appurtenances to the Said Alexander Berry his heirs and Assigns forever the said Thomas Davenport himself and his heirs executors Administrators the aforesaid tract of land Premises under the said Alexander Perry his heirs assigns Against the Claim and Claims of all Persons Whatsoever doth and Will Warrant and defend by the Presents.

In Witness Whereof the sd. Thomas Davenport has hereto set his hand and seal the day and date above Written.

Thomas Davenport.

Signed sealed delivered in Presence of Saml. Pryor, Jurt.

James Stewart

P-380.   State of Tennessee   May Session 1829.

    Marion County Court

Then Was the foregoing deed of Conveyance From Thomas Davenport to Alexander Perry for 182 Acres of land in Marion County Was this day Proven in Open Court and execution thereof taken. James Stewart a Subscribing Witness tone to and ordered to be Certified for record.
        Probate Test.

Jno. Kelly
By Geo. W. Rice D. Clk.

P-380.   State of Tennessee   August Session 1829.

    Marion County Court

Deed of Conveyance from Thomas Davenport to Alexander Perry for one hundred and eighty two of land in Marion County Was this day Produced in Open Court execution further Proven by the Oaths of Samuel N. Pryor one of the Subscribing Witnesses thereto and Ordered to be Certified and Admitted to record

Jno. Kelly Clk.
By G. W. Rice   D. Clk.

P-380.   Thomas Kell Sr.   Known all Men by these Pres-
            To   Power of Attorney   ents that I Thomas Kell Sr.
         Thomas Kell Jr.   of the County of Marion and
State of Tennessee have Made Constituted and appointed Thomas Kell Jr. of the County and State Aforesaid My true and lawful attorney for me and in My Name and in My Place and Stead to take and receive of and heirs of Loudon Carter deceased in the Counties of Green Washington and Carter All in the State aforesaid or of any from their Attorney or Attorneys in their behoof lawful Authority I do Authorize Thomas Kell Jr. to receive a deed of conveyance to three hundred acres of land lying on the noth side of Sequachie River be it More or less in said lines Which the said heirs are bound to me for and also to Make deeds to such Part of said tract as I have Conveyed to different Persons Viz.: To David Stewart

p-581. to two miles of the bank of Dry Creek then down the said creeks
meanders to the Valley road 100 Poles; thence with said road to the line
of Griffiths 50 Acre Survey 20 Poles thence west thirty six Poles to
Pointers thence with B. D. Griffith line to the beginning fifty Acres be
the same more or less together with all and singular the Woods Water Mines
hereditaments and Appurtenances.

To have and to old hold unto the said Jesse Rogers, his heirs
And assigns forever lastly I the said James Jackson do bind myself my
heirs unto the said Jesse Rogers his heirs &c to Warrant and forever defend the sd. Tract of land with the appurtenances unto th said Jesse
Rogers his heirs forever free from the lawful Claims oof all and every
Person or Persons lawfully Claiming to Claim the same or any Part thereof.

In Witness Whereof I the said James Jackson have hereunto set My
hand and seal this day and date first above written Number of the Grant
13130 Ack.

Signed sealed and delivered in Presence of us,

Henry Greyson		his
his		James X Jackson
Dennis X Evans		mark
mark		

P-581.   State of Tennessee

Marion County Court   August Session 1829.

(P-582)   Then was the foregoing Deed of Conveyance from James Jackson
to Jessee Rogers for Fifty Acres of land in Marion County was this day
Produced in Open Court and execution thereof Acknowledged by the Conveyor and ordered to be Certified and Admitted to record.
Test.

Jon. Kelly   Clk.
By Geo. W. Rice D. C.

Registered Feby 5th. 1830.

Jno. Kelly D. Register.

P-582. W. H. Standifer
         To   Deed.   This Indenture Made the 9th day
        Amos Griffith   of August in the Year of Our Lord
                             eighteen hundred and twenty eight
between William H. Standifer of the County of Marion and State of Tennessee of the One Part and Amos Griffith of the County and State aforesaid of the Other Part,

Witnesseth that or ad in Consideration of the sum of four
hundred dollars to me in hand Paid the receipt of which is hereby Acknowledged hath and by these Presents doth grant bargain sell alien enfeoff and Convy Unto the said Amos Griffith his heirs and assigns forever
a Certain Part of a tract of lnd granted by the State of Tennessee to
the sd William H. Standifer for five hundred acres it being the nst end
of a two hundred and two Acres that the said William H. Standifer transferred to Nathaniel Davis and David Oats which Seventy Acres of the Same

P-382. has since been transferred back to the said William H. Standifer the above mentioned grant No. 8717 bearing date th first day of August 1854, situated lying and being in the said County of Marion the Above Seventy Acres lying and being in the said County of Marion and bounded and described as follows

Beginning on a White oak on the bank of Sequachie River and on the line of the lot of School field No. 2 then up the said river as it Meanders North 53 degrees east twenty six Poles thence North 28 degrees forty two Poles; thence North Nineteen degrees east thirty six Poles to a sweet gum thence east alto line running due south to the School line and West to the beginning as Will include Seventy Acres to-gether With all and Singular the woods, Water, Water course, Profits, Commodities hereditaments and appurtenances to the Aforesaid tract of land.

To have and to hold to the said Amo Griffith his heirs ad asigns forever free and Clear of the lawful title Claim and Demand of him the said William H. Standifer Person or Persons Claiming said Seventy acres tract of land forever Will Warrant and forever defend the aforesaid tract of land Said Amos Griffith his heirs &C.

In Witness I the said William H. Standifer have in Presence of James Standifer

Isreal Standifer   Attest

                                        Wm. H. Standifer

P-382.   State of Tennessee

          Marion County Court

          August Session 1829.

Then Was the foregoing deed Conveyance from William H. Standifer to Amos Griffith for Seventy Acres of land in Marion County Was this day duly Proven in Open Court and execution th ereof Proven by James Standifer one of the Subscribing Witnesses thereto and ordered to be further Proven by

                              Jno. Kelly   Clk.
                              By Geo. W. Rice   D. C.

P-382.   State of Tennessee

          Marion County Court

          November Session 1829.

Deed of Conveyance from William H. Standifer to Amos Griffith for seventy Acres of land in Marion County Produced in Marion County Produced in Open Court and execution thereof further Proven by the Oaths of Isreal Standifer a subscribing Witness thereto and Ordered to be Certified and Admitted to record. Let it be Registered

                              Jno. Kelly   Clk.
                              By Geo. W. Rice   D. C.

Registered Feb. 5th. 1830.

                              Jno. Kelly D. Register.

P-383.   Samuel M. Pryor
               To Deed of Con.
          Arthur Frogg

          This Indenture Made this the fourteenth day of August One Thousand eight hundred and twenty Nine between Samuel M. Pryor and of the

County of Marion and State of Tennessee of the one Part and Arthur Frogge

P-383. of the County of Marion and State aforesaid of the Other Part.

Witnesse h that the said Samuel M. Pryor for and in Consideration of the sum of one hundred dollars to him in hand Paid the receipt of Which is hereby Acknowledged hath bargained nd sold unto the said Arthur Frogg his heirs and Assigns forever a tract of land containing forty Acres More or less situated in Marion County aforesaid on the South east side of Sequachie River bounded as follows to Wit:

Beginning at a Stake and Pointers a North West Corner of a fifty Acre survey of John Maxwell's then With the same south 636 Poles to a White Oak Poplar Marked as Corner forSaid Maxwell on the brk of aid river then up the Same as it Meanders North 38° West 19 Poles North 48° West twelve Poles North 44° West sixty Poles North 29° West forty Poles to a dogwood And Pointers on the bank of said river and George Lanes Line then With th same east one hundred and sixteen Poles to a Swamp Oak said Same Corner of the line of Another survey Made in the name of said Lane Now in the Name of Thomas Maxwell or a part of it thence south With the same forty eight Poles to Pointers to said John Maxwell fifty Acre Survey then West With the Same to the beginning including house built by Benjamin Thomas Jr. on said 40 acre.

To have hold and enjoy the above Mentioned granted and bargained Premises to the said Arthur Frogg, his heirs and assigns forever and the said Samuel M. Pryor, his heirs &c do and Will Warrant and forever defend the title of the said land to the said Arthur Frogg his heirs and Assigns forever against the legals Claim of any Person or Persons Whatever.

In Witness Whereof he hath hereunto set his hand and affixed his seal the day nd Year first above Written.

Signed sealed and delivered in Presence of us

Mathew M. Pryor, Ggr.
Seth Pryor

Samuel M. Pryor

P-383. State of Tennessee

Marion County Court

August Session 1829.

Deed of Conveyance from Samuel M. Pryor to Aurther Frogg for fifty Acres of land in Marion County Was this day Produced in Open Court and execution thereof Acknowledged by the Conveyan and Ordered to be Certified for registration.

Jno. Kelly
By G. W. Rice D.C.

Registered Feby. 5th. 1830.

Jno. Kelly   D. Register

P-383. Henry J. Ternell
To   Deed
Austin Hackworth

This Indenture Made and entered into this the twenty fourth day

P-383. of July in the Year of Our Lord one thousand eight hundred and twenty Nine between Henry Yarnell of the County of Marion and State of Tennessee of the first Part and Austin Hackworth Jr. of the County ad State Aforesaid of the Other Part,

Witnesseth that for And in Consideration of the Sum of three hundred dollars to Me in hand Paid the receipt Whereof is hereby Acknowledged the said Henry J. Yarnell hath granted bargained Old and Conveyed And by these Presents doth grant bargain sell ad Convey Unto the S id Austin Hackworth And his heirs and assigns forever a Certain tract or Parcel of land lying in the County of Marion Aforesaid on the Northwest Side of Sequachie River Containing one hundred and six Acres More or less bounded as follows Viz.

Beginning at Corners the southeast Corner of Amos Griffith Survey of Ten Acres thence south sixty four degrees east Ninety Poles to Pointers thence South Ninety two Poles to a White oak thence east eighteen Poles to Pointers thence North Ninety three Poles Passing the South West Corner of Yarnells two hundred and ten Acre Survey and running a line of the same to black Oak thence East With the same thirty one Poles to Pointers thence North one hundred and twelve Poles to a Post oak the Northwest Corner of said forty Acres Survy. Then West With the Condition between (P-384) said Yarnell And said Hendren thirty two Poles to a Post oak thn North With said Condition twenty four Poles to a hickory on said Conditional line West fifty Poles to a stake And Pointers then south twenty one Poles to a stake thence thirty eight Poles to a stake and Pointers; thence south twenty Poles to Pointers at the foot of the Mountain thence With same forty sx degrees, West forty five Poles to a black haw bush; then east twenty four Poles thence south fifty five Poles to the beginning.

To have ad to hold the aforesaid tract or Parcel of land Unto the Said Hackworth and his heirs forever from the Claim and demand of all and every Person or Persons Claiming by through from or Under Me the said Henry J. Yarnell My heirs and assigns and from the Claim and demand of All and every Person or Persons Whatsoever I the said Henry J. Yarnell Will Warrant and forever defend.

In testimony Whereof I the said Henry J. Yarnell have hereunto set My hand ad seal the day Above Written.

Signed and delivered in Presence of

Alford Standifer
John Chiles
Jane Standifer
James Dunlap

Henry J. Yarnell

P-384. State of Tennessee

Marion County Court

August Session 1829

Deed of Conveyance from Henry J. Yarnell to Auston Hackworth for one hundred add six Acres of land in Marion County Was this day Produced in Open Court and execution thereof Acknowledged by the Conveyor and ordered to be Certified and admitted to record.

Test

P-384.

Jno. Kelly Clerk
By G. W. Rice D. Clerk

Registered February 6th. 1830.

Jno. Kelly, D. Register.

P-385. Fredrick Oyler
   To Deed
  James Chaudoin

This Indenture Made this 20th day of April in the Year of Our Lord one Thousand eight hundred and twenty Nine between Fredrick Oyler of the County of Marion and State of Tennessee of the first Part and James CHaudoins of the County And State Aforesaid of the other Part,

  Witnesseth that for and in consideration of the Sum of one hundred Dollars to him the said Fredrick Oyler in hand Paid the receipt Whereof is hereby Acknowledged hath and by these Presents doth grant bargain and sell alien enfcoff and Confirm unto the said James CHaudoins his heirs and assigns forever a Certain tract or Parcel of land Containing on hundred Acres lying and being in the County of Marion on the Southeast side of Sequachee River being a tract of land granted by the State of Tennessee to the said Fredrick Oyler by Grant No. 13342

  Beginning on a Post Oak thence east twenty four Poles to a black oak Near Rocky Ridge thence South ten ° West ninety Poles to two White Oaks thence south forty five West forty Poles to a black oak and White oak thence north eight ° West Ninety Poles to a hickory thence North thirty eight Poles to a post oak thence Noorth thirty east one hundred and fifty two Poles to a post oak; forty two Poles to a stake thence South forty Poles to the beginning including a Spring With all and singular the Woods Waters Water courses Profits, Commodities hereditaments and appurtenances Whatsoever to the said tract of land belonging or any Wise Appertaining and reversion and reversions remainders and remainder rents, and issus thereof and all the estate rights title Claims and demand of him the said Fredrick Oyler his heirs and assigns forever of in and to the same and every Part and Parcel thereof either in law and equity.

  To have and to hold the said one hundred Acres of land With the Appurtenances unto the said James Chaudoin his heirs and Assigns forever against the lawful title Claim and demand of him and every Person or Persons Claiming from by and Under Will Warrant and forevery defend by these Presents and the said Oyler covenants and agrees that the said tract of land above described Should hereafter be taken by any Older or better title than the one by these Presents Conveyed then and in that Case the said Oyler is to refund the same by him reced with legal interest from the time the said James Chaudoin Might be legally disposed of the aforesaid Premises by any Course of law.

  In Witness Whereof I hereto set My hand and seal the day and year first above Written.

  Signed and Acknowledged in Presence of Wm. I. Standifer.

Burgess A. Mathews

Fredrick Oyler.

P-383. State of Tennessee ⎬ August Session 1829

   Marion County Court

      Deed of Conveyance from Fredrick Oyler to James <u>Chaudoin</u> for
100 Acres of land in County of Marion Was this day Produced in Open Court
and execution Proven by the Oaths of William I. Standifer and Burgess A.
Mathews the subscribing Witnesses thereto and ordered to be Certified for
registration.
      Test.

                                    Jno. Kelly   Clk.
                                    By G. W. Rice   D. C.

Registered Feby. 7th. 1830.

P-386. Jerard Bronson ⎬

      To   Deed
   David Rankin

This Indenture Made the fourth day
of September in the Year of Our
Lord eighteen hundred and twenty
Nine between <u>Jerord</u> Bronson of the
County of Marion and State of Tennessee of the one Part and David <u>Rankin</u>
of the County and State aforesaid of the Other ͘

      Witnesseth that for and in Consideration of the sum of four
hundred dollars to him in hand Paid the receipt Whereof is hereby Acknowledged hath and by these Presents doth grant bargain sell Alien en-
<u>fooff</u> and Confirm Unto the said David Rankin his heirs a Certain tract
or Parcel of land Containing four Acres Situated lying and being in said
County of Marion on the West side of Little Sequachie it being a Part
of a tract of land granted by the State of Tennessee to Alexander Coulter for 160 Acres by Grant No. 1767

      Beginning at a Persimmon tree of the bank of said Sequachie
the beginning Corner of Said Grant then up Said Sequachie as it Meanders
S. N. 430 N. 36 Poles N. 31° W. 20 Poles; N. 11° W. 45 Poles; N. 6°
W. 22 <u>Pooles</u>; N. 3° E. 10 Poles to Hendrix Corner then With his line,
N. 16 Poles to a Stake thence S. 62° W. 12 Poles to a hickory then N.
60° W. 30 Poles to a Walnut then S. 72° W. 22 Poles to hickory then S.
16° E. 38 Poles to stake then S. 2 Poles 25° W. 30 Poles to Gum Hendrix
Corner in all 43 Poles to Pointers then With Wheelers line S. 34° E. 72
Poles to Pointers E. 27 Poles to a Hickory then N. 49° E. 19 Poles to
Pointers then running a Direct line to the beginning including fifty four
Acres be the Same More or less With all and singular the Woods Waters,
Water courses and the Appurtenances to the Said Rankin his heirs forever
free from the lawful Claims of the said Jerard Bronson his heirs and from
the lawful Claim of every Other Person or Persons Whatsoever.

      In Witness Whereof the Said Jerard Bronson hath hereunto set
his hand and seal the day & Year first Above Written.
      Signed sealed and delivered in Our Presence.

William Rice
James Rankin   ⎬   Jerord Bronson

P-386. State of Tennessee   ⎬
                                            November Session 1829
   Marion County

P-386

     T Deed of Conveyance from Jerard Bronson To David Rankin form fifty Acres of land in Marion County Was this day Produced in Open Court And execution of same Proven by the Oaths of William Rice and James Rankin subscribing Witnesses thereto and Ordered to be Certified and Admitted to record. Let it be registered.
     Test

                      Jno. Kelly Clk.
                      By Geo. W. Rice D. Clk.

Registered Feby. 7th. 1830.

                      Jno. Kelly D. Register

P-386. Thomas Brantley
        To   Deed
        Humphreys West

This Indenture Made this the twenty first day of _____ in the Year of Our Lord one thousand eight hundred and twenty seven between Thomas Brantley of the County of Marion and State of Tennessee of the one Part and Humphreys West of the Other Part

     Witnesseth that the said Party of the first Part for and in Consideration of the sum of fifty dollars to him in hand Paid at and before unsealing and delivery of these Presents by the said Parties of the Second Part the receipt Whereof is hereby Acknowledged hath granted ad bargained sold remise released conveyed and confirmed by these Presents doth grant bargain sell remise release conveyance Confirm unto the said Party of the second Part and to his heirs and Assigns forever a Certain Piece or tract or Grant situated lying in the town of Jasper known and (P-387) designated in the Plan of said town as lot No. 99 Containing one Quarter of an Acre to-gether With All and singular the tenements hereditaments Appurtenances thereto belonging oor Any Wise Appertaining and reversion and reversions remainder and remainders rents issus and Profits thereof and also all the estate right title interest Claim or demand Whatsoever of him the said Party of the first Part otherwise law or equity.

     To have and to hold to the said Party of the Second Part to the Sole and only Proper use benefit and behoof the second Party of the second Part his heirs and assigns and the said Party of the first Part for himself his heirs executors administrators and assigns doth hereby Warrant and Will forever defend the ever title of the above bargained Premises to him the said Party of the Second Part his heirs assigns forever free from the Claim or Claims of all and every other Person or Persons Whatsoever, as also from the Claim of the general Govement.

     In testimony Whereof the aforesaid Party of the first Part hath hereunto set his hand and affixed his seal the day and Year Above Written

G. W. Rice   his
John Rice   Thos.X Brantley
                       mark

P-387. State of Tennessee

        Marion County Court

May session 1829.

P-387. Deed of Conveyance from Thos. Brantley to Humphrey West for Lot
No. 99 in the town of Jasper Was this day Produced in Open Court and execution thereof Proven by the O ths of George W. Rice and John Rice Jr.
subscribing Witnesses thereto and Ordered to be Certified and Admitted
to record.

   Test

            Jno. Kelly Ck.
           By G. W. Rice D. Clk.

Registered Feby. 7th. 1830.

           Jno Kelly D. Register.

P-387. Andrew Bronson
    To Deed   This Indenture Made the 14th day
  David and Wm Rankin   of September in the Year of Our
              Lord one thousand eight hundred
and twenty Nine by and between Andrew Bronson of the County of Marion
and State of Tennessee of the one Part and David Rankin and William Rankin
of the County and State aforesaid of the Other Part,

   Witnesseth that the said Andrew Bronson for and in Consideration of the sum of Seven hundred dollars to him in hand Paid by the
said David and William Rankins the receipt of Which is hereby Acknowledged
hath and doth by these Presents doth bargain sell release and Convey unto the said David and William three Certain tracts or Parcels of land
Situated in the County of Marion and State Aforesaid the first Containing
one hundred and eleven Acres of Aand A bounded as follows, Viz.

   Beginning at a black oak the North east Corner of said Bronson survey of 49 Acres thence North 52 Poles to an Oak; thence East 70
Poles to a stake and Rawlings line thence along the same S. 74° East 38
Poles to a stake and Pointers thence east 36 Poles to a stake thence
South 116 Poles to a stake and Pointers thence West 146½ poles to a stake
on Said Bronson line and with the same North to the beginning. The next
49 acres and bounded as follows Viz.

   Beginning at the West Southwardly Corner of a survey Mad for
Luke Hendrix issue of Polly Corkem John Bronson at a black gum thence
With Said line North 37° east 20 Poles to a hickory thence east 42 Poles
to ablack Oak thence south Poles to a hickory thence West 114 Poles to
Pointers thence East to the beginning.

   The next Containing fifty Acres and bounded as follows, Viz.

   Beginning at a sake and Pointers on Said David Rankin line
of a tract of land he Purchased of Isaac Stanlifer thence West along the
Sma___ Poles to Pointers at the foot of Cumberland, thence With said
Mountain as it Meenders North thirty ° east 60 Poles north 67° East 40
Poles to Pointers at the foot of said Mountain thence east 34 Poles to
Pointers a Corner of Jonathan Popes Survey that he Purchased of Polly
Cox thence Along his line South fifty four east 52 Poles to a Stake on
the line of former survy of aid Bronson then With his line West 60 Poles
to Pointers then South 68 Poles Crossing the Wagon road ito the Corner of
the same the East With the said twenty four Poles to Pointers on the Same
then South leading in Part on a subway of Said Rankin 62 Poles to a stake
on the Same then West thirty Poles to a stake North With his line 93
Poles Crossing Said road to a stake Corner of Said Rankins then West With
his line 6 Poles to the beginning, Making in All two hundred and_____

P-389.   Land.

To have and to hold the Said tract or Parcel of land With their Appurtenances to the said David Rankin and William Rankin and their heirs forever from the lawful Claims of the Said Andrew Bronson And his heirs & from the lawful Claims of every Other Person or Persons Whatsoever.

In testimony Whereof I the said Andrew Bronson hath hereunto set his hands and seal the day and date first Above Written.

Signed sealed and delivered in Presence of us

William Rice   Andrew Bronson   (seal)
James Rankin

P-389.   State of Tennessee

                                                             November Session 1829.

         Marion County Court

Deed of Conveyance from Andrew Bronson to David Rankin and William Rankin for two hundred and ten Acres of land Was this day Produced in open Court and execution thereof Proven by the Oaths of William Rice and James Rankins Subscribing Witnesses thereto and Ordered to be Certified and Admitted to record. Let it be registered.
         Test

                                                    Jno. Kelly   Clk.
                                                    By Geo. W. Rice   D. C.

Registered Feby 7th. 1830.

                                                    Jno. Kelly   D. Register.

P-389.   Wm. Jones   D. Sheriff
              To   Bill of Sale
         David Oatts

Know All Men by these Presents that James Jones. Sheriff of the County of Marion by William Jones D. Sheriff has this day Sold at Public Sale as the Property of Polly Ann Holt a Certain Negro girl named Sarah and Whereas David Oatts became the highest bidder at two hundred and Seventy Nine dollars the receipt of Which is hereby Acknowledged And in Consideration of Which I do hereby Warrant and defend the title of the Said Negro Girl to the aid David Oas so far as Im Authorized to do as Sheriff Aforesaid and by Virtue of the Precepts on Which the said Negro Girl

In Witness Whereof I hereunto set My hand and seal this the 10th day of March 1828.

                                                    James Jones   Sheriff
                                                    By William Jones   D. Sheriff

Jno. Kelly D. R.
Rewling and D. Rankin

P-389.   State of Tennessee

                                                             August Session 1829.

         Marion County Court

Bill of Sale from Sheriff of Marion County by his Deputy Wil-

P-388. liam Jones to David Oats for Negro Girl named Sarah Was this day Produced in Open Court and execution thereof Acknowledged by the said William Jones and Ordered to be Certified for registration.

Test.

Jno. Kelly Clk.
By Geo. W. Rice D. Clk.

Registered Feby 8th 1830.

Jno. Kelly D. Reg.

P-388. Robert B. Cann
          To
       David Oats

Bill of Sale

For and in Consideration of the sum of three hundred dollars to Me in hand Paid by said David Oats I have and delivered unto the Said David Oats a Certain Negro girl named Elphy Slave during life about sixteen Years old Said Negro I Will Warrant and defend the right title Claim or demand of any Other Person or Persons Claiming by or through Me My heirs Under said David Oats and his heirs also I Warrant her to be sound in every Part clear of ani impedments Whatever.

In Witness whereof I hereto set My hand and seal the 4th day of June 1829

Signed and Acknowledged in Presence of A. Kelly Jr. Jurat Iac. Mins, John Ward Jurat

P-388. State of Tennessee

August Session 1329.

Marion County Court

Bill of Sale from Robert B. Cann to David Oatts for a Negro Girl named Roby Was Produced in Open Court this day and execution thereof Acknowledged by the said A. Kelly Jr., Iac. Mins and John Ward, Subscribing Witnesses and Ordered to be Certified for registration.

Test

Jno. Kelly Clk.
By Geo. W. Rice D. Clk.

Registered Feby. 8th. 1830.

John Kelly D. Register.

P-389. Burton Cooper
          To   Deed
       Samuel C. Francis

This Indenture Made and entered into this the thirty first day of July in the Year of Our Lord one thousand eight hundred and twenty Nine betwixt Burton Cooper of the State of Tennessee and County of Marion of the one Part & Samuel C. Francis of the same Place of the Other Part,

Witnesseth that the sd. Burton Cooper for and in consideration of the sum of two hundred dollars to him in hand Paid at or before the sealing and delivering of these Presents the receipt whereof is hereby Acknowledged have given granted bargained & sold and by these Presents doth give grant bargain & sell unto Samuel C. Francis his heirs add assigns a

P-389. Contain tract or Parcel of land Containing fifty Acres entered at
one cent per Acre Paid into the office of Entry of Marion County & entered on the 7th day of January 1826, Pursuant to a Provision of an Act of
the General Assembly of sd. State Passed of the third day of December one
thousand and twenty by No. 555 thence granted by the said state bearing
date the fifteenth day of June 1827 lying in the sd. County on the North
West side of Sequachie River Adjoining lands of Isabella Cooper; Jas. C.
Mitchell & Joseph Francis & Abner, Phillip and bounded as follows

Beginning at a stake and Pointers Isabella Cooper North east
Corner thence east two Poles to a stake said Mitchell Corner thence With
his line North twenty one Pooles to Pointer sd. Francis Corner thence
With his line West seventy seven Poles to his Corner thence the same course
Contained sixty Seven Poles in All one hundred and fifty four Poles to
Pointers thence south one hundred and four Poles to Pointers, thence east
eighty two Poles to Pointers on Phillips line thence With said Phillips
line North eighteen Poles to Pointers thence east eighty two Poles to Pointers thence east eighty two Pols to the beginning together With all and
singular the receipt Members and appurtenances thereof or any Wise appertaining thereunto the sd. tract of Parcel of land Unto Samuel C. Francis
his heirs and assigns forever and the sd Burton Cooper doth Warrant & forever defend the right title of sd land from himself his heirs executors
Administrators &c assigns & from all other Persons Whatever to the sd
Francis his heirs & assigns from their own Proper use benefit &C behoof.

In Witness Whereof I have set My hand and affixed My seal this
day and date first Above Written.

In Presence of Thomas Maxwell and Joseph H. Francis

Burton Cooper   (seal)

P-389.   State of Tennessee

Marion County Court

August Session 1829.

Deed Conveyed from Burton Cooper To Samuel C. Francis for fifty
Acres of land in Marion County Was this day Produced in Open Court and
execution thereof Ackd. by the Conveyor and admitted to be Certified for
registration.

Jno. Kelly Clk.
By Geo. W. Rice D. Clk.

Registered Feby 8th. 1830

Jno. Kelly D. Register

P-389.   Isabella Cooper
          To   Deed
         Samuel C. Francis

This Indenture Made this the
thirty first day of July in the Year
of Our Lord one thousand eight
hundred & twenty Nine between Isabella Cooper of the State of Tennessee
Marion County of the one Part & Samuel C. Francis of the same Place of
the other Part,

Witnesseth that the sd Isabella Cooper for and in Consideration of the sum of two hundred dollars to her in hand Paid at or before
the sealing and delivering of these Presents the receipt Whereof is hereby Acknowledged hath given granted bargained & sold & by these Presents

P-389. doth give grant bargain & sell unto Samuel C. Francis his heirs
& Assigns forever a Certain tract or Parcel of land Containing fifty acres
it being an Entry Made With the Entry Takers office of Marion County and
in the Act of twelve and one half cents per acre of No. 260 dated the
fifteenth day of July 1822. Situated lying in the State & County Aforesaid on the North West Side of Sequatchie River beginning at a stake &
Pointers on the bank of sd river thence the same as it Meanders North
five Poles North East twenty four Poles North fifty eight East forty Poles
North thirty East two Poles to a sweet gum on the bank of the river; thence
West eighty two Poles to a stake, thence South one hundred & twenty five
Poles to a stake thence East twenty Nine Poles to the beginning including
the Improvements Where the sd. Cooper now lives surveyed the 1st day of
May together With All & Singular the receipt Members & appurtenances thereunto the said tract or Parcel of land unto Samuel C. Francis his heirs
and Assigns forever to sd. Cooper do Warrant and forever defend the Right
& title of Said land from herself heirs executors Administrators & Assigns & from All Other Persons Whatever to the said Francis his heirs and
Assigns for their own Proper use benefit & behoof.

Witness Whereof I have hereunto set My hand and affixed My
seal the first above Written in Presence of

| Thomas Maxwell | | | |
| J. L. Francis | | Isabella Cooper | his X mark |

P-390. State of Tennessee

Marion County Court

August Session 1829.

Deed of Conveyance from Isabella Cooper to Samuel C. Francis
for fifty Acres of land in Marion County Was this day Produced in Open
Court and execution thereof Acknowledged by the Conveyance and Ordered to be Certified for registration.

Jno. Kelly Clk.
By Geo. W. Rice D. Clk.

Registered Feby 8, 1830

Jno. Kelly, D. Register

P-390. Abner Hargess
         To   Deed
     J. H. Akens

This Indenture Made this the 12th
day of July In the Year of Our
Lord one thousand eight hundred
and twenty eight between Abner
Hargiss of the one Part and John H. Akens of the Other Part noth of the
County of Marion and State of Tennessee,

Witnesseth that Abner Hargiss for And in Consideration of two
hundred to Me in hand Paid by said J. H. Akens the receipt Whereof is
hereby Acknowledged doth bargain Alien and Enfeoff and by these Presents
doth bargain sell Alien and Convey demised Certain tract of land Containing Sixty six Acres and 136 Poles lying and being in the County of Marion
in the State of Tennessee on the bad Waters of Battle Creek on a beech
at the foot of the Mountain thence North 50 West forty four Poles to

P-390. Pointers thence North 66 West forty Pointers thence North 58 West twenty four Poles to a black gum at the foot of the Mountain thence south 77 West twenty Poles to a stake in the dry branch thence twenty seven Poles to a Poplar and sugar tree at the foot of the Mountain South 52 East forty four Poles to Pointers at the foot of the Mountain South 43 East fifty six Poles to Pointers at the foot of the Mountain 21 East thirty three Poles to a Poplar thence Southwest twenty Poles 1 West twenty six Poles to a Sugar tree at the foot of the Mountain then Seven Poles to a Poplar at the foot of the Mountain then North And four Poles to the beginning at the foot of the Mountain said land lying and being in the County of Marion on Battle Creek.

To have and to hold With its rights Members and Appurtenances or any Wise to the same belonging to the said John H. Akens his heirs and assigns Administrators and Assigns forever the said Abner Hargess for himself his heirs Assigns executors and Administrators doth Coveyenent and the said J. H. Akens that the Said bargained Premises he Will Warrenty forever from him his heirs and assigns a Certain and a dministration and All Other Person or Persons lawfully Claiming as to Claim.
(P-391)   In testimony Whereof I do hereby set My seal the day and date above Written.

Signed in Presence of James R. Akeln and I. W. Salmon

his
Abner Hargess X
mark

P-391.   State of Tennessee

Marion County Court

August Session 1829.

Deed of Conveyance from Abner Hargess to John H. Akens for said six and one hundred and thirty six Poles of land in Marion County Was this day Produced in Open Court and execution th ereof Acknowledged by the Conveyor and Ordered to be Certified and Admitted to record.

Test

Jno. Kelly
By Geo. W. Kelly D. C.

Registered Deby. 8th. 1830

Jno. Kelly D. Register

P-391. Commisisioners
   To   Deed
   Samuel B. Mead

This Indenture Made this 19th day of April in the Year of Our Lord One thousand eight hundred and twenty eight between William Stone, David Oats Burgess Mathews Alexander Kelly William Stephens and David Miller Commissioners in trust for the County of Marion and town of Jasper and their successors in office of the one Part and Samuel B. Mead of the County of Marion and State of Tennessee of the Other Part

Witnesseth that for and in Consideration of the Sum of two hundred fifty dollars to us in hand paid the receipt Whereof is hereby Acknowledged hath and by these Presents doth grant bargain alien Enfcoff and Confirm unto the said Samuel B. Mead his heirs executors and administrators a Certain lot of land in the town of Jasper known and designated in the original Plan of land of said tgen by Lot No. 580 Containing one Quarter of an acre sold at Public Auction as the law directs.

P-391   To have and to hold the Aforesaid Lot of land With all and singular the right and Profits emoluments Appurtenances belonging or any Wise appertaining to the same to the only use and behoof of him the said Commissioners in trust as aforesaid and Will as far as they are Authorized as Commissioners forever Warrant and defend to the said Samuel B. Mead his heirs &c the Above recited lot Against the right title interest Claim and demand of all and every Person or Persons Whatever.

In testimony Whereof We hereunto set our hands and seals this day and date afore Written.

S. Hicks
Jno. Kellt   Attest

Wm. Stone	(seal)
Burgess Mathews	(seal)
William Sephens	(seal)
David Oats	(seal)
Alx Kelly	(seal)
David Miller	(seal)

P-391.   State of Tennessee
         Marion County Court

August Session 1829.

Then Was the Within Deed of Conveyance from William Stone, Burgess Mathews Alx Kelly David Oats David Miller, William Stephens Commissioners in trust for the County of Marion and Town of Jasper Was this day Produced in Open Court and execution thereof duly Proven by the Oaths of John Kelly and the Subscribing Witnesses thereto and ordered to be Certified for further Probate.
         Test

Jno. Kelly Clk.
By Geo. W. Rice D. Clk.

Registered Feby 8th. 1830

Jno. Kelly D. Register

P-391.   Samuel B. Mead.
             To   Deed.
         James Whiteside

This Indenture Made and entered into the 6th day of June 1828 between Samuel B. Mead of the County of Marion and State of Tennessee of the One Part and James A. Whiteside of the County of Bledsoe and Stae aforesaid of the Other Part

Witnesseth that the said Samuel B. Mead for and in Consideration of the sum of Two hundred and fifty dollars to him in hand Paid by the said Whiteside the receipt of Which is hereby Acknowledged hath and by the Presents doth grant bargain sell and Convey unto the said James A. Whiteside his heirs &c forever a Certain lot of land in the town of Jasper known and designated in the Original Plan of said town by Lot No._____Containing one quarter of an Acre it being the same Whereon George W. Rice lives.
(P-392)   To have and to hold the aforesaid lot of land With all and singular the rights and Profits emoluments and appurtenances belonging or any Wise appertaining to the same to the Only use and behoof of him

P-392. James A. Whiteside his heirs & assigns forever and the said Mead
Will Warrant and forever defend to the Whiteside his heirs &c the above
cinted Lot Against the right title interest Claim and demand of all And
every Person or Persons.

In testimony Whereof I have hereunto at My hand and seal this
date above Written.

Signed and delivered in Presence of I. G. Chambers, M. Luper
Witness

Samuel B. Mead

P-393.   State of Tennessee |
                                           | August Session 1829.
          Marion County Court |

Deed of Conveyance from Samuel B. Mead to James A. Whiteside
for lot No. 52 Jasper Was this day Produced in Open Court and execution thereof Acknowledged by the Conveyor and ordered to be Certified
for registration.

Test

Jno Kelly
By Geo. W. Rice

Registered Feby. 8th. 1830

Jno Kelly   D. R.

P-392.   Henry Lawrence |
            To   Deed | This Indenture Made this the thirteth
          Arden Griffith | day of November in the Year of Our
                                       | Lord one thousand eight hundred
and twenty seven between Henry Lawrence of the County of Marion and State
of Tennessee of the one Part and Arden Griffith of the County and State
aforesaid of the Other Part

Witnesseth that for and in consideration of the sum of two
hundred and fifty dollars to him the said Henry Lawrence in hand Paid
the receipt of Which is hereby Acknowledged hath and by these Presents
doth grant bargain sell alien snfcoff and confirm unto the said Arden
Griffith his heirs and assigns forever a Certain tract or Parcel of land
Containing seventy five Acres lying in the County of Marion adjoining a
forty acre entry of William now lives the place Where Lewis Johnson once
lived

Beginning at a black oak on a ridge northwardly from Mary
Heards and east Part of the said Ridge thence East seventy eight Poles
to Pointers thence south one and fifty four Poles to a Oak on the North
boundary of Brumleys fifty acres survey thence West in Part With the same
sixty eight Poles to a stake and Pointer North one hundred and fifty four
Poles Including _____ Acres bethe same More or less it being a tract of
land granted the said Henry Lawrence by the State of Tennessee for Seventy five acres by Grant No. 13350 With all and singular the Woods Water
Watercourses Profits Commodities hereditaments and Appurtenances Whatsoever to the said tract or Parcel of land belonging or any Wise appertaining and the reversion and reversions, remainder and remainders specie
thereof and all the estate right title interest property Claim or demand
of him the said Henry Lawrence His heirs and Assigns forever of in and to

P-392. the same and any Part and Parcel thereof Within law or equity to him the same Seventy five Acres of land With all the Appurtenances Arden Griffith his heirs and assigns forever against the lawful title Claim and demand of all and every Person or Persons Whatever Will Warrant and forever defend by these Presents.

In testimony Whereof the said Henry Lawrence doth hereunto set his hand and seal the day and date above Written.

In Presence of James Smith   David Griffith
Attest

Henry Lawrence

P-392.   State of Tennessee
                                                    November Session 1829.
             Marion County Court

(P-393)   Deed of Conveyance from Henry Lawrence to Arden Griffith for Seventy Acres of land was this day Produced in Open Court and execution thereof Proven by the Oaths of James Smith and David Griffith subscribing Witnesses thereto and Ordered to be Certified and Admitted to record. Let it be registered.
             Test

Jno. Kelly Clk.
By Geo. W. Rice D.C.

Registered Feby. 8th. 1830.

Jno. Kelly D. Register

P-393.   Churchwell Jackson
                 To   Deed
             Gabriel Lavorn

An Article of Agreement Made and entered into this the 15th day of August in the Year of Our Lord one thousand eight hundred and twenty Nine between Churchwell Jackson of the County of Marion and State of Tennessee of the one Part and Gabril Lavorn of the County and State aforesaid of the Other Part. The Condition of the Abouve Obligation is such that the said Churchwell Jackson hath bargained and sold and doth by these Presents bargain and sell unto Gabriel Lavorn a Certain tract or Parcel of land Containing one hundred and twenty Acres by survey bearing date the 27th day of February 1827 for two hundred dollars to him in hand Paid for the said tract or Parcel of land lying in said County on the southeast side of Sequachie River adjoining land of Arden Wilson and Charley Reeds and bounded as follows

Beginning at a beech on said Wilsons line thence West six Poles to Pointers on the bank of said river thence down the same With its Various Meanders Which is When Produced to a straight line three hundred and fifty five Poles to a beech a Corner of an eighteen Acre tract of said Reed Made in the name of Paul M. Williams thence With the line of the same East thirty Poles to Pointers thence South twenty eight Poles to Pointers on the line of said eighty eight acre survey at the goose Pond branch thence up said branch east fifty eight Poles to a sweet gum at said goose; thence With said Pond as it Meanders North sixteen degrees east sixteen Poles Northwardly sixty five east twenty two

197

P-393. Pol s North sixty E st twenty seven Poles North eighty two ° east twenty one Poles to a ogwood and hickory thence South fifty six east twenty four Poles to a White Oak at the head of said Pond thence East one hundred and six Poles to a south red oak thence North said Wilsons line in Part one hundred and six Poles to the beginning With said tract or Parcel of land the said Churchwell Jackson doth Will and truly Warrant and forever defend from the Claim or Claims of him his heirs forever.

Signed sealed and delivered in the Presence of us the day and date above Written.
Attest

Ephriam Brannon, and
James Jackson

his
Churchwell X Jackson
mark

P-393. State of Tennessee

August Session 1829.

Marion County Court

This Was the foregoing Deed of Conveyance from Churchwell Jackson to Gabriel Lovern for one hundred & wtenty Acres of land Was this day Produced in Open Court and execution thereof Proven by the Oaths of Ephriam Brannon and James Jackson the Subscribing Witnesses thereto and ordered to be Certified and Admitted to record.
Attest

Jno. Kelly Clk.
By Geo. W. Rice D. C.

Registered Feby. 9th. 1830.

Jno. Kelly D. R.

P-393. The Last Will and Testament
of
Jacob Watson Deceased

Now in the Name of God Amen.

Be it remembered that I Jacob Watson Senior of the County of Marion and State of Tennessee boing Weak in body but of sound Memory - Bless be God - do this day the twenty sixth day of August in the Year of Our Lord one thousand eight and twenty Nine Made and Publich this My last Will and Testaments in the following Manner Viz.

First of all I leave My body to be buried My lawful debts to be Paid and My furnal expenses. I offer up My Spirit to God Who gave it.

2nd. I Ordain that Nelly that all her increase be left With William Watson My first son and Sarah his Wife and there be remain as free With them till their death And the rest of the Children and their suving relations and never to be sold nor traded but remaining With the family from one to the other Shall remain free.
(P-394) 3rd. To Thomas Watson the second son a note of the Amount of One hun red and fifty dollars or his heirs signed by the said Watson and Now remain for use.

4th. I further more do bequeath to John Watson My fourth son My big Bible.

5th. I further more do ordain that Jacob Watson fourth son

P-394. to have berry the hogs and Cattle one feather bed and furniture
that he live with William Watson and that at his death Berry is to remain
his serving relative

6th. I furthermore do bequeath the remainder of My Property
that remaining in the hoes to be equally divided Among all My Children
by the judgement of the executors

I also Make and Ordain William and Aaron Watson sole Executors
of this My last Will and trust for the Proposes in My Will Contain.

In Witness Whereof I the said Jacob Watson Sen. have this day
to My last Will and Tesaments set My hand and seal the day and date Above
Written.

George W. Roy   Jacob Watson   (seal)
Wm McHeny:
John Watson   Attest

P-394.   State of Tennessee |
                                     | November Session 1829.
         Marion County Court |

        The last Will and Testament of Jacob Watson Deceased Was this
day Produced in Open Court execution thereof Proven by the Oaths of George
W. Roy, William McHenry and Watson the subscribing Witnesses thereto it
being examined Separately and apart said that the same Was the last Will
and Testament of Jacob Watson and that he signed sealed and Acknowledged
the same in their Presence that they believe that the said deceased Was at
the same time in Possession of all his Mental faculties Whereupon the
same is Ordered to be Certified and Admitted to record.
        Test

                                            Jno. Kelly Clk.
                                            By Geo. W. Rice D. Clk.

Registered Feby. 9th 1830.

                                            Jno. Kelly D. Register

P-394.   Daniel O. Baker |
            To | Bill of Sale
         Jno. Kelly |

        Known All Men by these Presents that I Daniel O. Barker of
the County of Marion and State of Tennessee for And in Consideration of
the sum of four hundred dollars have this day bargained and sold unto
John Kelly of the County and State aforesaid a Certain Mulatto by name
Edward about twenty Years of age and do by these Presents delivered
said boy to the said Kelly as soon as I am entitled to the Possession
of him by Heirship by My Fathers Will and deceased My Brother together
With a Certain and agreement between Myself and Joseph Martin an equal
heir With myself a boy Edward I Do Warrant and defend to the said Kelly
free and Clear of the Claim and demand of all Manner of Persons Whatever
and a lawful slave Whereof I hereunto set My hand and seal this the
10th day of January m. 1829,
        Signed and Ack. In Presence of

Robert   X Kirkline   D. L. O. Baker

P-394. State of Tennessee

Marion County Court

August Session 1829
Bill of Sale

Daniel O. Baker to John Kelly for Negro by named Edward Was this day Proven in Open Court and Acknowledged by the said Daniel O. Baker and Ordered to be Certified for registration.

Test.

Jno. Kelly Clk.
By Geo. W. Rice D. Clk.

Registered Feby 11th. 1830.

Jno Kelly D. Register

P-394   John Walker
            To
        Ferrell Belsher

This Indenture this the eight day of November in the Year of Our Lord One thousand eight hundred and twenty four between John Watson of the County of McMinn and State of Tennessee of the One Part and Ferrell Belsher of the County of Marion and State Aforesaid

Witnesseth that the said John Walker for and in Consideration of the sum of five thousand dollars to him in hand Paid said Ferrell Belsher the receipt Whereof is hereby Acknowledged hath bargained granted and by these Presents doth bargain and sell and alien unto the said Ferrell Belsher a Certain tract or Parcel of land containing six hundred and forty acres situated lying and being in the County of Marion and State of Tennessee and on the North side of Tennessee river and bounded as follows to Wit

(P-395)   Beginning at a hackberry Marked this I. W. and Lockust elder of the bank of Tennessee river under a rocky clift Opposite the Mouth of running Water Creek thence along the foot of a steep Rocky Mountain North sixty two West three hundred and forty Poles to a Spanish Oak in the rocks thence south five hundred and five Poles to a sweet gum hickory and Maple sappling on the bank of said river; thence up the river as it Meanders four hundred and eighty five Poles to the beginning With All and singular the Woods, Water Water Courses and Profits thereunto belonging or any Wise appertaining.

To have and to hold unto the said Ferrell Belsher his heirs and assigns forever from the said John Walker Jr. his heirs and assigns forever and from all and every Person or Persons Whatsoever Will Warrant and defend the title to the said Ferrell Belsher Against all Manner of Persons Whatsoever.

In Tes-emony Whereof I have hereunto set My hand and seal the day first Above Written.

Signed sealed and delivered in the Presence of

Hopkins L. Terry
P. Rob
Allen Belsher Jr.

John Walker

P-395.   State of Tennessee

Marion County Court and Circuit

April Term 1830

P-395.   Deed of Conveyance fisk John Walker to Ferrell Belsher for six hundred and forty Acres of land in Marion County Was this day duly Proven in Open Court by the Oaths of Hopkins L. Turney a subscribing Witness thereto and having been heretofore Proven in Court by the Oath of Allen Belsher the subscribing Witness is ordered to be Certified for registration (Seal) I Certify that the foregoing Probate of the Deed therein Specified is a true and complete Copy of the record in My Office.

Given under My hand and Private seal not having a seal of office at office in Jasper this 15th day of April 1830.

Wm Standifer Clk.

Registered the 16th day of April 1830

P-395 Elijah M. Hall
     To   Deed.
    John C. Everett

This Indenture Made this the 12th day of April in the Year of Our Lord one Thousand eight hundred and thirty between Elijah M. Hale of the County of Morgain and State of Alabama of the one Part and John C. Everett and William Arnett of the County of Marion and State of Tennessee of the Other Part,

Witnesseth that for and in Consideration of the sum of Fifteen hundred dollars to us in hand Paid the receipt Whereof is hereby acknowledged Hath and by these Presents doth grant bargain alien enfeoff and Confirm unto the said Everett and Arnett their heirs executors and administrators two Certain Lots of land in the town of Jasper known and designated in the Original Plan of Said town as Lots No. 63 and 71 Containing one Quarter of an Acre of each on Which there is a Unfinished Story Brick house.

To have and to hold the Aforesaid lots of land With all and singular the rights and Profits emoluments and Appurtenances belonging or any wise appertaining to the same to the only use of them the said Everett and Arnett their heirs &c and I the said Elijah M. Hall Will Warrant and forever defend to the said John Eyrett and William Arnett their heirs &c the Above recited Lots Against the right title Claim in trust and demand of all and every Person Whatsoever.

In Testimony Whereof I have hereunto set My hand and seal the day and date first herein Written.

Elijah M. Hall.

P-395.   State of Tennessee

       Marion County Court

April Term 1830.

Deed of Conveyance from Elijah Hall to William Arnett and J. C. Evertt Was this day Acknowledged in Open Court for Lots No. 63 and 71 in the town of Jasper by the bargainor and Ordered to be Certified for registration.

Copy TesT

Wm. I. Standifer Clk.

Registered and examined April 27th. A. D. 1830.

Jno. Kelly   D. Register.

P-396.   William Oscar   }
              To   Deed.   }   This Indenture Made this the
         Larken Bethel   }   twenty fifth day of April in
                                 }   the Year of Our Lord one thou-
sand eight hundred and twenty Nine between William Oscar and Larken Bethel of the County of Franklin and State of Tennessee

     Witnesseth that the said Oscar for and in Consideration of the
sum of _____ dollars to him in hand Paid by him the said Bethel the receipt Whereof is hereby Acknowledged hath Given, granted bargained and
sold and by these Presents doth grant, bargain sell and confirm unto the
said Bethel his heirs and Assigns a Certain tract or Parcel of land situated in Marion County and the State of Tennessee on the top of Cumberland Mountain and on the head Waters of Battle Creek on the road leading
from the State of Georgia and Belfast in Jackson to Calwell in Franklin
County and State of Tennessee including the burnt stand being the same
tract of land Granted to sd. Bethel and sold to Me the sd. Oscar and
Confirmed on the 31st day of December eighteen hundred and twenty three
     Beginning on a black oak near the head of a spring Marked L.
D.B. forty Nine Poles to a black oak thence East sixty six Poles to four
sourwoods thence south forty Nine Poles to a Maple thence West to the
beginning Containing twenty Acres be the same More or less
     To have and to hold the before recited land and bargained Prem-
ises With all and singular rights, Profits, rents hereditaments and appurtenances to the Only Proper use and behoof of him the said Larken
Bethel forever and the said William Oscar doth further Warrant and agree
to and With the said Bethel his heirs and Assigns that the before recited
land and bargained Premises he Will Warrant and forever defend the right
title Claim interest and demand of all and every other Person or Persons
Whatever.
     In Testimony Whereof I the said William Oscar hath hereunto
set his name and affixed his seal the day and date above Written.
     Signed sealed and delivered in Presence of us

Burnett Thompson   }
Isaac Read   }   Wm. Oscar.

P-396.   State of Tennessee   }
                                    }   February Session 1830.
         Marion County Court   }

     Deed of Conveyance from William Oscar to Larkin Bethel for
twenty Acres of land in Marion County Was this day Produced in Open Court
and execution thereof Proven by the Oaths of Burnett Thompson and Isaac
Read subscribing Witnesses thereto and Ordered to be Certified for registration a true Copy Test

                              Jno. Kelly   Clk.
                              By Geo. W. Rice D. Clk.

Registered 6th day of May 1830

P-396.   Nathaniel David   }
              To Deed   }   This Indenture Made and entered
         A. M, Carter   }   into this the Seventh day of May
                                    }   in the Year of Our Lord one thou-
sand eight hundred and thirty between Nathaniel Davis of the County of and
state of Tennessee of the One Part and A. M. Carter of County and State

T-396. aforesaid of the other Part

  Witnesseth that the said Nathaniel Davis for and in Consideration of a tract of land Conveyed to said Nathl Davis by A. M. Carter Containing one hundred and forty acres lying in Marion county in the state Aforesaid where Davis now lives as a consideration to him Paid before the unsealing and delivery of these Presents by the Conveyance of the aforesaid Mentioned land in consideration whereof doth Acknowledged himself fully Sattisfied doth give Grant bargain sell Convey and Confirm unto the said A. M. Carter his heirs executors Administrators or Assigns forever a Certain tract or Parcel of land lying and being in the County of Washington on the Waters of Boons Creek North _____ borough About three Miles the same place Whereon

  Beginning at a White Oak to Boons Creek thence south fifty two Poles to a black gum sappling thence south Nine East twenty six Poles to a White oak Sappling thence south twenty two degrees twenty Poles to a (T-397) White Oak thence West twenty two Poles to a stake in a field thence south one hundred and twelve Poles to a White and black Oak stump thence West two hundred and fifty Poles two Poles to a White Oak thence North Eighty Nine Poles to a black oak thence south twenty four degrees East Ninety one Poles to a beech near a small branch thence south twenty five degrees thirty two Poles to two dogwood thence north seventy five East forty one Pole to a Mullberry & dogwood then north forty degrees East fifty two Poles to a White oak and black oak and dogwood thence With Fifty eight Poles to a Post Oak and dogwood thence south forty four degrees East seventy two Poles to a Red Oak then south sixty seven degrees East twenty two Poles to a red Oak stump; thence East forty Nine Poles Crossing boons Creek to the beginning containing two thousand and eighty five Acres Which said Premises to-gether With all and singular rights Privileges and Appurtenances as thereto belonging.

  To have and to hold the said Bargained Premises unto said A. M. Carter his heirs executors Administrators and assigns for & I the said Nathl. Davi for Myself my heirs executors Administrators and Assigns do by these Presents for We Warrant and defend the Above bargained Premises from all Claim Whatever as a indefensable right in fee simple Unto the said A. M. Carter his heirs executors Administrators and Assigns forever.

  In testimony Whereof I have hereunto set My hand and affixed My seal the day & Year First Above Written in Presence of

        Nathaniel Davis

F-397. State of Tennessee   1830
    Marion County Court

  Then Was the foregoing deed of conveyance from Nathaniel Davis to Afod M. Carter for two hundred and eighty five Acres of land in Washington County Tennessee Was this day Proven in Open Court and execution thereof Acknowledged by the Conveyor and Ordered to be Certified for registration in the County of Washington.
  Test

        Jno. Kelly Clk.

Reg. 20th. of May 1830.

        By Geo. W. Rice

P-397. Mary Barker
        To   Deed.
  P. H. Butler and
  C. B. Raines

This Indenture Made this 14th day of April in the Year of Our Lord one thousand Eight hundred and twenty Nine by and between

Pleasant H. Butler & Charles B. Raines of the County of Marion and State of Tennessee of the One Part and Mary Barker of the County and State aforesaid of the other Part

      Witnesseth that for and in consideration of the sum of forty dollars to Me in hand Paid the receipt Whereof is hereby Acknowledged I the said Mary Barker hath and doth by these Presents grant bargain sell and convey Unto the said P. H. Butler and C. B. Raines and their heirs and Assigns forever a Certain lot or piece of land in town of Jasper known and designated in the Original Plan of said town as lots No. 34.

      To have and to hold the aforesaid lot or Parcel of land unto the said P. H. Butler and C. B. Raines With its Appurtenances to them and their heirs &c forever from the Claim and demand of All and every Person or Persons Claiming by through or under Me the said Mary Barker My heirs or assigns and from the Claim and demand of all and every Person or Persons Whatsoever, I the said Mary Barker Will Warrant and forever defend

      In testimony Whereof I the said Mary Barker have hereunto set My hand and seal the day and Year first herein Written.

      Signed sealed and delivered

Hall;
Wash Hendrix   Attest

                     her
              Mary X Barker
                   mark

P-397. State of Tennessee

Marion County Court

      April Session 1829

      Then Was the Written deed of Conveyance from Mary Barker to Pleasant H. Butler & Charlie B. Raines for Lot No. 34 in the town of Jasper acknowledged in Open Court by the said Mary Barker and Ordered to be Certified for registration.

      Given under My hand and Private seal their being No. seal of Office at office in Jasper this 25th day of July 1829.

                         Wm. I. Standifer Clk.

Registered 27th. May 1830.

P-398. Beny K. Hudgins
        To Power of Atty.
  Robert Woody

Known All Men by these Presents that We Benjamin K. Hudgins and Emily Hudgins Wife of the said

Benjamin K. Hudgins of Marion in the State of Tennessee do hereby constitute Ordain and Appoint Our Attorney for us and in Our name to sell a Certain tract of land in the County of Middlesex and State of Virginia Which descended from Dawson Hudgins the Father of the said Benjamin K. Hudges do hereby authorized My said attorney for Me and My Wife in My name to relinquish all My right of Dawson Which I might have in or to the afore-Mentioned tract of land by the laws of Virginia and we the said Benjamine K. Hudgens and Emily Hudges do hereby further ordain Constute and Appoint the Aforesaid Robert Woodey our true and lawful Attorney for us and in

P-398. Our names or Either of them as May seem Proper and best to act demand sue for and obtain All or any interest we may have in or to the estate of the said Dawson Hudgins further of the said Benjamin K. Hudgins Whether the same be real or Personal estate and further to settle all Matters and controversies Which may arise in reference to any interest We May have in either in the real or Personal estate of the said Dawson Hudgins and We the said Benjamin K. Hudgins and Emily Hudgins do hereby satisfy and Confirm every Act and deed of our said Attorney in regards to the Matters and things hereon Mentioned in as ample and full a Manner as we or either of us could do if we were Personally Present and transacting the same in Ourselves.

In TesTimony Whereof we have hereunto set our hands and affixed our seals this 17th day of May in the Year of Our Lord one thousand eight hundred and Thirty.

Benjamin K. Hudgins
Emily Hudgins

P-398.   State of Tennessee   ⎬   May Session 1830.

    Marion County Court   ⎬

Then Was the within Power of Attorney from Benjamin K. Hudgins and Emily his Wife to Robert Woody this day Produced in Open Court and execution thereof Acknowledged by the Said Benj. K. Hudgin to be his Act and deed for the Purpose therein Contained and expressed And the said Emily his Wife having first been Privately examined sitaratily and a Part from her said husband Acknowledged that she Voluntarily signed the same Without fear thereto or Compulsory from her said husband and that the same is her Act and deed for the Purpose therein contained And expressed Whereupon the same is ordained to be Certified for registration. Let it be registered (L.S.)

Given under My hand and Private seal of office not having an official seal at office in Jasper this 30th day of May A. D. 1830.

Jno. Kelly   Clk.

Registered 27th May 1830.

P-398.   Sand. D. Riggles   ⎬
    To Deed of Trust.   ⎬   This Indenture Made and entered
   H. L. Torney   ⎬   into this day 18th of _____ be-
               tween Solomon and Daniel Riggle
of the County and State of Tennessee of the one Part and Hopkins L. Turney of the County of Franklin and State of Tennessee of the other Part

Witnesseth that Solomon and Daniel Riggle for and in consideration of one dollar to them in hand Paid hath bargained and sold and by these Presents doth bargain and sell to said Hopkins L. Turney and his heirs a Certain Lot or Parcel of land it lying and being in the town of Jasper Marion County Tennessee known and designated in the Plan of said town as lot No. and being on the north side of Public road and being the same on Which said Solmon and Daniel Riggle now lives and Which said Riggle Purchased of William Arnett also five feather beds and four bedsteads one bureau and Cupboard and the furniture therein two Chairs Small penning table three trunks five Window Chairs Nine Common Chairs three pair And irons one cow & Calf one bay horse one grey Mare two Pot racks one

P-303. lot & one Hut a stable all of which Property I Warrant to the said Hopkins L. Turney and his heirs Against the Claims of all Persons whatever. In trust nevertheless that Whereas the said Solmon and Daniel Riggle is justly Indebted to Willis Estill Jr. in the following Sum to wit; One Note executed by them to the Commissioner for the County of Marion and State of Tennessee for the sum of $270.00 and Which Note was transferred by said Commissioners to said Estill and Which note is dated the 10th day of February 1821, & due twelve Months after date also n Note executed by said Riggle to said Turney on the 6th day of April 1829 & due one day after date for the sum 191.25 and Also a note executed by Daniel Riggle & William Jones to Scott Terry for $90.00 due the 25th day of Dec. 1828 and dated the 25th day of April 1828 and Which Note belongs to said Estill also said Solmon and Daniel Riggle is justly indebted to B. and P. L. Dechard in the sum of $52.50 due by Note dated 19th of April 1828 now therefore if the said Solmon And Daniel Riggle Shall pay said Several debts above Mentioned on or before the first day of March A. D. 1831 With interest then this indenture and every Part thereof Shall be Void and in further trust if the said Solmon and Daniel Riggles Shall fail to pay said debt and every Part thereof on or before the 1st day of March 1831 It shall be lawful for said trustee at any time Where required to Proceed to sell said Property or so Much thereof as May be necessary for ready Money to the highest bidder before the Courthouse door in the town of Jasper After ten days Privous of the time and Place of sale by Putting up Advertisements for that Purpose at the Courthouse door in Jasper and at such Other Places said trustee shall think best and out of the Proceeds of the sale Pay Whatever May be due and owning on the said debts aforesaid and the expense of said sale and the surplus if any Pay over to the said Solmon and Daniel Riggle for their legal representatives and the trustee to convey the Property sold in fee simple to the Purchaser or Purchasers.

In testimony Whereof the Party to these Presents have hereunto set their hands and seal the day and Year first Above Written.
Signed and delivered in Presence of

Alford Henderson
Jno. Dechard

Solmon Riggle
Daniel Riggle
Hopkins L. Turney

P-303.   State of Tennessee

Franking County Circuit

July Term 1830.

Then the Within deed of trust from Solmon Riggle and Daniel Riggle to Hopkins L. Turney for the Purpose therein Mentioned Was this day duly Proven in Open Court by the Oaths of Alford Henderson and Jonathan Dechard the subscribing Witness thereto and was thereupon Ordered by the Court to be Certified for registration. Let it be registered.
In testimony Whereof I Jonathan Spyke Clerk of the Circuit Court of the said County have hereunto set My hand this the 28th day of July 29th 1830.

Jno. Kelly D. Register

Registered July 29th 1830

Jonathan Spyke Clerk
By P. S. Dechard D. Clk.

P-393. Carter Hins)(
     To Deed.) This Indenture Made and entered
   Absolom Deakins (into this 29th day of January in
) the Year of Our Lord on thousand
eight hundred and thirty between Alford M. Carter, William B. Carter George
W. Carter James P. Taylor and Mary C. Taylor his Wife Benjamin Brewer &
Sallie L. Brewer his wife of the County of Carter in the State of Tennessee
George T. Gillespie & Eliza M. Gillespie his wife of the County of Grey
in the State aforesaid of one Part and Absolom Deakins and George Stewart
of the County of Marion and State Aforesaid of the Other Part.

      Witnesseth that the said Aford M. Carter William B. Carter
George M. Carter James P. Taylor and Mary C. Taylor his Wife Benjamine
Brewer and Sallie Brewer his Wife George T. Gillespie and Eliza M. Gillespie his Wife for and in consideration of the sum of One thousand dollars
to them in hand paid by the said Absolom Deakins & George Stewart the
receipt Whereof they do hereby Acknowledged have granted bargained sold
released and Confirmed and by these Presents do grant bargain sell release and Confirm Unto the said Absolom Deakins and George Stewart a Certain tract or Parcel of land situated lying and being in the County of
Marion aforesaid being a Part of a Ten Thousand Five hundred acre tract
Originally Patented by the Name of John Sevier on Sequachie Creek bounded
as follows.

      Beginning at a Point in the Center of Sequachie river opposite
Maple the south bank then North 57 degrees East one hundred and thirty
seven Poles to a Spanish Oak thence north thirteen degrees East fifty six
Poles to a black oak thence East Poles to a stake and pointers in a
Wagon road thence North fifteen degrees East along said road Ninety four
Poles to small Walnut and Pointers on the of division between heirs of
Loudon Carter decd. and John Southgate said line North fifty degrees West
One hundred and twenty six Poles in said center of Sequachie river thence
along the same as it Meanders half of a spring on the opposite bank opposite Blakely landing south 57½ West fifty four Poles south 45 West 32
Poles south 57 West fifty four Poles South 27° West eighteen Poles south
24° West fourteen Poles south 31° West twenty Poles south 25 twenty Poles
south one degree West twelve Poles south twenty Poles south 11° East
sixteen Poles south 11° West thirty eight Poles a direct line to the
beginning.

      To have and to hold the said tract or Parcel of land contain-
ing two hundred and forty three Acres be the same More or less With the
appurtenances thereto belonging to them the said Absolom Deakins and
George Stewart their heirs & assigns forever and the said Grantor herein
before for themselves and their heirs do Covenant and Agree to and With the
said Absolom Deakins and George Stewart their heirs and assigns that in
Case they the said Absolom Deakins and George Stewart their heirs and Assigns shall at any time by Virtue of an older and better title by due Course
of law by Which of or land or any Part thereof that then and in that
Case they the said before grantors and their heirs Will forever refund
to of four dollars and forty of said land from Which they may be Which With
interest thereon from the date of such eviction Until Paid.

      In Witness Whereof the before Mentioned Grantors have hereunto
set their hands and seal the day and Year first Above Written.

P-400.   Sealed and delivered in the Presence of Wm. D. Carter

                                      Mary C. Taylor

                                      Brewer B. Brewer

                                      A. M. Carter

                                      G. W. Carter

                                      George T. Gillespie

                                      Eliza M. Gillespie

P-400   State of Tennessee   0

                                       February Session

       Carter County   X   One thousand eighty hundred and

                                       thirty three

      Then Came the Within deed from William B. Carter Mary C. Taylor James P. Taylor Sallie S. Brewer Benjamine Brewer Alford M. Carter George W. Carter to Absolom Deakins and George Stewart; Exhibited in Open Court the M and the said Mary C. Carter Wife of James P. Carter Brewer Wife of Benjamine Brewer were examined by the Court separate and apart from their husbands and Acknowledged that they executed the same Without the threat Court or Furswasion of their said husbands thereupon is Amitted to record and Ordered to be Certified for registration in the land lies.

      Test

                                                C. B. Williams Clk.

P-400.   State of Tennessee   X

       Greene County   X

      ton John Belch and RoBert / Malory

(401)   Whereas Absolo Deakins & George Stewart hath Produced a deed of Conveyance Made to them by the heirs and representative of Loudon Carter decd of a Certain tract or Parcel of land lying and being in the County of Marion and State of Tennessee and Produced the same to be Acknowledged by George P. Gillespies of the representatives of Loudon Carter of Court of Pleases and Quarter Session of Green County and it being represented to our said Court the Elizabeth M. Gillespie Wife of the said George P. Gillespie & One of the heirs of Loudon Carter is an inhabitant of Our said County of Greene and that from in desposition she is Unable to Come into our said Court of Pleas & to be Privtely examined as to her free Consent in executing the said Conveyance Know Ye that we in Confidence of Your Prudent and fidelity have appeared you and by these Presence do Give Unto you full Power and Authority to take the Private examination of the said Eliza M. Gillespie Wife of the said George P. Gillespie concerning her Consent in our executing the said Conveyance and thereupon We Command you that You go to the Eliza M. Gillespie and Privately and apart of her said husband examine her the said Elizabeth M. Gillespie Whether she executed the said Conveyance freely of her own record Without force or complusion of the said George P. Gillespie her husband and the examination being distinctly and Plainly wrote on the said deed or some Paper annexed thereto and When you shall have taken the said examination You are to and the same Closed up Under your seal to-gether With this Writ unto our said Court now holding for the County of Greene

          Witness

Andrew Patterson Clerk of said Court at office the fourth Monday in January 1830.

P-401. April 29th. January 1830.

A. Patterson
By V. Sevier. D. C.

P-401. State of Tennessee

Greene County

     We John Belch and Robert Malaway do hereby Certify that by Virtue of the annexed Commission we have Purchased to take the Private examination of Eliza M. Gillisper Wife of George F. Gillespie touching her execution of the deed of conveyance hereto annexed and we having examined Eliza M. Separately and part from her husband George T. Acknowledged She executed the said Conveyance freely and of her record Without fear or Compulsion of the said George T. Gillespie her husband.
     Given under our hands and seal this 29th day of January 1830.

John Balch and R. **Malaway**   (seal)

P-401. State of Tennessee

Green County Cour   January Session 1830.

     Then Was the execution of deed duly Acknowledged in Open Court by George P. Gillespie and also duly Acknowledged by Aliza M. Gillespie his Wife an Commissioner as appears this Certificate of examination Which With Commissioners are hereto Annexed all of Which appear and record and are Ordered to be Certified for registration as to the said George P. Gillespie Eliza M. Gillespie his Wife.
     In testimony Whereof I Andrew Patterson Clerk of said Courthouse hereto set My hand and seal of office at office the 29th January 1830.

A. Patterson
By V. Sevier D. Clk.

Registered 16th of August 1830.

P-401   Adam Hall
          to   Power of Attorney
     Joshua Stewart

     Known All Men these Presents that I Dai Hall of the County of Marion and State of Tennessee do hereby Consitute Ordain and appoint Joshua Stewart My true and lawful Attorney in fact for Me and in My name to act demand in for the Sum and obtain All and All Manner of debts dues demands or from Claim that I May have Against or that May be Coming to Me from the Estate of My father Adam Hall lately a residence of the County My Attorney to sue for or otherwise obtain Whatever legicy Distribution Share or Shares May be Owning to Me from the estate of the Said Adam Hall (P-402) deed Whether the name be real or Personal Property and I do hereby ratify and Confirm all and every act My Said Attorney May do in relation do the estate of the said Adam Hall Decd. in Survy for obtaining and giving receipts for Any Claim demand distribution Shares or Shares that I May have Against the said estate or that May be to Me therefrom

P-402. is as ample and Complete a Manner as I Myself Would do if Personally Presents and transcribing the same

In testimony Whereof I have hereunto set My hand and seal the 20th day of August 1830.

his
David X Hall
mark

P-402. State of Tennessee   August Session 1830.

Marion County Court

Power of Attorney David Hall to Joshua Stewart was this day Produced in Open Court and execution thereof Acknowledged by the said David Hall Whereupon the Same Was Ordered to be Certified and Admitted to record. Let it be registered.
(L.S.) Given Under My hand and Private Seal (Not having an official Seal in Jasper this the 20th day of Aug. 1830.

Jno. Kelly Clerk

Registered 18th Sept. 1830.

P-402. John Strictland   This Indenture Made and entered
       To Deed.   into this the eighteen day of
    Andrew Bass   _____ in the Year of Our Lord
One thousand eight hundred and twenty Nine between John Strictland of the State of Tennessee Marion County on the One Part,

Witnesseth that the said John Strictland for and in Consideration of the sum of one hundred dollars in hand paid the receipt Whereof is truly Acknowledged by these Presents doth grant bargain sell alien devise and convey unto the said Andrew Bass his heirs and Assigns a Certain Place or Parcel of land situated in the County of Marion and State of Tennessee lying on the Waters of Battle Creek and is bounded as follows, to Wit,

Beginning at a black gum running southwest between the spring Oak Corner thence With said Bass line eastwardly to the upper boundary of a entry entered by John Washington thence to Klipper dogwood Corner thence With said Klippers line Crossing the Cove to a Sugar tree thence up the Cove to a buckeye and Ash thence Northwardly to an Elm thence to the beginning, Containing forty Acres be the same More or less.

To have and to hold the said Piece or Parcel of land and bargained Premises With All and singular the rights hereditaments and Appurtenances of in and belonging to or any Wise Appertaining to the Only Proper use benefit and behoof of him the sd Andrew Bass his heirs and assigns forever and the Said John Strictland himself his heirs executors and Administrators doth Warrant and Agree With the Said Bass his heirs and Assigns that the Afore recited Parcel of land and bargained Premises he Will Warrant and forever defend from the Claim or Claims of all and every Person or Persons Whatsoever Claiming the same or Any Part thereof.

P-402.   In Witness Thereof I the said John Strictland set My hand and Seal this day and date Above Written.
Signed sealed and delivered

Bluford Bethel   his
Adam Overturf   John X Strictland
                                                mark

P-402.   State of Tennessee
                                            August Session 1830.
         Marion County Court

         Deed of Conveyance from Strictland to Andrew Bass for forty Acres of land in Marion County Was this day Proven in Open Court and execution thereof duly Proven by the Oaths of Adam Overturf the sub-scribing Witnesses thereto who swears he saw Bufford Bethel Attest the Concurring Witness and that said Bethel is a non-residence of this State Whereupon the said Deed of Conveyance was Ordered to be Certified And Ad-mitted to record. Let it be registered.
         Test

                                            Jno. Kelly

Registered 1st October 1830

                                            Jno. Kelly D. Reg.

P-402. James Johnson
            To   Deed.   This Indenture Made this 18th day
        Andrew Bass   of Dec. 1829 one thousand Eight
                                       hundred and twenty Nine between
James Johnson and John Wooten of the County of Marion and State of Ten-nessee of the one Part and Andrew Bass of sd. County of the Other Part
P403.   Witnesseththat in Consideration of the sum of One hundred and thirty dollars to the sd James and John in hand Paid by the sd. Andrew they the sd. James and John hath bargained and sold and by these Presents doth bargain sell alien release and Convey unto him the sd Andrew a Cer-tain Piece of land situated lying and being in the County Aforesaid on Battle Creek
         Beginning at a black lynn John Strictland Corner thence North sd. line to an Ash thence Crossing the cove to a sugar tree a Corner of the Old Survey thence up the Cove East Wordly to a beech a Corner; thence North Crossing the Cove With sd. Johnson line to a stake thence North West With a Boundary to the beginning for Compliments be the same thirty Acres More or less said land being a Part of a sixty acre tract and Part of a hundred Acre entry and a Part of a fifty Acre entry deeded to sd. Wooten by William Harris.
         To have and to hold the Aforesaid Parcel of land together With all & singular the appurtenances or in any wise appertaining to the same belonging or in any Wise appertaining unto him the sd. Andrew his heirs and assigns forever & the Said James and John for themselves their heirs executors Administrators doth Covenant and Agree to and With the sd. Andrew Bass that the bargained Premises they Will Warrant and forever de-fend Against the Claim or Claims of all Persons Whatsoever Pretending to Claim or hold the same by Virtue of a deed of Conveyance from the said James and John.

P-403.   In Witness thereof We the sd. James and John has hereunto set
our hands and seal the day and Year first Above Written. Containing the
Above named

Adam Overturf,   Attest   Jams Johnson
Bufford Bethel   John Wooten

P-403.   State of Tennessee   )
)   August Session 1830.
         Marion County Court   )

        Deed of Conveyance from James Johnson and John Wooten to Andrew
Bass for thirty Acres of land in Marion County Was this day Produced in
Open Court and execution thereof duly Proven by the Oath of Adam Overturf
one of the subscribing Witnesses thereto who swears he saw Bluford Bethel
Attest the same as a Concurring Witness and that the said Bethel as a
non-resident of this Stae Whereupon the same is Ordered to be excepted
and Admitted to record. Let it be registered.
        Test
                                         J. Kelly   Clk.
Registered the 1st of Oct. 1830.

P-403.   Ferrell Belsher   )
             To   Gift   )   For and in Consideration of the
         Wiley Belsher   )   tender love and affection that
)   I have and bear toward My son
Wiley Belsher I Give and bequeath to him the following named Negroes (to
Wit)

         Dubling   Hardy   Isaac
         Lon   Will   Charlie
         Charlotte   Big Cynthia and her Children
         William   Dela   Betsey
         Cela   Delpha & her Child   Sarah
         Dock & Lizzie   Eliza & their Sons

and also the following named Negroes at My and My Wife death to Wit

        Cap --Cynthia Ladoc & Martha & their increase

Which said Negroes the title of I Warrant and defend from Claim or Claims
of Any Person Whatsoever.
        In Witness Whereof I have hereunto set my hand and seal this
10th day February the Year of Our Lord One thousand eight hundred and twenty Nine
        Signed and sealed in Presence of
                                                 his
James Hall   )   Ferrell X Belsher
Wm. I. Standifer   )   mark

P-403 State of Tennessee   )
)   August Session 1830
       Marion County Court   )

P-403.   a deed of Gift from Ferrell Belsher to Wiley Belsher for twenty
One Negroes Was this day instituted in Open Court and Was duly Provided
by William I. Standifer one of the subscribing Witnesses thereto to be
the Act and Deed of the Said Ferrell Belsher said Witnesses also State
that James Hall the Other subscribing Witness Who now lives in the State
of Georgia Was also Called upon to Witness said deed at the same time he
Standifer Attested. Impression is that he did see Hall Witness it though
he has no distinct record of seeing him Subscribed his name and Benjamine
R. Montgomery and John Everett Proved that the Signature of James Hall to
said deed is in his Halls Proper handwriting Whereupon it is Ordered by
the Court that said deed be admitted to registration. Let it be registered.
(P-404)   I John Kelly Clerk of the County Court of Marion County in
the State of Tennessee do Hereby Certify that the Above is a true Copy the
record now of the same in My Office.

          Given under My hand and Private seal Not having a seal of
Office at Office) at office in Jasper the 30 - day of November A.D. 1830.

                              Jno. Kelly Clk.
                              By Wm. I. Standifer D. C.

Registered and examined the 29th day of Nov. 1830 in the Registers Office of Marion County.

                              Amos Griffith Register
                              By Jno. Kelly D. Reg.

P-404. Andrew Bass
           To Deed.
        William Stone

                         This Indenture Made and entered
                         into this the Seventh day of __
                         in the Year of Our Lord One thousand
eight hundred and thirty between Andrew Bass of the State of Tennessee
and County of Marion of the one Part and William Stone of sd. State and
County of the Other Part.
          Witnesseth that the said Andrew Bass for and in Considera-
tion of the sum of three hundred dollars to him in hand Paid the receipt
Whereof is hereby Acknowledged hath and by these Presents doth grant bargain sell alien Convey and Confirm unto the Said William Stone his heirs
and assigns a Certain Piece or Parcel of land situated in the County of
Marion And State of Tennessee lying on the Waters of Battle Creek and is
bounded as follows to Wit
          Beginning at an elm running South east to a hackberry And blue
ash thence Westward to Klippers line thence With Same Southeast to a dogwood a Corner thence North east to a stake thence Northward to a sugar
three a Corner thence eastward up the cove to a beech a Corner thence
Across the Cove With Harris line to the upper boundary of a entry thence
Westward With the Upper Boundary of a entry thence Westward With the upper
line of said entry to the beginning Containing Seventy Acres More or less.
          To have And to hold the Above named Parcel of land And Bargain-
ed Premises together With all singular the rights Proper Hereditaments and
Appurtenances of in and to the Same belonging or any Wise appertaining to
the Only proper use benefit and behoof of him the said William Stone his
heirs and Assigns forever and I the Said Andrew Bass for himself his
heirs executors and Administrators Covenant and Agree to and With the said
William Stone his heirs and assigns that the before recited Parcel of land
And Bargained Premises he will forever Warrant from the lawful Claims of

P-404   all Persons Whatever or any Part thereof And I will Warrant
and forever defend by these Presence Whereof the said Andrew Bass hath
hereunto Set his hand seal this day and date first Above Written.

Signed sealed and delivered in Presence of us.

```
                    his
Noble L.   X   Stone                        }
            mark                            }    Andrew Bass
James Holly        Attest                   }
```

P-404.   State of Tennessee   }
                                           }   November Session 1830.
              Marion County Court   }

Deed of Conveyance from Andrew Bass to William Stone for Seventy Acres of land in Marion County as this day Produced in Open Court and
execution thereof duly Proven by Oaths of Noble L. Stone and James Holly,
Subscribing Witness thereto and to be Certified for registration a Copy
Test

Jno. Kelly   Cl.
By Wm. I. Standifer   D. C.

Registered January 25, 1831.

P-405.   William Watson   }
            To   Dee   }   This Indenture Made this 23rd day
         John K. Tate   }   of October in the Year of Our Lord
                                 }   one thousand eight hundred and twen-
ty eight between William Watson of Marion County and State of Tennessee
of the one Part and John K. Tate of the State and County Aforesaid of the
Other Part,

Witnesseth that for and in consideration of the sum of two
hundred and fifty dollars to the Said Watson in hand Paid by the said
Tate The receipt Whereof is hereby Acknowledged he the said Watson has
bargained and sold, and by these Presents does bargain and sell release
and Convey unto the Said Tate a Certain tract or Parcel of land Containing twenty Acres 34 Poles Situated lying and being in the County of
Marion And State of Tennessee on the Waters of Battle Creek Near the
Mouth of Fiery Gizzard

Beginning and remaining as follows Viz. on a Stake on David
Martins south boundary line running due east With said line fifty three
Poles to a beech, thence due south along the foot of Cumberland Mountain
Seventy five Poles to a White Oak thence due West on the Conditional line
between David Hill and said Watson fifty three Poles to A White Walnut
on Susans Lowery east boundary line thence due North along said line
to the beginning.

To have and to hold the said Tract or Parcel of land to-gether
With all and singular rights Members and hereditaments to the said tract
belonging or any Wise Appertaining unto him the said Tate his heirs And
assigns forever and the Watson doth Warrant and Agree to and With said
Tate heirs executors Administrators that the said bargained Premises he
Will Warrant and forever defend free from the lawful right title interest
or Claim of all & every Person or Persons Whatsoever Claiming or Pretending to Claim the same.

P-405.   In Witness Whereof I the said Watson have hereunto Set My hand
and Seal on the day and Year first Above Written.
          Signed and sealed and delivered in Presence

I. H. Roberts   ◊
Phillips Bible   Attest   ◊   Wm. Watson
                                                 ◊

P-405.   State of Tennessee   ◊
                                                 ◊   November Session 1830.
     Marion County Court   ◊

          Deed of Conveyance from William Watson to John K. Tate for twen-
ty five Acres of land in Marion County Was this day Produced in Open Court
and execution thereof duly Proven inOpen Court by the Oaths of Isaac H.
Roberts and Phillips Bible the Subscribing Witness thereto & Ordered to
be Certified for registration.
          In Testimony Whereof I John Kelly Clerk of said Court have
hereunto Set My hand and Private seal (Not having a seal of office) at
Office in Jasper the 8th day of Dec. 1830.
          (seal)

                                        Jno. Kelly
                                        By Wm. I. Standifer D. Clk.

Registered January twenty sixth 1831.

P-405.   Jesse Grayson   ◊
            To   Deed   ◊   This Indenture Made this 7th
         Amos Griffith   ◊   day of September in the Year of
                                                 ◊   Our Lord one thousand eight hun-
dred and thirty between Jess Grayson of the County of Marion and State of
Tennessee of the One Part and Amos Griffith of the County and State aforesaid of the Other Part.
          Witnesseth that for and in Consideration of the sum of two
hundred Dollars to him the said Jesse Grayson in hand Paid the receipt
Whereof is hereby Acknowledged hath and by these Presents doth grant
bargain sell alien enfeoff and Confirm unto the said Amos Griffith his
heirs and Assigns forever a Certain tract or Parcel of land Containing
two hundred Acres lying in the said County of Marion on the North West
side of Sequachie river Adjoining a tract of land of one thousand five
hundred Acres granted to John Sevier by the Stateof North Carolina also
Adjoining Andrew Still and Henry Lyda and bounded as follows
(P-406)   beginning at a black Oak and Pointers the Northwest boundary
of John Sevier tract Where the south boundary of the said Lyda 50 Acres
Survey intersects the same then With said Sevier lines South thirty five
degrees to hundred and two Poles to Pointers a Corner of an 80 Acre survey
of Hill then With his line West on hundred and Nine Poles to a black __
then North eighty two Poles to Pointers at the foot of the Mountain
Along the Same West ten Poles to a stake on Stills lines then along the
Mountain then east one hundred and fifty seven Poles to a stake on said
Lyda then With his line South twenty Poles to Pointers then east Seven-
ty Seven Poles to the beginning including the Premises Where the said
Jesse Grayson now lives including two hundred Acres be the same More or
less it being a tract of land Granted to the said Jesse Grayson by the
State of Tennessee for two hundred Acres by Grant No. 1633 With all And
Singular the wood water water courses Profits Commodities hereditaments and

P-405. Appurtenances Whatsoever to the Said tract or Parcel of land belonging or any Wise Appertaining And the reversion and reversions remainder and remainders, rents and issue thereof And all the estate right title
interest Property Claim and demand of him the Said Jesse Grayson his heirs
and Assigns forever of in And to the Same of every Part and Parcel thereof Within law or equity.

To have and to hold the said two hundred Acres of land With the
appurtenances Unto the Said Amos Griffith his heirs forever Against the lawful title Claim and demand of all and every Person or Persons Whatever Will
Warrant and forever defend by these Presents.

In Witness Whereof the Said Jesse GRayson hath hereunto set his
hand and seal the day and Year and first Above Written in Presence of

David Oats   Jesse Grayson
A. Kelly Jr.

P-405.   State of Tennessee
                              November Session 1830.
       Marion County

Deed of Conveyance from Jesse Grayson to Amos Griffith for 200
Acres of land in Marion County Was this day Produced in Open Court and
execution thereof Proven in Part by Alexander Kelly One of the Subscribing Witness thereto and Ordered to be Continued for further Probate Deed
of Conveyance from Jesse GRayson to Amos Griffith for two hundred Acres
of land in Marion County Was this day Produced in Open Court and the execution thereof Proven full by David Oats a Subscribing Witness thereto
and Ordered to be Admitted for registration.

A Copy test.

                                   Jno. Kelly Clk.
                                By Wm. I. Standifer D. C.

Registered January 26 1831.

P-406.   William Trussell
        To   Deed.   This Indenture Made this 15th day
    Samuel Lemon   of February One thousand eight hun-
                             dred and thirty between William Trus-
sell of the County of Marion and State of Tennessee of the one Part and
Samuel Lemons of the County and State Aforesaid of the Other Part,

Witnesseth that the Said Trussell for and in consideration of
the five Dollars to him in hand Paid before the sealing and delivering
of these Presents hath granted bargained and sold and by these Presents
doth bargain sell unto the said LeMons his heir and Assigns a Certain
tract or Parcel of land Containing sixteen Acres lying in the third district
in Marion County on Battle Creek Adjoining the farm of Asher Trussell and
said William Trussell and bounded as follows to Wit,
(P-407)   Beginning at a sycamore his lower Corner and running With the
Mountain South 33° east thirty four Poles to a Stake on the West bank of
Said Creek then Crossing at Pointers on the east bank and With a Conditional line With Thos. Bullin North 71° east fifty eight Poles to a beech
then With the Mountain North 37° West fifty two Poles to a stake in a
line of said Trussell survey and With it South fifty two° West sixty

P-407. two Poles to the beginning.

To have and to hold the said tract or Parcel of land to-gether
With All and Singular the tenements appurtenances and hereditaments thereunto appertaining or belonging and every Part and Parcel thereof unto and
for the Only uses and behoof of him the said Samuel LeMons his heirs and
Assigns forever and the said Trussell for himself his heirs &c The Premises hereby bargained and sold unto the said LeMons and his heirs or Assigns Against Him said Trussell and his heirs Shall and Will Warrant and
forever defend by these Presents from the lawful right title Claim of
every Person Whatsoever and the said Le Mons his heirs &c hath hence forth
lawful Power and Absolute Authority to grant bargain and sell the same in
Manner and form aforesaid that the said Premises now are and forever Shall
remain free and Clear of and from all former gifts, Grants bargained sale
judgements execution and incumberance Whatever.

In Witness Whereof the said Trussell hath hereunto set his
hand affixed his seal the day and date first Above Written.

William Trussell   Seal.

P-407.   State of Tennessee

          Marion County Court   May Session 1830.

Deed of Conveyance from William Trussell to Samuel Lemon for
sixteen Acres of land in Marion County Was this day Produced in Court and
execution thereof Acknowledged by the Conveyor and Ordered to be Certified
for registration.

          A Copy Test

Jno. Kelly Clerk
By Wm. I. Standifer D. Clk.

Registered January 26 1830.

P-407.   Churchwell McNew
          To   Deed.   This Indenture Made this 7th day
          David Lane   of August in the Year of Our Lord
                                         1829 between Churchwell McNew of
the County Aforesaid Marion and State of Tennessee of the One Part and
David Lane of the County and State Aforesaid of the Other Part

Witnesseth that for and in Consideration of the sum of two
hundred dollars him the sd. Churchwell McNew in hand Paid the receipt
Whereof is hereby Acknowledged hath bargained and sold and do by these
Presents Acknowledged hath bargained and sold and do by these Presents
Alien Anfcoff sell convey unto the said David Lane a Certain tract or
Parcel of land Containing twenty three Acres Situated in Marion County
on the North West side of Sequachie river on Halls branch Adjoining lands
of Thomas Brannson; James Blevins and others,

Beginning at a Post Oak on Bronson line it being a Corner of
a tract Conveyed to Isaac Cooper for twenty Acres then along said Bronson line North thirty Nine Poles to a Post oak in Blevins then With his
line east forty Poles to a stake then North two Poles to a Stake then
east thirty four Poles to a Chincapine Oak Blevins Corner then With his
line North nine West twelve Poles to a White Oak then east thirty Poles to
a stake on Edging line and With the same South twenty five Poles to

P-407. Pointers then West twenty Nine Poles to a stake said Lane twenty three Acres be the same More or less it being the said Churchwell McNew Will Warrant and forever defend so far as the title of the same invested in Me by the Grant from the State of Tennessee Above specified and No urther as this is the express Contract,
(P-408)   In Witness Whereof I hereunto set My hand and seal this day and date above Mentioned.

Signed and Acknowledged in Presence of (Churchwell McNew.

Charles Kilgore
George W. Lewis

P-408.   State of Tennessee   )
)   Session 1830
              Marion County Court   )

        Deed of Conveyance from Churchwell McNutt to David Lane for twenty Acres of land in Marion County Was this day Produced in Open Court And execution thereof duly Produced by the oahts of Charles Kilgore & George W. Lewis, subscribing Witnesses thereto and ordered to be Certified for registration.

        In Testimony Whereof I John Kelly Clerk of said Court do hereby set My hand and Seal not having a seal of office) at office in Jasper the 24th day of January 1831.

                                    Jno. Kelly Clk.
                                    By Wm. I. Standifer D.Clk.

Registered Jan. 27, 1831.

P-408.   John Southgate   )
             To   Deed   )   This Indenture Made this eighth
          Elisha Kirklin   )   day of January in the Year of Our
)   Lord one thousand eight hundred
and twenty Nine between John Southgate of the City of Norfolk and Commonweath of Virginia by his Attorney in fact McIver of the one Part and Elisha Kirklin of the County of Bledsoe and State of Tennessee of the other Part

        Witnesseth that the said John Southgate by his attorney in fact Aforesaid for and in Consideration of the sum of two hundred and eighteen dollars to him in hand Paid by the said Elisha Kirklin at or before the Sealing and delivering of these Presents the receipt Whereof is hereby Acknowledged hath granted bargained and sold aliened released and Confirmed and by these Presents doth granted bargained and sold alien release and Confirm unto the said Elisha Kirklin his heirs and assigns forever a Certain tract or Parcel of land situated lying and being in the County of Marion Containing eighty Acres on the South east side of Sequatchie Creek being Within of said Southgate Part (being the Upper half) of a tract on said Sequachie Creek Originally granted by the State of North Carolina to John Sevier bounded and described as follows to Wit:
        Beginning on a Black Oak at the foot of the Mountain Corner to William Cooper line north fifty four degrees West One hundred and fifty Poles and Pointers then North thirty degrees east twenty six Poles to

P- 408. Dogwood to the Hatfield tract then With a line of Said tract North forty degrees sixty eight Poles to a hickory then With a line of Alexander Lamb three degrees east One hundred and twenty Poles to a hickory at the foot of the Mountain then a direct line to the beginning being the same tract Emanuel Rogers and Aaron Smith now lives to-gether With all and singular the appurtenances Whatsoever to the Said tract of land belonging or any Wise appertaining and the reversion or reversions remainder or remainders rents issues and Profits thereof and every Part thereof and all the estate; right title interest Property Claim and Whatsoever of him the said John Southgate his heirs and assigns of in and to the Same and every Part and Parcel thereof either in law or equity.

To have and to hold the said tract of eighty eight Acres of land herein before described With the appurtenances Unto the Said Elisha Kirklin his heirs and assigns to the Only Proper use and behoof of him the said Elisha Kirklin his heirs and Assigns forever free and Clear of All Claim and demands of him the said John Southgate his heirs executors and Administrators and of all and every Person Whatsoever Claiming by from Under him themselves or either of them and the said John Southgate for himself his heirs executors and Administrators doth hereby Covenant Premises and Agree to and With the said Elisha Kirklin his heirs and assigns that if he the said Elisha Kirklin his heirs or assigns Shall at any time hereafter be evicted from the Said bargained Premises or any Part thereof in Virtue of any title Whatever More Valid in law than the title Now Conveyed to him in Virtue of these Presents that then and in that Case he the said John Southgate hall pay nd refund Unto the said Elisha Kirklin his heirs or Assigns at the rate of two dollars twenty seven Cents Per Acres for each and every Acres from Which he or they Shall be so evicted by due Course of law With interest thereon from the time of such eviction.

In Witness Whereof the said John Southgate by his Attorney in fact aforesaid hath hereunto set his hand and seal the day and Year first herein Written.

John Southgate
By his Attorney in fact
John McIvins

Signed sealed in Presence of

J. Bridgeman
A. S. Rillum

P-409. State of Tennessee

Bledsoe County Court

February Session 1829.

Then Was the Within deed of Conveyance from John Southgate to Elisha Kirklin for eighty eight Acres of lad in Marion County duly Proven in Open Court by the Oaths of John Bridgeman and Anderson S. Killim Witness thereto and Ordered to be Certified for registration.

In testimony Whereof I Scott Terry Clerk of the Court of Pleas and Quarter Session for the County of Bledsoe have hereunto set my hand and Private seal (not having an Official seal of office) at office in Pikeville this 1st day of April 1829.

Scott Terry Clerk

Registered January 27, 1831.

P-409.　　　John Southgate
　　　　　　　　Co　Deed.
　　　　E. & A. Kirklin

This Indenture Made this eight day of January in the Year of Our Lord one thousand eight hundred and twenty Nine between John Southgate of the City of Norfolk and Commonwealth of Virginia by his Attorney in fact John McIver of the One Part and Elisha Kirklin of the County of Bledsoe and Allen Kirklin of the County of Marion and State of Tennessee of the Other Part

Witnesseth That the Said John Southgate by his Attorney in fact aforesaid for and in Consideration of the sum of eighteen hundred and fift dollars to him in hand Paid by the said E. & A. Kirklin John Hatfield & James Rogers at or before the sealing and delivery of these Presents the receipt Whereof is hereby Acknowledged hath granted bargained and sold aliened released and Confirmed and by these Presents doth grant, bargain and sell Alien released and Confirmed unto the said Elisha Kirklin and Allen Kirklin their heirs and Assigns forever a Certain tract of land situated lying and being in the County of Marion Containing two hundred and sixty six Acres on the South Side of Sequachee Creek known as the Hatfield Place

Beginning at a Walnut tree Corner to John Heard Senr. and Alexander Kelly on the line of Lot No. Sixteen thence along the line of said Heard North seventy degrees West sixty Poles to a black oak Corner to the James Rogers tract thence With a line of said tract South thirty eight degrees West One hundred and forty Seven Poles to a beech and elm thence along Isaac Story brick the same Course fourteen Poles to White Oak thence South thirty degrees East Seventy two Poles to a White Oak thence South twenty Six degrees West One hundred and thirty five Poles to Pointers on a line of the tract occupied Davis and Foster then With the same South fifty degrees east three Poles to a hickory thence Sith a line of William Cooper South fifty degrees east forty one Poles to a black Oak; thence south fifty four degrees sixty two Poles to a dogwood; then With the lines of Alexander Lamb Vals tract south Forty degrees east one hundred and fifty three Poles to a black gum then North twenty Seven degrees West fifty eight Poles to_____ then North fifty degrees east eighty eight Poles to Pointers in the line of said Lot No. 16 then With the Same North fifty degrees West Seventy Poles to the beginning

Also another tract of land adjoining the Above known as the James Rodgers tract Containing sixty three Acres Beginning at a Point in the Center of said Sequachee Creek opposite to and ant the S. E. bank John Heard Corner thence With said Heards line South Seventy degrees east Ninety five Poles to a black Oak a Corner the Above described Hatfield tract then With a line of the same thirty eight degrees West One hundred and thirty one Poles to a beech and elm on a branch thence down the branch (Being a Conditional line Stower) N. 42° W. 27 Poles thence N. 89° W. 67 Poles to the Center of Said Sequachee Creek Opposite the Mouth of said branch then up said Creek N. 21 East to the beginning both said tracts being Within the bounds of said Southgate Part of a Certain 10500 Acre tract of land Originally Granted to John Sevier the upper Part thereof having been laid off by Partition Southgate to-gether With all and Singular the Appurtenances to said land belonging or any Wise Appertaining and the reversion and reversions, remainder and remainders rents issue thereof and every Part and Parcel thereof and all the estate interest Property Claim and demand Whatsoever of him John Southgate his heirs and

P-410 Assigns forever of in and to the every Part and Parcel thereof either in law or equity.

To have and to hold the said two tracts of Two hundred & sixty six and land herein before described With the Appurtenances unto the said Kirklin and Allen Kirklin their heirs and Assigns to the Only use and behoof of them the Said Elisha Kirklin and Allen Kirklin their heirs and Assigns forever free and Clear of all Claims and demands of all and every Person and Persons Whatsoever Claiming by from or Under him them or either of them and the said John Southgate for his heirs executors and Administrators doth hereby Covenant And agree to and With Elisha Kirklin and Allen Kirklin their heirs and Assigns that if they the Said Elisha Kirklin and Allen Kirklin their heirs and Assigns Shall at any time hereafter be evicted from the Said bargained Premises or any Part thereof in Virtue of any title or titles Whatsoever Now Valid in law than the title now Conveyed to them in Virtue of these Presents that they and in that Case be the said John Southgate Shall Pay and refund unto the said Elisha Kirklin and Allen Kirklin their heirs or assigns at the rate of Five dollars sixty two Cents Per Acre for each and every Acre from Which he or they Shall be so evicted by due Course of law With interest thereon from the time of such eviction.

(P-411) In Witness Whereof the Said John Southgate by his Attorney in fact aforesaid hath hereunto set his hand and seal the day and Year first Above Written.

Sealed and delivered in Presence of

J. Bridgeman	John Southgate
A. S. Killin	By his Attorney in fact
	John McIver

P-411. State of Tennessee

February Sesion 1829

Bledsoe County Court

Then Was the Within deed of Conveyance from John Southgate to Elisha Kiklin & Allen Kirklin for three hundred and twenty Nine Acres of land in Marion County duly Proven in Open Court by the Oaths of John Bridgeman and Anderson S. Killen Witness thereof and Ordered to be Certified for registration.

In testimony Whereof I Scott Terry Clerk of the Court of Please and Quarter Session for the County of Bledsoe have hereunto set My hand and Private seal (Not having an Official seal) affixed at office in Pikeville the 1st day of April 1829.

Scott Terry Clerk

Registered January 28th. 1831.

P-411. Anothy Street
            To   Deed.
         John Kelly

This Indenture Made the 17th day of October in the Year of Our Lord One thousand eight hundred and twenty (1828) between Anthony Street of the County of Marion and State of Tennessee of the One Part and John Kelly of the County and State Aforesaid of the Other Part,

P-411.   Witnesseth that for and in Consideration of the One hundred Dollars to Me in hand Paid by the Said John Kelly the receipt Whereof is hereby Acknowledged hath bargained sold & Conveyed by these Presents to the said John Kelly his heirs and Assigns forever a Certain tract or Parcel of land Containing fifty Acres situated lying and being in the County of Marion Immediately on the North West bank of Tennessee River on Kellys turn Pike road; it being a tract of land granted by the State of Tennessee to Anthony Street for fifty Acres by Grant No. 20840 dated 4th Dec. 1824.

Beginning at a blue ash and hackberry on the bank of said river it being the upper Corner of Alexander Kelly's Survey then along the line N. 28° E. 60 Poles to a White oak at the foot of the Mountain then along the same as it Meanders S. 40° E. 20 Poles 73° E. 101 Poles N. 15° E. 22 Poles to a Stake at the head of a Small Spring then S. 33° E. 20 Poles then E. 74 Poles to a Stake then S. 18 Poles to a stake and Pointers on the bank of said river then down the Same as it Meanders to the beginning including the Place Now in Occupation of Amos Mitchell With all and Singular the hereditament and Appurtenances thereunto belonging or in any Wise Appertaining either in law or equity.

To have and to hold the aforesaid tract of land & PrMixes to him the said John Kelly his heirs and assigns forever free and Clear of the lawful title Claim and Demand of Mr or My heirs or any Persons Claiming Under Me or My heirs I will Warrant and forever defend so far as the right of the same is Vested in My by the said Grant from the State of Tennessee.

(P-412)   In testimony Whereof I hereunto set My hand and seal the day and date Above Written.

Signed and Ackd. in Presence of

Erasmus Alley	Anthony Street (his X mark)
E. Hornbeak	

P-412.   State of Tennessee

Marion County Court

August Sesion 1830.

Deed of Conveyance from Anthony Street to John Kelly for 50 Acres of land in Marion County Was this day Produced in Open Court and execution thereof duly Proven by the Oaths of Elijah E. Hornbeak and Erasmus Alley Subscribing Witnesses thereto and Ordered to be Certified for registration.

(Seal)

In testimony Whereof I John Kelly Clerk of said Court hereunto set My hand and Private Seal Not having a seal of Office at office in Jasper the 24th day of January 1831.

Jno. Kelly
By Wm. I. Standifer D.C.

Registered January 28th 1831.

P-412. Phillip Kraft
　　　　To　　Deed.
　　　John Kelly

This Indenture Made this 18th day of June in the Year of Our Lord 1829 between Phillip Kraft of the County of Marion and State of Tennessee of the one Part and John Kelly of the County and State aforesaid of the Other Part,

　　　Witnesseth that for and in Consideration of One hundred dollars in hand Paid the receipt Whereof is hereby Acknowledged and by these Presents bargain sold and Conveyed unto the Said John Kelly a Certain lot in the town of Jasper known and designated in the Original Plan of the aforessaid town by Lot No. 72 it being the lot Where said Kraft saddle shop now Stands With all and Singular the hereditaments and Appurtenances thereunto belonging or in any Wise appertaining.

　　　To have and to hold the Said John Kelly his heirs and assigns forever the Above lot and Premises free and Clear of the lawful Claim and demand of All Manner of Persons Whatever, I the said Kraft doth Warrant and forever defend of Which of these Presents.

　　　In Witness Whereof I hereunto set My hand and sealthis day and date first Above Written.

　　　　　　　　　　　　　　　　Phillip Kraft

D. R. Rawlings
J. C. Everett

P-412.　　State of Tennessee

　　　　　Marion County Court

August Session 1831.

　　　Deed of Conveyance from Phillips Kraft to John Kelly for Lot No. 72 in the town of Jasper Was this day Produced in Open Court and execution thereof and duly Proven by the Oaths of Daniel R. Rawlings and John C. Everett subscribing Witnesses thereto and Ordered to be Certified for registration.

　　　Whereof I John Kelly Clerk of said Court have hereunto set My hand and Private seal (not having a seal of office at office in Jasper this day of January 1831.

　　　　　　　　　　　　　　Jno. Kelly
　　　　　　　　　　　　　　By Wm. I. Standifer　C.

Registered Feby. the 1st. 1831.

P-413. Alford M. Carter　et al.
　　　　To　Warranty Deed
　　　　Thomas Kell

This Indenture Made and entered into this 29th day of January in the Year of Our Lord one thousand eight hundred and thirty between Alford M. Carter William B. Carter George W. Carter James B. Taylor & Mary C. Taylor his Wife Benjamin Brewer & Sallie S. Brewer his Wife of the County of Carter & State of Tennessee and George T. Gillespie & Elisha M. Gillespie his Wife of the County of Greene and State Aforesaid of the one Part and Thomas Kell of the County of Marion and State aforesaid of the Other Part,

　　　Witnesseth that the said Alford M. Carter William B. Carter George W. Carter James P. Taylor and Mary C. Taylor his Wife Benjamin Brewer & Sallie S. Brewer his Wife George T. Hillespie & Eliza M. Gillespie

P-413   his Wife for and in Consideration of the Sum of One thousand and
twenty Five dollars to them in hand Paid by the said Thomas Kell the receipt Whereof they do hereby Acknowledge have Granted bargained Sold released and Confirmed and by these Presents do grant bargain sell release
and Confirm Unto the Said Thomas Kell a Certain tract or Parcel of land
Situated lying and being in the County of Marion and State Aforesaid Containing three hundred Acres be the Same More or less being Part of a tract
of a ten thousand five hundred Acres on Sequachee Creek Granted to John S.
Sevier and bounded as follows,

        Beginning at a Point in the Center of Sequachee River on the
south boundary line of the aforesaid tract of ten thousand five hundred
acres thence along the Said line North fifty degrees West one hundred and
thirty degrees West one hundred and thirty Poles to a Stake thence North
Nine degrees east two hundred and Ninety six Poles to a stake thence eighty
six degrees east one hundred & three Poles to a Pointer in the Center of
Sequachie River Opposite to an elm on the Northwest bank as it Meanders
South 130° east 30 Poles thence South 33° West 15 Poles south 38° West
28 Poles South 11° West 15 Poles south 18° West 12 Poles south 45° east
24 Poles South 13 Poles South 34½° West 15 Poles south 20° West 14 Poles
South 29 West 32 Poles South 7° east 15 Poles South 71° east 30 Poles South
20° east 24 Poles south 9° West 32 Poles South 46 degrees east 10 Poles
east 9 Poles South 54° 17 Poles South 23° east 9 Poles South 19° West 8
Poles South 57° West 18 Poles South 76° West 16 Poles North 85° West
29 Poles North 79 degrees West 17 thens a direct line to the beginning.

        To have and to hold the said tract or Parcel of land With the
Appurtenances thereto belonging to him the said Thomas Kell his heirs and
assigns forever and the said grantors herein named for themselves and their
heirs do Covenant and agree to and With the said Thomas Kell his heirs
and assigns that in Case he or they shall at any time hereafter by Virtue
of an older or better title by due course of law by evicted of or from said
land or any Part thereof that then and in that case they the said before
named grantors & their heirs Will refund said Thomas Kell his heirs or assigns at the rate of three dollars and fifty cents for each Acre of said
land from Which Others May be so evicted With interest thereon from the
time of such eviction Until Paid.

        In Witness Whereof the before Named Grantors have hereunto set
their hands and seals the day and Year first Above Written, Signed sealed & delivered in Presence of

(P-414)   W. B. Carter
                                          Mary C. Taylor
                                          J. P. Taylor
                                          Sally S. Brewer
                                          A. M. Carter
                                          G. W. Carter
                                          Geo. T. Gillespie
                                          Eliza M. Gillespie

P-414.   State of Tennessee |
                                  | February Sesion One thousand eight
            Carter County | hundred and thirty

        Then Was the Within deed from William B. Carter Mary C. Taylor
James P. Taylor Sally S. Brewer Benjamine Brewer, Alford M. Carter and

P-413. George W. Carter to Thomas Kell exhibited in Open Court by them
and the Said Mary C. Taylor Wife of James M. Taylor and Sally S. Brewer
Wife of Benjamine Brewer were examined By the Court Separate and apart
from their husband and Acknowledged that they executed the same freely
Voluntarily Without the threat Courtin or Purssion of the Said husbands
Whereupon said deed is Admitted to record and Ordered to be Certified for
registration in the County Wherein the land lies.
    Test

                                    Geo. William Clark

P-414.   State of Tennessee   § To Robert Maloney and
                                  § Daniel Kennedy Esquire
            Grundy County   §

    Greeting Whereas Thomas Kell hath Produced the Deed of Con-
veyance Made to Him by the heirs of Landon Carter decd. a Certain tract or
Parcel of land lying and being in the County of Marion & State of Tennessee
& Procured the Same to be Acknowledged by Geo. T. Gillespie one of the
representatives of Landon Carter decd in the Court of Please & Quarter
Session of Greene County and it being represented to Our said that Eliza
M. Gillespie Wife of the said George T. Gillespie and one of the heirs
of Landon Carter decd. is an inhibitant of Our Said County of Greene and
that from and Indisposition she is unable to Come into Our said Please
& to be Privately examined as to her free Consent in execution of the Conveyance Know Ye that we in Confidence of Your Prudence have appointed
you and byy these Presents do give unto you full Power and Authority to
take the Private and Separate examination of the Said Eliza M. Gillespie
Wife of the said Geo. T. Gillespie of her execution to said Conveyance &
therefore we command you that you go to the Eliza M. Gillespie and Privately & Apart from her husband examination said Eliza M. Gillespie Whether she
executed Said Conveyance free and of her own accord Without fear or Compulsion of the said Go. T. Gillespie her husband and examination being
distinally and Wrote on said deed or some Papers Annexed thereto and When
_____ have taken the Said examination you are to send the same under
Your seal together With this Writ unto Our said Court Now holding in the
County of Greene Witness Andrew Patterson Clerk of said Court at the
fourth Monday in January 1830

                                    A. Patterson
                                    By V. Sevier D. C. C.

P-414 1 S A 29 January 1830.

P-414   State of Tennessee   §
                                 §
           Greene County   §

    We Robert Malony and Daniel Kennedy, that by Virtue of the
Annexed Commission Proceeded to talk the Private examination of Eliza
M. Gillespie Wife of Geo. T. Gillespie touching her execution of the
deed of Conveyance hereto annexed and We having examined the said Eliza
M. Gillespie Separate and Apart from her husband Geo. T. Gillespie Ack-
nowledged that she executed the Said Conveyance freely and of her Own

P-414   Accord Without fear or Compulsion of the Said George T. Gillespie
her husband.

Given Under Our hands and Seals this the 29th day of January
1830.

R. Maloney
By Daniel Kennedy D.

P-415.   State of Tennessee

Greene County Court

January Session 1830.

Then Was the execution of this _dedd_ duly Acknowledged in Open
Curt by George T. Gillespie his Wife on Commission as appears by the Certificate of examination Which With its Commission Are hereto Annexed All
of Which Appears of record and are Ordered to be Certified for registration as to the said George T. Gillespie And Eliza M. Gillespie his Wife.

In testimony Whereof I Andrew Patterson Clerk of Said Court
have hereunto set My hand and seal at office the 29th of January 1830.

A. Patterson
By V. Sevier D. C.

Registered February 2, 1831.

P-415.   John Southgate
          To   Deed
          Davis and Foster

This Indenture Made this twentieth
day of December in the Year of Our
Lord One thousand eight hundred add
twenty five between John Southgate of the City of Norfolk And Common Wealth
of Virginia by John McIver his attorney in faayt of the One Part and William Davis and William Foster of the County of Marion and State of Tennessee of the Other Part

Witnesseth that the said John Southgate for and in consideration of the sum of Nine hundred dollars to him in hand paid by the said
William Davis and William Foster at or before the sealing and delivery of
these Presents the receipt Whereof is hereby Acknowledged hath granted
bargained and sold aliened released and Confirmed and by these Presents
doth grant bargain and sell, Alien; release and Confirm unto the said
William Davis and William Foster their heirs and assigns forever a Certain tract or Parcel of land situated lying and being in Said County of
Marion Containing two hundred and thirty four and a half Acres (being
Part of a tract of Acres Originally Patented in the name of John Sevier)
bounded and described as follows to Wit --

Beginning at a Point in Sequachee Creek Opposite a hackberry
and persimmon on the South east bank on a line With William Stewall then
along said north fifty five degrees east two hundred and thirty to Poles
to a black then north twenty Seven degrees east thirty eight and a half
Poles to a hickory then north fifty degrees West one hundred and forty
seven Poles along a line With John Hatfield and Isaac Stoner to a stake
thence along a line With Elijah Chambers South forty eight degrees West
two hundred and twenty five Poles to a black Oak then South fifty four
degrees West thirteen Poles to a Point in the Center of said Sequachee
Creek Opposite to a White Oak and Black Oak then down the same as it
Meanders South thirty six degrees east one hundred and thirty eight Poles

P-415.	to the beginning together With All and singular the appurtenances Whatsoever to the Said tract of land belonging or any Wise appertaining and the reversion and reversions, remainder and remainders rents issues and Profits thereof and every part or Parcel thereof And All the estate right title interest, Property Claim and demand Whatsoever of him the said John Southgate his heirs and Assigns forever of in and to the same and every Part and Parcel thereof either in law or equity.

To have and to hold the Said tract of two hundred and thirty four and a half Acres of land herein before described With the Appurtenances said William Davis and William Foster their heirs and assigns to the Only Proper use and behoof of him the said William Davis and William Foster their heirs and assigns forever free and Clear of All Claim and demand of him the said John Southgate his heirs executors and Administrators of all and every Person and Persons Whatsoever Claiming by from or Under them or either of them and the said John Southgate for himself his heirs executors and Administrators doth hereby Covenant Promise and Agree to and With the Said William Davis and William Foster their heirs and Assigns that if they take the said William Davis and William Foster their heirs or Assigns Shall at any time hereafter be Vested from the said Bargained Premises or any Part thereof in Virtue of any titke or titles Whatever Mor Valid in law then the title now Conveyed to them in Virtue of these Presents that then and in that case he the said John Southgate Shall Pay and refund Unto the Said William Davis and William Foster their heirs or Assigns at the rate of three Dollars and eighty four Cents per Acre for each and every acre from Which he or they Shall be so evicted by due Course of law With interest thereon from the time of such eviction.

In Witness Whereof the said John Southgate by his Attorney in fact Aforesaid hath hereunto set his hand and seal the day and Year first herein Written.

Sealed and delivered in Presence of

Jno. Bridgeman
Aaron Schoolfield

John Southgate
By his Attorney in fact
John McIver

P-416.	State of Tennessee

Bledsoe County Court

November Session 1830.

Then Was the Within deed of Conveyance from John Southgate by his attorney in fact John McIver to William Davis and William Foster for 234½ Acres of land in Marion County Was this day Proven in Open Court by the Oaths of John Bridgeman and Aaron Schoolfield the Subscribing Witnesses thereto and Ordered to be Certified to the for registration.

In Testimony that the foregoing is truly Copied of the record in My office I Scott Terry Clerk of the Court of Pleases and Quarter Session for the County of Bledsoe have hereunto set My hand and Affixed the Private seal of My office not having an official seal at office the 12th of Nov. 1830.

Scott Terry	Clerk

Registered February 3rd. 1831.

I am the one Chargeable With the registers fees on all deeds that May be registered by Me hereafter the fees on the foregoing deeds having to the former deputies.

February 4th. 1831.

P-417.   Wm. I. Standifer
        Finalsettlement Made between Amos Griffith and Jno. Kelly
June 6 1831 for deeds &c registered previous to that date on Book
A. & B.

                                        A. Griffith
                                        By John Griffith
                                        Jno. Kelly

P-417.   Last Will &c
             or   )   In the Name of God Amen.
          Ferrell Belsher   )

        I Ferrell Belsher of the County of Marion & State of Tennessee
being in the sixtieth Year of My Age & Considering the Uncertainty of
this Mortal life & being of Sound Mind & Disposing Memory do Make and
Publish this My last Will & Testament in Manner & form following hereby
revoking annulling & Making Void all former Wills and any former deed
or deeds of Gift of any kind Whatsoever by Me Made.first I give and bequeath unto My Wife Sally Belsher during her Natural life all My real &
Personal estate after My just debts are Paid except Maybe Coming to the
said Sally Belsher from the estate of her & her heirs Absolutely to be disposed of as she May think Proper.
        2. I give and bequeath & devise to My son Wiley Belsher his
heirs after the decease of My Wife Sally Belsher the two lots & houses in
the town of Jasper that I purchased of William Armett . I also give &
bequeath & devise Unto My son Wiley Belsher his heirs & Assigns All that
tract or Parcel of land that I bought of Alexander Coulter containing two
hundred & Nineteen Acres adjoining lands of said Coulter & Roswell Hall
after the decease of My Wife Sally Belsher. I Also give & bequeath to
my son Wiley Belsher & his heirs after the decease of My Wife Sally Belsher
the following Negroes to Wit;
        Will. I   Big Cynthia & her daughter Betty
        Delphia & her Child   William Selab;
        Hardy   Charlotte
        Charles;   Isaac;
        Sarah;   Ciley;
        Eliza and   Liza.
        3rd. I give bequeath & devise to My son Allen Belsher his
heirs & Assigns after the death of My Wife Sally Belsher three hundred
and twenty Acres of land; Which is to be the Northern half of the tract
of Which I now live including the ferry landing & dwelling houses. I
also give & bequeath to My son Allen Belsher & his heirs the following
Negroes to Wit -
        Cap,   little Cynthia;
        Martha;   Zadock;
        Dick;   Tom;
        Nelly;   Fanny;
        Malinda;   Dublin;
        Big Nancy   Little Nancy
        I further Give bequeath & devise to My son Wiley Belsher &
his heirs the Southern half of the tract of land on Which I now live Containing three hundred and twenty Acres also two tracts of land Containing two hundred two and half acres each No. Not known in Twigg County
State of Georgia.I give and bequeath to son Allen Belsher & his heirs
one tract of land in the County of Irwin When surveyed & State of Georgia

P-417. Containing Four hundred and Ninety Acres. I also Give & bequeath to My Son Allen Belsher & his heirs one Other tract of land in the County of Wayne When surveyed & State of Georgia containing four hundred & hundred & Ninety Acres.

I give & bequeath to My son Wiley Belsher My Cotton Gim in the town of Jasper.

I Give & bequeath to My son Allen Belsher & his heirs All the household & Kitchen furniture Utensils & hogs after the death of My Wife Sally Belsher her It being My Will & Pleasure that the horses Cattle & Crops that May be on hand at My death Shall be equally divided between My Sons Wiley and Allen Belsher.

(P-418)   It is My Will and direction that My two Sons Shall Contributely pay an equal Proportion of all my just debts & Particularly the debt Due John Walker of the Cherokee Nation.

Lastly I hereby constitute & Appoint My friend William I. Standifer and My two sons Wiley Belsher & Allen Belsher executors of this My Last Will and Testament.

In Witness Whereof I have hereunto set My hand and seal the 2nd day of March 1829.

his
Ferrell X Belsher
mark

Signed sealed Published & declared by the Above Named Ferrell Belsher to be his last Will and testament in the Presence of us Who have hereunto subscribed our names as Witnesses in the Presence of the testator.

Jacob Riggle
Howett Mitchell

P-417.   State of Tennessee

Marion County Court

August Session 1830.

The Last Will and Testament of Ferrell Belsher deceased was this day Produced in Open Court Whereupon Came Wiley Belsher by his Counsel Withdrew his Please by him Pleaded to the Validity and execution of the last Will and Testament of said Ferrell Belsher, deceased also Came Howell Mitchell and Jacob Riggle the subscribing Witnesses thereto Who swears they saw the said Ferrell Belsher signed seal Acknowledged delivered the same as his Act and deed for the Purpose therein Contained and expressed and that the said Ferrell Belsher at the time of signing sealing and delivering the same Was in Possession of all his Mental facilities Whereupon the same is Ordered to be Certified and Admitted to record. Let it be registered.

In Testimony Whereof I John Kelly Clerk of said Court have hereunto set My hand and Private seal (Not having a seal of Office) at Office in Jasper the 25th day of January 1831.

This 3rd day of January 1896.

Jno. Kelly
By Wm. I. Standifer
By E. H. Craven 2nd Deputy Reg.

THE END
OF BOOK A & B 1819-1830

www.ingramcontent.com/pod-product-compliance
Lightning Source LLC
Chambersburg PA
CBHW080235270326
41926CB00020B/4241